# LEGAL POWER

## FOR
## SMALL BUSINESS
## OWNERS and MANAGERS

### EASY-TO-READ GUIDE

by
**RAYMOND J. MUNNA**
*Attorney*
LL.M. (Corporation Law), M.B.A.

A ★ Granite Publisher
Kenner, LA 70065

# Legal Power for the
# Small Business Owner and Manager
by Raymond J. Munna

A★Granite Publishers
80 Granada Drive
Kenner, Louisiana 70065-3145
(504) 443-5765

**Also by Raymond Munna**

Handbook for the Potential Franchise Purchaser
*Franchise Selection: Separating Fact From Fiction*

**LIBRARY OF CONGRESS CATALOGING-IN-PUBLICATION DATA**

Munna, Raymond J.,
        Legal power for small business owners and
        managers: easy to read guide / by
        Raymond J. Munna.
                p.              cm.
        Includes bibliographical references and index.
        ISBN 0-935669-10-8: $19.95
        1. Business law—United States.
        2. Small business—Law and legislation—United States.
        I. Title.
        KF889.3.M86    1991
        346.73'0652—dc20
        [347.306652]
                                            91-8838
                                            CIP

        0 9 8 7 6 5 4 3 2 1
        Copyright 1991 by Raymond J. Munna
        Printed in the United States of America

# EASY POWER REFERENCE GUIDE

| ACTIVITIES | CHAPTER |
|---|:---:|
| Buy or Sell Services or Goods<br>Design your own contract or<br>Defend yourself against some else's contract | 1 |
| Starting a Business—<br>What form should it take?<br>Overview and Comparisons | 2 |
| Forming a Partnership<br>(2 or more partners) | 3 |
| Forming a Corporation<br>Want to Protect Your Assets | 4 |
| Buying or Selling a Business—<br>"Must" Rules to Know | 5 |
| Want to multiply your business quickly or<br>want to buy a franchise | 6 |
| Competitors doing unfair things—<br>Criticizing your product or services,<br>engaging in deceptive practices, restrictions or competition | 7 |
| Competitors lying about their products or services,<br>Bait and Switch advertising | 8 |
| Quality may be your best product or service.<br>Increase your market share and profitability.<br>Federal Trade Commission Rules | 9 |
| Competitors fixing prices or colluding in some way.<br>Large competitors acting like bullies—<br>Check out the antitrust rules. | 10 |

| | |
|---|---|
| Borrowing or lending money. Buying a car.<br>Selling inventory with time payments.<br>Learn about promissory notes | 11 |
| Learn how to transfer risks to an insurance carrier.<br>Fire, business interruption, life, health, general liability.<br>Everyone needs this information. | 12 |
| Raising capital from the public.<br>Learn the treacherous rules for selling securities.<br>Possible exemptions from some rules. | 13 |
| Want to protect a name, ad copy or<br>a special manufacturing process. | 14 |
| Leasing commercial real estate for your office. | 15 |
| Borrowing or lending money with security for the loan. | 16 |
| Employees and working conditions have special rules. | 17 - 19 |
| Need an attorney.<br>"Must" information. | 20 |

# Table of Contents

## CHAPTER 2
STARTING YOUR BUSINESS—WHAT FORM CAN IT TAKE? . . . . . . . . . . . . . 62

# CHAPTER 3

# CHAPTER 4

# Acknowledgement

I'd like to thank James M. Garner, Esq., Eve B. Masinter, Esq., and Alex McIntyre, Esq. for many helpful suggestions.

# Introduction

I heard the story about a young man who became a partner in a bar. The bar experienced financial difficulties. The partners were sued on a debt and the young man had to make good on the debt since the other partner could not. The young man thought he learned a difficult lesson but paid the debt of about $1500.

Later the young man was sued again on an unpaid debt of the unsuccessful bar business. This time he had to stand good for almost $100,000. He vowed he would not let this happen to him again.

Well, he became a lawyer to stop from being caught by legalities of which he was unaware.

That leads us to the theme of this book—

| | | |
|---|---|---|
| Legal Knowledge | ⇨ | Legal Power |
| Legal Power | ⇨ | Legal Tender |

By the way, the young man above was young in 1835. His name was Abraham Lincoln.

# CHAPTER 1

ENTERING INTO A CONTRACT:
A BASIC GLUE FOR DOING BUSINESS

# CHAPTER 1

## ENTERING INTO A CONTRACT: A BASIC GLUE FOR DOING BUSINESS

We will examine a foundation for doing business—or for being in business. Each person's rights and duties are frozen at that one point in time. This makes those rights predictable, in general and it makes those rights knowable.

Let us look at your entering into contracts with other persons from the viewpoint of an ongoing business. A business person buys goods and services from other individuals or entities. A business person also sells goods and services to other individuals or entities. All contracts that an individual makes are those that point out the importance of becoming familiar with contracting.

Let's play a guessing game for a moment. Try to determine what may be the first contract you enter into in any day. It may be tonight. We enter into contracts at the beginning of most days.

Would you have any idea what the first one may be? Are you using an alarm clock to wake up? Did you watch television after midnight? Are you buying electricity from the power company? You may also be using natural gas.

You may buy gasoline for your automobile in the morning. You may get the newspaper in the morning. You are entering into many contracts each day. All of us are entering contracts, because they are part of the lifeblood of doing business. You cannot get away from contracts and laws. Unfortunately, you can't always have an expert by your side, so you have to become familiar with contracts and the law. Obviously, we would not have the time

or the money to afford to have a full-time legal companion with us. Having a lawyer around you that much could cause your life insurance rates to go up.

Let's take a look at the law of contracts. The best way to view a contract is as a photograph. It is like a snapshot of one point in time. Both parties (assuming only two) are agreeing to certain required behavior that will set the tone for their agreement.

You cannot assume that your duties under this agreement can be changed at some later date. A contract requires that we want to have some predictability about the relationship. One way to view the handshake is that the agreement is written in concrete and the concrete is now dry. You have to examine the law of contracts and the different ways of viewing it. If you understand the law of contracts, you can be a better manager.

Contract law is derived from the English common law. Its genesis goes back hundreds of years. Common law grew out of case law. English judges decided many cases and the accumulation of these cases created a body of law that is called common law. Within the common law there are several different roots, but they are not terribly important for our purposes now.

More recently, many problems have cropped up when lawyers and laymen try to piece together many cases to determine what the law is. A major problem with the "common law" (case law) is that it contains a large number of gaps. If there is no reported case for a given situation, then there is no existing law for the problem. With all these gaps, our legal engineers had to help solve the gap problem.

In the contract area, one early solution involved proposing a theoretical statute that provided answers. I say *theoretical* because it was not created by legislators or judges; it was created by legal scholars and lawyers for the benefit of any state legislature that chose to adopt it. It was not, however, a *law* in the binding sense. One of the first proposals to solve business problems was the Uniform Sales Law. Subsequent to that, a more comprehensive body of law called the Uniform Commercial Code (UCC) was developed.

The UCC applies to contracts for the sale of tangible goods. We are interested in what the UCC says about personal property that is tangible. The UCC modifies the law of contracts. Contract law covers other property including real estate, services and any personal property question not covered by the UCC. Therefore, we have not only the common law to examine but also the UCC for those things that are goods.

What is a contract and how does this apply to any of us? It can be considered a mutual agreement between parties. One party is agreeing to *do* something or *not* to *do* something; for example, to pay money or not to sue, to transfer goods or to refrain from transferring goods, to exercise a legal right or to refrain from exercising a legal right. One party does this or *promises* to do this in return for the other party doing something or *promising* to do something. This agreement is enforceable by the public authorities, i.e., courts.

What is the key way to look at this? If you are buying goods for your business, such as inventory or office supplies, and you agree to buy them with the supplier agreeing to provide them at a certain price, you are generally committed to this bargain. There can be obvious breaches of this agreement. If you do not accept delivery of the office supplies, you may have breached this contract. If you believe you can get it cheaper someplace else, you do not

necessarily have a right to then change the contract. It is as if it were cast in stone.

Many things happen in a business which might cause you or your supplier to bend or give in even though there is no legal obligation. This might be good public relations or marketing, but first we must examine basic contractual rights and obligations. A contract is like a snapshot in time. It is as if you are creating your own law between you and the other party. This is one of the better ways of viewing it. Keep this in mind.

What are the important elements to discuss? What is necessary to have a contract? Basically, there are five requirements.

## MUTUAL ASSENT: Guts of the Agreement

The first and most important criterion, whether it be a common-law contract or UCC contract, is that there must be a mutual agreement between the parties: Who is going to transfer what goods or services, or refrain from exercising a legal right, in return for whatever goods, services or withholding a legal right by the other party? What is the deal? Certainly this deal has to be communicated to the proper party or to the proper party's agent and must be understandable, must be communicated with intent to be committed to a contract, and the other party must accept it. That is the mutual agreement.

We discussed the requirements of the most essential requirement of a contract, and that is what is the deal and who are the parties to it? And that is where we discussed the mutual assent.

### OFFER

The offer is typically the portion of the contract that contains all of the terms and conditions of the agreement. The offer contains *who* is going to do *what* including *when* and *where*. In other words, it is the deal. It is not just "Where's the beef?" The offer must be communicated to the proper parties, and it must be communicated with the intent to be bound. Let's take a look at some of the elements.

The essential elements of an offer include, first, that it must be communicated. Now, who has to send this message and what does the message have to say?

## A. COMMUNICATION

First, the message must come from the person making the offer or the person's agent. It doesn't have to come from that particular person, but it must be communicated to the proper party, meaning the potential acceptor of the contract or that person's agent. On the other hand, it cannot be communicated to John Smith and John Smith goes and tells one of his friends about the potential cutting of the grass and the friend then cuts the grass.

That would not meet the requirements of having communicated it to the proper party or the proper party's agent.

## B. INTENT

Even though many of us have entered into what appear to be a zillion and one contracts, we may not want to be bound by the burdensome part of the contract, but in order to get the good part of the contract we have to be committed to what would be considered the downside. An example is: Most of us have bought houses, and in the process of buying a house we end up having to commit ourselves to a mortgage, those ghastly beasts that may last for 30 years, or what seems to be an eternity at best. The point is, if we want to get the house, we end up having to sign a mortgage to get the purchase money in order to get enough money to be able to buy the house. So even though we may have some mental reservations, hoping that the mortgage will disappear, we want to buy the house, so we have to be committed to the burden of that mortgage and the payments and the interest. Therefore, the deal must be communicated to the other party, but with intent to be committed. Now, this can be distinguished from an invitation to make an offer.

Why did I even bring this up? Because there is no way of bringing in every case and all of the nuances that businessmen may come into contact with, but some of the more prominent ones are important. An example we see day to day could involve our own advertising, such as advertisements by stores in the newspaper. These are generally not considered offers to us. If we read the newspaper and see that we can buy office supplies at some discount, 30 percent off, *et cetera*, again we are talking about generally; those are not considered offers to us at a specific price. The courts and the genesis of advertisements have resulted in these generally being considered a suggestion to us, that if we are interested in those office supplies, we can approach that particular office supply vendor or store and make an offer. They need not necessarily accept it at that particular price. There can be exceptions. An example of which you ought to be aware is that if the offer is too specific, "we have three of

---

### *POWER POINTS* _____

MUTUAL ASSENT GENERAL REQUIREMENTS

▶ You MUST communicate to your intended audience.

▶ You MUST intend to contract with one or more persons/entities in your audience.

▶ Your EXTERNAL behavior may control over your INTERNAL intent.

▶ You must be definite in your words/actions.

these left," three of a certain type of binders that are bargains, then that particular store is making an offer with regard to those three; but if no particular quantity sells out, then they are generally not considered to be an offer.

## C. OBJECTIVE STANDARDS

The courts generally have to wrestle with the appearance of the words, facts and circumstances of a potential offer. If something is offered "in jest," then it may not meet the requirements of being a valid offer with intent to be committed. If someone is telling a joke, which might imply an offer, the courts might look at these facts and circumstances and determine that it was just that, a joke. On the other hand, we may have this internal reservation but have made all the external motions of being committed to a deal, and the courts might say from all of the external facts and circumstances that we have committed ourselves to that deal, no matter what we have communicated to other parties, maybe to family members or friends. If we didn't communicate the reservations, if we didn't tell the other party that we really didn't mean it and if it would appear to a third person (or to a jury, for that matter) that we were intended to be committed to that deal, then guess what: You probably have a deal. There have been numerous cases, some of which have become classics in the law, which covered that fact.

## D. DEFINITENESS

One of the important additional features of the offer is that it must be definite. Some of the essential items of the contract are that there must be an agreement on price, an agreement on quantity, generally an agreement on when each of the parties is going to perform his particular duties; and in any absence of this, there must be some legal mechanism to supply whatever is missing, or there can be no contract. Therefore, definiteness is an essential factor.

We see that under the UCC a number of factors can be supplied, for instance, when they have not been specifically mentioned. An example might be that there is no statement as to where the object is. Let's assume someone is buying television sets from a wholesaler, but there has been no discussion of the place where they must be picked up. Now, generally that would to the buyer that, if the seller has a place of business, it is implied that that is the place where the buyer will have to pick up the television sets.

Another example might be that no price was set, but that one of the parties can be allowed to set the price. The UCC can make provisions for this and both of the parties, or that particular party must act in good faith, because without a price there can be no contract. The UCC has been developed and designed to allow one of the parties, or both of the parties for that matter, to agree based on some objective standard. For instance, if we are talking about grain—wheat or corn—you could use a reference pricing in that particular local market or a particular grade of that type of grain. So even though the parties have not agreed to a price today or on the date the contract was created, they could agree to use a price two weeks hence and let one of the parties select it, subject to a good-faith standard.

---

## POWER POINTS _____

▶ You MUST state the price, quantity and other essential terms in your offer.

▶ Sometimes these essential factors can be derived from other facts or sources—BUT be very careful.

## IMPLIED OR INFERRED TERMS - OUTPUT AND REQUIREMENTS CONTRACTS

Even the common law has identified certain circumstances whereby the quantity term can be supplied, even though it has not been specifically agreed to in the contract. An example might be that an automobile manufacturer has agreed to buy all the aluminum a particular manufacturer at a particular plant can produce in one year. The courts have allowed such agreements to supply the definiteness that is needed or the quantity term by these "output" contracts, meaning that one of the parties will purchase all of the output that the other party produces. The courts have read into these agreements certain good-faith standards, meaning that the producer of the goods cannot manipulate the outcome by drastically increasing or decreasing the output so that the party that is purchasing the output is then made to buy much more or not receive the quantity needed.

## REQUIREMENTS CONTRACT

These are virtually the converse of the output contract. An example might be that the aluminum manufacturer would be willing to produce all the aluminum required by a particular automobile manufacturing plant. In other words, all the requirements and all the aluminum that the manufacturer requires for his plant operation for the coming year or two years or six months will dictate how the aluminum producer agrees to supply. Now, the courts have said that even though it is impossible to predict what the requirements would be, given a reasonable range or good faith implied by both parties, the courts will consider this a definite agreement and therefore one that could ultimately be considered a valid offer and part of a valid contract.

Your offer can end and no acceptance is possible under these circumstances:

1. Lapse of reasonable time since your offer.

2. You decide to revoke your offer.

3. Your offeree rejects your offer.

4. Offeree makes counteroffers that are changes to your offer.

5. Destruction of the subject matter of the potential contract.

6. Subsequent illegality of what you are trying to do in the contract.

The next significant question is: How long is this offer good for? Does it last forever, for a day or just for a limited time?

Offers can terminate for several reasons, which include lapses of time and revocations by the person making the offer. There can be some exceptions, which are (a) rejection by the person receiving the offer, (b) counteroffers by the person receiving the offer, (c) death or insanity of either party, (d) destruction of the object of the contract, and (e) subsequent; legality of the object of the contract.

Let's take a look at these.

## LAPSE OF TIME

The contract offer may itself contain an expiration of time, such as next Tuesday or the first of next month, in which case the offer will expire.

What if no time has been described? Then the passing of time would have to be derived from the way that particular business is conducted. In other words, if you have a real estate business it may be a longer time, and if we are talking about the purchase or sale of commodities such as wheat, silver or gold, where those markets change almost by the minute, it may be a shorter time.

# REVOCATION OF THE OFFER BY THE PERSON MAKING THE OFFER

A person who may have thrown the offer out, for instance, has communicated to the teen-ager we mentioned before that I have decided to cut the grass myself and I am withdrawing my offer to any of you. There can be some exceptions to the ability of the person making the offer to pull it back.

One of these is known as an *option contract*, whereby an individual is paid a price to keep the option open. Thus, either of the parties could pay to require the other party to keep their end of the bargain open for a certain time. These are called option contracts, and are generally paid for; and there must be some consideration, either money or services or goods, and so forth.

There can also be an exception without consideration under the UCC. This area is one of which any businessman should take note. If you would be considered a merchant or if the other party might be considered a merchant—that is, someone knowledgeable in that particular business or someone who has an employee who is knowledgeable in that business or someone who just advertises to the public that they are knowledgeable in that business—under certain circumstances they can be required to keep the offer open even though they may have changed their mind. Under the UCC, a merchant who has made a signed written offer which gives assurance that the offer will be kept open for a certain period up to three months may be committed to this even though the other party has not paid to keep that offer open. This relationship would not be considered an option, but is considered a firm offer under the UCC, in which case the person making the offer may not be able to hold it back.

Another limitation on the ability of the offeror to pull back the offer or to revoke it may depend on state or federal statutes. In certain states, for instance, the offeror may not be able to revoke the offer for certain periods or for certain reasons; therefore, there can be limitations on that.

Finally, in unilateral contracts there are time periods where one of the parties has begun to perform. There must be some time period on withdrawing the offer. We were given the example about the teen-agers and the grass cutting. If one of the teen-agers began cutting the grass, typically the homeowner would not be in a position then of revoking the offer even though the young man cutting the grass has not finished. Of course, a few hundred years ago under the common law that was the nature of this particular beef, meaning that if the offeror revoked before the person cut the last blade of grass there would be no agreement. We consider this unfair, and the courts have eventually placed some restrictions on what could be a totally unfair result. Nevertheless, the unilateral agreement or offer does contain some restrictions on the ability of the person making the offer to pull it back or revoke the offer.

## REJECTION BY THE OFFEREE OR THE PERSON RECEIVING THE OFFER

If the person receiving the offer decides to reject the offer, that particular offer is generally considered defunct for all purposes. There can be some exceptions; one that crops up occasionally is that the offeree may have sent a rejection in the mail, yet minutes after placing the rejection in the mail calls up the person making the offer and says, "I accept the offer." Under those particular circumstances, sometimes in some courts, the offer might be considered outstanding and the party who would have received the oral acceptance cannot refuse it.

## COUNTEROFFERS

The party receiving the offer is generally considered the offeree, and can also terminate the nature of an offer—or an entire offer—by counteroffering. For instance, someone would offer their automobile to you for $2,000 and you tell them you will only offer $1,950. Such an exchange is a rejection of the initial offer, which would now be dead, and for most intents and purposes is a counteroffer. In this particular case the initial offer is terminated and you are now the person making the offer, which would require the other party, the owner of the car, to then accept or reject the offer.

Death or disability of either of the parties: It is possible, under most circumstances, if either of the parties dies or becomes disabled, be it by insanity or some other cause, this would possibly result in the termination of the offer. It is difficult at times for either of the parties to carry out a contract if they are incompetent. In most cases, death makes it extremely difficult to carry out any contract. It is not always impossible, but it does make it more difficult.

## DESTRUCTION OF THE SUBJECT MATTER

Destruction of the subject matter can terminate a contract. It does not necessarily affect it 100 percent of the time, but here is a specific example. Let's assume you are going to a dealership to buy a particular car and you see one on that particular lot which is exactly what you want. It has four doors and the proper color, and there may be some other extra items, but this car has everything you want. You contract with that dealership to buy that car. You go back the next day to put your money down, and through no fault of the dealership the car has been part of a fire that started spontaneously, or possibly was started by an arsonist or third parties totally unrelated to the dealership. In that case, the initial offer would probably be dead. Not only is the car burned up, but your offer may be down the tubes. In that case, because the subject matter of the contract has been destroyed, there can no longer be a contract with regard to that car. Now, that does not necessarily mean that given more or less the same circumstances you might not have an enforceable contract.

An example of where you would still have a legitimate offer open would be if you had gone to the same dealership and contracted for a certain make and model of car, but had not specified that particular car. Possibly the one on the lot was not exactly what you wanted; therefore, you contracted for the dealer to go and find one for you. In that case, even though the car that you might have taken burned up, it was *not necessarily the one that was identified with your particular contract*. Therefore, the offer is still open. So take note: The identification of that particular car with the contract can make a tremendous difference as to who wins.

## SUBSEQUENT ILLEGALITY

An example of this might involve buying some peaches from someone in another state and then there is a law change while the offer is still open. There is now a ban on delivering those particular peaches in your state. In effect, it is illegal for that particular delivery of peaches. That offer is now dead.

## ACCEPTANCE OF THE OFFER

Now that we have gotten into the general requirements for the offer, what does it take to end up with a valid and enforceable contract, or what are the stipulations with regard to an acceptance?

First, an acceptance must be definite. It cannot be kind of a namby-pamby acceptance. The courts probably would use objective standards, meaning that they look at it objectively, from the viewpoint of a third party.

## UNILATERAL OFFER

How do we determine whether there has been an acceptance of a unilateral offer? The example given before, of the homeowner and the teen-agers will be used here. In that case, the method of acceptance is by performance. Here we are dealing with services, not goods; however, the UCC covers this kind of transaction, that even a unilateral type of agreement can be accepted by two methods. One would be actual performance; a second would be notification to the person who made the initial offer that proper performance would follow. So we see that as far as the unilateral offer is concerned there can be two methods of accepting it. One, if we are talking about common law—meaning that the UCC does not apply because it does not involve goods—then there is generally only one method of accepting, and that is by doing it. On the other hand, if the UCC applies there are basically two ways of locking down this contract.

## BILATERAL OFFER

Whether the offer is unilateral or bilateral, the acceptance must be definite. Again, this offer can be accepted only by a person to whom it was communicated, and the person to whom it was intended to be communicated or by that person's agent. Thus, if an offer was made to a specific person, the acceptance is restricted to that particular person or that person's agent. A bilateral offer is looking for an exchange *promise* from the offeree, not necessarily an act.

Some offers can be made to the public in general. An example of that might be a reward to the public: One which might provide information leading to the conviction of a bank robber. Anyone in the public would be an eligible person who could accept the offer.

A requirement of the acceptance must be that the acceptance must be done by an individual or an entity acting in reliance on the offer and who has knowledge of the offer, even though the person might be accepting the offer. For instance, given the example of Party *A* offering a car to Party *C* for $2,000. Party *B* is totally unaware of the fact that Party *A* offered that, but Party *B* goes to Party *A* and says, "I would like to buy your car for $2,000." We still would not have a contract. There would be no contract because, even though Party *B* is making an identical offer, Party *B* is not the party to whom the offer was communicated and could not accept it.

Second, generally the acceptance, at least under the traditional common law, must be identical. Commentators say it must be a mirror image of the offer. It cannot be changed; it must look the same identical way. You cannot change any of the terms or conditions or provide any gifts or other material things. In the automobile example, you could not offer $1,999.95 plus two pencils, which might be worth more than 5 cents. There would be no acceptance even though the value, on an objective basis, might be more than the $2,000 that the person wants in order to sell his car.

## THE UNIFORM COMMERCIAL CODE

The Uniform Commercial Code (UCC) changed the common law of contracts as it pertained to *goods*. Let's take a look at some of these changes in determining if or when the other party has accepted an offer.

## MIRROR IMAGE RULE

Most of the time, if we are talking about tangible personal property, we are talking about goods. There can also be other substances, such as minerals or trees or crops, that can be considered *goods*. If the UCC applies, it is possible to have a locked-in contract even though acceptance has not been a mirror image of the offer.

There is no way for us to discuss in any summary fashion all of the nuances of this; but we ought to be aware of this change from the common law, because it applies in business.

## BATTLE OF THE FORMS

The battle of the forms comes into play, and you have to know the havoc that can result. Why is it important? Here is, in a nutshell, why; and hopefully you will see why it becomes important.

Let's assume you happen to be a retailer of appliances and you are buying some television sets from your distributor. You request they give you a quotation on a particular brand of television sets with the delivery requirements you would like. The distributor will then come back to you with, in effect, an offer at a certain price with certain terms and conditions, typically on the front and back of the form.

---

## *POWER POINTS* _____

▸ If you want to win the contract game, you must make sure that your contract prevails or there is *no deal*.

▸ If you want to win strategic contract points, make sure your specific provisions are accepted or there is *no deal*.

▸ You must *communicate* your contract requirements clearly and crisply.

▸ You will lose some deals if you insist on the above.

▸ If the deal is enough to make or break your business, prepare for the worst up front or it may be too late later.

This process begins the battle of the forms. Now you may send back an acceptance with some conditions on it. You may accept the price and most other terms, but you may exclude certain terms that were included in your distributor's form or price quote. Now the question (which cannot be answered simply) may be: Is there an acceptance? Your form is very different from the form of the distributor. Do you have a deal at all? Have you accepted the distributor's terms and conditions, or have you killed the deal by offering terms that are not a mirror image of the offer?

The courts and the UCC will look at the number of items to which the parties have clearly agreed. If the number of items and the objective intent are that the parties are to be bound, the courts may say, "Party A and Party B, you have a deal. The basis of the deal that we have here is the eight items that you have clearly agreed to. You have intended to be bound by it. You want to buy these television sets. There are enough elements that you have agreed to that there is clearly a deal."

But what may be in dispute are the terms and conditions on the *back* of the distributor's form and the terms and conditions on the back or front of your form. The courts will end up having to examine those conflicting terms. It may be necessary for a jury or the judge to determine what other terms and conditions are included. Those terms that were "different," those terms that were "additional" may become important. That is the source of any dispute. Other questions might include limitations of liability or limitations of warranty (guarantees) on the distributor's forms.

The distributor might have language that says he is not responsible if the television sets explode immediately upon your receiving them. The distributor is trying to limit his responsibility. Your form might say that the seller is clearly guaranteeing, according to the manufacturer's warranties, that if the TV's blow up on your dock, the manufacturer or distributor has to take them back.

That is when a court fight might erupt. You will not get to court unless there is some dispute.

If the court concludes there is a deal, you have to take the television sets and you also have to pay for them at the price that was stated on the forms. You may have a bunch of trash TV's that are unsalable. Do not say it is unfair or cannot happen. It does happen. You can get stuck royally if you ignore those forms. There is no formula for deciding what additional terms are included. If you want *your* form to prevail, you have to make sure you state clearly in your form that there will be no change in conditions. Your strategy is to require the other party to accept all of the terms and conditions of your form or there will be absolutely and unequivocally no deal.

The most important thing to remember is that if you want your form to prevail, make sure you do not do anything until the other party accepts your terms and conditions. In big business and with thousands of forms flying about, it may be difficult.

The problem of marketing or of getting people to buy your product makes the ideal answer unworkable, and sometimes difficulties of competition for business may change your best protective stance. If you are dealing with a much larger business organization, you may not be able to force your deal (forms) unless you are willing to accept the risk that you could lose the entire deal.

Do not for a minute disregard the thousand words placed on the back of forms. Please be aware of the fact that this could adversely effect your deal or your personal financial success. Do not ignore it and do not assume for a minute that it is business as usual. If you end up in a dispute, you can assume you will end up getting the raw end of that particular deal. Remember Murphy's Law. This applies particularly if the other party is bigger than you are. That may not always be the case, but that is the best battle information I can give you.

## TIME OF ACCEPTANCE— WHEN DOES IT ACTUALLY OCCUR

How do we determine if the acceptance has been effective? It does not make a difference which side of the transaction you are on. You have to know. Furthermore, it depends on the offer—the means that have been authorized for the acceptance.

Sometimes the person making the offer does not specifically state how it should be accepted. In that case, once the acceptance is placed in the mail or placed in the mailbox, there is an acceptance. The post office becomes the agent of the offeror (person who sent the offer); as soon as the agent receives the acceptance there is a deal (enforceable contract).

The offer may say nothing with respect to the acceptance being placed in the mail. If it is not specifically mentioned, the courts have held that the *same means* that was used to *transmit* the *offer* can be used for an acceptance. If the offer was placed in the mail, then for purposes of determining an acceptance, the courts say using the same means results in an acceptance.

Under the common law, if you used a different means (*e.g.*, carrier pigeon) there was *no acceptance* until the original party received the acceptance.

If the UCC applies (dealing with goods), then the acceptance would be immediate as long as the acceptance is sent by using a *reasonable means*. It would not have to be *identical*. If the offer was sent in the mail and was returned express mail service, then you have a deal as soon as you give the acceptance to the express mail service.

If you used an "unauthorized means" or one that was not reasonable under the circumstances, then possibly there would be no acceptance until it was *received* by the *other party*.

The original rule whereby the post office, for instance, became the agent of the offeror is sometimes called the *mailed-acceptance rule*. It is good only for acceptance purposes.

It does not work for purposes of rejecting an offer. Therefore, if the person who receives an offer rejects it, then it makes no difference what means is used. The rejection is not good until it is *received*. If you put a rejection in the mail but an hour later call up the other party and say "I accept," it is possible for there to be a valid contract, because the rejection would not be effective until the other party received it.

## SPECIFIC KEYS IN THE OFFER

It is possible that you require an acceptance by using a carrier pigeon or by using express mail. If so, you can restrict the acceptance to that means. No other means would be acceptable. On the other hand, you may be on the other side, and if that is what the other party says, then you'd better use exactly those means. The offeror can be that specific. If the offeror says it must be accepted in the mail and you use an express service, the court might interpret that as being inadequate and therefore an invalid acceptance.

## METHODS OF ACCEPTANCE

The basic method of acceptance is by clear and unconditional language. The offeree agrees to enter into the contract.

*Silence.* Generally, silence cannot constitute an acceptance. We have all seen occasions where individuals attempt to say, "If I do not hear from you, I will consider your silence your acceptance of my offer to sell the Empire State Building."

In general there can be no "jamming" of any individual by their *silence*. It is possible for a prior relationship to exist such that silence *may* be sufficient for an acceptance. In general, silence or inaction will not constitute an acceptance of an offer. The offeror cannot impose any obligation of the offeree to speak or to do something to keep out of a contract. In general, no matter what the offeror says, the offeree does not have to do anything to deny a contract.

---

### *POWER POINTS* _____

▶ Silence is usually, but not always, not an acceptance.

▶ Auctions and newspaper ads are generally requests that *you* make an offer.

---

## SOME EXCEPTIONS

There can be some exceptions. Some examples would be the following:

1. It is possible for a person to deliver services or goods for the benefit of another person who knows that any reasonable person would interpret their acceptance of such services as creating an *expectation* of payment. All the facts here would be important.

2. If there is a *prior relationship*, there is reason to believe that the offeree understands that the silence may constitute an acceptance. In addition the offeree acts in a way that leads the offeror to believe that any subsequent inaction would constitute an acceptance. Again, the facts and circumstances are important.

3. If the parties have a past relationship or past dealings where silence or inaction has been accepted as a "yes," then silence may tie the two parties to the deal. If there are some facts in addition to the "silence," it is possible to have an enforceable contract. Mere silence, however, generally will not create an acceptance.

## ANNOUNCEMENT OF AN AUCTION SALE IS NOT AN OFFER

There are some unusual sides to the formation of a contract. You should be aware of the fact that auction sales have a certain amount of similarity to a newspaper advertisement, in that the auctioneer at an auction sale typically is not making the offer, despite what it may sound like to the public; he is merely inviting an offer, so that the person who is bidding is making the offer and it is up to the auctioneer to accept or reject the offer under the circumstances. I might add this writer's brief experience when attending an auction involving furniture and numerous antiques. I pointed out to a friend of mine who regularly attends these auctions, some additional items behind the auctioneer. In the process of merely pointing out something, I almost ended up making an offer on an oak table, which I certainly did not need and did not intend to make an offer on. I managed to pull down my hand just in time. In effect, I was saved by the bell, by someone else making a superseding offer. I guess we could have ended up with significant questionable litigation if I had unintentionally caught the auctioneer's eye. Nevertheless, the point is that at an auction the auctioneer is the party who accepts the offer, and not the audience member.

## VALIDITY OF CONSENT

Much of the law involving contracts is couched in the experience of the judges who are involved in litigation involving contracts. We see that it is based mostly on good sense and fairness. We see that even though there may be apparent consent to an agreement, in fact, for reasons, there should not be an enforceable contract. Courts have often concluded that because of one or more significant problems there was no agreement.

For someone to accept, acceptance must be *clear* and *not conditioned*.

Let's take a look at some of the times where they do not often crop up. Certainly they have cropped up enough times. Considering the many millions of contracts that are formed each year, there is significant litigation involving acceptances. Every business person must be aware of the requirements for an enforceable contract including valid consent to an agreement. You'll have to learn when an "acceptance" may be invalid.

## MISTAKE

The first mistake would be that it is possible for one or more parties to an agreement to have been mistaken about some portion of the agreement but there still may be an enforceable agreement. On the other hand, there are certain types of mistakes which might vitiate or deny the enforceability of this particular contract or any particular one.

First, the mistake is as to the existence of identity of the object of the contract. Let's try to decide what we mean by mistake. A mistake would generally be considered a misunderstanding of some of the facts or one of the parties having a state of mind or certain understanding of what the deal is supposed to be which happens to be incorrect or not in accordance with the actual facts. It may be both of the parties have it, or it may be that only one of the parties has it. It makes a big difference. I would like you to realize that a mistake here is not the same thing, and is not intended to be the same distinguishing factor, as an innocent misrepresentation. It essentially involves a misunderstanding of a significant fact.

There can be mutual mistake, meaning both of the parties have a misunderstanding, or mutual mistake, which can render the contract *void*. If the contract is void, that means there was never an agreement to start with, because one of the essential features or essential motivating reasons for the contract does not exist. The parties could not have had an accurate meeting of the minds when both of them are mistaken about some important aspect of the contract. This generally means a material aspect of the contract.

A classic example might be where both of the parties believe that Party *A* is selling a Stradivarius violin to Party *B* (who happens to be a violin student with a large pocketbook). These particular violins sell in the hundreds of thousands of dollars and probably could easily get a seven-figure mark price under the right circumstances. If Party *B*, the buyer, thinks the seller's price is in excess of what would be a typical price for a typical current- day manufactured violin, in the mistaken belief that this is not one of the exquisite classics made by the renowned maker, then there would be no agreement; and this mistake—assuming that both of the parties are sincere in their mistake—could still vitiate or void the contract.

Of course, if the contract was induced by some dishonesty on one or the other party's part, that particular person would probably not be able to get out of the contract.

Therefore, if there is some mistake through the existence of this particular violin, or if it is not in fact a Stradivarius violin, then it is possible that one or both of the parties would be able to void this agreement. For instance, if the party happened to be the buyer, then the buyer would be able to get his or her money back.

## MISTAKE AS TO QUALITY OF VALUE

A problem that crops up on occasion involves quality of value of a product. Even though the mistakes are mutual, this generally does not effect the validity of the contract. An example might be, an automobile that you are buying from an automobile dealer; you might both consider that it is an extremely good value and that you are certainly getting your money's worth or more than your money's worth. This is generally not considered to be a mistake. There are no other circumstances other than just the seller's opinion of what the value is or the buyer's opinion of whether or not the buyer is getting a bargain and the seller agrees with it.

The bottom line is that if both are wrong there is no rescission based on only that. This is particularly true where each of the parties has the means of getting correct information. For instance, if the buying party has the opportunity to get an item appraised, it may be, unless it is extremely difficult or expensive to get it appraised, that the courts are not likely to invalidate that particular contract. Facts versus opinions of value can change. The courts acknowledge the fact that most sellers would certainly communicate that they are giving you a good deal. In fact, that may not be the case. The question of fact versus opinion will be discussed next.

## FACT VERSUS OPINION

Someone is giving you an opinion about whether or not you are getting a good deal; if it is the seller, the courts allow what is called "puffing." Puffing would not invalidate the sale, nor would it constitute fraud or misrepresentation or otherwise. On the other hand, if you are buying jewelry from someone who has been in the jewelry business for 20 years and represents that he or she has enough experience to be virtually an expert (even if they do not characterize themselves as expert), then the courts might decide that that might be a misrepresentation of fact. Even if they are telling you that it is their opinion of quality, if they have the credentials and have told you how great they are, how knowledgeable and how honest they are, and that they have the background in that particular business, then there may be misstatement of fact which can result in an invalid or voidable contract.

## UNILATERAL MISTAKE

Generally the courts do not help a party who has made a unilateral mistake. For instance, let's assume you are buying a diamond and believe it is one heck of a value because you understood it was a two-carat diamond selling for some 30 percent of what you thought two-carat diamonds sold for, when in fact you misread the card that, described the diamond and possibly it said 1.2-carat diamond. The courts would generally not allow you to rescind that contract based on a misrepresentation of fact.

## KNOWLEDGE OF OTHER PARTY'S MISTAKE

On the other hand, the courts have created several well recognized exceptions where, for instance, there has been a mistake in a calculation of the figures which is apparent to the other party. In the example just mentioned above—believing that the diamond was a two-carat diamond when it was a 1.2-carat diamond—the courts generally would not allow any damages or rescission to the party who was mistaken. On the other hand, if the seller of a diamond in this circumstance knew that the party was mistaken and never owned up to it or called the mistake to the attention of the potential buyer, then the courts probably would allow the innocent mistaken party to be able to rescind the transaction.

The most important thing to remember is that this may exist even though there is no fiduciary relationship between the seller and the buyer. This may be an arms-length transaction, but the courts would say that normally they are not going to help the mistaken party who is unilaterally mistaken. On the other hand, the courts are not going to allow a more knowledgeable party or the party who has caught the mistake to benefit to the detriment of the party who is mistaken. If in this dealing you can see that the other party has made a mistake and it is apparent or should be apparent to a knowledgeable

party, then the courts are possibly going to balance the scales of justice and allow the contract to be voided or rescinded. This has happened when the courts have discovered that there has been a calculation in a bid or contract and the party receiving the bid could obviously tell that there has been a mathematical error in calculating the total amount of concrete that would go into a bid. This indicates that an obvious mistake had been made.

## MISTAKE OF LAW

If the parties are mistaken about the governing relationship, there are no grounds for rescission. The opinions from a layman of what the law is that pertains to a case generally would not rescind the contract. Keep in mind that exceptions to all this can be made by specifically placing conditions into the contract such that if there is a mistaken belief about a particular point of the law or fact, the contract can be rescinded. Then even though the law might not allow a rescission or damages, the contract can allow it as long as it is not against public policy.

Nevertheless, the general rule in the common law is that a mistake or lack of knowledge of our laws would not constitute a mistake of fact that the courts would use to invalidate an agreement. Some courts have to distinguish domestic law from foreign law, meaning that if you do not know a law in the United States, it would be in the same category as not knowing a fact or being incorrect about a fact. On the other hand, those courts may say that if you make a mistake as to a foreign law, it may be considered a mistake of a fact and therefore might allow one of the parties to void this particular contract.

## SIGNIFICANT EXCEPTION

If one of the parties states in definitive terms that they know what the law is, even if they are not a lawyer, it is possible for the misstatement of law to be considered so important to this particular contract that the courts might allow the innocent party to get out of the contract. This can happen even when the person is stating that the law is a fact.

There are many areas that deal with the law, for instance various things where laymen can become extremely knowledgeable in a particular area in which they deal. I have seen people who deal in the insurance area who can be very knowledgeable about tax law involving financial planning, and many times they give extremely sophisticated and in-depth advice based on a well-steeped knowledge of the law. On the other hand, if someone were to rely on this particular individual or individuals, this might be a detriment. It is then possible for the innocent third party to claim a mistake of law, which might allow the innocent party to get out of a contract. Again, if you are a businessman and you are relying on it, the solution is to put the statement of the law—your understanding of the law on which you are basing this contract—in the contract.

## FAILURE TO READ THE DOCUMENT

Unfortunately, many of us have on occasion signed contracts without having read or understood all of the details, and under many circumstances we have signed contracts with large companies. It would not make any difference whether we read the contract or not, because they probably would not allow one dot or "t" to be changed or any periods, or commas, or any other change to be made. So for all practical purposes, in most cases it will not make any difference.

For example, when I bought my first house, I was reading the details of the Act of Sale and Act of Mortgage and the notary/attorney knew that I was a lawyer, and he also probably knew that I was not a specialist in this area. He told me nicely to hurry up so that we could get this matter over with, because he had no intention of changing one iota in the agreement no matter what I wanted and no matter what my opinion was, so I should quit wasting his time. The point of all of this is that often we are truly intimidated or even pushed by social means into hurriedly signing an agreement. Another example is, if there are a number of people in the room who are witnesses and who may be part of a transaction, there is a lot of social pressure to get the deal over with. There are always one or two people that have ants in their pants and are pushing to move forward with the transaction. Many times lawyers use this social pressure to get matters over with with a minimum of discord.

## FRAUD

There are essentially two types of fraud, and the difference is very important.

### FRAUD IN THE EXECUTION
Fraud in the execution of a contract would make the contract void (dead for all purposes, unable to be cured). The type of fraud we are talking about here is not the type of fraud most of us would come across.

This type of fraud involves an innocent party who without his or her own fault is unaware of the fact that he or she is entering a contract and who had no intention of doing so. An example of this might be where someone believes they are filling in a form for a survey, but they are not told that there is a second or third carbon which contains a contract. Thus if the party signs a space on the top form, it might appear that the party signed the carbons which contain a contract. Though uncommon, it has been known to happen, especially tied together with such intimidating circumstances as having other people around and being under some social pressure to hurry up and sign the form. You can imagine this happening when there is some incentive, such as a gift certificate, and a line waiting to do the same. This particular agreement would obviously result in no meeting of the minds whatsoever. This agreement is totally void and therefore rescindable.

### FRAUD IN THE INDUCEMENT
What is fraud in the inducement? Many times this might be considered little more than "puffing." It is fraud, however, when an innocent party knows he or she is entering a contract, but is given misrepresentations of important facts by the other party to the contract. In this particular case, a contract is voidable by the *innocent* party. The party

who is making the misrepresentation has no option but to rescind the contract.

What are the requirements? *First,* there must be a false representation of a fact. Either the party knows that the statement of fact is a lie, or he is stating something as being factual when he does not know if the statement is true. The offending party might make no effort to find out if the statements are true. In other words, the party does not mind handling the truth loosely.

*Second,* we must be dealing with statements of *fact* and not statements of *opinion* or value.

*Third,* the fact being stated must be *material,* meaning it must be important enough to a reasonable person under the circumstances. A reasonable person must consider the statement valuable to him in determining whether to buy or sell the product, or to buy or sell the service, or to enter into the contract. Materiality is determined on the basis of a reasonable person under the circumstances.

*Fourth,* the party making the statement must have the *intent* to deceive or to take advantage of any potential misstatement.

*Fifth,* there must be justifiable reliance by the innocent party. The innocent party must have done something in reliance on these statements. The party might buy an automobile or a television set, sell a car, *et cetera.* This type of fraud can also result from *suppressing* the truth. Fraudulent concealment when a party is in control or knows that a fact would be material would also result in fraud in the inducement.

One example that has popped up involves elderly, wealthy individuals and dance studio lessons. Several cases have surfaced where individuals who were very uncoordinated have purchased a block of lessons. Then they were induced to buying *additional* blocks of lessons, even though the first block of lessons have never been used. To add to the tragedy, courts have determined that several of these elderly women were falsely complimented, and in all truth they were probably total klutzes. The courts have held these incidents to be examples of fraud in the inducement and allowed the innocent parties to rescind these particular contracts.

Two additional concepts are important if you are defrauded. You have to return whatever it is you have received, if that is possible, and you must seek to rescind the contract within a reasonable amount of *time* after you have discovered the fraud. You cannot sit on your potential rights. If you discover that you have been defrauded and you have not performed your part of the contract, you can seek to rescind it and you may not have to perform your part of the contract. Again, you must act within a reasonable time. You cannot wait forever.

## INNOCENT MISREPRESENTATION

It is possible for someone to misrepresent the facts innocently. How this is distinguished from misrepresenting the facts by reckless disregard of the truth may be difficult to determine, but nevertheless the courts have said that if the misrepresentation or the omission of facts was innocent, but the other party relied upon it to their detriment, the innocent party may be able to rescind the contract. Now, some courts have said that unless the contract involves a material fact or is in some area of special contracts that state law points out or involves a fiduciary relationship, the contract would not be voidable even though there has been some misrepresentation. Generally the innocent party would be allowed to rescind the contract, but state laws may vary and many of the circumstances may not be good enough for your particular case. We are discussing innocent misrepresentation— these are known as material facts, important facts such that any reasonable person would consider them of value in making a decision.

## DURESS

If someone has been forced into entering into an agreement, there has been no true, willful assenting or agreeing to enter this particular contract. What is duress? Duress is a form of unlawful force or constraint imposed on a person by the offender, whereby the innocent person or the victim is placed in circumstances where he or she is compelled to do some act or agree to a particular contract. Duress can be, under the law, of two kinds. Although we do not have a value scale, I call it big duress versus little duress.

## "BIG DURESS" VERSUS "LITTLE DURESS"

"Big duress" (my term) generally consists of threats of physical violence or imprisonment or actual physical violence or imprisonment which would force the victim into nominally assenting or agreeing to a contract.

There can also be much lesser types of duress, which would include economic duress, whereby someone would agree to enter into a contract and thereby give up a legal right he might have in order to protect his business, his person, his family, etc.

A contract procured by big duress (non-economic duress) is generally *void*. This exists when someone's life is threatened, as with a gun. On the other hand, there can be "little duress" whereby the agreement might be *voidable*.

Economic duress can be one example. There might be subtle hints of firing a relative if an individual does not enter into a contract. This might be "little duress." The agreement would be voidable. However, you would have to act timely, in that you have to seek to have your money returned and return whatever benefits you have received under this contract.

## THREAT TO BRING CIVIL SUIT

A threat by a party to sue the victim in a civil action generally would not constitute duress, either big or little. Here we are trying to distinguish a civil lawsuit, even if there is no right to bring a civil suit. We are assumed to know what our rights are. If someone incorrectly states that they might sue us, or have a right to sue us or a right to collect from us in court in a lawsuit, we are *not protected if we guess wrong*. A person is allowed to threaten to sue us civilly even if they do not know what they are talking about, even though they actually have no right or cause of action against us under the law.

On the other hand, threats of duress or prosecution or imprisonment in a *criminal forum* may constitute *actionable duress*. In such states, a threat by a party that they will have a person ar-rested to induce the victim to sign a contract or to agree to a contract—even if the party is guilty—may constitute illegal duress and render a contract void.

In some states it is possible for the opposite to be true. A party might agree to adjust a contract or sign a contract under such duress and the contract might be legal. This would probably be a minority position; few states would protect the offender. Most businessmen should be aware of this threat. We have seen numerous cases in which individuals have violated the law in their behavior within a company; for instance, have been threatened or forced to sign documents at the cost of the company exposing them to the District Attorney. In effect, the only safe ground is for a party to steer clear of trying to use the *criminal* prosecution right for their own individual *civil* purposes. Keep these two jurisdictions separate.

I have seen lawyers threaten defendants with "criminal prosecution" if they do not pay a civil debt. This has the potential of being *extortion*.

Many times individuals will threaten to go to the authorities so they can settle a civil lawsuit. In fact, the courts generally do not like individuals attempting to utilize what is a *public means* of *punishment* for their own personal benefit. When someone commits a crime they are offending the community, not just the victim. Victims have their own civil rights, and in some cases the law distinguishes that by creating a criminal right without creating a con-comitant civil right. So for a lawyer or for you as a business person, avoid the threat of "criminal any-thing" to solve your civil or economic problems. There is a path that works, but it's a lot like mating porcupines—a sticky subject.

## UNDUE INFLUENCE

What is undue influence? That is where a weaker or subservient party is induced by a *stronger* or *dominant* party to agree to a contract which, given different circumstances, this party might not enter into. An example might be where an individual is relying on, for instance, a relative. It might be an elderly aunt relying on her niece. The niece leans on the aunt or misrepresents some of the facts to the aunt, or tells the aunt that she should enter into a contract. Later we discover that this contract was not for the benefit of the aunt, but the dominant party has in some way benefitted to the detriment of the aunt. The court may allow a rescission of this contract. It is considered *voidable*. If the subservient person is relieved of the dominant-subservient relationship and is no longer under that pressure, then the law requires this person to act timely to rescind the agreement or lose the right to get out of the agreement. Examples of these cases include parents and children, confidential or fiduciary relationships, husbands and wives, lawyers and clients, physicians and patients, clergy and their parishioners, principals and agents, guardians and their wards, or even relationships that have developed from social needs.

## FAIRNESS EXCEPTION

The courts have often taken the position that when a transaction results from undue duress, the burden is on the *dominant* party to prove that the transaction was *fair*. The dominant party has to disclose all of the facts. It is important to realize that the subservient party, being the weaker of the two, does not have the burden of proof.

## CONSIDERATION—WHO IS GETTING WHAT? WHAT IS HE GIVING UP?

It is generally called valuable consideration. This means one party has to give up something of value to get the other party to commit to doing or giving something of value in return. The values may not be the same. The courts do not care whether they are the same. Also, if the values are grossly different, there is still a contract. So beware: Fairness in your eyes or in the other party's eyes is irrelevant.

The courts often use the term "valuable consideration." One of the necessary elements supporting the contract involves a party receiving something from the other party. That party might also negotiate to have the other party give up something that is of value.

Consideration can be your receiving something that benefits you or the other party giving up something that creates a detriment or costs the other party, in time or money or services or legal rights. Neither party may actually receive the consideration personally. They do not have to get the consideration themselves. A party might want someone else to receive the consideration he or she is getting.

Consideration is the *quid pro quo* of a contract. It is important to be aware of what valuable consideration is and what it is *not*. One thing that it is *not*: It is not valuable if it is *past* or old consideration. Let's assume you already owe someone $1,000 because they sold you an automobile. You have received the automobile and now you owe them $1,000. That $1,000 debt will not support *another contract* for another car, pencil, balloon or anything else. The old consideration is no good for anything else. It is not valuable consideration for a *new* contract, though it was for the original contract. Or, for instance, if someone has *given* you something freely, that free gift would not constitute consideration for a new contract. Let us assume that an individual gave you a fancy racing bike. Two years later she (donor) needs a loan of $500. The initial donation of the bike would not constitute consideration for a $500 loan. She would still have to repay the $500 loan unless you agree to make the $500 a gift. The bike donor would not be able to say, "Oh, but I gave that person a bicycle that was worth $1,000. I certainly do not have to pay back the $500 that the individual loaned me." For legal purposes, the first gift would not constitute consideration to support the new contract.

There is no mutual assent if:

1. *Both* parties are mistaken about some important (material) aspect of the contract.

2. One party has fraudulently misrepresented some terms of the contract, including offer or acceptance.

3. One party has unduly coerced the other party to enter the contract.

4. One party (a subservient person) has entered the contract as a result of undue influence by a dominant person.

## LEGAL SUFFICIENCY

The basic approach we mentioned is that the courts will consider what is valuable or what is legally sufficient. It is what you bargained for, what you agreed to receive, or what the other person has bargained for or agreed to give up. As long as it is not *past* consideration or *illegal* consideration or a *prior gift* or something that is impossible to carry out, it may be *consideration.*

Also the courts will not try to *balance* the consideration. They will not make that judgment unless there are some rather bizarre circumstances.

Again, a key point to remember is that the courts do not try to look into the individuals' minds to determine whether or not the consideration is adequate. As long as the parties are not insane or disabled, the courts accept each party's determination of *value.* So if you agreed to take a six-pack of soft drinks in return for an automobile, the courts generally do not determine whether one of the parties came up short. There are exceptions, but they rarely apply.

## LEGAL SUFFICIENCY OF CONSIDERATION

Determining legal sufficiency depends to a certain extent on the type of contract and some of the other circumstances surrounding the contract.

## UNILATERAL CONTRACTS

In order to support a unilateral contract, the basic requirement is that one of the parties must *perform the act* (e.g., cut the grass). To meet the *consideration* requirement under the unilateral agreement, the party triggering it must *perform.* Once performance has taken place, we have an enforceable contract. This concept is modified if we are talking about the transfer of goods (UCC). It is possible for a "unilateral agreement" to be *performed* by *promising to perform.* This is another example of the UCC modifying the common law. All that the accepting party under the UCC need do is *agree* to *promptly perform.* Again, under the common law, the only adequate consideration is *actual performance.*

Under the UCC you have the option of the actual performance or the promise to perform.

## BILATERAL CONTRACTS

Don't forget that under contract law, a promise to perform by the first party and a promise to perform by the second party are sufficient to create a contract, even though all that has been exchanged are promises for promises to exchange money, to exchange services, to give up a legal right. Therefore, it is important to remember that under contract law you do not have to do anything but make promises in order to be locked into a contract.

In bilateral contracts, adequate consideration need only be shown by *promising* to give up a legal right, *promising* to deliver goods, *promising* to deliver services in return for the other party *promising* to deliver goods or services or to give up a legal right. The promise to do any of these is sufficient to support bilateral contracts.

## MUTUAL OBLIGATION

One important item to remember is that *both* parties must be *obligated* in an agreement. This does not mean they will each individually receive something from the contract. It is possible, for instance, for Mr. *A* to agree with Mr. *B*, who is an automobile dealer, to give Party *B*'s favorite charity $15,000 in return for the dealer, Mr. *B*, transferring to Mr. *A*'s niece an automobile. In this example, neither of the parties is receiving a *personal* benefit. The recipients are the third parties, the charity and the niece. Nevertheless, mutual obligation exists here. Also, both parties will be *bound* by the contract as soon as the parties *agree* to the deal. The promise to perform and the other party's promises to perform create a mutual obligation.

## ILLUSORY PROMISES

Each of the parties must be bound in a deal or neither is bound. If one of the parties does not owe any duty to perform, then the other party does not owe a duty either. An example of this might be where one of the parties agrees that *A* will buy all of the stepvans that she *wants* or *wishes* from *B* for $18,000 per stepvan with no other conditions. The courts would interpret this as being an illusory promise because it is based on somebody's wants or wishes. Therefore neither party is bound. The courts would not enforce this "agreement" if one of the parties does not *want* to perform.

What a person wants or wishes is *subjective* and incalculable. Contrast this with a deal to buy all the output of an aluminum plant. The aluminum plant output for last year would be an objective that would help control the quantity sold in an output contract.

## PREEXISTING CONTRACTUAL OBLIGATION

Consideration does not include past consideration or past debts or moral debts. There is one example that is very important to review; it is an important distinction between the common law and UCC in one area with regard to pre-existing obligations. I can best describe this by giving you an example.

Let's assume that you own a residential lot and you have negotiated with a contractor to build a house on your lot for $70,000. After beginning to build the house, the contractor comes back to you and says he found out he underbid the house and is going to lose $10,000 on the house. He will not go forward unless you agree to pay him $10,000 more. Under common law the contractor probably has no right to any additional consideration (the $10,000). The typical common-law case would involve the lot owner paying the additional money and then suing the contractor for a return of the $10,000 after the house has been completed.

On the other hand, under the UCC and under certain state laws, it is possible for the contractor to enforce the new $10,000 amount based on the *good faith* of both parties. These laws (UCC and certain state laws) are aimed at allowing legitimate uncoerced requests for modification of the contract. It is possible, therefore, for the lot owner to believe that the contractor legitimately tried his or her best to perform the contract based on the specifications, yet there had been some honest underestimating.

## SETTLEMENT OF DEBTS

### LIQUIDATED DEBTS

Under the classic common law, it is not possible for parties to settle a *known existing debt* for *less than the full amount*. Assume you owe a retail store $100, because you purchased clothing there. Under the common law, you would not be able to *settle* that debt for $90 when it is *undisputed* that you purchased $100 worth of goods there. A liquidated debt is one in which the debt amount is known or calculable and there is no reasonable dispute about the debt. Assume that there were no defects in the goods. You could settle for $90 plus a pencil or plus a case of soft drinks, for instance. You could not settle for $90 and nothing more.

On the other hand, also under the common law, it is possible for you to settle a *disputed* debt for less than the amount that may have been claimed. Because it is disputed or what is known as an "unliquidated debt"—meaning that the parties are not sure whether the dollar amount would exist—then it is possible, even under the common law, to settle it for whatever amount the parties both agree to. Obviously if neither party agrees, then the debt cannot be settled. The point I am trying to make here is that we are still adding to our picture of consideration. Let's go back to the fact that a contract is like taking a photograph of the parties' agreement at one point in time. The contract is "cast in stone." Therefore, to deviate from this would take a specific exception under the common law or under the UCC. Do not assume, for instance, that you settle *any debt* for any amount you want just by some language in a check.

Sometimes there may be bad faith, sometimes there may coercion. The courts in most states seem to be leaning toward allowing people to modify agreements despite what they originally agreed to, as long as both parties are acting in good faith. In other words, if there is no manipulation, no dishonesty, no concealment of material facts, courts will generally enforce modified contracts. The best thing I can tell you is that if you have something like this occur, check with your business lawyer for your state laws.

## CHECKS—PAYMENT IN FULL

Checks marked "payment-in-full" come into play because on occasions individuals attempt to slip one by another party. Putting "paid-in-full" on a check where the amount is less may or may not work. Most courts look to whether the common law or UCC applies. If common law applies, then the check drawer might be attempting to slip something past someone. Courts may allow the parties to sue even with the "paid-in-full" language on the check. It is not always cut and dried. I am telling you this because being cutesy with a check may not always work. If the parties agree to a lesser amount, the agreement is enforceable in most states but possibly not in *your state*.

## SUBSTITUTED CONTRACT

One distinction we can use as an example is bringing an automobile into an auto dealership to have additional convenience items placed in the car. You have agreed to a certain price and then you have a chance to discuss the matter with several other parties and you believe you would like to get a slightly different package than the one you initially contracted for. You therefore go back to the dealership and come up with a package in which you both agree that instead of getting package X15, you are going to get package YZ2, which may cost more or cost less. It is obviously best to make sure that in the new agreement you state that this is a substitution of the old contract. Should you not, the court still would probably take the posture that this new agreement is intended to substitute for the old agreement, and the old agreement would be non-existent or would be unenforceable now.

## CONTRACTS WITHOUT CONSIDERATION

There are several circumstances whereby the courts would enforce an agreement even though there has been no consideration. In these particular circumstances, we will see either that there has been a law passed or that there has been some basic inherent unfairness, which the courts will acknowledge or identify.

Assume the statute of limitations comes into play. In some states the statute of limitations for contracts is six years; that is, if a debt due under a contract has not been collected within six years, it is no longer *enforceable*. It is possible, if there was a valid contract at one time, for the courts to allow the resurrection of this debt by a simple promise to pay on that debt. This is a slightly different fact setup than the typical past consideration example. Assume you owed someone a debt ($500) previously; that would not support a new promise, a new contract to pay money. You owed somebody $500 and you did not pay it, and the statute of limitations has run. You do not have to pay them any more. Despite that, you promise to pay the $500. Depending on state law, you may be obligated to then make the payment, even though this might appear to fit the "past consideration" example given before.

## PROMISE TO PAY A DISCHARGED DEBT

The bankruptcy laws have been designed to give the debtor a break from the financial perils of having incurred too much debt. First, in bankruptcy the debtor may be discharged from paying existing debts. There is a procedure under the Bankruptcy Laws whereby a debt can be resurrected or reaffirmed. It is possible for this debt to be revived if the bankruptcy procedures that entail the judge's approval of the resurrection of this debt are followed.

## PROMISSORY ESTOPPEL

There are certain circumstances whereby a party takes advantage of another party to the victim's detriment. An example might be the following: Ms. *A* would like to buy an automobile from Mr. *B*. Mr. *B* is a dealer. Ms. *A* goes to the dealership and the dealer says if you give us a television testimonial we may be able to give you a discount price on the car. Ms. *A* agrees. And the dealer says if you will then sign your name in a booklet saying how great the dealership is, then maybe we will knock off another $1,000. In a third attempt the potential dealer, states that the buyer still does not have enough money. The dealer then says, well, if we can get your statement for radio we will knock off another $1,000. Assuming that Ms. *A* has given all these testimonials, the dealer will probably be bound to the discounts it offered to Ms. *A* even though not written in any agreement.

If the dealership is taking advantage of Ms. *A*, the dealership would not be allowed to plead the truth or hide behind it. There are numerous court cases where a party was not allowed to plead "the truth" because the party took advantage of an innocent person who acted on the offender's words. One classic example happened when an individual wanted to hide assets from his creditors. He "sold" a piece of property to a supposed corporation. He got three other individuals to be shareholders in the corporation with him. Then later on, he told these individuals, after his creditors had gone away, that there had been no corporation. He said the corporation could not have taken title to the property even though that is what he represented to the other shareholders. In fact there had not been a corporation. He now spoke the truth.

The court said this individual had created this false scenario and would not be allowed to take advantage of it. Therefore, for purposes of this individual, he was only one-fourth owner. He was not the 100-percent owner he claimed he was, even though there had been no valid purchase because the corporation did not exist. The bottom line of all of this is that for some purposes, even though there had been no consideration, some individuals will not be allowed to plead the truth. Thus, the courts might supply the consideration where there was none or the courts might supply the mutual or other part of the agreement where it did not exist.

In some states, it is possible for there to be firm contracts even though there may not in fact be consideration as the common law or UCC would define it. There are, however, exceptions.

In common law, a corporation that acted *ultra vires* (in excess of its power) could itself get out of the contract where it had exceeded its own powers.

Today between contracting parties neither party would be able to use *ultra vires* to get out of the contract, even though there may be some limitation contained in the corporate charter or the corporate bylaws. It is often possible for

shareholders to stop a corporation from entering a contract that exceeds its authority if it is caught beforehand. It is possible for shareholders to seek damages from the directors or officers who exceeded the authority, but neither the corporation nor the second party to the contract can utilize this as a defense to their entering a contract.

You have no contract unless there is consideration. Any combination of the following can solidify a contract.

| You Give Up | Other Party Gives Up |
|---|---|
| Property | Property |
| Services | Services |
| Legal Right | Legal Right |

There are some exceptions when courts will "force" a contract even though some basic element is missing.

Promissory estoppel is a major exception. This occurs when Party A has gotten Party B to perform while Party *A* knows he has never made any promise to perform for Party *B*. It is sometimes called detrimental reliance.

## LEGALITY OF OBJECT

A contract must have a legal object. Goods that are being sold, or services that are being performed, or the right that is given up, must be within acceptable grounds as far as public policy and legality are concerned. For instance, the agreement to perform illegal services, such as breaking into a building, would not create an enforceable contract. The following are some of the specific types of legalities.

## VIOLATIONS OF STATUTES

### LICENSING STATUTES—
### REVENUE VERSUS REGULATION

Certain statutes require that individuals apply for and procure a *license* before they are able to perform certain tasks.

Certain statutes are *regulatory* in nature. These would be those statutes that would require an accountant to pass certain tests before she can practice public accounting.

Attorneys, doctors, embalmers, nurses, dentists are all in that category; the statute requires that they not only pay a fee but prove a certain level of competence, including passing tests, before they are allowed to perform services involving their skills.

Certain other types of statutes are *not* regulatory in nature but are *revenue raisers*. For instance, to sell umbrellas or shoes to the public, an individual typically does not have to pass a test to show that he has skills in warding off rain or skills in knowing how to size shoes. Though many of us have other ideas as a result of ill-fitting shoes, no test is required. Usually he need only procure a license, which is a fee-generating license.

The state or municipality now has some means of assuring that it can collect taxes that may be involved with those occupations. There is no level of skill that is being required. If an architect has not received a license because he or she has not taken or passed the test to become a licensed architect, that individual would not be able to collect from anyone for having performed architectural services. That is the penalty for not having complied with the laws requiring licensing for architects. On the other hand, if the statute merely involved the purchase of a license for sales tax purposes, such as selling ice cream, an unlicensed individual would be able to enforce an agreement for the sale of his ice cream. The person could still enforce the agreement in a court of law if he or she has not been paid.

### GAMBLING STATUTES

In almost all states there are strict prohibitions against gambling in general. In some states there are certain limited types of *exemptions* which would allow someone to have race track betting within the perimeters of the specific track. We see lotteries, race tracks and some casino gambling exemptions. If there is no exemption, then a person's attempt to enforce a gambling debt would be illegal.

Certain types of contracts are not considered gambling contracts. Some contractual types have been distinguished by law and by precedent.

### CERTAIN EXCEPTIONS

An example might involve an insurance contract. If a person has an insurable interest in the life of the person being insured or in the property being insured, the contract is not considered a gambling or wagering contract. Also, futures contracts in wheat, corn, pork bellies, plywood and oil are not considered gambling contracts. In order for any activity to be accepted, hence legal, it must fit specifically the type of law that is exempting that particular behavior. If there is no exemption or exception from the law, any debt that may be due or any contract involving illegal gambling or wagering is unenforceable. It implies a *void* agreement.

### SUNDAY STATUTES

Generally, any contract made or performable on a Sunday is valid and often considered to be legal. Many states have passed "Blue Laws" to prohibit work by most businesses on Sunday. The majority of the courts look for ways around any illegality; however, since there is no public clamor for the enforcement of these laws, also known as "Sunday Business Closing Laws," their effect will continue to be limited.

Many courts have acknowledged that the Sunday closing laws were religiously based. Because of the constitutional problems with enforcing religiously oriented laws, we continue to have courts that ignore or overturn laws that attempt to provide for Sunday closing.

The federal and state constitutions prohibit establishment of any religion or prohibiting the free exercise of any religion.

## PUBLIC POLICY VIOLATIONS

### TORTS OR CRIMES

Any contract which directly or indirectly attempts to encourage or bargain for behavior that violates someone's civil rights including injury—physical, psychological, mental or economical—or attempts to encourage injuring families or violating laws protecting the public or attempts to encourage violation of criminal laws is illegal, hence *void*.

These contracts cannot generally be *resurrected* to be enforceable; however, there are rare exceptions.

Public policies are difficult to define in a contract. A minor legal violation (*e.g.*, a parking ticket) incurred in completing a contract may not limit enforcement rights of either party. On the other hand, things that seriously impede the public welfare, health and welfare result in a *void* agreement. Such an agreement might also be criminal in nature by anyone attempting to contract for such behavior.

### EXCULPATORY CONTRACT PROVISIONS

Some courts have struck down provisions in contracts "allowing" one party to eliminate any liability for that party's own tortious behavior. Courts scrutinize provisions that seek to completely shield one party from its own willful or reckless behavior. In summary, courts often refuse to enforce such provisions.

For instance, on occasion you may have seen in shops a sign saying they will not be responsible for items left in your automobile. In those particular circumstances, the shops are still responsible for the actions of their employees. These shops may be able to limit their responsibility for individuals not under their control. Thus, even with contract language that limits their legal exposure, they are responsible for their employees and agents. Attempts to eliminate this total responsibility are probably illegal or unenforceable. On the other hand, these shops can help reduce their size as a target for non-employees or non-agents.

## COMMON-LAW RESTRAINTS OF TRADE

Most of us are aware of the problems of restraint of trade in violation of the antitrust laws. You have learned about these laws from history and civics lessons. There are other types of restraints of trade that sometimes can be a violation of public policy or sometimes can be enforced by the courts. You ought to be aware of the keen distinction here, even though at times it can become a rather grayish area.

### SALE OF A BUSINESS AND RESTRAINTS

A typical example is a local supermarket which over the years has created good will in taking care of its customers. The owner wants to sell the supermarket and retire. Part of what he will sell is good will. Someone may be interested in buying Joe's Supermarket. The potential buyer would be paying for the ability of this store to attract customers. If he buys the store from Joe, he does not want Joe to re-enter the business and scoop up the customers. It is not uncommon to see in the sale of a business a general legal prohibition against the selling owner from competing with the buyer for a long period of time in the market area. This protects the purchaser from competition by the seller. Courts generally do not like restraints of trade. In instances involving the sale of a business the purchaser is generally paying *more* than the value of the *building* (if he is buying the building), or more than the inventory value. The purchaser is buying the business as an ongoing business and not on a liquidated value basis. The courts will enforce provisions on protecting the excess value that the buyer is paying for. He is not just paying for the $20,000 of inventory and $200,000 for the business; he, is paying for an intangible which has brought customers to Joe's Supermarket. This intangible is what generates profits for Joe's Supermarket.

Courts will enforce provisions to make sure Joe does not return to burn the buyer. If the territory and circumstances are reasonable, the courts will enforce that prohibition, the restraint of trade, keeping the seller of the business from competing with the buyer.

## EMPLOYMENT CONTRACTS AND RESTRAINTS

We have seen certain prohibitions applying to an individual's livelihood. Sometimes businesses have taken the posture that they will *train* an individual and make this individual *visible* at no cost to the employee, but the business wants to protect its investment. Let's assume that an individual works for a loan company and in turn they work with some of the local automobile dealerships. The finance company trains its new employee with finance courses and schooling on the latest financing techniques. The finance company also helps advertise the employee through brochures, business cards and paying the employee's dues in various organizations. The finance company then has an interest in making sure this individual does not turn around and go to work for a competitor. Here the courts are concerned with balancing any restraints against other employment with the employee's livelihood. Companies can obviously lean on employees and erase any employment opportunities an individual may have in the future.

The courts do not like employment contracts that contain these restrictions unless they are reasonable and balanced. These restraints must be more limited than those involved in the sale of a business. Under this circumstance the courts would look to see if the restrictions are reasonably *necessary* to protect the employer's interest. The courts would ask whether the employee can adversely affect the employer. This would indicate whether the restraint is necessary. Assuming the necessary threshold is met, the second factor is the reasonableness of the restraint. It must be reasonable in time and geography. The courts do not like to see restrictions that are *broader* than the *employer's territory*. If the courts look to see what was the relevant marketing area for the employer, the courts are not likely to allow a restriction which exceeds the territory of the employer. The courts sometimes have redone contracts, but generally courts will not step in and enforce the law of contracts if a contract is contrary to the public policy as a result of contract provisions that were overreaching.

In summary, some courts have used their equity power to reform (rewrite) the contract provisions.

Often the courts just strike down the entire contract if one of the significant provisos is not met. Thus if its time restrictions are for too long a period, the court may strike the entire contract. If any employer is interested in having such a restrictive agreement, he should be concerned about consulting his business lawyer to see what is the latest in enforceable provisions in his state and local courts.

## OBSTRUCTING THE LEGAL PROCESSES

Another type of contract that is illegal or unenforceable is the type that attempts to get parties to agree not to cooperate in any requirement for the administration of justice. On occasion individuals have agreed that if they settle their civil differences one of the parties agrees not to testify against the other party in a court of law. One party may agree not to initiate the disclosure of any activities that occurred. The courts have held that restrictions of this type, where a party would agree not to cooperate with a grand jury subpoena, are unenforceable and strictly illegal. These agreements are *void*.

One of the cases a few years ago involved an ex-husband and ex-wife. It seems the wife decided to use a pair of scissors to rearrange her husband's chest. The husband got the message and decided a divorce would be appropriate. The parties agreed to a property settlement and to a divorce. Part of the agreement was that the husband would not speak publicly or would not present to the public authorities any of the evidence of the wife's attempt at chest surgery on him! The courts held that this agreement was unenforceable and against public policy and the attempt to do such a thing was strictly illegal and void. That portion of the contract was *void*.

The object lesson is to note the distinction between civil and criminal law. We cannot make civil agreements that would adversely affect the public's rights to enforce criminal statutes or even to restrict someone else's rights under the law.

## ILLEGAL PERFORMANCE OF CONTRACTS

It is possible for a contract to be considered illegal even though it is legal on its face. For example, let us assume a contract has been struck with an individual who will distribute movies for a motion picture studio. The fee that the individual will receive is $10,000 plus a percentage of the gross revenues. Assume that the sales person used the $10,000 to bribe an employee of a large customer. Assume that the film studio learned of the commercial bribery and refused to pay the hired agent. If the agent sued the film company, he would probably lose because the agent attempted to *perform* the contract *illegally*. In this case, there was nothing wrong with the method of distribution. The courts, however, do not encourage individuals to break the law to perform a contract.

## UNCONSCIONABLE CONTRACTS

As mentioned in connection with legal capacity, the courts occasionally step in to protect an individual who is unable or incapable of understanding a contract. On the other hand, the courts do not usually step in to make sure that consideration is adequate.

The courts are not going to step in to see if a person is paying $10,000 for a car and has gotten $10,000 worth of value. The courts will not enforce "fair deals." The buyer must beware. None of us can be experts in all of the things that we end up buying on a day-to-day basis. Again, the courts generally do not step in to help us.

On occasion the courts have used the doctrine of *unconscionability* to *void* a contract. The UCC has such a provision, and on occasion common law courts utilize this concept. It works like this: If a contract or any clause of the contract is deemed to be unconscionable at the time the contract was made, the court may refuse to enforce the contract or may strike out the portion of the contract that is unconscionable.

This doctrine has its roots in the early common law in the courts of equity, where chancellors could fashion a remedy when a contract was unfair at least in part. One of the factors the courts will examine in determining if conscionability is involved is whether one of the parties dictated that a *printed* form be used.

The courts also look at whether the price is fair or if we are dealing with a top-of-the-market price. Was there a discounted price? The courts will also look at the capacity of the person forced to sign the agreement. Did the person give up all or most of their basic rights? If, the buyer has no right to return goods if the goods are proved to be duds, then the courts may step in. Do the contracts have a forfeiture clause so that a buyer loses whatever payments he has made even though the goods are repossessed? The courts do not like such provisions. The courts also look at the surrounding circumstances to see whether there would be any ethical and possibly grossly aggressive behavior that is repulsive to the common good.

The courts also look for the fine print and see if the contract is such that it would be very difficult to understand. If there were 200,000 words on one page, did the person have time to read the document? The courts have also looked at such things as how repetitive some of the phrases are. Some contracts are designed with repetitious phrases and penalties and other onerous clauses in several places. When you see contracts like these, it is easy for the party requiring the printed form to encourage people to strike out whatever they do not like. The party doing the striking may be striking it out only *once*, yet the contract is designed to have the offensive phrases in three or four different ways and places. I have seen this type of contract; even if you catch some of the "bad" provisions you may miss the other three or four times they appear in the contract. Therefore, the courts will look to see how manipulative was the approach taken to the contract and to the terms and conditions.

Last, the courts will look at the status of the individuals—whether they are unsophisticated, uneducated, illiterate, foreigners not at home in the language, or individuals who are unlikely to have much in the way of bargaining or economic power in order to fend for themselves. One example involved the sale of a freezer to a welfare recipient. The initial unit had a retail value of $300. By the time the completed contract was signed, including credit charges, the amount had risen to $1,439.69. The court held the contract to be unconscionable. On occasion the court will step in to stop such gross behavior.

You may not be able to enforce a contract if the object of the contract is illegal. The "illegality" might depend upon "degree of seriousness," or how bad the illegality is.

## EFFECTS OF ILLEGALITY

Not all contracts that contain *some* illegal provisions are necessarily totally illegal. Generally, if the contract contains a grossly illegal provision (one that would be violative of the criminal statutes), the entire contract is unenforceable. On the other hand, where part of a contract may be unlawful and the other part is legal, it is possible that the courts may enforce the lawful portion and prevent only the illegal portion from being enforced. In effect, the courts will sever the legal part of the contract if that is possible. On the other hand, if it cannot be severed the courts generally rule the entire contract is illegal.

There are some circumstances whereby if the potential illegality is such that it is not against public

You have to know the state public policy where the contract is made or to be performed.

e) Certain exculpatory provisions, to free a party from liability he might ordinarily have, may be unenforceable. Do not assume. Check with your lawyer.

f) Restraints of trade, e.g., non-compete agreements may be unenforceable. Different states have different rules.

g) Parties cannot agree to obstruct legitimate legal process in the courts. These types of agreements are unenforceable.

h) If Party *A* performs a contract in an illegal manner, *A* may be breaching the contract even though it is silent on how *A* is to perform the contract.

i) Contracts with provisions that are too one-sided or horrendous *might* be unenforceable. This does not happen often, but occasionally a court will view one of these as unenforceable.

policy, the courts may allow the basic contract to be enforced. For instance, where truck drivers are given some incentives to reach a destination within the speed limit, the contract is enforceable even if the drivers receive a few traffic citations. On the other hand, if the schedules were such that the drivers would have to constantly exceed the speed limit, the courts might not allow them to enforce their contracts for payment.

## OTHER EXCEPTIONS

There are some exceptions to the unenforceability of an illegal bargain. The courts make an attempt at trying to bring some justice to a potentially bad situation.

### 1. First Party Withdrawing Prior to Performance

On occasion the courts have allowed a party who withdraws from the potential illegal bargain prior to having performed, to be able to rescind the contract and get any money back and have their performance consideration refunded. The courts

---

# Here are some examples you should keep in mind:

a) Certain licensing statutes are required to practice in a field and hence be able to enforce a contract for services. CPA's and MD's are examples.

b) In some states gambling contracts are unenforceable even if they were legal in the state where made.

c) Contracts requiring performance on Sunday may or may not be enforceable.

d) Some contracts cannot be enforced because the state "public policy" prohibits them.

have to make tough decisions on these, but nevertheless it does happen.

### 2. Party in the Protected Class

Some laws are specifically made to protect a certain category of individuals. One example might be the federal and state securities laws. They are designed to protect investors primarily against a company or insiders selling the stock in violation of the disclosure requirement of the statute. Therefore, on occasion when an individual knows that he or she is buying stock that should be registered, courts have allowed some of these investors to recoup their investment by rescinding the contract. The purpose of the securities law was to protect this particular category of individuals (investors) from the stock issuer. Another example might involve child labor laws where even though the children know they are violating the law and the parents of the children know they are working more hours than they should, the courts have allowed those individuals and parents of these children to collect the amounts of money due. They are allowed to collect even though the children have worked hours in excess of what the law allows. The employer who violates this statute is the one who ultimately pays. The children are in the protected category.

### 3. Parties Not Equally at Fault

Generally, the courts will not aid a party in the recovery of consideration paid by that party in a deal if both of the parties are equally at fault. On the other hand, if the parties are not equally at fault the courts will allow the party who has "less fault" to get his or her consideration returned.

### 4. Party Ignorant of
### Material Information on Illegal Deal

Some courts have allowed a party who is innocent or who is ignorant of the facts of the illegality to be able to get his consideration back. An example might involve someone who is asked to take a briefcase to a friend who lives 400 miles from his house. The individual (Ron Q) does not know that the briefcase contains illegal contraband. Ron Q is offered $100 for the delivery and will be paid upon his return. Ron Q is given a round-trip airline ticket to deliver the "important documents" to his friend. Ron Q does not see or cannot examine the papers. He is told he has some "mortgage documents." Later on, his friend who receives the papers is arrested for possession of contraband in the briefcase. Ron Q can still recover the $100 upon his return. He could enforce this in court.

In summary, the courts will not encourage or enforce illegal bargains. They view these "bargains" as void, with some exceptions. The courts view exceptions very narrowly. Substantially all of the contracts that are enforceable in this country involve legal bargains, but "illegal bargains" do occur on occasion.

## FORM OF CONTRACTS; WHICH ONES MUST BE IN WRITING

There are certain types of contracts that are required by law (UCC or other laws) to be in a certain *form* in order to be *enforceable*. Generally, the state law will contain enough information so that we know what form the contract must be in to be enforceable. These agreements must be (a) *signed* the way we normally think of contracts being signed with the parties there and with the information contained in them; or (b) be evidenced by written documents which in total lay out the deal. The requirements need not be met in only one way.

You should be aware of these written requirements and pay attention to the type of contracts that are *unenforceable* if we do not meet this form requirement. These contracts can be *valid* even if they should be in writing but are not, but they would be generally *unenforceable*. In any event, if the deal should be in writing, but is not, you will probably *lose* your consideration.

Let's take a look at the types of contracts we are talking about.

## STATUTE OF FRAUDS—
## WHAT IS THE LAW THAT IS CAUSING ALL THIS WRITING HUMBUG?

### CONTRACT COVERED BY THE "STATUTE OF FRAUDS"

The term "statute of frauds" is used here as a generic term for most state statutes that require contracts to be in some written form.

There are basically eight types of contracts that are covered:

1. Executor or administrator of an estate agrees to pay the debts of the deceased.

2. Defendant agrees to pay the debts of another.

3. Agreements based upon a promise of marriage.

4. Agreements for the sale or transfer of any interests in land or real property.

5. Agreements that cannot be performed within a year of the date of the contract.

6. Agreements that involve no sale of goods, usually $500 or more.

7. Sale of securities or security interests.

8. Modification or rescission of contracts

There are other types of covered contracts, which vary from state to state, but these are the predominant subject matters. There are certain types of personal property that are covered by the UCC.

### Executor/administrator promises to pay the debts of another

The basic scenario is that the administrator/executor has allegedly agreed to *personally* pay for the debts of the deceased out of his or her *personal* funds. This type of allegation became fairly common some three or four hundred years ago in England. As a result, Parliament passed a law (actually called "Statute of Frauds and Perjuries") which prohibited a mere statement without written proof that the administrator/executor agreed to pay such bills. Obviously it is very easy for someone to testify that the administrator/executor who was administering/executing the estate of the deceased promised to *personally* pay the debts of the deceased. Parliament stepped in to stop the abuses. In those days it was easy to hire a "professional witness" to testify to anything—and they did. So, to remedy the fraud upon the courts, the plaintiff would now be required to produce a *writing* to prove his/her case or there would be no case. Now the creditor must get this evidence in writing in order to enforce it in court.

### Guaranteeing someone else's debts

In keeping with the previous example, when someone agrees to pay the debts of another, again there had been tremendous abuse in the early common law days. This was another of the areas where Parliament placed this higher standard to prevent the tremendous abuse that was taking place. Therefore, the creditor had better have this agreement or promise *in writing*.

There have been some exceptions created by the courts. They include:

### Main Purpose or Primary Beneficiary Exception

If the debtor in fact is the primary beneficiary, the courts have said that it is not the promise to pay the debt of another. It is in fact the promise to pay the debt of that party who benefits from the agreement. An example of this might be:

Mr. *X* is dealing with a lumber company, and says he would like to buy 240 board feet of 2 by 4 in 8-foot lengths. A friend of mine will pick them up. If the friend does not pay the bill, just send me (Mr. *X*) the bill. Here Mr. *X* is receiving the *benefit* of the purchase, because he has negotiated the deal. On the other hand, if the guarantor comes in *after* the debt is in existence and says if that individual does not pay, I will, there is a different deal. Now the creditor must get the promise in writing.

## Substitute of Guarantor

Another example is where the guarantor is substituted for the original debtor by the creditor. In other words, the creditor and the guarantor (Mr. *Z*) agree that even though Mr. *B* owes the money, the creditor will write off the debt from Mr. *B*, but will look primarily to Mr. *Z*. If they agree to this *orally*, the courts will enforce that. It is another exception to the guarantor/suretyship provision.

## Marriage as Consideration for Another Form of Consideration

An agreement to marry, wherein two parties agree to marry each other, does not have to be in writing. Agreements to marry plus something else are covered by the writing requirement. For instance, if there is some agreement that the future husband will transfer to the future wife some goods, as an incentive to marry, this agreement has to be evidenced in writing. It is not just the agreement to marry, but the agreement to transfer property, goods or services, or something additional to mere marriage, which would trigger the writing requirement. (This is not a common small business problem, but I thought you should know this before your next cocktail party.)

## Land Contracts—Including Sales or Transfers of Interest in Real Property

If a third party intends to sell, lease, or transfer or encumber any of these "bundle of rights" that an individual has in real property, the agreement generally has to be evidenced by a writing. If anyone owns real property, he or she has the right to mortgage it, sell it, or allow someone to grow crops on it. We have the right to allow someone to pick peaches or bananas off the trees. If someone is claiming such rights in real property, he or she would have to have that evidenced by a writing. There are some exceptions the courts have allowed. One of these is that no agreement in writing is required if an individual (a) has made a down payment, (b) has moved onto the property and (c) has done something to improve the property. Some courts have allowed these circumstances as an exception to the requirement that the transfer or sale of the property be evidenced in writing.

## Agreements that Cannot be Performed Within a Year of the Making of the Contract

Any agreement or promise that cannot be performed within one year of the making of the contract is covered by the statute of fraud. Therefore, it is not enforceable unless it is evidenced by a writing. It need only be *capable* of being performed within a year to be excepted from the statute of fraud. It does not make a difference if it is *probable* that it will be performed within one year. It is only important that it is *possible* to be performed within one year. If we have an agreement calling for employment of an individual for life, this agreement is enforceable without having to meet the standards required by the statute of frauds.

Another example might be a contract to work for someone for 52 weeks but the work does not begin for four weeks from the date of making the contract. This contract cannot be performed within one year from the making of this contract. Therefore, it must be evidenced by a writing within the standards of the statute of fraud. There is an exception that has been upheld in many courts. It says that if one of the parties (Mr. *W*) has completed all of his performance, even though it takes more than one year, and this performance has been *accepted* by the other party (Mr. *R*), then the entire agreement is now outside the statute of frauds. Mr. *R*, who is yet to perform, must now perform. In other words, if Mr. *W* has worked for over a year under a contract that should be in writing, all is not lost for Mr. *W*. If Mr. *R* (employer) has accepted Mr. *W*'s services but has not yet paid Mr. *W*, Mr. *R* must now pay. Mr. *R* cannot use the writing requirement as a shield for services he has used to his benefit.

## The Sale of Goods and Merchandise for $500 or more

Under the UCC a contract for the sale of goods and merchandise of less than $500 is enforceable without meeting the statute of fraud (*i.e.*, can be oral). If it is for $500 or more, it must meet the statute of frauds and must be evidenced by a writing. This applies to the sale of personal property, but does not apply to the sale of money, investment securities or other intangible things specifically defined in the UCC. The excluded things that we are talking about would include accounts receivable, bonds, notes, shares of stock and several other types of personal property.

## Other Statute of Frauds Provisions Within the UCC

The UCC requires that the sale of securities, no matter what the value, is included within the provisions of the statute of frauds. Security interests in personal property must be evidenced by a writing. In addition, the sale of other kinds of personal property in excess of $5000 must be evidenced by a writing. This provision does not cover goods. It covers rights under contracts, royalty agreements, patent agreements and certain intangibles as listed in the UCC.

## Modification or Rescission of Contracts Within the Statute of Frauds

A contract may not be covered by the statute of frauds initially but a modification of the contract might then bring it within the statute of frauds. One example is a six-month employment contract that is extended to two years. To enforce the contract as modified, the agreement must be evidenced by a writing. Nevertheless, if there is a modification or rescission of a contract that would bring it within the statute of frauds, we would have to see if the agreement met the statute of frauds provisions. If the contract was initially for a year and a half, any rescission would have to be evidenced by a writing.

If a contract comes *within* the statute of frauds or the other statutes we discussed, then it must be evidenced by a *writing*. There are some exceptions.

# REQUIREMENTS UNDER THE STATUTE OF FRAUDS; HOW DOES A BUSINESS OWNER/MANAGER MEET THE REQUIREMENTS?

There are several approaches to complying with the statute of frauds. We will examine the methods for complying with these.

## A WRITING OR MEMORANDUM

The UCC does not dictate that there be a *formal written contract* when a writing is required. It merely dictates that there be some written note or memorandum describing the deal and signed by the party who is attempting to *deny* the *existence* of such agreement. Any form will do, such as a letter, telegram or receipt which generally *identifies* the *parties*, the *subject matter*, the *quantity* and the *price*. It does not have to be in a single document. It can be in several documents. The documents do not have to be signed at the same time. Nor do the documents have to be signed when the contract is brought into existence. The documents may have been destroyed. But if there is some evidence to verify that the deal was in writing, then it is possible for the party who is seeking to enforce the contract to move forward in court. The writing must identify who the parties are, the subject matter, the terms and conditions, and the consideration that is being promised, and it must contain the signature of at least the party who is attempting to deny it. The signature can be initials, a stamp, an "x," a printed stamp. We only need evidence that the party has assented to that particular agreement. It is possible for the memorandum to omit certain essential terms as long as under the UCC its terms could be supplied. The UCC allows certain essential terms such as price and quantity to be supplied by external sources. That is OK, for statute of frauds purposes.

## OTHER METHODS OF COMPLIANCE

One of the features of the UCC is that there are two categories of individuals to whom it applies.

One is the average consumer. The other is the *merchant*. A merchant is assumed to be more knowledgeable than the average consumer. It can make a difference if one of the two parties to the agreement is a merchant.

As I mentioned before, the UCC says that the party attempting to *deny* the agreement generally has to be the one who signs it. There is an exception if one of the parties is a *merchant*. If, within a reasonable amount of time, the other party (also a merchant) sends a confirmation to the merchant and the merchant does not object in writing to the confirmation *within 10 days* after receiving the confirmation, then the merchant may be tied to the agreement. A merchant does not have to sign an agreement. Therefore there is a way of requiring a merchant to object to what another merchant confirmed. A memorandum or note is sufficient to tie the merchant to the agreement. The merchant is held to knowing the business. This confirmation rule makes it easy for merchants to do business. It also requires the merchant to take action within 10 days if he finds that the memorandum or note is inaccurate.

## SPECIALLY MANUFACTURED GOODS

Another exception in the UCC which minimizes the written-proof requirement of the complaining party involves goods that are specially made for a particular buyer. These particular goods must *not* be suitable for sale in the *ordinary course of business* to other parties. An example might be a specially manufactured glass entrance door or tailored clothing that could not easily be sold. One condition is that the goods cannot be sold in the *ordinary course* of the *seller's business*. In addition, the seller must have made a *substantial beginning* to *manufacture* these goods—not just taken the order. The maker must have expended money and time in either procuring the materials or making the goods. The buyer would not have to produce a note or memorandum to prove there was an agreement.

## ADDITIONAL EXCEPTIONS

If the party attempting to deny the existence of the contract *admits* in court pleadings or in *testimony in court* that a contract is made, then the requirements of the statute of frauds may be met even though there is no note or memorandum to prove the existence. This type of "proof" is limited to the extent that the admitting party actually admits. For example, if he admits to buying five TV's but the original deal was really for 15 TV's, the admitting party is bound to pay for five, not 15.

There are two circumstances under which the buyer may be committed to an oral deal. If the buyer has *received* and *accepted* the goods, he has acted as an owner of the goods and is *bound* to pay. If the buyer has *received* the goods and has made some *payment* for the goods, then he is bound to pay. To the extent a buyer has performed by receipt and acceptance or receipt and payment, the buyer cannot deny the contract.

*Some exceptions to the writing requirement include:*

a) Merchant is party denying existence of the agreement.

b) The goods are specially manufactured.

c) Denying party admits the existence of the agreement.

d) The buyer of goods has received and accepted the goods.

e) The buyer of goods has received and paid for the goods.

## THE EFFECTS OF NON-COMPLIANCE

If one party (Mr. *X*) accepts the benefit of another party's (Mr. *Y*) performance, the courts will require the performance by the denying party (Mr. *X*). Mr. *X* will have to perform to the extent to which he has received any benefits. Let us assume that there has been an oral agreement for Alpha to work for Beta for two years. Alpha has worked for Beta nine months. Then Beta may win on the two-year agreement but would have to pay Alpha at least for the nine months for which Alpha has worked so far.

(Perhaps Alpha should call upon the Greek muses for retribution.)

The court will not enforce the *entire contract* even though there has been *partial performance*. Partial performance will *not* in effect legitimize the *entire contract*. That would virtually erase the statute of frauds if there had been even one day of partial performance.

## PROMISSORY ESTOPPEL

This is a court-created rule. It sometimes prevents persons from taking advantage of the truth if they had been the perpetrators of a fraud or any kind of behavior that creates an unjust result. In a previous example about the person who represented to his co-shareholders that a corporation had been created and that they were shareholders in it, he then went to court to try to get his property back by saying there had never been a corporation (which was true). The court said, "No. You are not going to be allowed now to tell the truth since you duped your co-shareholders into believing they were originally buying into a corporation."

This doctrine occasionally will crop up in statute of frauds cases. An example might be where Mr. *O* has assured Mr. *P* that under no circumstances will Mr. *O* assert the statute of frauds (as in "trust me"). Mr. *O* says that is not his style. Mr. *O* assures Mr. *P* he would not mislead him and not to worry about the lack of a written agreement. On occasion the court will not allow the "city slicker" to take advantage of his own lies. The courts apply this rule depending on how disgusting or unfair the circumstances may be.

## PAROLE EVIDENCE RULE

Many contracts are created after preliminary discussions and negotiations. There may be much give and take. But when a deal is struck, these preliminary facts disappear. The prior facts or any contemporaneous agreements become invisible once a contract is formed. This is a description of the parole evidence rule.

The parole evidence rule is leaning toward a "photograph" concept. The photograph of that deal is what will control. The courts now look to that agreement as being the *final* agreement. The parties cannot dispute this deal by referring to preliminary negotiations, the haggling over price, the haggling over delivery terms, or the negotiating of the goods. Once the parties have put the agreement in writing, they have struck a deal. Everything else prior to that agreement, including any documents, becomes *irrelevant*. There are a few narrow exceptions wherein the parties may bring either oral proof or other written proof, but only within certain specific circumstances. Some of the conditions are:

## Fraud and Other Problems

Let us assume there has been *fraud*, forgery, misrepresentation, mistakes, duress or failure of consideration.

## Partially Written Agreement

An agreement is partially written and partially oral. Where the parties did not intend to *write* the entire agreement, some oral agreement may be part of the deal.

## Ambiguities

Some terms may be contradictory or may leave tremendous gaps that were not in the agreement.

## Condition Precedent

Some essential items may have been omitted which may trigger the entire agreement. One example involves the renovation of the leased space for a restaurant. The agreement was silent on the tenant getting the landlord's permission to renovate his restaurant. The court recognized that the contractor could not begin remodeling unless the landlord concurred. The court allowed parole evidence to show that the tenant had to get the landlord's permission. This condition precedent was not in the agreement with the contractor. It was an *oral* condition precedent. This is an exception. The court said that was a condition precedent to proceeding with the remodeling contract. Parole evidence could be introduced to prove that this was a necessary condition.

## Usage and Custom

The UCC allows the parties to introduce evidence that the parties had dealt with each other previously under this same contract. The court may allow evidence of prior performance of this contract to be introduced. The UCC allows evidence of prior usage and custom into a disputed contract case.

## Modification or Rescission of Contract

If there are modifications to the contract or if there is a rescission of the contract, the courts may allow oral or outside evidence to be introduced. The courts could use this outside information to determine whether the contract has been totally terminated even though it has been evidenced by a writing.

The parole evidence rule stops either party from contradicting the provisions in the contract by using other oral or written evidence.

Once the contract is written, prior negotiations, discussions or writings become irrelevant but for the exceptions we've discussed.

However, if there is evidence of fraud, duress, undue influence, ambiguity, rescission or modification, then other evidence of the *facts* or contract provisions may be allowed.

# THE INTERPRETATION OF CONTRACTS

It is important to get some idea of how contracts are interpreted. Party-goers often hear in cocktail conversation, or individuals when express-

ing their knowledge of contract law, how ludicrous some court acted when interpreting some particular contract.

It is generally not true that courts focus on commas and semicolons to interpret contracts. Often it is more accurate that courts pick up the flavor of an entire contract and then base their decision on minor things. It is more nearly accurate that courts interpret the entire contract and the meaning of specific phrases.

Sometimes commas and semicolons and other grammatical devices make a difference, but generally that is not the case.

Some of the rules pertaining to interpretation of contracts are the following:

## THE PLAIN MEANING RULE

Generally, courts interpret contracts so that they pick out what the obvious *intentions* of the parties were in a contract. Since there is a dispute, it may appear that one of the parties is attempting to "change the rules." The courts will not attempt to force a construction of a contract when an interpretation stands out.

There may be a different interpretation as to what is a "plain meaning." Nevertheless the courts attempt to say that an interpretation that hits them in the eye is the plain or unambiguous meaning in a contract interpretation dispute.

## ORDINARY MEANING

The court will attempt to interpret the words in such a manner that whatever is the ordinary interpretation of those words is the one that will apply. There are special words that have a special meaning. For these words, the courts might get the definition from a standard dictionary. Those definitions are generally accepted as being the most probable interpretation that the courts will use. Technical words that are unambiguous and have a precise meaning are generally accepted as such by the court. The courts would not, however, use peculiar interpretations if the result is an unreasonable interpretation. The courts try to pick interpretations that are in keeping with the nature of the contract, the nature of the parties being involved in the contract, the nature of the business, and prior dealings that the parties may have had with each other.

## WHOLE CONTRACT

It is extremely important to view or interpret a contract as a *whole*. This yields an overall strategy that fits all of the words and provisions together. This approach is used even when a contract is partly written and partly oral (assuming the parol evidence rule does not exclude the oral portion).

## AMBIGUOUS LANGUAGE

If there is some ambiguity in the language of the contract, the courts will probably interpret the contract strictly against the party who *prepared* the contract. If there is a reasonable interpretation, the court will interpret it that way no matter which party authorized the agreement. If there is still an ambiguity, then the party who wrote the contract will generally pay the price.

## CONFLICTS WITHIN THE CONTRACT

If there are conflicts between (a) words that are handwritten, (b) words that are typewritten and (c) words that are printed (by the printing press), the courts have a certain priority whereby they interpret the contract. Where there is an unresolvable conflict between the three types we have just mentioned, then the handwritten would control over a typewritten, and typewritten would control over a pre-printed, portion of the contract.

## GENERAL PROVISIONS VERSUS SPECIFIC PROVISIONS

Again, we are looking at possible conflicts within an agreement. Where there are general provisions in a contract and there are also specific provisions pertaining to a particular required performance, the specific provision would generally prevail. An example might involve a contract for building a swimming pool at someone's home. There is a general provision that a certain type of tile would be used. If a specific provision pertained to the tile that would be used above a certain level in the pool, the courts would interpret this specific language as modifying the general tile requirement under the agreement. The general tile specification would be modified for that specific area above a certain level in the pool. The pieces would then fit. Unfortunately, the pieces do not always fit as in this example.

## VALIDITY OF CONTRACT

The common law and the UCC generally encourage commerce. If it is possible to reasonably interpret a contract in more than one way, yet one of those ways would establish a valid contract, the courts will look to the interpretation that says there is *a contract here*. If one reasonable interpretation creates a valid contract and the other two or three ways lead away from a contract, the court will probably favor the existence of a contract. On the other hand, if a contract is clearly invalid, the courts are not going to choose some convoluted interpretation that is not very probable and would virtually insult the verbal integrity of the agreement to make it work. The courts will hold that it is invalid.

## ESTABLISHED MEANING

For terms used in a contract that have an established meaning, the court will generally interpret them in accordance with the established legal meaning unless the party has a contrary meaning where there is no doubt that they do not intend to go along with the established legal meaning.

Do not assume that a contract "means what it says." Few legal types and fewer lay persons can put all the rules of interpretation together easily. Even if you could put all these rules together, you would probably find gaps and contradictions.

Write your contract so an elementary grade student could understand it.

## REFERENCE TO EXISTING LAW

If the two parties to a contract make any reference to a state or federal law, it is presumed that they are contracting in keeping with the law *existing* when the contract was made, as opposed to some other law that may have been in force at some previous time. If there is a subsequent change in the law, the courts may apply the new law. Also if the contract specifies some specific version of the law, the court will probably apply that version even if it is outdated. Under certain circumstances, the court may dictate that the current law be used. Prior versions may be illegal now.

There are times when certain laws apply to a contract whereby the court must strictly construe the contract. If the original interpretation of the contract is such that it will violate the law, the courts will interpret the contract so it strictly meets the requirements of public policy, or the contract will fall.

An example might be where the securities law would apply to a particular contract and the parties should register this securities offering with the state securities commission. If it is possible to interpret the contract so that the company might avoid registering the securities, the courts would be bound to look for the intent of the securities law. If the contract could be interpreted two different ways, the courts would look to the intent of the statute and the public policy. If it is possible to interpret the contract several different ways, but there is strong public policy toward protecting the investors in that state, then any ambiguity about registering the securities would be resolved in favor of registration.

## CONFLICTS OF LAWS

There are certain times whereby the courts may have to apply various conflicting laws. Some contracts may involve the laws of the state where the contract is *made* and the laws of the state where the contract was *performed*. At certain times it may be difficult to determine which laws apply. The court then applies the *conflicts of laws* rule.

For contracts the traditional common-law rule has been that if the contract is established in one jurisdiction, then its laws generally apply.

If, however, the contract was established in the state of Kansas to build a building in the state of Nebraska, the courts would probably look to the laws of the state of Kansas to decide if there is a valid contract. The contract is being performed and the building is being built in Nebraska. The courts would look to the laws of Nebraska to determine if the contract is properly performed. If the nature of a contract is such that it is repugnant to the public policy of State *Y* where it is being enforced, State *Y* might refuse to enforce the contract. Some states may refuse to enforce a contract based on a gambling debt. The general rule is that if the contract is valid in the state where it was made, then it will have to be recognized in other states. Again, there are some exceptions.

## STIPULATION OF GOVERNING LAW

Sometimes a contract specifies the law that will be applied to interpreting it. There are some requirements, however, that one or both of the parties must have some *contacts* with this particular state. If a contract is formed in Kansas and if it is performable in Nebraska, it is probable that the courts would not apply the laws of New York even if the contract so states. Thus, if none of the parties nor the subject matter of the agreement results in any minimum contact with a state, it is unlikely that any court would allow the laws of that State to be applied.

## THIRD PARTIES IN CONTRACTS

Any valid contract can be established, as we have mentioned, without any party to the contract receiving any of the benefits of the contract. An example is as follows: Mr. *A* is willing to donate $15,000 to the favorite charity of an automobile dealer (Mr. *B*) on the condition that Mr. *B* deliver the car, not to Mr. *A*, who is making the donation to Mr. *B*'s charity, but to Mr. *A*'s niece. Neither of the parties to the agreement will receive any of the consideration. We see that even though neither the charity nor the niece has incurred any burden or obligation, they will receive benefit. There are also circumstances whereby these third parties are able to enforce the contract since each is an *intended beneficiary*.

## ASSIGNMENT OF CONTRACTS INCLUDING RIGHTS AND DUTIES

An assignment of *rights* under a contract is the transfer of one's property rights in the contract to another person. It may also entail the delegation of certain *duties* under the contract.

Let us assume that we have contracted with an individual to build a house on our property, the amount of the contract being $80,000. The contractor agrees to follow your plans and specifications. If the contractor has built the house, the contractor can assign his right to the $80,000 to a bank.

Assume that the contractor has not built the house. He may then be able to delegate the *duties* involved in building the house to various subcontractors. Please note the *rights* versus the *duties*. The contractor is always responsible for the *duties* he has under the contract, but he can give up his *rights* under the contract. An assignment is the transfer by the contractor to a third party, an *assignee*, of his property rights under the contract.

One way to view property rights is that the consideration *due* you is an *asset* you have. The consideration you *owe* is a *liability* against you. The contractor is always obligated to make sure that the house is built according to the plans and specifications. As we mentioned, the $80,000 due from the homeowner is an asset, and the duty to build the house is a liability.

Some contracts can be assigned *without* the *approval* of the first party, the landowner. Other types of contracts, which may be of a *personal service* nature or involve certain *confidential information* or a *trust relationship, cannot be assigned without the approval of the other party*. If an artist were painting a portrait of you, this artist could *not* assign the duties involved in painting such a portrait to anyone else *without your approval*. This is a personal service relationship. The courts would be very protective of your rights to object to anyone assigning the *duties* involved here. On the other hand, if the artist has already painted the portrait and you owe her $1,000 for doing such a portrait, there would be no detriment to you if she assigned her rights to a bank. Therefore, we must distinguish between rights and duties that *may be* assignable and rights and duties that *may not* be assignable.

If you are contracting with an out-of-state party, you should consider having your state law listed as the state law to be used to interpret the contract.

## RIGHTS THAT ARE NOT ASSIGNABLE

If an assignment materially increases the risk or burden upon the *non-assigning* party, the assignment is forbidden even if such are *not expressly forbidden* in the agreement. The courts would generally not allow such an assignment.

I will give you an example. Assume you are obligated to pay the other party money in *cash* within three days. If the other party lives in your area and you know where she lives and where to deliver the money, the other party cannot assign the right to receive this cash to a bank that is 1,000 miles away. If the money had to be paid in *cash*, this assignment would materially increase your duty. Therefore, there are some limitations on the assignment even of the right to receive funds. Generally, transferring money by check anywhere in the United States is not an additional burden. On the liability or duty side, again, a person could not assign the right to services where it would increase your burden. Furthermore, assume you contracted to clean someone's carpets in your town for $99.95. This person could not assign this right to someone in another town. Your burden would be increased, and this "assignment" would be null.

One thing that is important to realize is that only the legal or contractual *rights* that one may have under an agreement can be assignable. As to the *duties* involved, even if someone else does them, the original party is still legally obligated—has the *duty*— to perform up to the standards to which you have agreed.

## THE FORM OF THE ASSIGNMENT

An assignment may be contractual in nature, but it does *not* have to be a contract. Generally an assignment may be oral or may be written. If the subject matter of the assignment falls within the statute of frauds, the assignment must meet the statute of frauds requirements or any statute that may require that the agreement be in writing. In some states a wage assignment must be in writing.

## RIGHTS OF THE ASSIGNEE, THE PARTY WHO RECEIVES THE ASSIGNMENT

An example of an assignment might be: You have purchased an automobile from a dealership. The dealer has delivered the automobile to you. You now have the obligation of making payments on it. Assume that the dealer has financed through the bank the purchase of a number of automobiles, typically called the "floor plan." The dealer has assigned his rights to receive the money from your purchase to the bank. The bank becomes the assignee. What are the bank's *rights* which you owe it? We mentioned originally that third parties can be beneficiaries and have enforceable rights in an agreement to which they were not an original party. Here the assignee (bank) has the right to payment for the car. The bank has a right to sue you if you do not pay the money to the bank. The bank's rights are subject to any defenses that you may have under the law against the *dealer*. Assume you get a bum car, then the bank has to take it subject to any of the problems that may exist under the contract and subject to any defenses you may have. Therefore, if you have been defrauded or were subject to duress, mistake, undue influence, statute of frauds problems, statute of limitations problems, failure of performance, capacity problems, illegality, covenants not to sue, limitations of liability, limita-

tions of causes of action, a right to set off amounts of money, counterclaims, the bank would have to defend against all of these. Thus, the bank does not have any better rights than the dealership had in these circumstances. Here we are assuming that the bank is not a holder in due course, because that would give it special rights. (It has only been in recent history that I met any poor bankers. They do not need special rights, agreed?)

## RIGHTS THAT ARE NON-ASSIGNABLE

We have mentioned that certain types of personal service contracts, or contracts involving personal skills, confidence or trust, may not be assignable. If you do not want the other party to assign any of his or her duties in a deal, say so in the contract.

## EXPRESSLY PROHIBITED ASSIGNMENTS

Some contracts expressly provide that the contract is not assignable. The general rule under the circumstances is that the contract cannot be assigned. That is not an absolute protection, however. Most courts will back the validity of a provision that prohibits such assignments and makes such prohibitions enforceable. The UCC states that the assignment of rights under a contract of sale is *valid unless it is otherwise agreed to*. The UCC seems to indicate that any time that there is language *prohibiting* assignment, unless it is more specific, it only prohibits *delegation* of the *duty* of performance. Thus, a prohibition against assignment under the UCC would still allow contractor to assign his *rights to money* to the bank. It would prevent him from delegating any of his *duties*. The UCC does encourage flexibility under any form of assignment.

If you want to make sure your offeree *alone* must perform the contract, STATE THIS IN THE AGREEMENT.

## PROHIBITION OF ASSIGNMENT OF TORT CLAIMS FOR PERSONAL INJURY

Under the traditional common law, the courts generally do not like and do not enforce an assignment of tort claims. In other words, if a person has been injured as a result of negligence, defamation, libel, slander, assault and battery, false imprisonment or abusive legal process or malicious prosecution, the common law generally would not allow such an assignment. Generally, the courts are not keen on encouraging the purchase or sale of personal injury claims. But tort claims for injury to personal or real property usually can be assigned.

## ASSIGNMENT OF A PERSONAL RIGHT TO ALIMONY

The general rule is that the voluntary assignment of alimony not yet due is against public policy. In general the courts want to discourage the assignment of future alimony. But past-due alimony installments to which an individual has a right may be assignable.

## ASSIGNMENT OF PENSIONS AND FUTURE WAGES OF PUBLIC EMPLOYEES

Assignments of pensions and future wages of public employees are considered against public policy and are generally unenforceable. These rights (assets) are not usually assignable. Generally, in pension or profit-sharing plans the rights to benefits are *not* assignable. There are some exceptions.

## ASSIGNMENT OF CLAIMS AGAINST THE UNITED STATES

Generally claims against the United States cannot be assigned until they have actually been granted and a warrant for payment has been issued. The Federal Assignment of Claims Act of 1940, known as the "Anti-Assignment Act," provides that assignments of claims against the United States are valid if they are freely made and executed in the presence of at least two attesting witnesses. This assignment can occur only after the claims have been allowed and the government has ascertained the amount due and has issued a warrant for such payment.

## WAGE ASSIGNMENTS AND ASSIGNMENTS OF FUTURE WAGES

It is possible in most jurisdictions to assign future wages, but we generally have to look to state law. There are numerous prohibitions and restrictions or form requirements to allow such assignments. Over the years there have been numerous abuses of this assignment, especially for the benefit of credit and loan companies. Many states have placed limitations or strict requirements to have such future wage assignments enforced.

## ASSIGNABILITY OF COMMERCIAL AND OTHER LEASES

Because many businesses lease property or premises to house their businesses, it is important to be aware of the right of a lessee (tenant) to assign his lease. Some leases contain a prohibition against assignment. In many states, the lessor cannot *arbitrarily* withhold the right of a lessee to *assign* the lease. You should be aware of any provisions in a lease that speak about prohibiting the assignment of a lease or prohibiting a sublease, for instance. Some leases contain requirements that there must be prior written consent from the lessor. If you as a lessee intend to sign such a lease, you should be aware of the need to insert some objective standards for prohibiting an assignment.

Some leases may contain language saying that the lessor cannot *unreasonably* withhold his permission. This means that the lessor can require that the assignee or a sublessee meet certain financial standards.

If you are the lessee and you wish to sublease to someone else, or assign the lease to someone else, you still continue to be *responsible* for meeting the terms and conditions of the lease. Sometimes if you have a financially responsible assignee involved, the landlord might agree to look to the assignee. In effect, the landlord and your assignee might create a *new* lease and exclude you as a lessee. Nevertheless, you ought to be aware of lease provisions that could come back to haunt you.

## ASSIGNMENT OF AN OPTION CONTRACT

You can keep an offer open for a definite period if you purchase an option contract which provides that. Unless the option agreement prohibits an assignment of this right or unless there is some personal service nature or confidential or trustee nature, the rights under an option agreement are generally assignable.

If you own an option contract, you might want to put in specifically your right to *assign* the option.

## PARTIAL ASSIGNMENTS, INCLUDING THE RIGHTS OF THE PARTIAL ASSIGNEE

Generally under common law, partial assignments which *increase* the burden of the party who must act are prohibited. On the other hand, if the partial assignment would not increase anyone's burden, then generally the courts would allow such a partial assignment.

## IMPLIED WARRANTIES OF THE ASSIGNOR

Back to our auto dealer, Mr. *B*. Mr. *A* purchased an automobile from Dealer *B*, who assigned his rights. Assume he assigned his rights to $15,000, which is the value of the automobile, to a bank. What types of representations or warranties does the automobile dealer make to the bank? The common law has generally concluded that the following general warranties are being made if nothing is mentioned in the assignment:

1. That the dealer will do nothing to *defeat* or make it more difficult for the bank to collect on the assignment.

2. That the dealer is *guaranteeing* that the assigned right that he is transferring to the bank *actually exists*, subject to no limitations or defenses which are not disclosed. In other words, if he has disclosed everything and the bank is willing to accept the assignment, then he has not violated his implied warranty.

3. That any *document* that is the basis of the assignment is *genuine* and is exactly as it appears to be. For instance, if the assignment to the bank by the dealership is based on a series of contracts, including yours, the dealership is representing to the bank that each is a *valid* contract.

4. The dealer is warranting that he has *no knowledge* of any fact that would *diminish* the *value* of the bank's claim to the $15,000. Let's assume that the dealer sold you a bum car but has not revealed this to the bank. Then the bank would have a cause of action against the *dealership* if in fact you do not have to pay for the automobile because it is a lemon.

## SUCCESSIVE ASSIGNMENTS

What happens in the unlikely event that a dealer (not Mr. *B*, since he was reputable, but Mr. *C*, who is a crook) assigns rights to *several* banks, not just one? Mr. *C* goes to several banks and shows them copies of the contracts and says that in return for $150,000 in contracts, the dealer would like to borrow $100,000. The dealer does this to three banks in a row. Which bank has a right to your money and the money assigned under the agreements?

There are several approaches which could yield different results. One approach is the prevailing *American Rule*, which is generally considered the majority view. The prevailing American view is that the *first assignment* in *time* prevails. Any later assignments in *time* have second or third or subsequent *rank* to the *first* assignment. The minority view, also called the British Rule by some commentators, is that the first *assignee* to *give actual notice* to you and to each of the individuals who owe money to the dealer prevails.

But even under the American Rule, there are several situations whereby the first assignee rule would not necessarily prevail. If subsequent assignees have given *value* for their assignments in good faith, the American Rule may be modified.

Some of these exceptions are:

1. Where the second or third bank has already obtained payment from you on the assigned claim.

2. Where the second or third bank has already sued you for the money and has obtained a *judgment* against you.

3. Where the second or third bank has signed a new agreement with you to make such payments.

4. Where a subsequent bank or any other assignee actually gets the original contract pointing out your obligation where the document is necessary in order to enforce the agreement.

If you assign any part of your contract, it is wise to give the other party notice that you have done so

## THIRD PARTY BENEFICIARY CONTRACT

Assume that you go to your friendly television dealer and tell the dealer you are buying the television for your mother. You then pay the dealer the $500 for the television.

Does your mother have any right to enforce the contract if the television dealer fails to deliver the television to her when it's due? You have paid the purchase price for the television and you are on a six-week trip to Europe. Can your mother press the issue, since you have paid the money? The appliance dealer has the use of your money and has not produced the television one week after it is supposed to be delivered. Your mother has an *enforceable cause of action* in a court of law. She is an *intended* beneficiary.

The courts have identified, at least under the traditional common law, three types of beneficiaries. One is the *donee* beneficiary, who is *given* the benefit. Your mother is a *donee* beneficiary. You have donated or given your mother this contract. Therefore, she is considered a donee beneficiary under the traditional distinction. In more modern jargon, your mother is an *intended* beneficiary.

On the other hand, another example will illustrate a different type of beneficiary. Suppose you are going to take a loan from the bank. As part of the consideration you are going to take out an insurance policy. As part of the lending procedures, you are going to make the bank the *beneficiary* of the insurance policy. The bank is considered a *creditor beneficiary*. The relationship arises out of a creditor relationship where there is a financial arrangement. The bank would also be considered an *intended* beneficiary under the more modern term.

## THE RIGHTS OF INTENDED BENEFICIARY

This promise in the contract to name a person the intended beneficiary gives the intended beneficiary certain rights. Generally, the rights of the intended beneficiary become solidified or vested at the time you *make the contract*. In the case of your mother, she may not even be aware that you are giving her the television; nevertheless, even if she is unaware of it, she would have an enforcement right at the time you form the contract with the television dealer. It is possible for an intended beneficiary to reject such a promised benefit, in which case the intended beneficiary may be giving up any rights he or she may have under the agreement. In certain jurisdictions, your mother would not be able to sue *you* for the failure of the television dealer to perform, but could only sue the dealer for failing to perform.

If either type of *intended* beneficiary has done something in *reliance* on their having *rights* under this agreement, it is possible that you may *not be able to change* the *beneficiary*. There are some exceptions, such as insurance policies that typically reserve the right to the policy owner to change the beneficiary. There obviously can be some exceptions. You can have an irrevocable beneficiary, which cannot be changed without the beneficiary's consent. In that particular case you as an insured are giving up your right to change such a beneficiary.

In any contract in which you want to reserve the right to change intended beneficiaries, *reserve* this right specifically.

## INCIDENTAL BENEFICIARIES

We ought to be aware that certain individuals may receive benefits from a contract but they are *not* intended beneficiaries. Their rights are so distant that you did not intend for them to get such rights.

This might happen, for example, in municipal contracts where the city may contract to have sidewalks paved. Certainly the abutting landowners receive some benefit, but the city may be doing it for the benefit of *all* citizens and not necessarily to benefit that *specific abutting landowner*. These landowners might be *incidental beneficiaries* only.

Certain non-parties to a contract may have a legal right to enforce the contract in court.

These third party beneficiaries are called *intended beneficiaries*, or sometimes *donee* or *creditor beneficiaries*.

## DISCHARGE OF CONTRACTS

Fortunately for most of us (and the court system), substantially all contracts are performed adequately and disappear. Adequately performed contracts far exceed 99.999 percent of all contracts formed. We will examine what is adequate performance. How do we discharge a contract? If we know what adequate performance is, we can also determine when there may be a breach of contract. We will also look at the remedies available to you if someone breaches a contract.

## CONDITIONS

How do we determine if there are any conditions to a contract which may affect whether or not there has been adequate performance? Let us examine types of conditions.

### Express Conditions

Express conditions are provisions in a contract that provide that should an event occur, as long as the following do not occur the contract is fully discharged. An express condition might also be present in a contract if it contains wording such as

"while" or "as soon as." There are numerous examples of conditional language that can be used.

There is no one way to express all potential *conditions* possible in an agreement.

We are focusing on *express conditions*, the conditions that are *known*. Put them in writing. Conditions possibly could be oral. The parties to an agreement can specifically state the conditions and the parties are clearly aware of them. If there is a failure of one of these conditions to occur or to fail to occur, there no longer is an agreement. If the "as soon as" does not take place, then there may be no agreement.

## DISCHARGE BY AGREEMENT OF THE PARTIES

This is possible, and often happens where there are some problems. Problems may crop up because of delivery schedules, strikes or a multitude of other reasons whereby the parties cannot perform. The parties can agree to some alternative resolution of the problem. Here are a few of the examples.

### Mutual Rescission

Two parties can agree to dissolve the initial contract by *mutual agreement*. In this circumstance they are saying that there are no damages due. Sometimes that can be part of their resolution. This is so especially if neither party has lost anything yet. Hopefully, they still have time to go back out into the marketplace. Then they can mutually rescind it. Certainly, if they are going to be dealing with each other in the future, both parties should certainly attempt to reach an agreeable solution.

### Accord and Satisfaction

*Accord and satisfaction* is a method of resolving a dispute based on the reality of all the circumstances. Assume that someone owes you some money as a result of your having sold him some lumber.

This party has had a problem paying the bill. He hasn't been able to do it. He talks to you and asks if he can pay you 80 cents on the dollar. He admits he is going to get out of the construction business. He admits he owes you the money, but is on the verge of getting stuck financially.

The concept of accord and satisfaction is a dual concept meaning that the accord and the satisfaction must both be met. Assume you agree to take the 80 cents on the dollar. If the original amount due was $1,000, you have agreed to take $800 and release the buyer from the other $200. If he actually pays the $800, then the contract is *discharged* by agreement of the parties.

Because you have agreed to the lesser amount and the lumber buyer has actually performed, then the debt is discharged.

On the other hand, even if you have agreed to take the $800, but the lumber buyer reneges on the $800, he owes you the full $1,000, not the $800. Thus, the *accord* is your agreeing to take $800, and the *satisfaction* is the payment. It takes both of these to tango.

If you are agreeing to take less in a deal, make sure it is clear that the original amount is due if there is a dispute or the amount is unpaid.

## Substituted Contracts

Assume you had an agreement with a contractor to build a house for $78,000. Now you and your wife would like some additional features included in the house. You go back to the contractor. You tell her you want to put these additional features in. You request a cost estimate. The contractor needs an additional amount of $10,000. You sign a *new contract* for $88,000, covering the same house plus the additional items. This is a substituted contract, since

## *POWER POINTS* _____

▶ Discharge of a contract means terminating or completing it.

▶ Discharge occurs if both parties complete their respective obligations under the contract.

▶ You may be discharged from a contract if the other party fails to perform a *material* (not minor) duty under the agreement.

▶ Parties to a contract can be discharged (without damages or penalties) if they agree on "early" termination, reach some accord and satisfaction, substitute a new performance, or release each other.

▶ The law may discharge one or more of the parties without damages or penalties upon the running out of the statute of limitation, the bankruptcy of the debtor party, the illegality of the subject matter or the impossibility of its completion.

▶ Impossibility varies from state to state but it probably means a fairly strict definition of "impossibility."

▶ You might want to define "impossibility" to include "acts of God" and many other superior external forces.

it covers the *same subject* matter *plus some*. This *new* contract discharges the original contract.

Certainly it is wise for you to make sure that the new contract specifically discharges the original agreement. Nevertheless, should you fail to place that language in the new contract, the court would interpret it such that the first contract is discharged.

## Novation

Novation is a substitution of a new party in a contract. One of the parties is substituted. Let's assume our example about hiring a contractor to build a house for $78,000. Your contractor decides she would like to take a vacation for a month. She says she has a contractor friend who specializes in the type of home you want. She asks if this second contractor could be substituted. You and your wife agree. The new contractor is substituted for the original contractor. The original contract is discharged by novation.

## Release and Covenant Not To Sue

A *release* is a discharge of the initial obligation by the two parties releasing each other. In addition the parties agree that neither of the parties will have a right to sue the other party out of the same contract. A release discharges the parties.

A *covenant not to sue* does not necessarily discharge the parties. It just prevents either of the parties from suing the other party. Each party agrees to give up its right to *sue* the other party for any problems that may arise out of an event or contract.

If there is going to be a *release*, it should contain sufficient language to make sure nothing arises again. Most such documents do so.

Read it yourself. Should you ever have a contract dispute, do not assume a word to the wise is sufficient.

## Renunciation

Renunciation can occur where *neither* of the parties has yet *performed*. A party can renounce the contract because there has been an initial breach or non-performance by the other party. In other words, if no one has done anything yet, the non-offending party can renounce his or her rights under the contract and treat it as terminated. This contract is discharged.

## DISCHARGE BY OPERATION OF LAW

## Subsequent Illegality

Assume you have agreed to purchase some grapes from someone in a foreign country. Because of some problem it becomes illegal to complete the deal. The subsequent illegality, even though it was legal the day you signed it, can operate as a discharge of that particular contract. It is by operation of law that it is discharged.

## Impossibility

Impossibility crops up from time to time. We ought to be aware of two types of impossibility (thought you knew it all, huh?) *Subjective* impossibility involves a particular person's reason—judgment—versus *objective* impossibility.

The impossibility that we generally see is *objective* impossibility under the common law. Objective impossibility means that no one is able to perform. This contract is deemed to be discharged by operation of law.

An example of this might include the destruction of the subject matter. Assume you are purchasing a particular make and model of specific automobile that you have seen on the lot of a new dealership. Through no fault of the dealer the automobile burns up. This fire would make performance impossible and could be classified as a discharge—again, by operation of law.

## Subjective

*Subjective* impossibility does not discharge a contract. It also does not relieve anyone from liability under the contract.

Subjective impossibility means the total inability to perform of the non-performing party to the contract. If you cannot complete the contract but someone else with better equipment can, you can only argue *subjective* impossibility.

## Bankruptcy

Bankruptcy is another method of discharging an obligation under a contract. It is specifically done by operation of law. Most of us are aware of the fact that once a bankruptcy is filed, the bankruptcy courts take jurisdiction of any obligation the debtor had at that time.

## Statute of Limitations

The statute of limitations means that even though someone may have a cause of action, he must bring it to court within a certain time period. If you wait too long, you lose. The courthouse doors close.

Assume you paid someone in advance to paint your house. For whatever reasons the person never got around to painting it. If you wait too long—that is, beyond the statute of limitations period—you can no longer sue. The statute of limitations says that if you have not enforced your rights within a certain time period, you will not be able to enforce your rights at all. The law encourages you to act on your rights in a timely fashion. The statute of limitations means that there is a limited time for you to act. You may have one, two, six or 10 years to act; states vary. Assuming a six year statute of limitation then if you wait six years and one day after the contract is breached, you do not have a right to sue on it. This contract is effectively discharged.

## MERGER

If you sue someone, for instance, for breach of contract and you get a *judgment* against them, you cannot sue that person on that particular contract again. That contract is *merged* into the judgment. That judgment itself may possibly be the basis of another suit or of other legal action. That contract,

however, has been discharged because it is now part of a judgment. You will not see it again.

## REMEDIES

Part of a basic definition of a contract involves the exchange of promises by the parties, for the *breach* of which the law gives a *remedy*. Now we should look at different types of remedies that are available when someone breaches a contract.

If you have been damaged by the other party's breach of duties under the contract, you will have to prove three elements:

1. A contract between you existed;
2. The defendant breached the agreement; and
3. The agreement and defendant's breach resulted in legal injury or damages to you.

## MONETARY DAMAGES

If there is a breach of contract, there are often losses to the innocent party. There is usually a monetary value attached to a breach. It will cost money to straighten out the errors that have taken place. It costs money to cure any breach that has occurred.

## COMPENSATORY DAMAGES

Compensatory damages are those that result from the loss of value. The amount of these damages, once paid, should place the innocent party where she would be if the contract had been properly performed. Assume you have agreed to buy a hundred bushels of wheat at $3 a bushel. The party breaches the contract, so you have to go back into the marketplace and buy wheat for $4 a bushel. You have now lost the value of $1 per bushel. That $1 per bushel would be your compensatory damages. You would have to get $1 per bushel for each bushel that was part of the initial contract, to be in your original position.

Assume that you purchase a house and the seller has represented to you that the rents are at a certain level. Later you find out that the rents are actually 20 percent less than what the seller represented to you. It is possible that your compensatory damages would be the difference between what you paid for the house and what the house would sell for, given the accurate rental amounts. That is an example of compensatory damages. Those are *direct* damages.

There can also be *consequential* damages that can occur. An example of consequential damages might follow this scenario: Assume you have purchased a van for your business. You use your van on the weekends in your flea-market business. As you drive to the flea market the front left wheel falls off.

*Direct* damages would be the dollar value it would cost to repair the front wheel and to put the van back into shape. In addition to that you may have lost working time including wages. Those can be considered *consequential* damages. Not every breach of contract involves consequential damages, nor are these damages automatically due to you if these indirect injuries occur. It depends on the facts and circumstances.

Consequential damages may be due if the other party to your contract knew of your particular needs and breached your contract. In any event, you should know the difference between direct and consequential damages. Another type of compensatory damages is called *incidental* damages. For an example of incidental damages, we can go back to the example of the van. Incidental damages might include rental of another van you are getting your van repaired.

## DAMAGES BASED ON RELIANCE

At times it is difficult to calculate the loss of profit that occurred and that a reasonable person could foresee. It is possible for someone to collect damages which would place them in the same position as if the contract had not been made. An example might be where Mr. *F* is expecting to sell his business to Mr. *G* for a price of $100,000. Mr. *G*, the potential buyer, breaches the contract and Mr. *F* is able to get only $80,000 for the business. The

$20,000 difference is the loss that would take place as a result of relying on this particular contract. Some courts might call this compensatory damages; other courts might call it damages as a result of reliance on this particular agreement.

## FORESEEABILITY OF DAMAGES

It is extremely important in the calculation of damages that you be aware of the concept of *foreseeability*.

*Direct* damages are easy to calculate with the van example which I gave. The cost of repairing the wheel and any other damage as a result of the physical damage are easy to foresee. The question is, how far out will a court extend the damages so that we would be recompensed by the manufacturer of the van or the selling dealer? Foreseeability is based on an objective test in which the judge or the jury attempts to decide what a reasonable person under the circumstances would be able to foresee as a result of providing a buyer with a van with a bad left front axle. Some things resulting from the left front wheel collapsing might be obviously foreseeable. The van might tip over and might break glass and might injure you and your product. This broken wheel might also cause injury to a third person.

Could a reasonable person foresee lost profits? If that axle broke, how far out would the reasonable person be able to predict any resulting injury? We do not have a neat formula to give you. The courts do not extend liability.

Different states have different standards for foreseeability. Also, different states allow different types of damages.

## MISREPRESENTATION RESULTING IN DAMAGES

Fraud involves intentional *misrepresentation* or the reckless *disregard* of the facts by a party knowing that the other person is going to rely on the representations made and that the representations involve *material* or important facts.

Damages can be, in some states, only what is lost out of pocket. This is the difference between the value of what the innocent party has *received* versus the amount of value she *gave* to the other party. In other words the courts might in the minority of cases disregard any of the fraudulent representations made and only look at the two *objective standards*. So we go into the marketplace and find out the difference between what you got versus what you gave up.

On the other hand, the majority of states would take into account the representations that were made. In other words, it is possible that you may have gotten your money's worth, but you may have paid, say $2,000 for an automobile, but as described by the other party, you were getting a $3,000 car for $2,000. In that particular case, the calculation of damages under the benefit-of-the-bargain rule would be $1,000. In this case the damages are greater under the benefit-of-the-bargain rule ($1,000) than under the out-of-pocket standard.

## NON-FRAUDULENT OR INNOCENT MISREPRESENTATION

In the case of *innocent* misrepresentation, the courts do not seek to punish. The only remedy you have when someone has innocently misrepresented the facts in a material way is the out-of-pocket approach. If the other party was not acting recklessly, damages could be less. The other party may have been relying on facts they got from someone who was supposed to be reliable. If we can distinguish innocent from non-innocent misrepresentation and if the courts say it is innocent, then you just have a right to out-of-pocket damages, but not the benefit-of-the-bargain approach.

## PUNITIVE DAMAGES

Punitive damages are calculated by the trier of fact, be it judge or jury. These are not compensatory damages and not consequential damages. These damages do not involve foreseeability. These damages are strictly intended to punish. Some states do not allow these, but most common-law states allow punitive damages. There have been some recent challenges to the concept of punitive damages.

I might mention briefly that the reason for these, challenges is that there are different standards of proof in civil versus criminal verdicts. A civil case requires a lower standard of proof than a criminal case. Punitive damages create the same type of burden as a criminal punishment in the form of a fine. Civil punitive damages involve a lower standard of proof than criminal penalties. Therefore, there have been a number of challenges, and we will see more. The U.S. Supreme Court will re-examine this issue in the near future. We could end up with different results from the tremendous allowance of awards that we have seen in recent history.

## LIQUIDATED VERSUS UNLIQUIDATED DAMAGES

*Liquidated* damages are damages that are *calculable* and *known*. For instance, if you have agreed to purchase a fancy racing bicycle for $852.37, have received the bicycle and have not paid for it, the amount of damages here is known as *liquidated*. We know exactly what they are, which is what the agreement called for: $852.37. This can be contrasted with what are known as *unliquidated* damages. These are amounts that have not been calculated and are not easily calculated. An example of unliquidated damages typically exists when someone gets injured in an automobile accident. We might know what the medical expenses have been; however, we do not know what the other types of damages are, including physical pain and suffering. There is no neat formula for that. Therefore, it is unliquidated. In a business context, determining lost profits is extremely difficult. This is another example of *unliquidated* damages.

## MITIGATION OF DAMAGES

The courts do not seek generally to punish people, but generally seek to bring both parties to a fair result. The courts sometimes look to the *good faith* of both parties in *lessening* damages that may have occurred. When there is a breach of contract, the courts generally require that the innocent party who has been injured take whatever steps he or she can to *minimize* the *damages* that may have taken place.

Suppose you just purchased the van and the front left wheel breaks and you lose your flea-market profits until it is fixed. Yet you could continue to run your flea-market business with a rental van for the one week (optimistic, you say) that it takes to fix yours. If you do not lease a van, let's assume you lose $500. But if you leased a van, you might lose only the $100 you paid for the rental van. If you can easily lease another van during the period it takes to repair your van, then the courts would limit your damages to the loss that would occur if you had rented a van, which was $100. In effect you cannot totally stick it to the other person when you could lessen (mitigate) the damages.

There are basic legal requirements before you get damages for breach of contract. These requirements are threefold:

1. You must prove damage with reasonable certainty and not based on your imagination or beliefs.

2. Damages must be reasonably foreseeable at the time the contract is made.

3. You must attempt to minimize (mitigate) the damages. If you can rent a replacement truck for $150 to save a $5,000 shipment of bananas from your broken truck, a court might expect you to do so.

If you need the offeree's products or services for an urgent reason, make sure he knows that reason. Put it in your agreement. Now your damages are *foreseeable*.

## REMEDIES IN EQUITY

Sometimes monetary damages will not solve the problem. Therefore the courts, particularly the courts in equity (as opposed to the courts of law under common law), have fashioned certain remedies to cure situations that cannot be cured by *monetary damages*.

Assume you have agreed to purchase a particular painting by a famous artist. You have established a contract. There is a promise for a promise, and it is in writing. Now it is time for you to pick up the painting, and the gallery will not release the painting to you. In most states you can go into equity court and seek a remedy specifically fashioned to fit the problem.

## SPECIFIC PERFORMANCE

One of the approaches you can take and one of the remedies you can use is called *specific performance*. The courts would enforce your rights and *require* the gallery to deliver this one-of-a-kind painting to you. This required result is specific performance. If there were numerous identical paintings and there was nothing distinguishing them, the court might not require specific performance. The property for which this remedy applies must be clearly *unique*. If you have met any prerequisites for getting this unique property, the courts may under their equity powers grant you specific performance. The other party would either turn over the goods or sit in jail.

All pieces of real estate are considered unique. It is also possible under the UCC for even non-unique goods to be subject to specific performance. If you want this right, make sure you put it in your agreements. State specifically that you have a right to *specific performance*. Make sure that the goods are specifically described in detail. Second, put in the agreement that you want the right to specific performance. It is not an absolute guarantee that you will get it. It will certainly increase your chances, because you have addressed it.

## INJUNCTION

Injunction is another potential contract remedy. It is a court order that commands a person to refrain from doing a specific act or actually engaging in a specific act. Anybody who violates an injunction is guilty of violating a court order and is potentially guilty of criminal behavior.

We are all obligated to obey court orders. An individual who violates an injunction may be *fined* or *imprisoned*.

Assume you have sold a business with a non-competition clause covering the selling party and you have met your state's requirements for getting this non-competition agreement. Assume the selling party sets up a competitive business in direct violation of the non-competition provisions. It may be possible for you to seek injunctive relief against the selling party. A court order prohibits the other party from violating the contract. The option is to stop the competitive behavior that violates your agreement, or sit in jail.

## RESTITUTION

Another potential remedy for breach of contract involves restitution. In all, this generally means that it returns the parties to their prior condition before the breach occurred.

# PARTY INJURED BY THE BREACH

If you happen to be one of the parties that had been hurt by another party's breach of contract for *non-performance* or for *repudiation*, you may have a right to restitution. In other words, if you have fully performed and the other party has not, you have a right to either get your *money back* or have a *return* of your *performance*, if that is possible.

## THE PARTY IN DEFAULT

Believe it or not, on occasion even the party who *breaches* a contract may have a right to something back. For instance, assume that one of the parties has breached a contract by not delivering all the wheat he or she has agreed to. Assume that the damages are $10,000 that the breaching party owes the innocent party. Assume that the breaching party (bad guy) has delivered an excess amount of goods which should not have been part of the damages. Assume he has delivered $20,000 worth of wheat

yet the $10,000 constitutes a breach under the total contract—the total amount lost. The party breaching the contract can get this excess amount of wheat back. There is still no free lunch (more or less).

## STATUTE OF FRAUDS

It is possible where the statute of frauds applies to a contract, yet has not been complied with, that one of the parties may be able to get their consideration back. They would be able to get restitution as a result of the other party saying "We have no contract here." Therefore, the courts would not allow one of the parties to be *unjustly enriched*, meaning get something for nothing. It may be possible for the original party who has performed to get his or her performance or consideration returned.

## VOIDABLE CONTRACTS

A voidable agreement is valid until an eligible person avoids it.

It is possible for a party who lacked contractual capacity was subject to duress or undue influence, was defrauded, was subject to innocent misrepresentation or some mistake, to get back his or her consideration given up in a contract. A party who seeks restitution must return anything he or she has received. Thus, if someone was mentally incapable and received a benefit except for a necessary, this person must return the benefit to void the agreement.

A "necessary" is determined by the conditions of the person who received them. A "necessary" for one person might not be so for another.

## LIMITATION ON REMEDIES

This item is important for business people. A number of large businesses put these provisions in their contracts. What this does is limit your right to seek particular types of remedies. The courts do not like these types of provisions in consumer contracts; they do enforce them in business contracts.

## ELECTION OF REMEDIES

Many times the innocent party to a contract breach has several alternative remedies that may be available. In some cases, you may be able to seek specific performance yet there may be some incidental damages. In the alternative, you may want to forget the right to have specific performance and seek damages in a court of law. You cannot get all your money back and still force the other party to get you the television sets, for example. Sometimes remedies are mutually exclusive. Sometimes they are not.

## LOSS OF POWER OF AVOIDANCE

We saw that the law requires that an injured party make an effort to *lessen* damages that are due. We see the same type of thing when a party seeks an *equitable remedy*. If a party has a voidable agreement and has the power to void it, he or she must act timely. We previously talked about minors being in a position of voiding or disaffirming contracts. This power begins at the time of forming the contract and continues until a reasonable time after he or she reaches the age of majority. We also see the same thing when we talk about other types of incapacity, lack of competency, lack of the ability to truly assent to an agreement, as when there is duress or undue influence.

There are at least three circumstances whereby an individual will lose their legally granted power to avoid a contract. The first is when the individual *affirms* the contract; that is, agrees to accept the terms and conditions of the contract. The individual gives up the power to void it.

Second is when the person can *unreasonably delay* exercising that power. We talked previously about having a reasonable time after any disability is lifted. If it is duress or incompetency, there is a *reasonable time* period that the courts allow a person to act. On the other hand, if the person *delays* too long and is going well beyond that time period, the power to disaffirm lapses.

The third is, sometimes *third parties* may be involved in the transaction and *their rights* may intervene and cut off an individual's rights to disaffirm. Assume a minor sells a car to an individual. The minor receives $3,000 for the car. The individual does not know he bought the car from a minor. The individual then sells the car to a third party. Assuming that the third party did not know about the minor and paid fair value for the auto (a bona fide purchaser for value), the minor would not be able to get the car back.

If the second party to the transaction still had the car, the minor would be able to void the contract. So there are circumstances where someone with a disability who might have the power to void a transaction may not be able to because third parties have entered into the transaction.

## CONDITIONS

The essential obligations of each party are called conditions. Party *A* must meet her conditions before or at some time when Party *B* is obligated to perform. There are implied-in-fact as well as implied-in-law conditions.

## IMPLIED-IN-FACT CONDITIONS

Assume that someone is building a house and is allowed to choose appliances from one of three brands and a specific make and model. It is implied that the potential homeowner will tell the contractor which of the three models the homeowner wants installed in the home. It may appear to be obvious, but it is considered an implied-in-fact condition that must be met. Obviously if the homeowner does not make such a choice, the homeowner would be at fault in not complying with the conditions of the agreement.

## IMPLIED-IN-LAW CONDITIONS

There are certain conditions which may be neither express (meaning that the parties have not specifically discussed them) nor so obvious as the implied-in-fact types.

Let's say you are buying an automobile. Further assume that the agreement does not specifically state when payment has to be made. The law might imply that the payment has to be made at the time you pick up the automobile. The law further implies that the title will also be delivered then. In some areas the practices may be different. There may be some *conditions* required to make this deal which are express and some which are implied or unstated.

Pay attention to which conditions are not met or whether or not the contract has been adequately performed. These could adversely affect your pocketbook.

## CONCURRENT CONDITIONS

This type of condition is generally the more obvious one. This type of condition occurs when the parties have to perform at the *same time*. If you are buying a house the implication may be that you are going to pay for it at the time you take possession. Therefore, this is generally considered a concurrent condition.

## CONDITION PRECEDENT

A condition precedent is one whereby something must happen *prior* to triggering the duty of performance of the other party. A certain act or behavior must take place *first*, prior to a party owing the duty of performance. An example might be a buyer purchasing a house. Assume the purchase agreement requires a potential buyer to purchase the house as long as the buyer gets approval for financing the purchase. This is considered a condition precedent to the purchase.

## CONDITION SUBSEQUENT

A condition subsequent can yield the same results as a condition precedent, but they work from an opposite viewpoint. This subsequent condition occurs when a certain event does *not* take place *subsequent* to, for instance, the sale of property, in which case the ownership may revert to the original seller. An example of a condition subsequent might be where Party *A* (buyer) is willing to buy a house from Party *B*. The purchase might be with the con-

dition subsequent that within the following year Party *B* (seller) will pave the entrance road to the property. If the condition subsequent is that the seller has 12 months to perform, and 12 months and two weeks later the road still has not been paved, we have a failure to meet a condition subsequent. The buyer (Party *A*) is able to rescind the transaction or resell the property to the original seller, Party *B*.

Make sure you have met all of your duties (conditions) under the contract; otherwise you may not claim a breach or damages.

Certain conditions may not appear in a contract but are part of the contract regardless.

## PERFORMANCE

The major method of discharging contracts is by adequate or legally sufficient performance. Under some circumstances there must be *exact* performance for a contract to be discharged. There are other circumstances for discharging a contract whereby we need only *substantial* performance. An example of the difference is if you were selling your automobile to someone for $2,000 and they showed up with $1,995 plus a case of soft drinks which clearly would cost more than the $5, there would be no deal (inadequate performance). You could clearly reject the agreement and sell your car to someone else if you wished. In any event, that would be a rejection and a counteroffer of your original offer.

The agreement was that you wanted $2,000, and you do not have to take one penny less, nor do you have to take it in any other form than cash. You do not even have to accept a check.

On the other hand, the courts have identified the problems of *exact* performance in such areas as home construction and remodeling. There the courts look to a concept called *substantial* performance. Most of us have learned that there is no house built that exactly meets the specifications of any of the plans. Therefore the courts have taken the approach that as long as there has been *substantial* performance, you still have to pay the price asked. There is still a deal. If there are any costs associated with *curing* or *renovating* any problems with the construction of the house, you may be able to reduce the price you pay by the amount of money it would take you to fix whatever is wrong. The courts will not necessarily make the house perfect. In the case of discharging a contract by *performance*, the contract effectively *disappears*.

Performance for completing a contract may have to meet one or more of several standards:

a. *Substantial* performance may be sufficient in construction contracts.

b. *Perfect* performance may be required in some contracts.

c. *Satisfactory* performance may be required by provisions in a contract.

d. *Satisfactory* performance can be defined as what is *reasonable* or as what Party *A wants*.

Include in your contract the standard you and the offeree agree upon. Do not leave the definition to chance.

## DISCHARGE BY BREACH

Discharge by breach does not mean that the contract disappears. It merely means that one of the parties who is the good party will not have to perform. In addition the good and non-offending party may sue for damages.

## BREACH BY ONE PARTY AS A DISCHARGE OF THE OTHER PARTY

### MATERIAL BREACH

If one of the parties has in effect committed some major breach *without justification* by not performing under the contract, the innocent party will not have to continue to perform, or may not have to perform at all. What the courts look for is the definition of a *material* breach, not a minor breach.

If you are buying parts for your automobile, the part doesn't have to be perfect but it does have to work adequately in your automobile. So if we are talking about material breach, it might involve a part that does not adequately perform. There is no *material* breach if the part works does not look perfect— for instance, a carburetor.

There are at least three ways of viewing what a *material breach* is:

1. Partial performance that is essential to the contract.

2. A failure of performance that can be quantified (measured or counted), which is serious or significant.

3. Prevention of intentional performance.

Some of the courts, for instance, will look to see whether or not the breach has held up anything of a substantial nature.

In some contracts, time is important. If someone is dealing in the commodities market, where prices change by the minute, they have to act rapidly. If someone doesn't respond timely in that particular market—perhaps within minutes—we may have a material breach.

## SUBSTANTIAL PERFORMANCE

As we mentioned briefly, in some types of contracts, primarily construction contracts, the courts look to *substantial* performance as a standard. Did the contractor substantially perform, or did he botch the job so tremendously that performance is not even close to what it ought to be? In such a case if you as the homeowner believe that the contractor has not even met the substantial performance standard, the courts might say there has been discharge, and you would not have to pay. If there has been substantial performance, as we have mentioned, you would end up having to pay the full amount *less* what it would take to repair or remodel your home to meet reasonable standards in our imperfect world.

## PREVENTION OF PERFORMANCE

Prevention of performance does not happen often. On occasion we have seen that even business people will do things for ornery reasons or do things merely to prevent the performance of the other party, for whatever reasons. If that is the case, the party who is preventing the other party from performing—not necessarily totally but in any substantial way—discharges the other party.

Let us assume that Party *A* is a plumbing subcontractor and for some reason decides that he cannot stand the homeowner. The plumber makes it difficult for any of the other subcontractors to get in the home by tying up the property in some physical way. In this case, the homeowner may not have to pay the plumbing subcontractor at all. In addition the homeowner could collect damages from the plumber for the cost of having to get someone else to rectify the problem. Again, this action by the plumber could discharge the homeowner.

## ANTICIPATORY REPUDIATION

All of us ought to be aware of anticipatory repudiation. It is a party letting you know that he will breach the contract when performance is due in the future. Performance is not yet due. Assume you (retailer) have contracted with a distributor to deliver several television sets. The new models arrive in two months, and you will pay for them 30 days after they are delivered. You have a deal to purchase the TV sets. You get a call from the distributor one month later saying that he is not going to be able to honor the contract. He has had a dispute with the manufacturer and he is not going to be able to deliver. This is an example of anticipatory repudiation.

You are not going to get your television sets. He is not going to perform, and he is letting you know.

Essentially, under these circumstances you have at least two options. One is, you can treat the contract, when the distributor calls you, as being breached. You can go into the marketplace and attempt to purchase the same television sets from someone else. The damages, as we will see, would be whatever more you may have to pay for them.

Your other alternative is to wait until the contract is due to be performed and then treat it as being breached. Nevertheless, under either circumstance you as the innocent party are discharged from having to perform, and you can treat it as discharged at either time. You do not have a right to try to play the market against someone, but you would not necessarily have to continue waiting until something happens at the due date.

## COMPETENCY OR CONTRACTUAL CAPACITY OF THE PARTIES

All parties to a contract must have sufficient mental ability to reach mutual assent in a contract.

## COMPETENT PARTIES

Most of us are aware that it would be unfair to allow an adult to use the common law to protect parties who could not understand the substance of a contract in which they were involved. Contract law is based upon each party understanding what it is they become bound by.

A requirement would be that both parties be competent. The common law wisely looks out for an individual when he or she enters into a contract. If one of the parties is a minor, the common law steps in to protect the minor from his own innocence. A minor is not considered competent or capable or as sophisticated as adults who may be dealing with the minor. Minority is not the only problem that can create a problem in forming or enforcing a contract. There are other types of physical and mental disabilities also.

Some of the types of incapacities that we are talking about involve minors (or infants), insane persons, intoxicated persons, in some cases married women (don't blame me, ladies!), aliens, convicts and even corporations.

A 6 year-old or a 10 year-old under most circumstances could not understand a contract. The law that has developed takes into account circumstances of tender age, incompetent parties, intoxicated individuals and individuals who may be lacking contractual capacity. Each party must have that minimum amount of contractual capacity to understand an agreement. We all realize that for many one-sided contracts, having capacity may not help us; but let's examine this important contractual requirement. This *essential* element for having a valid contract is that the parties must have legal capacity to contract. They must be able to understand what they entering into. It does not mean that if an adult fails to understand every item in a contract completely he cannot enter into a contract. The courts are not going to look into and examine everyone's mental or thinking processes. That is not the nature of determining contractual capacity.

## MINORS

The general rule is that contracts into which minors enter are generally voidable. There are some exceptions to this exception. In other words, some contracts by minors are enforceable.

What do we mean by *voidable*? The minor is able to get out of these contracts. He or she may disaffirm (reject) these contracts from the time they've formed until a reasonable time after the minor becomes an adult. Once the minor comes of age he has a certain reasonable time (not defined in the law) to evaluate the contract and decide to clearly reject the contract. If he or she does nothing he or she will probably be stuck with the contract. This defense is not available to the other party, but only to the minor or the party that is incapacitated.

## EXCEPTION FOR NECESSARIES

A minor will be responsible for the fair market value of those things that are considered necessaries which are actually furnished to the minor. The courts do not have an automatic formula for what is necessary. They often take into account the facts and circumstances involving the living conditions of this particular minor. There may be some difference between the minor of a rich family and the minor of an average family in determining what is a necessary. The best way to view this relationship with a minor for necessaries is that the minor may be responsible for the *fair market value* for the subject matter of the contract. Some of the factors considered by the courts include things necessary for a minor's subsistence, including a minor's health, education, age and marital state. This might obviously include food and clothing, medical care, sometimes education, lodging, tools and equipment. One case held that the services of an employment agency were a necessary. In this case, the minor was married.

## LIABILITY ON CONTRACTS—HOW DOES A MINOR BECOME LIABLE?

The minor cannot ratify or agree to a contract until he or she is in a posture of understanding the contract when the minor becomes of age. In some states there is a process of emancipation of minors, whereby a minor can be treated as an adult after being legally "freed" (emancipated) from some of the legal burdens of minority. The courts will not review the contracts once the minor has been emancipated.

In some states minors may be emancipated for some purposes, as of some age (*e.g.*, 16) but not for all purposes. They may be emancipated from a business viewpoint but not necessarily for all personal contracts. There is no simple description to give.

## MISREPRESENTATION OF AGE

In some states it is possible for a minor to rescind the contract if it does not involve necessaries. The minor need only return whatever she or he has of the original consideration. Therefore, if a minor has an automobile from a dealership and the automobile burns up, the minor can return what he has of the automobile and get his money back. Some states will say that the minor need only return whatever he or she has to disaffirm the contract. On the other hand, in some states, if the minor has misrepresented his age, then the minor may be charged for any loss the other party may incur.

What would that mean? If an individual received an automobile and wanted to disaffirm the original contract, but had used it for a year and a half, the courts might charge the minor the *fair usage value* for that year. What would the car lease for; the courts might determine the loss in *value* during that year. In this case the minor will have to pay that *decrease in value*. If it had been a used car, for instance, we might look at the decline in Blue Book values during that time period. The minor would then be able to disaffirm the contract but would have to come up with the difference. The courts have taken the position that even if the minor has committed a tort, such as misrepresenting the facts for his purchase, the minor should be protected. The courts will still protect the minor and allow the rescission of the particular contract.

In some states the court may take the posture that the minor, when committing a tort, would at least have to make restitution. The minor must at least return all of the goods to be able to rescind the contract. Whereas in the typical circumstances, if the minor has not misrepresented his or her age or has not committed any tort, the minor may have nothing to return but would still be allowed to get his or her money back or be allowed to rescind the contract. In cases where the minor has committed fraud in conjunction with a contract, a significant number of courts would still allow the minor to rescind that particular contract.

## OTHER INCOMPETENT PERSONS

### INSANE PERSONS

A person suffering under a mental incapacity, more particularly insanity, or physical disability, at the time that he or she enters a contract would generally lack contractual capacity.

First, we have to distinguish between two types of insanity. One is actual insanity. The other is judicially declared insanity. There is a difference, especially in the results.

### ACTUAL INSANITY OR INCAPACITY

A person who was actually insane during his or her attempt to contract would have to take an active part in disaffirming the contract once he or she became *lucid*. This contract is voidable, hence subject to being cured. If he or she never became lucid, there would be a continual possibility of disaffirming it. Once this person becomes lucid, then he or she would have to take an active part in either ratifying or disaffirming the contract.

It is possible for someone dealing with this particular person to have a valid contract. If the second party dealing with this incapable person did *not know* about the lack of capacity and also had a *fair* and reasonable contract, the courts might declare this contract *valid*.

### JUDICIALLY DECLARED INSANE OR INCAPABLE

On the other hand, if this individual had been declared judicially insane, then most courts or possibly all courts would appoint a guardian or a tutor, or someone to enter into and declare any contract void if the incapable person tried to enter such an agreement. It would make no difference whether the contract was fair. Any contract entered into with this particular person would be *void*; it would not be valid. The necessaries would still be the obligation of the party, since that applies to everyone, be it minors or insane or disabled individuals; it would be possible for the person who supplied the necessaries to be able to collect or enforce the contract to the extent of the reasonable value of the necessaries. Contract price would be irrelevant.

### INTOXICATED PERSONS

A person seeking to enforce a contract against a person who was intoxicated when he entered the contract may be in the same posture as dealing with a minor. These particular contracts are voidable at the option of the person with the incapacity. Thus this person is in a posture of disaffirming the contract within a reasonable time after he has become sober and has knowledge of the facts. If that person were to take *no action* to disaffirm the contract, then the courts would probably say that the now sober party is liable for the contract. He is liable for the fair market value.

## MARRIED WOMEN

At one time under the common law, married women during marriage did not have the capacity to contract. Today women generally have the same capacity to contract as men. It is possible we may see some residual disabilities wherein a woman may not have the same state contractual capacity as men. It may only be a matter of time or subsequent litigation to negate any differences.

## ALIENS

In most states the contractual capacity of an alien from a country which is not at war with the

United States is substantially the same as that of a U.S. citizen. There may be some limitations on land ownership by aliens. If an alien is a citizen of an enemy state, he may not be able to enforce all of the same contractual rights that a citizen has.

## CONVICTS

In most jurisdictions a convict has the same contractual rights as any other citizen. In some states they may be prohibited from exercising all of the same voting rights, and that may be one of the existing limitations. At common law a person typically convicted of treason or a felony could not enforce a contract.

## SUMMARY

You can win the contract game, but you must concentrate on winning. You cannot let a proposal sent to you with lots of small print on the front or back go unchallenged. When you return your version of the deal or your acceptance, make the whole deal contingent on doing it *your way* or make it clear "there will be no deal."

Let's review the types of incompetency and the legal effects on enforcing the contract.

| Type of Incompetency | Curable Defect (Voidable) or Null (void) |
|---|---|
| Minority | Voidable |
| Actual mental or mentally disabled/physical defect | Voidable |
| Court-decided incompetency resulting in guardianship Intoxication | Void |

It is difficult to determine mental incompetency, since someone can be demented but not stupid.

## ANALYSIS AND CHECKLIST

We would like to point out contract features you might want to consider for your business agreements.

## CONTRACT

Let's discuss some of the provisions you should consider in any contract. You may use this as a checklist.

### INTRODUCTION
1. *OPENING OF THE CONTRACT*

a. *Names and Addresses of Parties.* I suggest you have complete names and street addresses, not just post office addresses. Several delivery services do not deliver to post office boxes; in addition, for purposes of legal process post office boxes are generally ineffective.

b. *Corporation Information.* If one or both the parties are corporations, you would want to have information regarding the state of incorporation, the principal place of business of the corporation, the principal office of the corporation and possibly the name of the party who is going to be signatory to this agreement.

c. *Date of the Contract.* There can be two different types of dates that are important. One would be the date of signing of the contract; another would be the effective date of the contract.

d. *Recitals.* It is often wise to state the purpose of each of the parties to entering this contract. Should there be any dispute it gives the court some guidelines, some bases for the motivation or thinking of the respective parties.

### 2. *REPRESENTATIONS AND WARRANTIES OF THE PARTIES*

Parties often make certain representations with regard to the quality of the product or service they are delivering or expecting to receive. These should be made part of the contract. If there is any sales literature involved, it can be included by reference, because it is often the basis for the agreement.

### 3. *RIGHT TO ENTER INTO AN AGREEMENT*

If one or both of the parties is a corporation or is a partnership, it is important to show evidence of the signing party having the authority to sign on behalf of the entity.

### 4. *QUALIFICATION OR REGISTRATION PURPOSE OF THE RESPECTIVE PARTIES*

If any legal qualifications, state registrations or federal registrations are required, they should be listed in the agreement.

## MERCHANTABILITY AND OTHER PRODUCT OR SERVICE QUALITY STATEMENTS

Merchantability generally means that a product used is of at least average quality and sold only by a merchant. There can be additional statements that the product or services are fit for a particular purpose. If you have specifications for a product, state them in the agreement. If the product or services are required to meet certain standards, the standards should be specified. If the agreement is going to negate any of the legal warranties or protections that might be generally available, they should be stated here.

## FUNCTIONAL LANGUAGE OF THE CONTRACT

1. *Sale, License, Employer/Employee Relationship, Requirement for Insurance.* All of these can be listed in this section of the agreement.

2. *The Rights and Duties of Respective Parties.* This may very well be the guts of the contract; that is why it is important to state it with as much precision as possible. In other words, if you can quantify what has to be done, do it here.

3. *Legal Compliance.* If a condition of the contract is that it be performed in a particular manner to qualify for certain state or federal laws or regulations, specify them so that there is clearly no doubt.

4. *Respective Rights of Parties.* If this is to be an exclusive versus a non-exclusive agreement, list it.

In addition, if the parties will be allowed to compete with each other or if this is a relevant provision, state it here. Again, you must be specific in terms of geographical area, types of products, brands of products, types of customers, types of services and other similar considerations.

5. *Exceptions to Performance.* These are often called *majeure.* For instance, is not uncommon to see in the contracts that performance will be delayed if there are strikes, acts of God, war and other similar types of events. Sometimes you might want to say that at least during that period there will be a delay.

6. *Payments.* It is very important that if you absolutely need payment to be made on a certain date, you must specify the dates and state specifically that they can be no later than a particular date. The method of payment, such as cash, check, certified check, bank check, cashier's check or money order, is important. The place of delivery for any payments must be specified so there is absolutely no doubt. Do not refer to another address; state it specifically here. You should list what effect late payments will have and how the contract will treat them. Will there be any withholding or taxes on any payments? As we all know, the Internal Revenue Service has broadened its hand, andcontract payments may often be subject to withholding of taxes.

7. *Security Required.* On certain types of contracts, you may be required to place a bond with a commercial insurer. You may require guarantees to protect you from the failure of performance— what would be your rights upon the breach of the other party to this particular contract.

8. *Option To Extend the Contract Period.* If there are any time specifications in the contract, for the initial contract or for the subsequent option period, you should state it specifically. Statements of an additional six months are effective but can also be risky. Specify when the year starts and ends or when the three- month period starts and ends. State what information is required and when the information is required and to whom it must be sent in order to extend any contract.

9. *Insurance.* The amounts of any insurance such as workers' compensation insurance or general liability insurance, and any companies that

may be specified in the effective dates of any insurance, should be denominated. In addition, if you are requiring the other party to have such insurance, you may want to receive a confirmation certificate of such insurance and require that a notice of cancellation be sent to you.

10. *Accounting.* If one of the parties is liable for any potential accounting for products, pricing or any other specifications, the party may be required to maintain certain books. They may have to be maintained in a certain fashion, such as "in keeping with generally accepted accounting principles." You may want to specify when the books can be examined, whether during normal business hours, who pays for the inspection or for any audit, who pays for any error and whether there is any triggering point; for instance, above a 2% error of their cost; it must be paid by the party making the error.

11. *Confidentiality.* Often information can be transferred without releasing it or giving up your rights to it; you should specify that the other party is receiving such information in strictest confidence and is subject to immediate injunctive procedure and damages if they violate it.

## TERMINATION

The specific date of any termination should be stated, and if there are notices to be sent to any parties the advance notice for any party should be listed and the precise default date or period should be stated.

1. *Breaches of the Agreement.* The contract can state what specific things will occur if the contract is terminated as a result of a breach. If there are automatic breaches or any time period for curing any breach, would there be any liquidated damages, what occurs upon the bankruptcy of one of the parties or insolvency of one of the parties or the assignment for the benefit of any creditors by one of the parties? What happens if there is a change of control, a merger or consolidation or a buyout?

2. *Rights and Duties of Parties Upon Termination.* What are the rights of each of the parties? Do they have the right to repurchase goods or similar goods or similar services, who pays for the additional freight costs, or what are the pricing problems of replacement items and what must be the condition of such items upon replacement? What happens to either party's use of trade names, trademarks, logos and trade secrets? What about listings on signs of product use or uses, listing in any directories or telephone yellow pages, and so forth.

3. *Waiver of Any Single Breach Will Not Be Construed To Be* a Continuing Waiver. Provision that if one of the parties allows a *single* waiver of any particular breach, this will not be construed as a *continuing* waiver.

## MISCELLANEOUS

1. *Entire Agreement.* This can be used for both good and bad. I have often seen this in contracts where there is a statement made that this is the entire agreement between the parties, which can be after a lengthy process of negotiation and education by sales people. It effectively says that anything my salespeople say can be fraudulent to you, but you are not to believe it because only what is on this particular piece of paper is what is to control. If you are to use such statements, I would strongly urge you to make sure any sales literature that you use can be legitimately included in the agreements—that you don't have anything to cover up. On the other hand, if the other party states that this is the entire agreement, though they have made extensive representations or warranties otherwise, I urge you to include those specifically or not sign such an agreement. It is often a business's attempt to cover up for the potential fraud of their salespeople. They do not mind if their salespeople lure you into a contract; they just don't want to be held responsible for it. It is not necessarily controlling in a court of law if it says that it is the entire agreement, but it does give the manipulative type an edge.

2. *Amendments Should Be in Writing Only.* It is possible for you to be very strict in an agreement by stating that any amendments must be strictly construed and must be written only and signed by authorized parties. One of the problems that should concern you is that if you make any oral modifications you may in effect be leaving this particular provision out.

3. *Notices.* As we have mentioned before, addresses are very critical, especially for notices of any default. You will want to state that any notices must be sent by certified or registered mail or by some express or delivery service by which a signature is required, so you know any changes of address.

4. *Arbitration.* One of the serious considerations in any contract is the size of the contract with regard to your company. There are also other considerations; you might be concerned about their doing future business with the same company. Arbitration can fit if this particular contract is small in comparison with your overall business. On the other hand, if it could be a significant portion of your business, I would strongly urge you not to sign an arbitration agreement. It is an effective method of resolving disputes, but you are also giving up most of your legal rights when you sign an arbitration agreement. If you are a farmer and you are selling grain to a grain broker, the disputes may only involve grades of grain. In that case you might want to consider having an arbitration clause, but I would say that if it involves or a substantial portion of your crop, you should pass on it. There are many provisions involving arbitration, and you may wish to state that you will follow the rules of the American Arbitration Association or the rules of another particular body in which one or both of you are members. On the other hand, if there is any doubt whether or not arbitration is beneficial to you, leave such an agreement out. If it fits you or your particular contract, then you should seriously consider it.

5. *Assignment.* Some agreements can be easily assigned because there is no esoteric duty. For instance, if you are attempting to buy a particular brand and model of a television set an assignment of the right of the supplier to another supplier would not necessarily hurt you as long as it is delivered to your premises at a particular time that you dictate. On the other hand, there are some types of contracts that would not fit the assignment mold. An example of an esoteric duty might be the commissioning of an artist to do a portrait for you. Not all artists perform in a similar manner, and certainly you should never allow that type of a personal service contract to be assigned.

You may wish to state which state law is controlling, and also you may want to consider stating that the contract provisions are severable. Generally this would mean that if one provision is considered illegal or unenforceable the other portions of the contract are still enforceable.

6. *Guarantors.* If there are any guarantors or additional parties who might play a part in this particular contract, you should state them here.

Advertising and promoting your products and services is the lifeblood of your current and future business. There are some rules which apply to the touting game. Telling *half*-truths could lead to whole body incarceration (upon conviction only). I am sure you get the drift.

## ENDING OF THE CONTRACT

This is the place for signatures and the titles of the individuals, their agent capacity, if any. It is very important that you make sure that if you are signing on behalf of a partnership or a corporation or any other entity, that entity be stated clearly and your capacity as an agent be stated. If you have an official title, so state; if you are an agent as a result of a power of attorney, so state; you might even possibly want to include a copy of the basis for your representation.

# CHAPTER 2

STARTING YOUR BUSINESS—
WHAT FORM CAN IT TAKE?

# CHAPTER 2

## STARTING YOUR BUSINESS—WHAT FORM CAN IT TAKE?

There are several approaches to starting a business. Some of the choices are dictated by the number of individuals involved. Some of the choices are dictated by legal requirements. Some of the choices are effected by the potential exposure to risk, such as tort risk. Are there loans? Are there customer risks? Some of the factors revolve around taxation. Some might revolve around financial considerations and projections. In any event, often we leave these choices solely up to our accountants and lawyers. It is absolutely imperative that we know enough about the workings of sole proprietorships, partnerships (limited or general partnerships) and corporations (general or Subchapter S).

It is not sufficient for us to merely dump this decision in the laps of our "experts." If we do not know enough to *ask* the *right questions* or to give them certain *information* or the proper information, we may end up with a result that is not the best.

We will examine some of the details in comparing the approaches to forming a business. Once you become familiar with these, you can sit down and plot your strategy with some insight. There are pluses and minuses. There are two or three different routes to the same goal. But please do not *dump* this decision in someone else's lap.

We will take a look at the three primary ways of doing business as opposed to all of the potential ways. These three are:

1. Sole Proprietorship.

2. Partnership, which includes general and limited partnerships.

3. Corporation, which can include a one-person corporation or one with millions of employees and investors.

## SOLE PROPRIETORSHIP

### COST OF CREATION AND EASE

A sole proprietorship is generally the cheapest form of doing business. From a tax viewpoint it does not generally entail much. The sole proprietorship does not entail any additional taxation from a federal or a state viewpoint. It is easy to form. If we do enough business and have any employees, we then get an employer identification number, which is different from your Social Security number (File Form SS-4, which the IRS or your accountant has). It does not typically require any permission to do business in your state. Nor does this approach require filing any complex documents with the Secretary of State or with the Clerk of Court.

### COST OF OPERATION

The sole proprietorship generally is under the fewest restraints and is often the easiest of the several approaches to operate. It is also the cheapest form from a cost-of-operation viewpoint.

### POTENTIAL LIABILITY

One of the drawbacks of the sole proprietorship is that the individual, meaning you, will have unlimited liability for any business debts or business torts. If someone is injured as a result of your business, everything you have is on the line. For most intents and purposes, there is no barrier between you and potential absolute liability that could wipe out your assets.

## MANAGEMENT AND CONTROL

A sole proprietorship is easy to control. There is only one person to control it. He or she is the boss. The boss has an exclusive right to manage the business unless he or she delegates some authority to someone else.

## CONTINUITY OF EXISTENCE

One of the problems of a sole proprietorship is that when the owner dies, generally the business also dies. If there is some preparation made to carry it on by another person, this end could be avoided. It is a risk, however, that each owner should confront.

## TRANSFERABILITY OF INTEREST

It is possible for the sole proprietor to transfer the interest in his or her business, but it is not quite as easy as selling shares in a corporation. Transferring these interests can be a problem. Transferring a sole proprietorship involves watching out for creditors. Often it involves complying with the Bulk Sales Act of your state.

## TAXATION

For taxation purposes, the sole proprietorship is not a separate entity. You usually only have to file an additional Schedule C with your federal tax return.

## LEGAL ENTITY STATUS

From the viewpoint of being a legal entity, a sole proprietorship can sue or be sued in its individual name.

You have the right to own property. You, as an individual. As an individual you can also do business in another state, most of the time without any particular problems or qualifications and at mini-mal expense. If you want to change your business purposes or how you do business, you do not have to take a vote. Just do it.

## AGENTS

A sole proprietorship can appoint individual agents and does not have to worry about it happening without your knowledge. There are no automatic agents in the sole proprietorship. This is not the case with partnerships, for instance. There is only a principal. Unless he or she creates agents, there are no agents to create liability for the owner.

# PARTNERSHIP

Let's examine the partnership from the same views as we did the sole proprietorship.

## COST OF CREATION AND EASE

A partnership can be created without a formal agreement. It is a consensual agreement between two or more parties to share risks in a venture for profit. It is certainly recommended to have a written agreement. It can be oral; however, this is obviously dangerous unless the relationship is fairly well defined. Even a well-defined relationship, which can be more expensive to form, does not give you absolute protection from unwanted or unintended results. A partnership usually is created with a formal agreement, which entails legal fees. Limited partnerships are more complex, usually involve greater fees, and usually have to be filed with the Secretary of State or other public authority.

## COST OF OPERATION

Partnerships generally can operate the same way as any sole proprietorship. There are fairly few prohibitions. This is a slightly more costly form of doing business than a sole proprietorship.

## POTENTIAL LIABILITY

Partners have unlimited potential personal liability. This liability exists for all of the business debts and obligations including tort obligations. Partners can have unlimited liability for the known or unknown acts of their partners or agents.

## MANAGEMENT AND CONTROL

All the partners generally have equal voice in management. There can be an agreement among the parties to modify this, meaning that all of the authority can be given to one person. One person can be granted all authority, for instance, with regard to renting out an apartment complex. Another partner can have responsibility for keeping the accounting records. Nevertheless, unless by a contrary agreement, all of the partners have equal voice in the management.

## CONTINUITY OF EXISTENCE

A partnership is, for legal purposes, dissolved by the death or withdrawal of any partner or by a number of other events. It is possible to create a partnership with the proper provisions that would continue the partnership even if a partner dies. This provision would immediately create a new partnership, and not continue the existing one.

## TRANSFERABILITY OF INTEREST

Unless there is some contrary agreement, a partner generally cannot easily transfer his or her interest in the partnership. Generally the partner must get concurrence or agreement of the other partners to do so. Transferring an interest in a partnership is *more difficult* than in a sole proprietorship. The other partners must concur to allow a new person as a partner. This is a fiduciary position. We will see that a person can transfer his financial interest but cannot unilaterally create a new partner without concurrence.

## TAXATION

A partnership, for most intents and purposes, is *not a taxable entity*. The partnership itself does not pay federal or state income taxes, although each partner pays tax on his or her pro rata portion of the net results of the partnership. The partnership has to pay sales and other taxes as anyone else or any other entity. In general it is *not* a taxable entity. It does file federal or state *tax information returns*, but taxes are not usually paid on this level.

## LEGAL ENTITY STATUS

A partnership in most if not all states can *sue* and be *sued* in its own name. It can own property. For bankruptcy purposes, it can go bankrupt. That does not necessarily protect the partners from unlimited liability.

A partnership itself can be bankrupt, but the individual partners are not protected just because the partnership itself does not have enough assets to cover its debts. The partners themselves would still have to make good on the debts.

Doing business in other states is allowed and normally does not require much paperwork.

Modification or amendment of a partnership agreement generally has to be done *unanimously* unless there is an agreement otherwise.

## AGENCY

All the partners are agents for each other with certain very limited exceptions. Even if there is a contrary, *internal* agreement, third parties may not necessarily know about it. This agreement may not protect the partnership from liability that can be created by one of the partners ignoring any internal agreement.

Partnerships can be formed by implication or without intention.

Partnerships give all partners a chance to commit other partners to liability, intended or otherwise.

Partners cannot take a "set it and forget it" approach to partnership business.

## LIMITED PARTNERSHIP

If there are two or more persons who want to start a business venture, a limited partnership is an entity that is formed under legal authority of the state.

### COST OF CREATION AND EASE

A limited partnership is created through the authority of the state. It has a special status. It is not just consensual in nature. The relationship is virtually anything the partners want it to be. Because certain of the partners have a *limited liability* status, the partnership must meet certain state requirements. Certain documents must be filed, generally with the Secretary of State. There are certain details that have to be dealt with.

### COST OF OPERATION

A limited partnership may be slightly more costly to operate. It needs more legal and other attention. The articles of limited partnership are a bit more complex than for an ordinary partnership. To have limited partnership status, the general partners have to file a certificate of limited partnership with the Secretary of State or comparable state officer. The general partners will then receive a certificate from such officer. This is a critical need and vitally important to anyone who is a limited partner (what you do not know can hurt you).

### POTENTIAL LIABILITY

In a limited partnership, general partners have *unlimited* liability for the business debts and all of the obligations. The limited partners' liability is generally *limited* to the extent of the investment that they have made or the investment for which they have committed themselves. On occasion partnerships make agreements with some of the partners to make investments of their *time*. For instance, a limited partner might invest $10,000 immediately and commit herself to invest $5,000 the following year and $7,000 the year after that. If that is the agreement a limited partner has made, then that limited partner could be liable to the extent of the entire financial commitment (here $22,000).

If a partnership has some financial problems prior to bankruptcy, the creditors could enforce that portion of the agreement.

If a limited partner exceeds his limited status and begins to participate in *management* or in *controlling* the business, it is possible that the limited partner might give up his or her limited liability status. Be careful if you are a limited partner.

### MANAGEMENT AND CONTROL

Control of a limited partnership is usually in the hands of the *general* partners. For most day-to-day activities, the limited partners do *not* have a say so. For major changes in the limited partnership agreement, the limited partners have a vote. Under some state laws (especially with the Revised Uniform Limited Partnership Act) the limited partners can kick out the general partner, given enough voting strength. Limited partners must take a back seat for daily management. They are more like minority shareholders.

### CONTINUITY OF EXISTENCE

A partnership is dissolved by the death of one of the partners. But the death of a limited partner has less of an effect for most intents and purposes. It may have no effect on the partnership itself. It is easy to provide for the continuation of a partnership with the death of a limited partner. It is relatively easy to require that the partner's estate sell back its shares, since the estate cannot take part in management.

### TRANSFERABILITY OF INTEREST

This revolves around how easy it is to sell your interest in a limited partnership. The people who lay it on the line in a limited partnership are the general partners. They are the ones who have unlimited liability. They are also the ones who are considered the *fiduciaries* of the business. They have to give their *best effort* and have to be scrupulously honest. They are an ownership interest of a general partner. On the other hand, since a limited partner does not do anything for a partnership—or usually does not—it is easier to allow another person to purchase that partner's investment. Therefore, it is fairly easy to allow the transfer of a limited partner's interest. He/she is *not a fiduciary*.

## TAXATION

A limited partnership is treated the same as a partnership. It is generally not a taxable entity. You do not have to worry about paying income taxes on that level. The limited partnership must file an information return with the Internal Revenue Service and the state. The individual partners and limited partners pay taxes on their level.

## LEGAL ENTITY STATUS

A limited partnership is treated the same as a partnership for purposes of a legal entity. For purposes of suing or being sued or for owning property, bankruptcy purposes or doing business in another state, the limited partnership is an entity. One thing that is a little more burdensome is that a limited partnership generally has to report certain additional information if it wants to do business in another state.

## MODIFICATION OR AMENDMENT

The ability to modify or amend the limited partnership is dependent on the concurrence of the limited partners with the general partner. Generally there is a requirement of total consensus. The partnership agreement can contain provisions requiring a lesser vote.

These modifications or amendments must be filed with the Secretary of State or similar official *just as the original* articles of limited partnership.

## AGENTS

Limited partners are *not* agents for the partnership. The general partners are agents for each other, just as they would be in a general partnership. If a *limited* partner represents himself to the public as a limited partner, then he or she would have no authority. On the other hand, it is possible for general partners to inadvertently give a limited partner agency status. Everyone has to be careful to maintain the intended status of limited partners.

# CORPORATION

If there are two or more persons entering a business venture, they can form this artificial entity.

## COST OF CREATION AND EASE

A corporation is created pursuant to state statutes or federal law, depending on the type of business it is entering. Generally, to create it takes some detailed information. Also some choices have to be made in creating a corporation. These articles of incorporation must be filed with the Secretary of State or some similar official in most states. Generally these documents must also be filed, along with a copy of the *certificate* of incorporation, with the Clerk of Court in the area where the corporation has its registered office.

## COST OF OPERATION

The cost of operating a corporation is a little higher than any of the other entities. The reason for this is that there are certain formalities that must be followed in maintaining a corporation as a separate entity. This area is often overlooked by individuals and professionals who deal with corporations. It is unfortunate, but numerous corporate directors and officers do not pay attention to the requirements of corporate behavior. Corporations require the director and officers to hold meetings for important decisions. These directors have to adopt resolutions approving important actions. Shareholders must elect directors and directors appoint officers. Operating a corporation is often more costly.

## POTENTIAL LIABILITY

Corporate shareholders, corporate officers or directors are generally *not* personally liable for corporate debts and obligations. They are only responsible for their own behavior, but they are generally not liable for the acts of the corporation. Certainly if an officer, for instance, is responsible for injuring someone, then that person may be personally liable in addition to the corporation if the injury is a business tort.

## MANAGEMENT AND CONTROL

A corporation has an advantage over the previous forms in that it lends itself to having many investors, but has control *centralized*. Management may be only a few individuals. Thus you can have thousands of investors, but only five or six individuals who manage the corporation.

## CONTINUITY OF EXISTENCE

A corporation as a legal entity can have perpetual existence in most jurisdictions. It is possible to have a corporation with a limited lifetime. On occasion, corporations are only designed to last for, say, five years or 10 years as stated in the corporate articles.

## TRANSFERABILITY OF INTEREST

Generally it is easy to transfer ownership in a corporation from one shareholder to another shareholder. In actuality in most small corporations, or closed corporations as they are called, the directors wish to make it difficult for any of the existing shareholders to sell to an unknown third party. Sometimes you will see restrictions on the ability of a shareholder to transfer the shares of stock to another individual or another entity. Often you will see shareholder agreements that state how, when, for how much and to whom shares can be sold. These agreements often require that the individual offer the stock either to the corporation or to the other shareholders or to both, based on whatever legitimate offers they may have received. There can be other complications contained in such agreements.

## TAXATION

A corporation *is taxed* as a *separate entity* on its own level. A corporation generally is a taxpaying entity. This is essentially the only difference between a regular corporation and a Subchapter S corporation.

A Subchapter S corporation is generally *not* a *taxpaying* entity, though it can be under certain circumstances. It is mostly a reporting entity. The income and expenses are passed through to the shareholder, and the shareholder pays income taxes on any net income.

## LEGAL ENTITY

A corporation can sue and be sued in its name. It can own property. It can file for bankruptcy (certain types of corporations are excepted). A corporation can do business in other states, but it has to comply with state qualification procedures.

## AGENCY

Shareholders are not agents for any of the other shareholders, nor are they agents for the corporation itself. Even a 100-percent shareholder who is not an officer or director of the corporation has *no* authority to commit the corporation to liability.

Let's review in the next two chapters the nature of partnerships and corporation.

# CHAPTER 3

## PARTNERSHIPS

# CHAPTER 3

## PARTNERSHIPS

A partnership is an aggregation of two or more persons as co-owners of a business for profit. Let's examine the workings of the partnership.

### NATURE AND METHODS OF FORMATION

If two or more persons intend to go into business, two approaches available for forming a business are a partnership (limited or general) and a corporation.

We would like to examine the basic principles of forming a partnership. What legal principles must you know if you are going to consider a partnership? Some of the principles applying to other areas of law are primarily in the relationship between principal and agent. We will see later that this is a very important relationship. Do not rely on your lawyer's knowledge. You have to spot any problems.

What is a partnership? A partnership can be defined. However, the definition alone does not give us a clue to all of the problems of defining it. It is generally defined as an association of two or more persons to carry on as co-owners of a business for profit. This definition comes from the Uniform Partnership Act.

### ENTITY VERSUS AGGREGATE

It is important that we get some idea under what circumstances a partnership is a *separate entity*, and under what circumstances is it strictly a *grouping* of *individuals*. It does have an effect on your potential liability and how you do business. So let's discuss some of the issues.

### ENTITY

For most purposes a partnership is an entity. A partnership can acquire, own and dispose of property (real or personal property), enter contracts, commit civil wrongs, commit criminal wrongs, and sue and be sued in its own name and as an entity.

### AGGREGATE

For other purposes a partnership is merely an association of individuals who have a common bond. All these individuals are part of the approval process and all part of the liability process. Whether a partnership is an aggregate and for which purpose depends on the state. In some states and for some purposes, a partnership cannot sue and be sued as an entity; each individual partner must be named in any lawsuit. Even if a partnership files under the bankruptcy laws, the individual partners can still be personally liable for unpaid debts. Therefore, for bankruptcy purposes, a partnership is an *entity* to a certain extent but an *aggregate* for liability purposes.

The U.S. Internal Revenue Code treats a partnership as an *aggregate*. It does not create tax consequences, in general, on the partnership level, merely on the individual level.

### RELATIONSHIP AMONG PARTNERS

1. Partners in a partnership are fiduciaries with regard to each other. Each partner is an agent for the other partners; hence they must treat each other with the highest relationship in good faith.

This relationship of partners to each other may be based on a contract but, on the other hand, can be informal and in fact may not be written.

1.Partnerships can be express or implied.

2. If you have any remote idea of forming a partnership, have it *expressly* formed and not impliedly formed.

3. An implied partnership could be detrimental to your financial health (even worse than an express one).

## CHARACTERISTICS OF PARTNERSHIPS

Partnerships generally have these characteristics:

1. They are limited as to duration. When any partner dies—or no longer exists in the case of a corporate partner—the partnership terminates.

2. In order for a partner to transfer ownership and create a new partnership interest in the new owner, all the partners must agree.

3. A partnership is not a distinct *entity* for many purposes, including liability and taxation. On the other hand, for certain purposes, including ownership of property, a partnership may be treated as a separate legal entity.

4. The partners have unlimited personal liability for partnership debts—both contractual debts and debts arising out of civil wrongs or torts.

5. Partnerships can be formed informally.

6. Since partnerships are based on personal liability, it may be easier for a partnership to raise funds than for a corporation to raise funds.

## TYPES OF PARTNERSHIPS

1. *General Partnership.* This is the type of partnership of which most of us are aware: All of the partners are personally liable for all the debts, and all generally take part in the management of the partnership.

2. *Limited Partnerships.* Limited partnerships involve general partners, but in addition there is a new category of partner called a limited partner. Limited partners merely contribute capital to the partnership and usually have no additional liability, under the rules of the Uniform Limited Partnership Act or whatever state law applies.

## FORMATION OF A PARTNERSHIP

Partnerships may be formed by various methods. Let's take a look at some of the methods:

1. By express or implied agreement.

2. By informal creation, which can be done either orally or in writing.

3. By a rebuttable presumption under some laws, including the Uniform Partnership Act, whereby a person who receives a share of the profits may be presumed to be a partner.

## PARTNER'S RIGHTS

If we are trying to determine what the rights of each partner are, we can look to several sources. One of the sources would be the state law. Another source would be the partnership agreement.

Often a state law will define what a partner's rights are in the absence of a specific provision in any agreement.

The partnership agreement, whether it is formally written or informally created, can modify the state law "default" positions.

In every state, the partnership law defines certain elements of the relationship of partners to third parties and of partners to each other. Many of these elements can be changed by an agreement between the affected parties. If the parties do not change these elements, these are called "default" positions. Some computer buffs might appreciate the significance of "default" more than others.

Thus, a partner would have an ownership interest as defined by the agreement. The partner would have a right to share in the profits and receive a return of his or her contributions upon dissolution.

A partner would also have the right to participate equally along with other partners in the management of the partnership.

A partner would also have an equal ownership interest, unless defined otherwise, in any partnership property—not for personal use, however, but as a part of the partnership assets.

## PARTNERSHIP PROPERTY

How can we determine what property is owned by the partnership? We may have to examine numerous factors and we can look to the following to point us in the right direction:

1. Property acquired by the partnership with partnership funds, unless there has been some specific exception to the property being owned by the partnership.

2. Any property or capital contributed to the partnership by any particular partner, which then would be considered partnership property.

3. Profits from the partnership before such profits are distributed.

4. The partnership name and any good will.

Some of the factors that the courts have used to determine ambiguous situations include whether or not partnership funds were used to acquire the good or the property, the manner in which any property was used, the owner of record of property, if there is such ownership, and other factors that may indicate who pays taxes on the property.

All partners have equal rights to use partnership property for partnership purposes, as we have mentioned; it cannot be used *per se* for personal purposes.

A partner cannot assign his or her interest in particular partnership property, nor can partnership property be seized by an individual partner's creditors. The creditors can, however, seize the partner's interest in the entire partnership.

## MANAGEMENT RIGHTS OF A PARTNER

Each partner has a right to participate equally in the management of the partnership. For instance, a majority vote of the partners would be needed when we consider the ordinary business decisions that have to be made on a day-to-day basis.

On the other hand, if there are major changes proposed to a partnership, for instance entering a new line of business, then under most circumstances a unanimous vote would be needed.

Unless the agreement states otherwise most partners may act as agents for the partnership in partnership business.

Partners also have the right to inspect the books and records and therefore have knowledge of all partnership business.

## SHARING PROFITS AND LOSSES

Unless an agreement states otherwise, each partner has an equal right to share—and an equal duty to share in the losses—of any partnership. This is true even if capital has not been contributed equally, but an agreement may specify otherwise.

## OTHER PARTNER RIGHTS

A partner has the right to be reimbursed or indemnified for expenses incurred on behalf of the partnership. In other words, if he or she has spent $1,000 on legitimate partnership business, he or she has the right to be reimbursed that $1,000.

The partner also has the right to receive interest on any loans or advances made to the partnership. This is not the case with regard to capital contributions, however, unless the partnership agreement so states.

A partner does not have a right to any salary for work performed for the partnership. It is con-

---

### POWER POINTS _____

▶ Partners have equal management rights, unless otherwise agreed.

▶ Partners are agents for each other. (Do you want your partners to be able to ruin you financially?)

▶ Partners are fiduciaries to each other. This requires a high duty of care and complete disclosure involving the subject matter of the partnership.

sidered another part of the contribution of that particular partner to the partnership.

## DUTIES AMONG PARTNERS

1. *Fiduciary Duties.* The most important duty among partners is the fiduciary duty: Each partner owes the others a fiduciary duty.

A partner cannot gain personally, financially or otherwise, from any partnership transaction without getting the agreement of all the other partners. He or she cannot profit directly or indirectly from any partnership transaction or partnership potential. Each partner must turn over any profits made out of partnership business— again, directly or indirectly—to the partnership.

Partners cannot compete with the partnership. A partner may enter into other businesses, but not into any business that would be a direct or indirect competitor of the partnership. Also, in keeping with this, a partner must abide by the partnership agreement.

2. *A Partner Is Required To Exercise Reasonable Skill in Carrying Out His or Her Duties.* This would not mean perfection but merely exercising a reasonable level of skill.

3. *Partners Owe Each Other a Formal Accounting for Any of the Assets Over Which They May Have Had Control.* They also owe an accounting for their financial and non-financial behavior with regard to the partnership.

## LIMITED RIGHT TO SUE OTHER PARTNERS

Generally partners cannot sue other partners while the partnership is ongoing. There are some limited exceptions, but generally the law takes the view that the situation must be bad enough to have a termination before allowing such a suit.

## RELATIONSHIP OF PARTNERS IN PARTNERSHIP TO THIRD PARTIES.

*Agents.* The partners are agents not only of the partnership but, in effect, for each other.

A partner can bind the partnership to contracts with third parties. This can be the case even when the partner has no actual authority, but has only ostensible or apparent authority.

A partner can bind the partnership to torts committed by the partner. Any actions that violate someone else's rights, including personal injury or financial torts, can become liabilities of the partnership. These torts would be those committed in the course of the partnership's business. They can also include a breach of trust by a partner, such as stealing money received from a third party in payment for some goods sold to that third party.

Partners also typically have authority to buy and sell goods, receive money and pay partnership debts; they do not, however, have implied authority to use the partnership as a surety or guarantor of someone else's debts.

Partners usually cannot create liability for the partnership if their behavior is outside what would be considered either express or implied authority.

## LIMITATIONS WITH REGARD TO THIRD PARTIES

The law implies that third parties will know that there are some limitations to a partner's behavior or ability to commit the partnership to some liability.

These would include:

1. Behavior which is not reasonable under the particular circumstances.

2. The admission of a new partner into the partnership;

3. The assigning of any partnership property if the property is in the partnership's name.

4. Sale or disposition of the good will of the partnership.

5. Making the partnership a guarantor or a surety on another party's debts or obligations.

6. Admitting a claim in court which has been filed against the partnership.

7. Submitting a partnership claim to an arbitrator.

8. Performing any act which would make carrying on the partnership impossible. The partnership, hence the individual partners, may be bound to an agreement with a third party if the partner binds the partnership.

This binding can occur:

a. If the partner had *apparent* (but unauthorized) *authority* to act on behalf of the partnership.

b. If the partner had *express* authority.

c. If the partner had *implied* authority (e.g., as general manager), even if he *exceeded* his authority under an internal agreement.

## PERSONAL LIABILITY

Remember that a general partner's liability is personal to him or her. In other words, all of his or her personal assets, including personal property and real property, may be at risk for any partnership debt or partnership liability.

*Contractual Liability.* Partners are jointly liable on any contractual or debt obligation of the partnership. What this means is that all parties must be sued or named as defendants in any lawsuit against the partnership. The creditor cannot sue less than all of the partners if the partners are individually named.

Before any individual partner's personal assets are attached (liened) or seized, all of the partnership assets must be exhausted.

In addition, you should note that the release of any partner by the creditor releases all the partners unless there has been some specific reservation of rights.

Another noteworthy item is that if a majority vote has affirmed the partnership's entering into a contract, then all of the partners are liable even if they were not there to vote or voted against the proposition.

*Tort Liability.* With regard to civil torts, the relationship among partners and their assets is affected slightly differently than with regard to contractual obligations and debt obligations of the partnership.

Partners are jointly and severally liable for torts or breaches of their fiduciary obligations with regard to each other or with regard to third parties.

What this basically means is that if one of the partners injures someone in an automobile accident in the course and scope of doing partnership business, then the third party can sue any one of the partners and hold that partner liable for the entire liability. In effect the injured party does not have to bring all of the partners to the table or to the lawsuit.

The injured party can satisfy his or her judgment, assuming he or she is successful, out of the assets of any party he or she finds.

It is then up to the partner sued and held liable to seek contribution from the other parties; but an injured person who has a cause of action against that partner and the partnership can get his or her judgment satisfied out of that one partner's assets.

## INTERNAL AGREEMENTS DO NOT AFFECT THIRD PARTIES

Often the partnership agreement will split up losses or profits under certain circumstances in ways that are different than what a third party may envision. Nevertheless, that internal agreement does not adversely affect the third party's dealing with the partnership. In other words, internal limitations basically do not affect a third party's dealing with the partnership.

## ENTERING PARTNERS

Entering partners generally are not personally liable for debts created previous to their entry, although their partnership assets may be at risk. They are, however, personally liable for debts created after they have entered.

Withdrawing partners should be concerned about putting third parties on notice. If you are a partner in a partnership and plan to leave the partnership, you should make certain that all current customers know; otherwise your liability may continue.

The rule is to give *actual notice* to actual or current customers, and *constructive notice* (e.g., in a newspaper) to let the rest of the world know. With constructive notice, the *effort* to let everyone else know is probably sufficient under the law.

## CRIMINAL LIABILITY

Generally, partners are not criminally liable for the acts of other partners. That is not an absolute statement, but it is generally accurate. The basic reason is that criminal intent is required for criminal liability, and the law does not automatically assume that other partners know what the partner who committed a criminal act had on his or her mind.

There are exceptions, however, where parties have conspired to commit criminal acts.

## LIABILITY OF WITHDRAWING PARTNER

The liability of a withdrawing partner may be limited by some agreement among the partners, for instance in the partnership agreement. This agreement, however, is not necessarily binding on third parties. If a third party is on notice of the agreement and somehow concurs in it or acknowledges its existence and its potential limitation on the third party, then it is possible for this agreement to have an effect on the third party. Typically, it does not. Therefore if you are withdrawing from a partnership, you should be aware of this black hole. Before entering or leaving a partnership, you should do everything to discover all current financial liabilities as well as any potential liabilities.

You should inspect partnership books and records to avoid any hidden land mines.

## TERMINATION OF A PARTNERSHIP

Partnerships are generally composed of individuals, but they may also be composed of other entities, including other partnerships and corporations. They are generally not intended to last forever.

What is a termination of a partnership? The termination of a partnership comes about when the assets are turned into liquid assets (usually cash) in winding up of the partnership's affairs. It is not always true that a partnership needs to wind up its business; for instance, it is possible to transfer the business to a succeeding partnership or to another entity. Nevertheless, in general, termination is turning the business assets into liquid assets.

## METHODS OF TERMINATING A PARTNERSHIP

1. When partners cease carrying on the business together as an ongoing business, then dissolution must occur.

2. Termination occurs when the partners engage in winding up the business affairs of the partnership, for instance the termination of an ongoing sale of inventory or the sale of the inventory as a bulk item.

3. Termination occurs when the partnership is no longer in existence.

## DISSOLUTION.

Dissolution is the ceasing of the partnership from carrying on its business as an ongoing business and winding up of the business. It can occur in the following manners:

1. By prior agreement of all of the partners or within the partnership agreement. Some of these include having a specific term of years or days or months in the agreement, which has been reached. Another approach is by the partnership having accomplished its purpose: for instance, to develop a subdivision and all of the lots are developed. Another method can be expulsion of a partner from the business based on some provision in the partnership agreement.

2. By an agreement among all of the partners to terminate the partnership. This can be done by admitting a new partner, which can dissolve the existing partnership and create a new partnership. This can also be done by all of the parties agreeing to a dissolution and the ending of the partnership business.

## WITHDRAWAL BY A PARTNER

Withdrawal by a partner effectively works a dissolution of the partnership. Although the partnership may look and act like the previous one for legal purposes, it can be deemed to be dissolved.

Also, if there is no specific term in a partnership agreement, then any partner may be able to withdraw at any time. This would be the withdrawal of a partner within the provisions of the agreement, and this would work a dissolution of the partnership.

## DEATH OF A PARTNER

The death of a partner effectively dissolves the partnership. Under these circumstances the executor or administrator of the deceased person's estate may require an accounting from the other partners and the payment or repurchase of the deceased partner's interest in the partnership.

## BANKRUPTCY OF A
## PARTNER OR THE PARTNERSHIP

The bankruptcy of a partner will typically dissolve a partnership. The trustee legally seizes control of the bankrupt partner's interest in the partnership. The creditors of the bankrupt partner may receive the benefit of any assets.

## A COURT DECREE CAN
## DISSOLVE THE PARTNERSHIP

This can occur in cases where a partner has been guilty of misconduct or conduct detrimental to the business. It may also occur where a partner continually or seriously breaches the provisions of the partnership agreement. A court might also decree a dissolution where a partner violates his duties to the partnership. A court may also decree a dissolution where a partner is declared insane or is disabled for a considerable term. At least one of the partners would have to seek the court decree.

## SELLING, PLEDGING OR
## ASSIGNING A PARTNER'S
## INTEREST IN THE PARTNERSHIP

Selling, pledging or assigning a partner's interest does not necessarily dissolve the partnership. But any one of these would allow a third party who becomes the owner of the partner's interest to seek a dissolution of the partnership. This new party will usually have to wait until there is an expiration of the term of the partnership.

## RIGHTS OF EACH OF THE PARTNERS
## ON DISSOLUTION

*Dissolution in Accordance With Agreement.* If the dissolution of the partnership is done in accordance with the partnership agreement or in accordance with the law and not in violation of the agreement, then there are no damages due and no causes of action against any of the other partners as a result of the dissolution. In this case each of the partners

has a right to have the partnership assets applied to the partnership liabilities and possibly used to discharge the individual's liabilities, first to the partnership.

If there is any balance after the liabilities are met, there can be a distribution to the partners of their respective interests. We would obviously have to look at the partnership agreement to see how this distribution is done. If there is no specific provision in the partnership agreement, we would generally look to the state law on partnerships.

*Dissolution Contrary to the Partnership Agreement.* The partners who do not violate the agreement generally have a right to damages against the violating partner. They may also have the right to purchase the partnership and continue it in the partnership name as it exists. Also, the non-dissolving partners would have a right to wind up the partnership and arrange for any distribution of assets. The offending partner would not have any such rights.

An important distinction between the offending and non-offending partners is that the offending partner would have a right to residual partnership assets, but not a right to the value of any of the good will which the partnership may have or may have created.

## PARTNERS' RIGHTS UPON DISSOLUTION

During the dissolution process, the partners have no actual authority to act on behalf of the partnership. You must be mindful of the fact that under dissolution the partnership is changing from an ongoing business to one that is being wound up. Typically, you would not see a dissolving partnership buying new inventory unless, of course, there is work in process and it would be more valuable to complete the manufacturing process. Thus, there is a possibility of buying supplies, but not usually the purchase of inventory.

During this period all of the partners are still liable to creditors for existing debts and for any new debts that may be created.

The partners are also responsible for distributing the assets and paying off creditors. Legal or financial obligations cannot be avoided just because the partnership is being dissolved.

## PRIORITY AT DISTRIBUTION

When a partnership is being dissolved, the following parties are paid in the following categories and order:

1. Outside creditors.

2. Partners who are owed money: partners who have made loans to the partnership which is not capital and which is not undistributed profits.

3. Partners are repaid for their capital; that is, if there is anything left after any losses have been allocated, then the partners are repaid for their capital contributions.

4. Residual monies or assets are distributed to the partners as profit.

## PARTNERS LIABILITY FOR DEFICITS

Upon dissolution, if there are insufficient assets to cover the first three categories listed above, each of the partners must contribute toward any deficiency which may exist in category No. 3 above capital contributions. Generally, the partnership agreement would state how the losses are shared among the parties.

You may recall that losses are generally shared in the same proportion as profits unless there is something contrary in the agreement.

## PARTNERSHIP CREDITORS VERSUS PERSONAL CREDITORS OF A PARTNER

It is possible, when there is not enough money to go around in the partnership, that the partnership's creditors will seek a partner's personal assets.

What happens if the creditors of the individual have used up all of the individual's assets and are now seeking the individual's residual value in the partnership?

Basically, there is a simple rule, which works this way: Partnership creditors have first crack at partnership assets and individual creditors have first crack at individual assets. Thus, if a loss still exists and the partnership creditor is still owed money by the partner, it can seek any individual

assets left after individual creditors; are paid off and vice versa.

## CONTINUING A DISSOLVED PARTNERSHIP

It is possible for a partnership agreement to provide that even though a partnership is dissolved, meaning effectively discontinued as an ongoing business, the existing partners can continue without having to liquidate all of the assets. This is not uncommon in a partnership, and does occur as partners move in and out of a partnership.

The continuation, however, works a bit like a phoenix in that it sparks a new entity. Not necessarily the old one, but a new partnership which may have the same name. In addition, creditors of the old partnership continue as creditors of the new partnership. There is also no easy way of evading the debt obligations of the initial partnership.

## NOTICE TO THIRD PARTIES

It is extremely important that an exiting partner make sure that the customers of the partnership know that he or she is no longer a partner. Otherwise the existing partners may be able to bind that outgoing partner even without his or her consent.

The general rule is for the outgoing partner and the partnership to make sure that the actual customers or creditors are put on notice of the termination in the relationship. If there are actual customers or actual suppliers, both the ongoing partnership and the partners should let either the suppliers or the customers know.

For those potential customers, most courts have been satisfied with constructive notice, such as a newspaper ad or some general circulation method of letting potential customers or suppliers know that the partnership is changed and a certain partner is no longer involved with the partnership.

## HOW TO FORM A PARTNERSHIPASSOCIATION

Generally it is not too difficult to form a partnership, in terms of what information we need and what information we would be willing to disclose publicly. A partnership can be oral or written. It can also be created inadvertently by your actions. I heartedly recommend that any time you join another individual for business purposes, you put it in writing. There are some times, however, when it is easier to say than to do. In any event, if you have a business association with someone, make it express and written.

## ARTICLES OF PARTNERSHIP

I would like to give you some idea of the types of information that you want in the articles of partnership. This listing will force you to *think through* some of the important items in your relationship to other business partners.

### 1. THE FIRM NAME AND THE IDENTITY OF THE PARTNERS

The firm name can be different from its "doing business as" name. It does not have to contain all the partners' names, but it generally will have one or more of the partners' names. Again, the firm name could be different from the fictitious name. The partnership can use a fictitious name, but usually you will have to file the business name with the Clerk of Court or a state official or both. Check your state law.

### 2. NATURE OF THE PARTNERSHIP BUSINESS

What type of business are you going to enter? It is impor- tant for you to think about this, because you do not necessarily want to put "in any business." If you are going to do a *specific* type of business, you may want to consider *specifying* a type of business that you are in. If you want to expand the scope of the business later, you can amend the articles of partnership.

If you (personally) get involved in any other business, stating the partnership's purpose too broadly could create problems if you are in your own *different* business or if you are also involved in a corporation or other partnership in a *different* business. If your partnership is in the chicken business,

state it that way. Otherwise you may be violating your *fiduciary* duty to a chicken partnership. Assume this partnership also gets involved in *any type* of *real estate*. Also assume you are involved in real estate. You may be violating your fiduciary duty to the chicken partnership if you continue to stay or get involved in real estate projects *on your own*, even if these projects are non-competitive. You would then have to constantly get your projects "cleared" with the chicken partnership. This is an important consideration that is often, and I repeat, often overlooked—by lawyers too.

### 3. DURATION OF THE PARTNERSHIP

You may want it as long as possible. On the other hand, it is limited to the lifetime of the first partner who dies or becomes disabled. You may want the duration limited to a certain time when the project should be completed. If you need more time, you and the other partners can amend the original agreement.

### 4. CAPITAL CONTRIBUTIONS OF EACH PARTNER

You may want to think this through, because some partners may put up cash, some partners may put up equipment and some partners may put up expertise. One thing that is important is that putting up expertise, for instance, or putting a value on it, can create a potential tax consequence.

If someone is going to put in effort and be repaid at a certain rate based on their effort, they will be *taxed* on the payment.

Say one partner is putting up $5,000 in cash, another partner is putting up $5,000 worth of equipment and the third partner is putting up $5,000 worth of time at $50 an hour. As this last working partner accumulates her hours, those earnings will be taxable to that particular partner.

### 5. DIVISION OF PROFITS AND SHARING OF LOSSES

The fact that an individual puts up half of the contributions in the business does not necessarily mean that he or she is going to get half of the profits and suffer half of the losses in a partnership. There are many types of relationships. Sometimes there are *changing* percentages based on the *years*, based on the annual *cash flow*, or based on the *cumulative* cash flow, based on the *cumulative operating results*. So it is not like there is a neat little formula that we can address here. If there are five people, each person does not necessarily get 20 percent. Some individuals put in more effort, more time, more expertise, and they expect and should get more of the pie. Many people, especially those who have little business investment experience, believe they are worth as much as the other person in the same deal. Put all the percentages of profits and of capital in writing.

## 6. DUTIES OF EACH PARTNER

There may be, as in most businesses, specialization. It is generally more efficient. Partner A might keep the books, B will be the salesperson and Partner C will be the operations manager. Often it is the blending of expertise that can create a winning business.

## 7. SALARIES

A partner does not have an automatic right to a salary or even to a draw. If there will be either, for example if one of the partners is going to spend full time and get a salary or draw, this agreement should be specified in the articles of partnership.

## 8. RESTRICTIONS ON ANY PARTNER'S AUTHORITY

If you are going to have a *managing partner*, it is imperative that you define it that way. This does not mean that just because you started out with one particular arrangement, you cannot change it as time goes on. Certainly you want to consider this if you are going to give one person most of the burden. Also if you have a managing partner, you may want to restrict the other partners' activities or abilities to act for the partnership. This should be in writing, and third parties should be placed on notice of any restrictions on any partners.

## 9. RIGHTS OF PARTNERS TO WITHDRAW

How would you calculate the withdrawal price? What will be the method of calculating a withdrawing partner's interest? Is it based on book value? Will it be based on some calculation as a *going value*, where you might include multiples of earnings? The partners might want a fair-market-value method of valuing a partner's interest. The agreement may dictate the lower or the higher of two methods. The partners might want an arbitrator or an appraiser to determine value. Some partnership agreements require the partners to set a value once or twice a year. If the parties fail to set a value, then it would revert to the previous valuation.

## 10. CONTINUATION OF THE BUSINESS

You might want to include provisions for the continuation of the partnership should one of the partners die, withdraw or become disabled for a certain or extended time period. If a partner is totally and permanently disabled or out of the business for six months or a year, you may want to consider starting up a new partnership or buying out the inactive partner. Such a provision should be in writing. You may also want to purchase insurance to protect against some of these eventualities.

## WHO MAY BECOME PARTNERS

Generally any person who has legal competence is capable of being a partner, but no partner can become a partner of the other partners. I mean you cannot take on new partners unless there is unanimity. All existing partners must agree on accepting a new partner.

## STATUTE OF FRAUDS

It is possible for the statute of frauds to apply to a partnership, but generally it does not. You can form a partnership by an *oral* agreement or by a *written* agreement. On the other hand, if the partnership is going to last longer than a year, for instance, then in order to enforce any type of an agreement like that, it must be evidenced by a writing.

## LIMITED PARTNERSHIPS

### STATUTE REQUIRED

One of the major differences between a general partnership, which we have discussed above, and a limited partnership is that a limited partnership involves a statute that limits liability.

The general partnership is basically an agreement among parties to act in a certain manner as a partnership. They are co-owners of the business.

The new wrinkle is that in a limited partnership the limited partners are given a privileged status, which arises out of a law. The law will state certain requirements that the limited partner in the limited partnership must meet. If those requirements are met, then the limited partner will be liable only for the amount of money he or she has invested or agreed to invest in the partnership.

It is important to remember, however, that both the partnership and the limited partner must obey and observe the state laws.

### CREATING A LIMITED PARTNERSHIP

In order to create a limited partnership, the potential partners must draft a certificate of limited partnership which is based on the entire agreement of limited partnership. This must generally be filed with the Secretary of State and becomes an official record.

It is important for you to remember that if you are involved in a limited partnership you must make sure the certificate of partnership or the articles of partnership are filed in each state where the partnership is doing business. Various states have different requirements. Generally you would not have to file the entire partnership agreement, but you would file a certificate which contains certain abstracted information from the limited partnership articles or agreement.

Usually a limited partnership must have the term "limited partnership" in the name or title of the business. It is best to have the entire word spelled out as opposed to using initials. Some states may not identify the initials as giving limited liability status.

Each limited partnership must have at least one general partner who has unlimited liability and it must also have at least one limited partner.

A limited partner can contribute cash, property, debt obligations or services to the partnership. A limited partner may agree to make certain contributions in the future. In any event, if the limited partnership follows the rules, this limited partner would not be liable for any more than his or her commitment.

One of the things to pay careful attention to is that the purchase of an interest in a limited partnership by a person who is a limited partner can be deemed to be a security. Therefore, the limited partnership will have to pay attention to the securities laws not only of the United States, but also of any state in which a potential partner is offered an interest in the partnership.

### SHARING OF PROFITS OR LOSSES

Sharing of profits or losses is generally governed by the articles of limited partnership. However, the losses, to a limited partner are limited to his or her capital contribution.

The partnership agreement may state in what exact fashion the losses may be allocated. They certainly can be different than being based on the percentage of capital contribution that Partner $X$ has made in relation to the total capital contributions.

You should be aware of the fact that the losses are not shared on an equal basis as they would be in a general partnership.

This is because of the nature of the interest held by the limited partner.

### MANAGEMENT OF A LIMITED PARTNERSHIP

The general partners have the total right to manage on an ongoing basis the business of the limited partnership.

The limited partners have no right to partake in the management.

As a matter of fact it is dangerous for a limited partner to attempt to engage in the management of a limited partnership. This is one of the several ways in which a limited partner may find herself or himself becoming a general partner despite the forms used to purchase the interest.

There are some rights that a limited partner has which would not convert the limited partner into a general partner. These include:

1. A limited partner may be an employee or an agent of the limited partnership or of the general partner.

2. A limited partner may be a consultant to the general partner.

3. Limited partners have the right to approve or disapprove of changes to the limited partnership agreements.

4. A limited partner may vote on the dissolution or winding up of the limited partnership.

5. The limited partner may have the right to vote on loans made to or from a limited partnership.

6. A limited partner may have the right to vote on any change in the business nature of the limited partnership.

7. The limited partners may have the right to expel or engage a new general partner.

## ASSIGNMENT OR TRANSFER OF A LIMITED PARTNERSHIP INTEREST

If a limited partner assigns or transfers all of his or her interest then he or she ceases to be a limited partner. The assignee or purchaser of such a total interest may or may not become a limited partner. Some partnership agreements allow the new purchaser to become a limited partner, since they effectively do not take part in the management of the partnership.

It would not be unusual for a purchaser of a limited partnership interest to become a limited partner; it usually would be automatic. It would be unusual, however, for a general partner to be given the authority to sell his or her interest and have the new purchaser become a general partner. That does not happen unless there is a specific agreement by all partners.

## WITHDRAWAL OF A LIMITED PARTNER

Most state laws require that a limited partner give at least a six-month notice of intent to withdraw from the partnership. The agreement can provide otherwise, and many of them do. Nevertheless this is a "default" or automatic position in a number of states.

## DISSOLUTION OF A LIMITED PARTNERSHIP

Just as there are several methods of dissolving a general partnership, there are also several methods of dissolving a limited partnership. They include:

1. By specific provision in the articles of limited partnership.

2. By the death or withdrawal of a general partner, the temporary or permanent insanity of a general partner, the removal of a general partner or the bankruptcy of a general partner. The agreement can provide for the existing partners to continue a partnership. Unless there is something specific in the agreement or some agreement among all of the general partners and the limited partner, then the partnership would be dissolved.

In contrast to the death of a general partner, the death of a limited partner generally does not dissolve a limited partnership.

## DUAL STATUS

It is possible for an individual or an entity to be both a general partner and a limited partner at the same time. There is no particular advantage for this partner from a liability viewpoint, since a general partner usually has unlimited liability. The dual status allows the individual partner to seek a court remedy against other partners who are obligated to make contributions to the partnership but have been delinquent.

## PRIORITIES UPON DISSOLUTION

Priorities in a limited partnership are slightly different from priorities in a general partnership. In general upon dissolution of a limited partnership, the assets are distributed in the following manner:

1. To creditors, including partners who are creditors.

2. To partners or ex-partners who according to the agreement are owed money in the form of either

income or capital upon their withdrawal from the partnership; in other words, a preference written into the agreement.

3. Unless there is a contrary agreement, the capital contributions of both limited partners and general partners.

4. Unless there is a contrary agreement, any remaining assets are paid to both general and limited partners for their interest in the partnership. This is effectively profits.

This scenario is according to what is called the Revised Uniform Limited Partnership Act. It is a general guideline, but you would have to consult your own state law, because there are some differences in the priorities.

## JOINT VENTURES

Joint ventures for most purposes are treated as a partnership but to carry out a single business purpose, such as building a subdivision or building one building or the creating some media event or promotional undertaking.

They can be called joint enterprises or joint adventures, and they are carried on for profit, which is a requirement for the partnership laws to apply.

At one time some states disliked corporations becoming partners in a partnership because of their limited liability status. Often in some states, a corporation could be a member of a joint venture even though it was not allowed to be a partner in a partnership.

You might want to check your state laws if you have corporation that might want to become a partner in a part-nership.Generally, the courts have applied the law of partnership to join ventures, but there have been some exceptions. Some states have limited the agency authority of joint venturers; it is obviously different from the agency status of general partners.

Also, in several states the death of a joint venturer does not necessarily dissolve the joint venture as an ongoing business relationship.

State courts often apply the Uniform Partnership Act to joint ventures, expect joint venturers to

act as fiduciaries, and require that joint venturers conduct themselves as fiduciaries in a trust relationship with regard to their other joint venturers.

Therefore, each of the joint venturers would have a duty to disclose completely any material information to the other joint venturers, and they would also have to avoid any conflicts of interest or pre-emption of any opportunity which the joint venture could undertake.

There is generally no requirement that formality be met, and often there is no name required.

That is the easy side. On the negative side, the liability for each joint venturer is unlimited, and each joint venturer would be liable not only for his or her acts of negligence, but also for the acts of negligence of the other joint venturers. A joint venturer also would be liable for the liabilities of the entire joint venture.

## ACCOUNTING

Each of the joint venturers has a right to an accounting. This is obviously an important right, to be able to verify what has happened with the business and with respect to the books and records of the partnership. This is a way for each of the joint venturers to be able to verify the legitimacy of any financial statements and of any distributions of profits or losses.

A joint venture is, therefore, a less formal association formed for a single or limited business activity. It is usually not formed through a partnership or corporation. It is also not an entity separate from the joint venturers. Joint ventures file a partnership (information) tax return. Lastly, the parties are fiduciaries and agents for each other.

A general partnership is a consensual agreement among the parties to the agreement. The agreement does not affect the rights of third parties.

A limited partnership, if properly formed, can affect the rights of third parties. Therefore, you must pay attention to state law requirements to receive the benefits of the state law.

# CHAPTER 4

## CORPORATIONS

# CHAPTER 4

## CORPORATIONS

The corporation has been around for possibly thousands of years. Each is, in effect, an *entity* as is any individual. Corporations are creatures that exist on paper and for legal purposes. Go find me the legal entity that is a corporation or the legal entity that is a city. These do not exist except as a legal creation or fiction.

So why should you be concerned with this? Certainly many businesses are corporations. There are millions of corporations which were created to do business.

If you are contemplating starting a business and using a corporate form or if you are in a business (regardless of its form), you ought to know, how a corporation works. It will help you to run your corporation properly and to get the most positive advantages out of the corporation.

With better information, you can run an effective corporation (from a legal viewpoint), limit your liability and keep the IRS and other wolves at bay. On the other hand, if you do not pay attention to the legal requirements, which I have often seen, and individuals do not know what they should be doing or do not pay attention to what they should be doing, problems by the bushel crop up. We are going to keep you out of trouble (knock on wood). Let us examine some of the specific conditions controlling corporate existence and behavior.

## CORPORATE NAME

A corporation must have a unique name or one that is not confusing between its own name and the name of another business entity, for that matter, or even the name of an individual. A corporate name should be distinguishable or not similar to other business names. There are some simple approaches to safeguard from a name clash or conflict.

If you attempt to form a corporation, generally, either you or your attorney can check with the Secretary of State to see if there is any other name that is similar to the one in which you are interested. It is possible in most states to actually reserve a corporate name, which gives you enough time to form the corporation. This name may not be safe from other similar names which might be trademarks or service marks which are legally protected.

A couple of additional items which come into play are that in order to have a proper corporate name—at least for a for-profit corporation—the name must contain the words "corporation" or "incorporated" or "company," as long as it is not "and company" or "limited" or any of the abbreviations for these.

## POWERS OF A CORPORATION

In most if not all states, it is possible to form a corporation and allow it to do anything that is legal. Often you look at a newly formed corporation and you will see words to the effect that it has "the power to enter any legal business."

Though you certainly will not typically hear this, it can be dangerous at times. We will see when we talk a little about the problems of being a director or an officer in a corporation. If someone is a director or an officer in more than one corporation, both of which have the above "general power" clause, then there can be a conflict of interest. These corporations potentially compete with each other. Another problem could erupt because a dual officer might be competing with another corporation in which he or she is an officer (or director). One of the ways of limiting conflicts of interest and other potential liability creating activities is to *limit* the powers of the corporation to specific powers. If the corporation makes shoestrings and cotton navel covers, you might think seriously about stating that specifically in the articles of incorporation. If you intend, however, to conquer the business world via one corporation, then consider the general purpose clause.

## GENERAL PROVISIONS IN ARTICLES OF INCORPORATION

Generally there are certain things you would want to have in the corporate charter. They are:

1. A corporation can have perpetual existence, or can be limited to a certain number of years.

2. It can sue and be sued in its own name.

3. It can have a corporate seal.

4. It can purchase, receive, lease, acquire, hold real or personal property or hold any interest in such property.

5. It can sell, convey, mortgage, pledge, lease, exchange, transfer or anywise dispose of any of its property and assets.

6. It can lend money and use its credit to assist employees.

7. It can purchase, take, receive, subscribe to interest in other corporations or general partnerships or limited partnerships, or invest or buy bonds, for instance, or obligations of governmental units.

8. It can make contracts and guarantee and incur liability, borrow money and secure money lent by mortgages.

9. It can lend money for corporate purposes, invest and reinvest its funds, taking hold of property as security for the payment of such funds or loans.

10. It can conduct its operations and have officers either in or outside of the state.

11. It can elect or appoint officers and agents of the corporation and specify what their duties and compensation are.

12. It can make and alter any of its bylaws in ways that are consistent with its articles of incorporation and with the laws of the state.

13. It can make donations for welfare or charitable or scientific or educational purposes.

14. It can transact any lawful business, through its Board of Directors, and aid any governmental policy.

15. It can pay pensions and establish pension plans, pension trusts, profit-sharing plans, stock bonus plans, stock option plans and other incentive plans for any or all of its officers, directors and/or employees.

16. It can be a promoter or partner, member, associate or manager of any partnership, joint venture, trust or other enterprise.

17. It can have and exercise all powers necessary or convenient to carry out any of its legitimate purposes.

These items are taken from the Model Business Corporation Act, which may not necessarily be the law in your state but is a general guideline. There are the generalities, and it may be incumbent upon you to find out the specific ones.

## PLACE OF INCORPORATION

Where should you incorporate? There is no neat little formula to give you the answer. Your home state, in all probability, would be adequate for most purposes.

On the other hand, there may be other considerations if you are seeking investors or if there are specific quirks in the law of your state or specific types of corporate provisions that you might need. Under those circumstances, you might want to look at incorporating in another state. It does, however, add another level of paperwork.

For instance, if you were to form a corporation in Delaware and you have your principal place of business in Kansas, you would have to qualify your Delaware corporation in the state of Kansas. You might also possibly have to pay at least some taxes or fees to both states. On the other hand, there may be some serious benefits to be gained by doing such. Again, you will have to consult with counsel who is *knowledgeable in corporations*.

## FEATURES OF A CORPORATION

There are several important items which reveal the benefits of incorporation. We would like to list them.

### LIMITED LIABILITY

This is a serious consideration. What it essentially means is that you as an employee or investor generally do not have to be concerned about personal liability (over and above what you have invested). This can apply to an officer or director who is also involved in a corporation or invests in a corporation. Directors or officers generally need not be concerned with personal liability.

One thing you have to remember is that every one of us is responsible for our own behavior. Therefore, if an officer is involved or responsible for an automobile accident while in the course and scope of his duties as an employee of the corporation, he or she may be *personally* liable. The corporation does not shelter all persons from personal liability for all purposes.

### TRANSFER OF SHARES

It can be easy to transfer the shares of a corporation. Most small corporations, however, choose to restrict the transferability of their shares. This feature is important in a small corporation, for instance, where the corporation is really a small collection of employees. If that is the case, then protecting jobs may be important. Especially in a small corporation, you do not necessarily want an outside shareholder. Certainly, you also would not want someone who is incompatible with the other employees to own stock. Therefore, it is fairly common in small corporations to have some type of restrictions on transferability. A most common approach is to require that shares must be offered to the corporation and existing shareholders before being offered to any outsiders.

### LIMITED LIFE.

It is possible to have perpetual existence for a corporation. This means it can last forever. It will not make a difference to the corporation if a particular shareholder dies or for that matter if all of them die.

That is not the case with a partnership. If a general partner dies in the partnership, that partnership is terminated. We mentioned that it is possible to automatically resurrect a partnership, but there has to be an additional provision doing such in the partnership agreement.

### CENTRALIZED MANAGEMENT

One of the benefits of a corporation surfaces when the entity needs lots of outside money. We might have to go to numerous investors. These investors can invest their money in the corporation in the form of common stock, preferred stock or

---

## POWER POINTS _____

▶ Corporations are legal entities or persons.

▶ Corporations are citizens for *some* but not all purposes. A corporation is not a citizen for self-incrimination (U.S. Fifth Amendment) purposes.

▶ A corporation is strictly a creature of a governmental authority usually state or federal.

▶ A corporation is liable for its debts as is any other person.

▶ A corporation usually has perpetual existence.

debt obligations, yet they do not have to take part in the management of the corporation. In fact, the investors generally have no right to manage the corporation. That is generally not the case with a partnership. With some provisions, a partnership can yield a similar result.

## CORPORATIONS AS CITIZENS

Without getting into the details of the law involving citizenship and personhood, for some purposes a corporation *may* be considered a *citizen*. For some purposes it is *not*. For instance, a corporation cannot stand behind the Fifth Amendment of the U.S. Constitution and refuse to testify. A corporation cannot withhold its books and records. For other purposes, for instance the Fourth Amendment, when we are discussing search and seizure, a corporation is a citizen and is covered by the same rules that generally would apply to searches and seizures regarding individuals.

## CLASSIFICATION OF CORPORATIONS

It may be of some help to paint a picture of some of the different forms or styles of corporations. In some ways these distinctions may not always make a legal difference. These descriptions may help you interpret the types of behavior that are common for particular corporations. On the other hand, sometimes these distinctions result in legal differences. That is why I would like to briefly mention them.

## PUBLIC VERSUS PRIVATE

Generally when we talk about public corporations, we are talking about creatures of a government. The government could be a state or municipal government or the federal government. A private corporation can be small or huge. When we are using this term, General Motors, IBM and Xerox are *private corporations*.

Though they may have what we typically call "publicly held stock", they are considered private corporations.

## CORPORATIONS AND LIMITATIONS ON CONTRACTUAL CAPACITY

Private corporations may have limitations of contractual capacity either express or implied, in their corporate charters. Nevertheless, corporations generally can contract for all purposes. Second, the concept that a corporation has exceeded its contractual capacity or what is known as acting *ultra vires* (beyond its powers) may be dying.

## FOR-PROFIT VERSUS NON-PROFIT

A for-profit corporation is one that is formed to make a profit. Even if that never happens, it is still subject to a slightly different set of rules in most states than would be the non-profit. On the other hand, a non-profit or a not-for-profit corporation might actually make profits, meaning that at the end of the year its revenues exceed its expenses, but it is organized specifically and exclusively for charitable, educational or scientific purposes.

A corporation may be non-profit for state law purposes, but still have to pay federal or state income taxes on its profits. It is important to realize that if any corporation is formed to be tax-exempt under the Internal Revenue Code, additional IRS filings have to be taken by senior management or the board of directors to qualify for this special tax treatment. Many times I have come across individuals that formed non-profit corporations but failed to comply with the Internal Revenue Code. The fact that you meet all of the *state* requirements for non-profit does not mean that your non-profit corporation meets the IRS requirements.

## DOMESTIC VERSUS FOREIGN

Generally when we talk about a domestic corporation or if we refer to a corporation formed in your state, we are referring to a *domestic* corporation. This is as opposed to a corporation formed in a neighboring state or in any of the other 49 states. Those are considered *foreign* corporations. We might assume *foreign* means outside the United States. For corporate law purposes, foreign refers to a Untied States corporation formed in a state other than our state. A corporation formed outside the

United States or its territories is called an *alien corporation*.

## CLOSELY HELD CORPORATION

Many individuals who start up new companies form closely held corporations. The reason they are put in a slightly different category relates to it being a corporation of a few employees who also own most or all of the stock. Often these corporate entities are vehicles for employment.

An example might be two brothers who form a corporation along with two cousins to open up a restaurant and lounge. They may all be working in it. They each have their own specialties.

We might expect them to form a closely held corporation with its internal peculiarities. In some states there are specific laws which would allow for dispensing with a board of directors, so you would not need to have a board of directors to meet on a regular basis or to pass on particular activities that the corporation undertakes. On the other hand, if it is in a state that has no specific statute, sometimes the court decisions are different. In summary, if a corporation has only a few shareholders, most of whom work in it, you have a close or closely held corporation. Furthermore, sometimes the courts treat them differently. The courts allow more informal behavior to prevail and protect employment more.

## PROFESSIONAL CORPORATIONS

At one time it was very difficult for a professional to form a corporation and receive all the tax benefits available to corporations. Distinguishing the corporation from the professional proved difficult for many courts. Hence "no corporation" was often the call.

Over a number of years, though, the law—including the tax law—settled down. Professionals have been allowed to incorporate even though not much internally has changed. There are a number of tax benefits which professionals can get by practicing in a corporate form.

Most states have developed certain requirements with regard to professional corporations which would not apply otherwise. These states allow professionals to incorporate and address their peculiar problems.

Assume you have a professional dental corporation with three dentists and one of the dentist dies. Assume that her husband is the surviving spouse. The husband is generally not allowed to keep stock in the dental corporation without having a professional license to practice dentistry. In that instance, many states require that the stock be sold by the non-professional over a certain time period.

1. A public corporation is formed for governmental or public purposes. Examples include the Federal Deposit Insurance Corporation and public housing corporations.

2. Many corporations are formed in states which have laws favorable to management (as opposed to shareholders).

## FORMING A CORPORATION

Forming a corporation is not particularly difficult, and in some ways is easier than forming a limited partnership. Nevertheless there are many rules that come into play. The corporate law in most states is a gap-filler, and in effect has a number of default provisions. What do we mean by default provisions? Many state corporation laws say if you *do not state otherwise*, your corporation will have a particular set of features. For instance, let us take a look at some of the things that take place whereby you have some control over them.

### Organizing the Corporation

It is important to pay attention to some of the rules when organizing a corporation, because an individual can be held personally liable for things that he or she might assume become corporate debts, when in fact they may never become totally corporate debts. This is a case of keeping your eye on the bouncing ball.

## Promoters or Individuals Who Make Things Happen

Corporations are generally conceived by some individual with an idea of making something work or developing a new idea. They are sometimes initiated to convert an existing business which has not been incorporated to take advantage of the corporate and tax laws. These ideas are hatched by promoters.

A promoter does not necessarily mean a high-pressure salesman who is promoting the stock of some new corporation. A promoter can be the idea person or the money person or the investor chaser.

It is important to realize that any contract formed by a promoter before the corporation is formed, for most purposes, creates personal liability for that promoter and possibly for all of the existing promoters. Even if after the corporation is formed the corporation adopts and "ratifies" the contract, the promoter will be liable until that contract is *totally discharged*.

There are some exceptions. It is possible for the language in the contract to be so strong and so clear that under no circumstances will the second party look to the promoter for payment. Then it will be possible for the promoter to be off the hook. This is a rare exception.

It is important for you to realize that for any contract, the promoters can be personally liable. This happens inadvertently; for instance, hiring someone to deliver potential plans or office supplies or to do something in anticipation of the corporation being formed. Since he creates debts, these debts, with rare exceptions, will be the debts of the promoter.

## Promoters as Fiduciaries

One of the most important things to realize is that you (or anyone as a promoter) are *fiduciaries* prior to the corporation's formation. For that matter any liabilities or duties that existed prior to the corporation's existence carry over even after the corporation is formed.

What is a fiduciary? It is someone who has to act with the highest good faith under the law for someone else's benefit. A fiduciary must subordinate his or her personal interest to the other party. This duty is not the lowest duty. It is not the one that we are typically used to with regard to our neighbors, friends or strangers. A fiduciary cannot potentially *compete* with the corporation.

Assume you are forming a corporation to buy and sell antique carpets. You as an individual cannot buy and sell carpets as a promoter without in effect giving the corporation (or the corporation to be formed) the first option on the carpet business you have done. This assumes you have other potential investors. Unfortunately, it is one of those things that individuals seem to somehow psychologically turn off. Some promoters think that as long as they can form a mental concept of their acts being *separate* from their corporate duty, they do not have to be concerned about the corporation. But a promoter is a *fiduciary* with regard to the corporation which is not even in existence and with regard to potential investors.

## Subscribers

It is not uncommon to have individuals who are interested in investing in a corporation prior to the corporation's formation. There can be some risk for the individuals *promoting* the corporation, for several reasons. A simple way to say it is that if someone subscribes to shares prior to the corporation's formation, the subscriber generally has the right to get out of it at any time. Several states have passed a law which, to a certain extent, protects the promoters and the corporation to be formed from individuals changing their minds willy-nilly. Assume that a subscriber agrees to invest $10,000 in this corporation. The shares will be $5 each, so he will end up with 2,000 shares. Under these newer laws the *subscriber cannot change* his or her position—meaning cannot decide to back out of this purchase—for at least six months after it has been signed. This exists where there is a statute which locks an individual in for at least six months.

## Procedure for Forming the Corporation

The procedure for creation of the corporation is simple. It includes:

a. Selecting a name.

b. Selecting of the incorporators.

c. Drafting of the Articles of Incorporation, which include the name, location and address of the corporation, the purpose of the corporation, the duration of the corporation (be it perpetual or limited), the number of authorized shares and any classes of shares, the number and names of the initial directors, the names and addresses of each incorporator, and any provisions that may be necessary.

## Holding an Organizational Meeting

Generally at this meeting the incorporators turn over the reins of the corporation to the initial directors, who then adopt bylaws, elect officers, often select a bank for a bank account, and perform any other tasks they have to do just to get the corporation kicked off; or they may make any of the subscriptions to stock or put into place a plan to solicit additional investors.

## Proper Formation of the Corporation

This is a complex area that generally requires corporate lawyers to resolve. It is an area, however, in which you should have at least a smattering of background. If a corporation is formed properly and all papers are properly filled in, drafted and filed, we won't end up with any problems. It is known as a *de jure* (by law) *corporation*.

In many if not most states, at least two sets of originals are signed by the parties. Generally you would have them signed in the presence of a notary public or have the signed document acknowledged by one of the witnesses before a notary public.

One of the signed originals is filed with the Secretary of State. Generally the Secretary of State will send back a *Certificate*, which is separate and distinct from the *Articles of Incorporation*. A Certificate of Incorporation says that the Secretary of State has received the document as of a particular date and time, and that is when corporate life is created.

An additional filing may be necessary. A copy of the Certificate is filed, along with another original of the Articles of Incorporation, with the local Clerk of Court in the county of the corporation's principal place of business.

Even though you may leave the details to the lawyer, make sure that these things have in fact *taken place*. Mistakes occur, and it is never wise to assume 100 percent of the time that everything that should take place does take place. Certainly you cannot be the lawyer, but you can ask the questions after the formation to make sure that all of the steps have been taken.

Your state may be slightly different from my description, but you can ask your lawyer to give you a written description of the steps necessary.

## *POWER POINTS* _____

▶ The corporation is a favorable form in which to do business.

▶ The laws allowing the creation of corporations are beneficial when viewing entity features, its duration, limitation of liability, ease of transfer of interests, management and agency aspects.

▶ The corporation law aspects of corporations are often much more important than the tax aspects.

▶ Both the corporate and tax aspects should be considered prior to incorporation.

## De Facto Corporations

It is possible for there to be some problem with the formation of the corporation. If the state law has been *substantially* complied with, it is possible for you to be protected by unlimited liability status. This means that even if there has been some mistake or failure in the procedure followed, you might still be safe. This type of corporation is called a *de facto* (in fact) corporation.

## Adverse Interests

One of the things I would like to bring to your attention is a conflict-of-interest situation when there are several shareholders. If there are several shareholders, you may end up with several different, competing interests. This means that these interests are *opposed* to each other.

It is common to have a corporation with two or three individuals who get together to form a corporation and have only one lawyer handle the entire thing.

The problem with this approach is that Shareholder A may have totally different interests from Shareholder B. It may be important for each of the individuals to get his own attorney to look out for his own interests. It is very difficult for one lawyer to protect the interests of more than one party. If you have only two persons forming a corporation, you have at least three conflicting interests. These interests are Party 1, Party 2 and the corporation. Though these interests may be similar in the case of a one shareholder corporation, if you have two or more parties who become shareholders and employees or just two or more shareholders, you have at least three interests involved.

What is best for the corporation may be different from the interests of Shareholder A and the corporation, and Shareholder A's interest may be different and adverse from Shareholder B. Therefore, it is important for you to be aware of this. If there is enough money at stake, get your own lawyer to protect your interest. Then get another lawyer to form the corporation. If there is not much money at stake, you may consider having one lawyer for everything worth the risk. If something goes wrong or if there is a lot of money made, it may

and probably will be *too late* to cure it later. I do not want to be an "I told you so," but remember that I told you so.

## CORPORATE POWERS

You ought to be aware of the sources of corporate authority or power: What authority allows corporations to be born and what authority gives guidelines for their behavior.

*Statutory Authority.* Corporations are generally formed pursuant to *state* law. Generally the state constitution will supply some of the authority for forming a corporation in some minimal way, giving the state legislature authority to pass statutes. The constitution gives the legislature some authority to fill in the details on how and when corporations may be formed and what authority, duties and rights each has. The constitution further allows the legislature to define what duties and rights shareholders may have and what gaps need to be filled through the state statutes.

*Express Corporate Powers.* The articles of incorporation may give the corporation additional powers or may place some limitations on the directors or officers with regard to the corporation. Some cases speak about *ultra vires* as the condition whereby a corporation through its directors or officers exceeds its authority. This concept, though it is a nice Latin phrase, generally does not stop a corporation from doing things even *in* excess of its powers. The corporate charter is the next source below state law for deriving the powers of a corporation.

*Implied Authority.* The corporation has certain authority based on the powers that are given to it by state law or by the articles of incorporation. We cannot come up with a neat little formula to tell you exactly what types of authority a corporation may have.

*Liability for Torts and Crimes.* A very important concept comes into play here with a corporation. We want to make sure we have communicated it properly. Let's assume that you are the president of your own corporation, possibly with no other shareholders. You formed the corporation and you have it adequately financed at the beginning. One of your employees gets into an accident while transporting merchandise to a customer. Generally, you as president would not be held *liable* for that particular accident. The corporation and its assets would generally be held liable for it. Certainly the driver of the car, meaning your employee, who is at fault is personally liable.

*Corporate Tort Liability.* Now, it is possible for you as the president to have directed the individual to drive recklessly, and you might also be personally liable.

Or an indirect approach can be where the driver comes in from lunch and is visibly intoxicated. You, as president, direct the individual to go out on delivery even though you can tell what condition he is in. In this case, for civil purposes, it is possible for you to be personally liable for not exercising your supervisory powers properly. Certainly the corporation is also liable if the employee is liable.

*Corporate Liability for Crimes.* In general, criminal law requires that a person have *criminal* intent to be held *liable* for *crimes.* Generally a corporation will not be held liable for crimes. Nor would any director or officer generally be liable for the crimes of an employee. Let's assume an employee's negligent behavior involves a drunken driver, and the employee is charged criminally. You, as president, would not be personally liable if you had no criminal knowledge or did not know that the employee was intoxicated or was driving recklessly. As long as you had acted properly, neither you nor the corporation would be criminally liable. But that is not an absolute. (If it's absolute there must be an exception, said Murphy or some similar sage.)

It is possible in certain circumstances and depending on the laws—the law may supply the missing criminal intent—for the president or a secretary, treasurer or director to be directly liable by encouraging someone to commit a crime. It is possible for any one of them to be liable indirectly or vicariously.

An example might be the president telling one of his drivers to go out and collect a particular

account and not come back unless he has the money. In other words, if he does not come back with the money he will not have a job. This is not a typical case, but it has happened, especially when accounts receivable are starting to become accounts deceivable.

It is possible for the corporation itself or the president of the corporation to be held criminally liable even without direct knowledge or implication. There are several famous cases which have so held, so do not assume that by forming a corporation you or anyone else is insulated from all potential liability.

# FINANCIAL STRUCTURE OF THE CORPORATION

There are essentially two types of investments made in a corporation. These types are debt securities, which are in effect loans, and equity securities, which include preferred and common stock.

## Debt Securities

Most corporations have authority to issue *debt securities.* Nevertheless, if this is something you are contemplating in your corporation, it is best to make sure that your corporate charter specifically allows it and that you have nothing prohibiting this in the corporate charter. If need be you can have the corporate charter amended to specifically allow this. Generally, you do not have to do that; just make sure you have authority to do it.

## Types of Debt Securities

There are several types of debt securities:

*Unsecured Bonds.* These types of bonds are typically the ones that look like unsecured loans. The individuals who buy these bonds become unsecured creditors and are usually considered *general creditors* of the corporation. They usually, for purposes of priority, are the same as trade creditors (who sell the corporation inventory on credit). These are unsecured.

*Secured Bonds.* These types of bonds result from individuals lending money to the corporation but who have a superior right over the *unsecured* creditors. How is their right superior? They have a lien, a potential ownership right, in some underlying security. It might be personal property. These secured creditors might have a lien or a security interest in one of the airplanes or all of the airplanes or in a certain class of airplanes in an airline company. They could have a security interest in real property. The security may cover all of their loan amount, but sometimes it does not. As an aside, the uncovered amounts are treated the same as amounts owed general creditors.

*Income Bonds.* You will not typically see this type of bond in a small corporation, but there is no prohibition against it. Generally, debt securities have a fixed rate, for instance 6 percent, 7 percent, 8.5 percent, etc. There are some exceptions, and they can be done legally. For income bonds, however, the payment of interest may be conditioned upon the corporation earning a certain level of income. The directors must pay this particular interest out of a certain pool of profit only.

*Convertible Bonds.* Some corporations like to have longer-term financing or permanent financing, but find that investors are more willing to invest in bonds. What they may do is sell bonds, but give the holder a right to convert those bonds into common stock. Assume an investor buys a $1,000 par value bond and is allowed to convert it into 20 shares of stock at some specific future date. This, in effect, is placing the value of the stock at $50 per share at that future date.

*Callable Bonds.* In this case the bonds generally look like any other bond. They have a par value and an interest rate that obligates the corporation to pay it at a certain rate. Certain bonds contain provisions which also allow the corporation to call (redeem) the bonds at some future time. The corporation would send you a check and you would have to return the bonds.

Some investors calculate this callability feature in financial projections. They might take into account the fact that should interest rates go down, the corporation may be prone to call the bonds so they can be refinanced, possibly at a lower rate. Sometimes this feature is a sticking point in getting

investors. This call feature, or redemption feature as it is sometimes called, is alive, around and well.

*Equity Securities.* These are securities that are considered ownership. This means a right to residual assets and profitability as opposed to loan repayment and interest rates.

## ISSUANCE OF EQUITY SECURITIES

*Authority To Issue.* Corporations have authority under the state law to issue common stock without complication. The articles of incorporation must generally state how many shares the corporation can issue. A corporation may be authorized by the charter to issue 10,000 shares. The corporation is not *obligated* to issue all of the shares. There can be some risk, depending on the corporation, in not issuing all 10,000 shares that are authorized, but not all authorized shares must be issued.

*State Securities Laws.* Though this is not the place where we are going to discuss in detail the state securities laws, you should be aware that most states have laws that prohibit the issuance of stock to the public *unless certain requirements are met.* The basic requirement, typically, is that the corporation must disclose all of the good and bad information about the corporation before any securities are issued. These state laws are called "blue sky laws." This is not a legal term but a "term of art." These laws are often overlooked.

I was formerly a lawyer with the U.S. Securities and Exchange Commission, which enforces the federal version of these laws, generally called the Federal Securities Laws. We found *numerous* violations, even in small corporations, whereby the state or the federal laws were overlooked or ignored. I cannot give you an instant formula for meeting these requirements. On the other hand, if you are aware of these laws, you can make sure that your lawyer who is helping you form a corporation assures that your corporation complies with your state laws and the federal laws. It is still a current problem today.

*Pre-emptive Rights.* This is a legal provision that applies to most corporations in most states. A pre-emptive right is the right that a shareholder has to maintain the percentage of ownership that he or she has in a corporation.

Assume there are 10,000 shares outstanding in the corporation. The corporation needs more working capital and wants to go out and sell another 10,000 shares. Assume you happen to own 1,000 shares in the corporation at present. If pre-emptive rights apply to your shares, you have a right to purchase an additional 1,000 shares in the new offering. You own 1,000 of the 10,000 shares, or 10 percent of the outstanding corporate shares. You have a right then to purchase 10 percent of the shares of the new stock issue.

Most, if not all, small or close publicly held corporations, the existence of pre-emptive rights in a small corporation may be vitally important. On the other hand, if a publicly held corporation still has pre-emptive rights, it may hurt the corporation's ability to get financing. Thus, publicly held corporations usually eliminate pre-emptive rights.

*Consideration for Shares.* You may be familiar with the terms "par value" and "no par value." Generally when a corporation issues shares of either type, there is a distinction without much of a difference. On occasion there may be some difference. "Par value" only means that the corporation has stated that the corporation either has or should have at least some minimal value in its treasury on behalf of each share.

Most corporations that have *par value* shares place the value at some nominal amount, for instance one cent a share. You may want $10 per share for the stock, but it is often easier to place a nominal value on it. Sometimes the corporation may do this to reduce state taxes based on par value. On the other hand, you may want to issue *no par value* stock. Again, for the same share you might want to get $10 per share. You may have no par value stock with a *stated value* of $10. Or you may have par value stock with a par value of one cent, but with a stated value of $10. Thus, if you want a particular price per share, the corporation can get it either way.

## TREASURY STOCK

Treasury stock is stock that has been issued to a party and has been reacquired. Possibly a party

donated the stock back to the corporation. (Such a donation does not happen often.) Treasury stock is not voted by the corporation, and it has to be handled in a particular way for accounting purposes. Basically it is taken out of the realm of being *issued stock* for *some purposes*, though not for all purposes. It is still considered issued stock. (If you have a chance to review a balance sheet where there is treasury stock, you will see it is not counted in the total number of shares when earnings per share are calculated.)

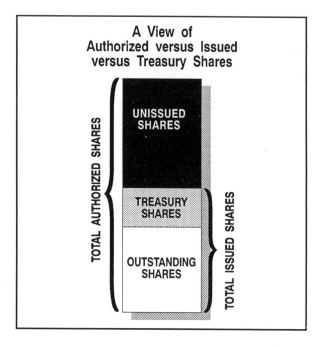

**A View of Authorized versus Issued versus Treasury Shares**

TOTAL AUTHORIZED SHARES

UNISSUED SHARES

TREASURY SHARES

OUTSTANDING SHARES

TOTAL ISSUED SHARES

1. *Authorized shares* are the total number of shares authorized or permitted to be issued under the articles of incorporation.

2. *Issued shares* are those that have been sold or transferred to shareholders.

3. *Treasury shares* are those that have been issued and later reacquired by the corporation.

4. *Outstanding shares* are shares issued reduced by treasury shares.

## PAYMENT FOR SHARES

It is important for you to realize a little wrinkle that comes into play in paying for shares. For most intents and purposes, shares must be purchased with cash on the barrelhead or in the form of property. The property can be real property<$Ireal property$Iproperty or personal property. It can be in the form of *already completed services*. You cannot purchase securities from a corporation based on a *promissory note* to the corporation or based on services to be performed in the future for the corporation.

## VALUATION OF CONSIDERATION FOR PURCHASE OF SHARES

One of the duties of the board of directors is to place a value on *non-cash purchases*. The corporation may set a price of $10 per share. The board of directors does not have to pass on every purchase for which $10 per share is given to the corporation. On the other hand, if shares are exchanged for *property*, then the board of directors is obligated to make sure that the value is fair and that there is some reasonable basis for the exchange of the consideration (property) for the shares issued.

If you are issuing 1,000 shares at $10 per share, the board must ascertain that $10,000 of property has been received by the corporation in return for those shares. If that is not the case, meaning that the board of directors over-valued the property which the corporation received, then it is possible for the directors to be *personally liable* for diluting the stock, or *watering* the stock, as it is sometimes called.

## CLASSES OF STOCK

Corporations can have different classes of stock with different features, just as they can have different types of debt securities. The categories are not the same, but let's take a look at them.

## PREFERRED STOCK

"Preferred" means stock which has some preference with regard to either the *dividends* received *or* the *assets* that the preferred stockholder may receive if the corporation is liquidated. Sometimes preferred stock is preferred for both dividends and residual assets. Several different wrinkles appear in the look of preferred stock.

*Dividend Preferences.* Some types of preferred stock are specifically called preferred because the preferred stockholder will get a dividend *before* any

of the common stockholders can receive a dividend. An example of this might involve $100 par value preferred stock with a 5-percent dividend. The preferred stockholder will receive that 5-percent dividend each year *before* the common stockholder can receive any money. It is also possible to have another version called *cumulative preferred stock*. In this case the common stockholders may be prevented from receiving any dividends until the 5 percent is paid for *each prior* year for which the corporation did not pay that particular dividend. The corporation must catch up any years missed before a common stock dividend can be declared. A corporation is not obligated to pay that 5 percent in any year unless the board of directors declares it. But nevertheless, with the cumulative preferred stock we are discussing, the common stockholders would not be able to receive a dividend until every year that the 5 percent should be paid and has in fact been paid. That is where the term "cumulative" comes from.

No dividends are owed to preferred stockholders unless the board of directors *declares* such a dividend.

*Liquidation Preferences.* Some preferred stock is called preferred only because the preferred stockholders would receive their par value back before the common stockholders receive anything. But this might work only when the corporation is *liquidated*. Outside creditors, secured and unsecured, would receive their money back first. Next, if there is anything left, then the preferred (as to residual assets) stockholders would receive their money back. Now, if there is no money left after paying off the preferred, then the common stockholders lose all of their value. Again, preferred stockholders are prior or preferred over the common stockholders. That is where the liquidation or residual asset preference comes in.

*Other Features of Preferred Stock.* Generally preferred stockholders do not vote. It is possible in many states to allow preferred stockholders to vote. Sometimes this will crop up where the preferred stockholders are allowed to vote if they have not received a dividend in a certain number of years.

*Call Features.* Preferred stocks can have some of the features of bonds. They can be callable. It is possible that the corporation may have placed that particular right in the corporate charter, so that everyone is on notice that the corporation has a right to buy those shares back at some future time and at a certain price.

*Convertibility Feature.* Some corporations provide a feature that will allow shareholders to convert preferred stock to common stock. On occasion some preferred stockholders might even be allowed to convert their preferred stock to bonds of a certain type.

*Participation Feature.* Preferred stock can also be participating. Here a dividend might be split between the preferred stock and the common stock.

Preferred stock generally looks like a fixed-income security (*e.g.*, a bond). It is, however, a bit of a hybrid.

## DESCRIPTION OF COMMON STOCK

Common stock is the ultimate ownership form and represents the lowest form of any preference but the highest form of ownership. The common stockholders traditionally vote.

Corporations sometime have several classes of stock. Some corporations name them in alphabetical order, as Class A, Class B and Class C. They may all have general voting rights, but not every class has to have voting rights.

At least one class of shares must have voting rights in a corporation. Each class can have slightly different features. Class A may be twice as valuable as Class B. The classes can have different par values, different voting rights. These classes can have different preferences with regard to dividends or with regard to residual value. They can have different rights with regard to the number of directors they can elect.

It is also possible to allow the board of directors to determine the specific features of the different classes. Usually a smaller corporation would not allow the board to determine such open-ended features. The simplest approach is to state in the articles of incorporation the features you want.

Unless there is some very strong contrary reason you will generally see just one class of shares. Again, this is not cast in stone. In fact, sometimes an investor in a smaller corporation may expect to have power to elect one or more directors in return for his or her investment in the corporation. One solution is to issue to this person all shares of a particular class.

## LEGAL RESTRICTIONS ON DIVIDENDS

There can be legal restrictions on the amount of dividends which can be declared by a corporation or more specifically by the board of directors. If a dividend would make a corporation insolvent, then each director who voted for this dividend may be responsible for an illegal dividend. Even if the dividend is legal but unwise financially, the director may have violated his or her fiduciary responsibility to the corporation. If you are a director, do not vote for dividends when it is not the wisest thing to do.

On the positive side, dividends can come out of current profits of the corporation or accumulated profits of the corporation. States vary on the sources of dividends. In some states, a board can declare a dividend this year even though it lost money, as long as it has a surplus in its cumulative earned surplus account. If you have any financial troubles in a corporation, do not vote for a dividend unless you want to personally pay it back if it ends up being an unwise or illegal dividend.

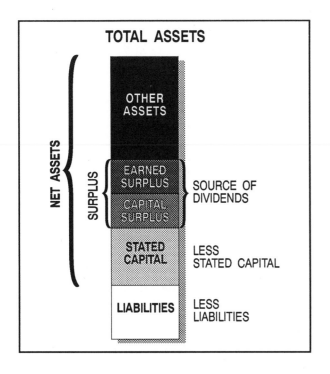

1. Total Assets are composed of several pieces.

2. Net Assets are Total Assets less Liabilities.

3. Stated Capital is composed of contributed capital, which includes the par value (e.g. 1 cent per share) of par value shares and the stated capital value of no par value shares.

4. Liquidation preferences come from any stated capital remaining upon liquidation.

## DECLARATION OF DIVIDENDS

No dividend is automatically due from a corporation, nor is it a *debt* of the corporation until it is *declared* by the board of directors. This is also the case with dividends on preferred stock.

The corporation may have money floating in from all over, falling out of the bank or flowing off of the tables. The corporation may be able to use money to light cigars. There is, however, no dividend due unless it has been *declared*. There are only a few legal cases in which the courts have forced a corporation to declare dividends when there was no reason to hold the money. One of the classic cases involved a Mrs. Dodge who sued the Ford Company for a dividend. By the way, she won. (Mrs. Dodge must have smiled in her grave when

Lee Iacocca filled the Chrysler/Dodge sails after leaving Ford.)

## TRANSFERRING OF SECURITIES

You should be acquainted with the minimal formalities that you have to follow to transfer securities.

All states apply the general rules that are contained in the UCC with regard to transferring securities. All securities transactions must be evidenced in writing. A corporation has a record of the ownership of each share, and the individual shareholders have such evidence in the form of stock certificates. The shares can be transferred in at least one of two ways:

*Transfer of Actual Certificate.* The *seller* of a certificate can place the name of the buyer on the back of the certificate and sign the certificate. Then, given the proper language, he or she can negotiate the transfer of ownership to the new party.

*Stock Power.* Another way of transferring the ownership of shares is to sign a document that allows the corporation to transfer on its books the stock certificate to the purchaser.

In either case the stock certificate is sent to the corporation or its transfer agent so a *new* stock certificate can be issued. This process allows the corporation to keep track of the names and addresses of the new owners.

Many smaller corporations have restrictions on the transfer of their securities. It is important that *notice* of those *restrictions* be placed on the stock certificate, so that anyone who sees the certificate (a) would know first that there are such restrictions, (b) might be given a brief idea of what the restrictions are, and (c) would know where to find a description of the restrictions (generally the registered office of the corporation).

Under certain state laws no certificate need be issued for shares. However, the corporation must register shares on its books.

## PROBLEMS WITH SECURITIES

On occasion securities are lost or accidentally destroyed. Securities are sometimes stolen. State laws provide a means of documenting the loss and a means of possibly reissuing shares. The fun really starts when the shares show up later with new owners. The UCC also provides for that scenario—but that is for another day.

## CORPORATE MANAGEMENT

Directors, officers and shareholders are the bodies that make up the management of the corporation. The directors and officers are the direct part of management, and the shareholders have an indirect role in the management of the corporation. Let us take a look at these functions separately.

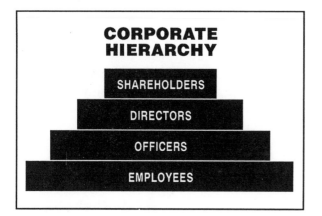

## BOARD OF DIRECTORS

*Selection.* The board of directors has the authority to carry out the day-to-day operations of the corporation. The board has the authority to hire and fire officers. It has major impact on the capital structure of the corporation, and it generally approves any fundamental changes of the corporation.

As we have seen previously, the board of directors must declare any dividends, and the dividends must come from sources that are financially feasible (or legal). The board cannot declare dividends that would bankrupt the corporation. The board also determines any management compensation.

*Qualifications.* The articles of incorporation or the bylaws may require that the directors be residents of a state, or sometimes require that the directors own a certain number of shares in the

corporation, or list other requirements for being a board member.

*Election, Number and Term of Directors.* Generally the articles of incorporation will state when directors are to be elected. It is possible for there to be a *certain number* of directors (less than all) which ought to be elected each year. It may be part of a *classification* system. Class A directors might be elected during even-numbered years and Class B directors during odd-numbered years. If there are no classes, then the directors would be elected in accordance with the state corporate law statutes or the articles of incorporation. In some states, the term for directors can be as long as five years, but are no shorter than one year. Nevertheless, the articles of incorporation or the bylaws would state when the election is, the number of directors to be elected, and their terms of office.

*Selection and Removal of Directors.* Shareholders elect directors for complete terms. Directors can select a director to fill an unexpired term. A corporation and shareholders do not have to keep directors who are not doing their job. No corporation has to keep a director who is damaging to the progress of the corporation. Directors can be removed at any time "for cause." This means "for legal cause." On the other hand, directors can also be removed without legal cause, because this is a right of the shareholders. There can be some complications with exercising this feature at times. Nevertheless, shareholders have the authority to remove directors.

There may be some rules with regard to calling a special meeting for that particular purpose, and state laws have different requirements for that. Sometimes the bylaws may contain conditions whereby a director can be removed under certain circumstances. It is unusual to allow directors to remove one of their peers, but it *may* be possible.

I have been on the board of several non-profit corporations, and this question arose several times. The answer, however, is not an easy one.

*Vacancies During an Unexpired Term.* In most states, it is possible for the board of directors to appoint a director to fill a vacancy for an *unexpired* term. Or, if a directorship has been created recently by the shareholders or in accordance with the bylaws, the directors generally have the authority to appoint someone to fill that vacancy for the *unexpired term*. All positions on the board of directors are voted upon prior to the beginning of a director's term of office.

*Directors' Functions.* Directors, as we have mentioned, have the power and the obligation to run the corporation on a day-to-day basis. Generally they choose to *delegate* this authority to officers. Nevertheless the only method that the directors can exercise power is *as a board*, meaning a single body. Directors, as individuals, have *absolutely no authority* as directors to tell any director, officer or employee to do anything. They can act only as a board.

*Quorum.* At any meeting of the board of directors, in order for them to act, they must have the legally defined *quorum*. Sometimes state law requires a certain *minimum*. Sometimes the articles of incorporation or bylaws state otherwise. So you will have to pay attention to what the *quorum* is to determine whether or not there is a *legal meeting*. The meeting (or a written substitute) is the only way the directors can operate. It is generally the way directors operate.

*Action Taken Without a Meeting.* In some states, the board of directors may act *without* a meeting. Again, they can act only as a single body. Assume that all of the directors agree to a particular resolution or particular action. A resolution could be sent to all the directors whereby they all agree on that particular resolution. If they all sign off on the resolution, then the resolution can be effective without a meeting.

*Executive Board.* On occasion, a board of directors may appoint a portion of the board to act during the time between board meetings, if necessary. The board may give temporary authority to an executive board so that if action has to be taken between meetings, the executive board may be able to act.

*Directors' Right to Inspection.* Directors have the ultimate obligation to take care of the corporation and to vote their best conscience. They also have an absolute right to inspect all of the books and records of the corporation. In other words, no one can tell them "no," certainly as long as they are directors. In some cases, even after they have left the board, if there has been some question about their having acted properly, pursuant to litigation, a director still has a right to inspect the books and records of the corporation.

Directors in general get their direction from the shareholders. Directors, however, have certain obligations, dictated by law, which are not derived from nor can be contravened by shareholders.

## OFFICERS

The directors are in a position of electing all or most of the officers or any proportion that they wish. The directors generally select the major officers of the corporation or at least *ratify* the selection made by someone else. Generally the directors select at least the president, vice president(s), secretary and treasurer. The president *generally* is the chief executive officer. Vice presidents have various duties, usually in a specific area, such as sales, distribution or manufacturing. The secretary is generally the person who keeps the records of the meetings of the shareholders or of the board of directors. He or she also may keep track of the contracts of the corporation.

The treasurer is the person who takes care of the finances of the corporation, deals with the resolutions needed for banks and is responsible for the accounting functions of the corporation.

*Authority of Officers.* Officers of the corporation may have *actual, express,* authority in keeping with the articles of incorporation and bylaws. They may have *implied* authority, which means it is not specified but can be derived from a position or title. The treasurer will generally have certain *implied* authority as a result of his position.

*Apparent Authority.* Apparent authority is created as a result of the behavior of a party. Assume the president of a corporation expresses to a third party that the treasurer may have a certain type of authority, then the treasurer may have what is known as apparent authority even if the bylaws state that he or she does not have such authority. If you are a third party dealing with a corporation and

---

### POWER POINTS _____

▶ Directors and officers are fiduciaries to the corporation.

▶ Directors and officers cannot:
   a. "Scoop" a business opportunity which the corporation could consider.

   b. Use corporate assets for personal purposes.

   c. Deal unfairly in corporate shares.

   d. Exercise unreasonable judgment in managing corporate affairs.

▶ As a director, make sure the board reviews and authorizes all important or significant corporate action.

▶ Directors should expect a complete disclosure of important corporate activities from the chief executive officer.

---

an important member of the corporation, such as the president, creates the appearance that the treasurer can sign a particular promissory note on behalf of the corporation, then you as a third party may have a right to *rely* on the president's statements. (The board might want to tan both of their hides later.)

*Ratification.* This process occurs when someone who *could* have *authority*, such as a treasurer, acts *without authority*. Later the corporation agrees to go along with what happened. The corporation must find out all of the facts. Then, after getting the facts, it agrees to accept the results. This process gives a person authority to act for the corporation. Furthermore, the corporation is bound to the transaction. Assume that the treasurer without authority sold a corporate-owned car to a third party. Later the board gets the facts and agrees that the transaction was OK. Then the corporation is bound to the deal and the treasurer is in the clear.

## DUTIES OF DIRECTORS AND OFFICERS

The directors and officers of a corporation have a *high duty* which is owed to the corporation. Many individuals are unaware of this duty. Many directors or officers of a corporation seem to be unaware of it. There are several types of behavior which

describe a director's or officer's duties to the corporation.

*Obedience.* A director or an officer of a corporation is obligated to follow the reasonable dictate of the board or of his superiors. The directors of the corporation, for instance, must fulfill their duties as dictated in the bylaws. If there is a meeting once a month at a certain place and time, it is the directors' obligation to show up. There may be a reason why someone does not show up, but nevertheless, their duty is to be *obedient*.

The same principle applies to officers. If they are supposed to show up at a certain time and place and perform certain duties, then the officers must be obedient in keeping with the *reasonable* and legal dictates of the corporation.

*Diligence.* The officers must exercise reasonably prudent care in keeping with their duties. Sometimes this is defined as being the same type of care you would exercise in conducting *your own affairs* (assuming you act responsibly). Also, under the duty of diligence, you as a director should exercise your *reasonable business judgment*. In general, courts will not second-guess directors in business judgment. Directors can make mistakes, as we all do, and the court will not grade them. The courts will not determine that an act would not get a passing grade. As long as you are acting reasonably under the circumstances, the court will not second-guess an officer or director's judgment.

The business judgment rule protects directors or officers if they exercise due care, act in good faith and reasonably believe they are acting in the best interest of the corporation.

*Duty of Loyalty.* Directors and officers of the corporation owe the corporation their fiduciary duty. They must look out for the best interests of the corporation, possibly even ahead of their own. They cannot favor themselves over the corporation. They owe a high duty to the corporation. What are examples of this fiduciary duty? The directors and officers must subordinate their own self-interest to the corporation. Assume that the corporation could handle a project if it were presented to the corporation. Further, assume that an officer knows about the project and could handle it personally. Then the officer has the duty to present this option to the corporation first.

What happens if a director or officer violates this duty? He can be subject to suit *by the corporation* or by a *shareholder* on behalf of the corporation. Violations of this duty of loyalty are sometimes hidden. At least if you are aware of these duties, you won't have to worry about this.

*Conflicts of Interest.* If a director or an officer has any interest which is adverse to that of the corporation, he or she may have a legal obligation to *disclose* this conflict of interest to the corporation. I have been annoyed at the reluctance of many directors or officers to disclose such conflicts.

*Pre-Emption of a Corporate Opportunity.* There is a concept whereby a director or an officer must give the corporation the first shot at any particular deal which he or she might want personally. A director or an officer could not buy property, for instance, right next to a real estate development of the corporation without disclosing to the corporation prior to such purchase. The individual must allow the corporation the first shot at that particular deal.

*Duty Not To Compete.* A director or an officer of a corporation has a duty not to compete with the corporation for any type of business or potential business into which the corporation has entered or could enter.

*Liabilities of Directors and Officers.* Even though a director has not violated any duties such as obedience, diligence or loyalty, he or she can still be personally liable for corporate liability.

The directors or officers could be liable for defects in corporate behavior. If the board has supervisory authority or if it has urged someone to commit a tort or if they (collectively) have violated the state or federal securities laws or antitrust laws, it is possible for the directors to be personally liable.

*Contracts.* Generally, directors or officers are not responsible for the contracts of a corporation, but if they urge someone to violate the contract or if they cause the corporation to enter a contract knowing that the corporation cannot carry it out, then it is possible for the directors or officers to be personally liable.

---

## *POWER POINTS* _____

▶ Shareholders have the right to attend shareholder meetings and to vote on matters.

▶ Shareholders have the right to elect directors and to vote on fundamental matters involving the corporation, including mergers, consolidations and sales of major assets.

▶ Shareholders (even a 100% shareholder) as shareholders (and not as directors or officers) have no authority to manage the corporation or commit it to liability.

## SHAREHOLDERS

### ROLE OF SHAREHOLDERS

Shareholders are the owners of the corporation. Their right to vote is the most fundamental right to the concept of ownership of the corporation. That does not mean that some shareholders cannot own non-voting shares of common stock. Our discussion, however, is geared toward the typical common shareholders.

Shareholders have the right to vote on everything from the most important activities or changes to the corporation all the way down to the most menial. It would be ludicrous for shareholders in large corporations to vote on the menial things. Generally they concentrate on the activities of greater importance to the corporation.

Shareholders vote at *annual meetings,* which in most jurisdictions must be held annually. They also vote at *special meetings.* Under certain circumstances, shareholders with a certain percentage (*e.g.,* 20 percent) of the total shares may call a special meeting in most states.

At any meeting of the shareholders, there must be a *quorum.* What is a quorum? A quorum is a stated minimum of shares present to be voted, either by a shareholder in person or by proxy, at a meeting of shareholders to vote by proxy, and in counting up the quorum, you count those shares that are actually there, and those that are represented by proxies.

Typically management solicits proxy votes from shareholders who may not be able to attend. In large corporations, it might be virtually impossible to hold a meeting with every one of the shareholders present. (On the other hand, most shareholders are not interested in attending such meetings.)

### ELECTION OR REMOVAL OF DIRECTORS

Shareholders generally elect directors each year. In most if not all states, directors can serve for periods longer than one year. A typical maximum is five years. None allow perpetual directors. As we alluded to before, corporations can have several classes of stock. An example of classification might be two classes of directors, half of whom are elected one year and half the next year.

### EXTRAORDINARY MATTERS

It is generally the right and responsibility of the share-holders to vote on fundamental changes or little things that are considered *extraordinary.* For instance, if the corporation were to expand into a new line of business or add five directors or stop doing business in a major field, the board might be wise to present this to the shareholders for concurrence.

### VOTING POWER

There are various approaches to voting. It is not quite as simple as one share, one vote, though it can be.

*Straight Voting.* This type of voting involves one vote for each common share held. For each share of stock that you own in XYZ Corporation, you have one vote. This is known as straight voting. A problem with straight voting involves a shareholder with less than a majority. He or she may never get a chance to elect any directors.

*Cumulative Voting.* There is another form of voting that is known as cumulative voting. Cumulative voting allows an individual to *multiply* his or her *number* of *shares* by the *number* of *directors* being elected or re-elected. It can produce a different result.

Here's an example. Under straight voting, if an individual holds 25 percent of the shares of the corporation and there are four directors being elected, that particular individual would probably not be able to elect any *directors.* She certainly could not do it unilaterally. She could only do it with other votes which would total a majority.

On the other hand, if this corporation has cumulative voting, there could be a different result. That individual would be able to multiply her 25 votes that she has times the four directors being elected. Now this shareholder would be able to cast up to 100 votes for one of her choices. In effect, that would result in that individual being able to elect at least one director as long as she has 25 votes.

There are methods of concentrated voting power, meaning collecting the votes from several individuals and pooling them in one place. An example of this is called a *voting trust*. Each of the shareholders turns his shares over to the voting trust. He then receives an interest in the voting trust, generally equal to the interest he has in the shares except for voting power. The trustee or trustees of the voting trust now have voting authority.

Generally the shares are transferred on the books of the corporation to the name of the trustee. The trustee becomes known as the *nominal* owner. The shareholders become what is known as the *beneficial owners*. In this case, it is possible for a number of shareholders to vote as a bloc.

An example of where this can work well is where shares of a company are distributed throughout a family. It might be virtually impossible to educate all of the family members on the benefits to be gained by a particular mode of action. Some families have created a voting trust, transferred their shares to it and made sure that the trustees are knowledgeable in business.

## SHAREHOLDERS' AGREEMENT

Another method for concentrating voting power is a shareholders' agreement. Such an agreement may be to vote in a specific manner for the election or removal of particular directors or regarding extraordinary changes at a shareholders' meeting.

Shareholders' agreements do not have to be limited in terms of time.

## RESTRICTIONS ON TRANSFER

Most closely held corporations have strong restrictions on transferring shares. These provisions come from the article of incorporation or bylaws and must be noted (not detailed) on the share certificate. Courts uphold these if reasonable.

## ENFORCEMENT OF SHAREHOLDER RIGHTS

There are several specific rights that shareholders have, and they are important for you to know.

## EXAMINATION OF BOOKS AND RECORDS

Basically shareholders have a right to examine the books and records of the corporation. Depending upon the state, there can be certain limitations on this right. Shareholders in most states have a right to examine the basic books and records of the corporation. This does not mean they have a right to examine every journal and every ledger that a corporation creates.

The corporation is obligated to keep sufficient books and records so the shareholders can examine the financial condition of the corporation. Generally the shareholder has some economic reason to examine the books and records. In many if not most states, the shareholder does not have to state any reason. There have been some cases involving individuals who have had non-economic reasons for examining the books and records (*e.g.*, Vietnam War). Sometimes they have been refused access to books, but not often. As long as the individual has a proper purpose which could ultimately be examined by a court, then the individual generally can examine the books and records. It is not for the corporation to determine what is a proper purpose. Some stockholder may want to find out whether or not management has been doing a decent job, with the ultimate goal of kicking them out. That can be a *proper purpose*. It is not something for management to define.

Some states require that the shareholder hold a minimum number of shares or be a shareholder for a number of months (*e.g.*, six months) to be allowed to examine the books and records.

## SHAREHOLDER LAWSUITS

Essentially there are two types of lawsuits pertaining to corporations and shareholders.

*Direct Action.* A shareholder may want to enforce an individual claim that the shareholder has against the corporation. For instance, in a rare instance where the corporation has tons of money lying around and has not declared a dividend, a shareholder may want to file a suit against the directors and officers directly.

A shareholder may want to sue the corporation directly to inspect the corporate books.

There have been examples in small corporations where the majority stockholder was also the president. He did not realize that shareholders have these rights, and arbitrarily refused to allow the inspection. The shareholder, in these cases, can have a direct cause of action against the corporation.

Another example might be a shareholder who is denied the right to vote. He or she can sue the corporation to enforce this right. This is a direct suit.

*Derivative Suits.* Another important type of remedy for shareholders which has been derived from the common law, and not specifically corporate laws, is known as the *derivative suit*. This type of suit is addressed in the corporate statutes in most states. It involves a shareholder bringing a suit against a third party who has damaged the corporation. A shareholder may bring a cause of action on behalf of the corporation to enforce some right that the corporation should have enforced.

An example might involve a director who has done business with the corporation and who has misrepresented the facts to the corporation. Assume a director is a supplier to the corporation in which you are a shareholder. A shareholder discovers that this director has violated his duty to the corporation by selling product to the corporation through fraudulent representations. If the other directors of the corporation know about the fraudulent sale but do nothing, a shareholder may be able to sue the directors *and* the offending party. Therefore, despite the directors' willingness to go along with an illicit deal or a deal where the corporation may have paid too much, a shareholder may sue the "villains," because the shareholder's power is *derived* from the corporation.

One of the basic requirements is that the shareholder first demand that the board of directors take action against the offending party or parties. In rare instances this step can be eliminated. It is an obligation of the shareholder in most cases to make such a demand on the board.

If after notification the board nothing happens, then it is possible for a shareholder to sue on behalf of the corporation. Many times courts approve naming the directors as defendants for not having taken any action. Under some more recent state laws, courts may require a plaintiff shareholder to put up a security bond for the reasonable expenses that may be incurred by the corporation. This in effect creates a guarantee for the corporation's litigation expenses.

If the plaintiff wins, he gets his money back. However, if the plaintiff is incorrect then the corporation would not be out of pocket for its expenses or its attorney's fees. Some state laws might require a small shareholder who holds 5 percent or less of the shares of the corporation to put up security. If he holds more than a certain percentage of shares, he may get the security waived.

## APPRAISAL OR DISSENTER'S RIGHTS

We have a feature of some stocks that had been popular at one time. It is still in existence. It involves shareholders' appraisal rights.

This comes into play when a shareholder objects to a possible merger or consolidation. This right recognizes a shareholder's limited power to reject becoming an unwilling shareholder in *another* or a *new* corporation. To receive this right you have to object *timely* to a *forthcoming* vote on a merger or sale of assets. You must demand that you be bought out.

There are certain limitations in many states. If the vote is too high (for instance, if the vote is 90 percent or more), you may not have a dissenter's right. If it is less than 60 percent, you may not have these rights. In effect there is a corridor of rights, in this example it exists between 60% and 90%. In exercising these rights, you are clearly giving up your right to the shares. You must vote "no" against the merger at the meeting or by your proxy and make sure you have a demand for being bought out under your dissenter's right. You will have to tender the shares to the corporation. In any event, most states have this appraisal right.

Shareholders often have appraisal rights if they vote against certain corporate acts which may affect the value of their shares. These rights often include acting against corporate mergers.

## POTENTIAL LIABILITY OF SHAREHOLDERS

One of the best reasons for incorporating is based upon our understanding that a corporation is a *separate entity*. The corporation is created under state or federal laws. Liability can be personal for shareholders under certain circumstances.

*Wage Claims.* Statutes in a few states provide that shareholders may be *personally* liable for wage claims of corporate employees. This liability may be aimed at major stockholders in the effected corporation.

## DEFECTIVE OR IMPROPER INCORPORATION

Occasionally the corporation has not been properly formed. Under these circumstances the shareholders, especially the active ones, may have some personal liability. Some courts hold them jointly and severally liable with other shareholders, promoters, officers and directors. If there is a serious defect in the incorporation process, all these persons may be liable as partners. The default result is similar to a partnership.

If a corporation has not been properly formed, but meets substantially all state requirements and has done business, there may be no danger to shareholders. This is called a *de facto* corporation.

A corporation which meets all state requirements is called a *de jure* corporation.

## IGNORING CORPORATE ENTITY

Generally when a corporation is formed, it is treated as an entity separate from the shareholders. The law does not look through the entity.

On the other hand, if directors do not hold regular meetings or do not take action on important issues or if the corporation is undercapitalized initially, or the directors do not keep the corporation's business separate from their own, the courts sometime *ignore* the corporation as an entity. The courts will do this to prevent fraud or injustice. In these cases the courts hold shareholders personally liable. This is the noted concept of "piercing the corporate veil." It has also been called penetrating the corporation.

## ILLEGAL DISTRIBUTIONS

We have mentioned briefly that, if directors declare dividends which exceed the legal limits or are paid from capital, the shareholders may be personally liable to creditors.

Where the dividends would increase the liabilities over the assets of the corporation, the dividend would probably be considered illegal and the shareholders may be personally liable for returning such distribution.

## CONTROLLING SHAREHOLDERS

It is possible for those shareholders who have controlling interest in the corporation to have a special type of liability. Sometimes if individuals have a controlling interest in a corporation, they are able to sell their shares for *more* than the *market price* of the shares.

They are also transferring the right to *control* the *corporation*, which obviously can have a separate value. Several cases and commentators have looked at this from the viewpoint that the right to control a corporation is not an asset of any one shareholder; it is an asset of the corporation itself and should not be sold by any shareholder. It is not a feature of that particular individual. Therefore, being a controlling shareholder puts that person in the posture of having to look out for the interests of the minority shareholders. Not all courts take this position.

Sometimes when the courts view the sale of control at an excess price or a premium, as it is called, the court may require a return of the *excess* to the corporation or sometimes distribute it to the other shareholders on a rateable basis.

## FUNDAMENTAL CHANGES

Shareholders have a right to exercise their managerial powers in deciding fundamental or unusual matters. These are matters that do not occur in day-to-day operations. It is extremely important to realize the nature of *fundamental* or *extraordinary* changes of a corporation. The reason for this is that in this area any director, officer, shareholder or controlling shareholder must act in the highest, best interest of all of the parties involved.

It is totally incorrect to believe that because someone controls more than 50 percent of the votes in a corporation he or she can do anything he or she wants. That is *false*, though the courts will generally not step in and re-examine a business judgment, they will step in at times when the minority interest is being abused. Thus, majority shareholders can still get their ears boxed if they ignore minority shareholders' rights.

## CHARTER AMENDMENTS

Amendments to the articles of incorporation are considered fundamental or extraordinary changes. No matter what is being changed, even if just the name, the shareholders have a right to pass judgment on the proposed transaction.

Some of the examples of what are considered fundamental changes include:

1. Changes to the corporate name.

2. Changes to the corporation's period of duration.

3. Enlarging or diminishing the corporation's purpose.

4. Increases or decreases in the number of shares or par value of the shares.

5. Reclassification of any shares and change of any preference right, including preferences with regard to dividends and preferences with regard to residual assets.

6. Creating new classes of shares.

7. Tinkering with pre-emptive rights.

*Sale of Substantially All of the Assets.* Any change to the corporation or any proposed change of the corporation to sell any or all of the assets of the corporation must be voted upon by all of the shareholders. Every shareholder must get notice of the meeting. The meeting notice must go to at least the last known address of every shareholder.

*Purchase of Shares.* If your corporation is interested in purchasing all the shares of another corporation or all the assets of another corporation, the shareholders must typically vote on it. There can be exceptions if there is a difference in size. If General Motors agreed to purchase a company worth only $25,000, GM would not have to get shareholder approval, since $25,000 is not an un-usual or extraordinary expenditure for such a large corporation.

*Merger.* A merger is the combining of the assets and liabilities of two or more corporations with only one being the surviving corporation.

If your board of directors has proposed your corporation's merging with another corporation, this is a fundamental change. This would be the case even if it's with a minor corporation. Here you are changing the charters of the two corporations. Shareholders would have to vote on such a merger.

*Consolidation.* This is the combining of two or more corporations into a new corporation. The original corporation cease to exist.

Consolidation works similar to a merger. An example might be if Corporation *A* consolidated with Corporation *B* to come up with the new Corporation *C*. The shareholders would have to vote on this extraordinary change.

## DISSOLUTION

### NON-JUDICIAL DISSOLUTION

Certain non-judicial dissolutions do not require court determination. These can result from an act of the legislature or from expiration of the term (*e.g.*, 10 years) of the corporation. Assume that your corporation is good for a term of only 10 years. It is now one day past the 10th year. That day can be the basis for a non-judicial dissolution of the corporation. It is also possible for the shareholders to work a non-judicial dissolution. It is also possible for the directors to initiate a non-judicial dissolution with the approval of the majority of the shareholders.

### JUDICIAL DISSOLUTION

The state or the shareholders or creditors can sometimes force a judicial dissolution of the corporation. Though it is rare, it is possible for the Attorney General of the state to force a dissolution in court when a corporation has failed to file annual reports or pay taxes, or has been responsible for numerous other types of state violations.

---

### *POWER POINTS* _____

▶ When buying a business, you will want to get the facts about the business.

▶ The name, logo and slogan of the business could be important.
  a. Are there any trademarks, service marks or trade names?

  b. How are these protected?

  c. Get copies of any registration papers from local, state or federal authorities.

▶ What licenses are necessary to run the business? Can you get them transferred?

▶ Are all local, state and federal taxes paid?

▶ Are there any potential lawsuits or claims outstanding?

▶ Are there any legal violations outstanding, such as OSHA, fire inspections or similar problems?

▶ Are there any zoning problems? Do you need a certificate of occupancy?

▶ Are there any related trade associations you can join?

▶ Do you have complete financial statements?

▶ Do you know what the current replacement cost of equipment is? How about furniture and fixtures?

▶ Can you transfer insurance policies?

▶ Who are the major customers, what percentage of the business do they compose, and will they "walk" when the current owner sells?

---

## LIQUIDATION

Dissolution does not necessarily mean that the corporation ceases existence. It only means that there is an attempt to wind up or sell the assets of the corporation. Dissolution requires the board of directors to wind up the affairs of the corporation and liquidate the assets by turning them into liquid assets.

After a corporation has been dissolved, it must cease doing business. That should be its end goal if it is terminating. After liquidation, the creditors must be paid off. The creditors' rights must be examined and paid off prior to distribution of any assets to the shareholders, directors or officers of the corporation. It is possible for creditors to step in when there is a dissolution of the corporation, so that their rights are protected.

## DIVIDENDS AND OTHER DISTRIBUTIONS

Shareholders are entitled to receive dividends once the board of directors declares them.

Generally, investors are looking toward eventually receiving not only their capital return, but additional amounts. This is why they have taken a risk by investing in the corporation. There are several types of dividends, and there are restrictions on them, and we would like to take a brief look at this.

## TYPES OF DISTRIBUTIONS

### Cash Dividends

Most of us are aware of the cash dividends that are declared by many major corporations. This is the major approach to dividends even in smaller corporations.

### Stock Dividends

Corporations can issue shares of stock to its stockholders. The corporation transfers retained earnings to capital for accounting purposes.

### Property Dividends

Property dividends are not common. These are received in various forms. On occasion, for instance, a large corporation that has several subsidiaries may distribute the stock of one of the subsidiaries to the shareholders of the parent corporation. The shareholders here receive dividends *in-kind* in the form of additional shares. Property dividends may be in the form of some of the products that are developed or manufactured by the corporation. The corporation may make contact lens cleaner and may distribute some of its products to its shareholders.

### Liquidating Dividends

Occasionally a corporation is dissolved. Upon that occurrence it will then distribute the liquidation assets in cash or in-kind (personal or real property) to the shareholders.

## REDEMPTION OF SHARES

Just as we mentioned that bonds and preferred shares can be callable if the corporation has the proper provisions in its charter, it is also possible for common shares to be redeemed.

---

## *POWER POINTS* _____

▶ Forming a corporation will protect the owner from financial harm only if the directors and officers continually keep it clean. If you think it is like an atomic clock that you can set and forget, you are asking for a nuclear (financial) explosion. The fallout may reach your pocketbook.

▶ Buyers must check several additional areas:
1. Make sure known creditors are notified. This is self-defense.

2. Provide in the agreement some protection against hidden or undisclosed creditors.

3. Check leases in detail. This includes personal and real property leases.

4. Check licenses.

5. Check trademarks and trade names.

6. Check insurance policies.

7. Check sellers' purchase records.

▶ There are many facets to corporations which we did not cover. Our discussion is intended to pique your interest in corporate "finery" so that you can avoid corporate chicanery.

# CHAPTER 5

## BUYING OR SELLING A BUSINESS

# CHAPTER 5

## BUYING OR SELLING A BUSINESS

Most if not all states have laws that focus on buying or selling a business in bulk. There are a number of different ways to do it. In this chapter we will address selling all the assets of a business as opposed to selling the capital stock in a particular business. In effect, the law has requirements designed to protect everyone's interests in the sale of a business. The parties in interest are the seller, the seller's creditors and the buyer. Typically if a buyer is new at the business, he or she has not incurred any new creditors. New creditors would generally not be terribly concerned about what had happened previously as long as they have their interest protected in the new business.

It is typically called, under the UCC, bulk sales or bulk transfers of merchandise or similar assets which is *not* in the *ordinary course* of *business*. In other words, when you typically sell inventory as automobiles one at a time or occasionally might sell a fleet, but you would not sell 95 percent of your inventory at one time. This applies to virtually any business.

The primary purpose of the Bulk Sales Act is to prevent any fraudulent activities which would affect the creditors or the potential buyer in the sale of merchandise or any other similar type of assets.

The bulk sales portion of the UCC gives the *seller's creditors* an opportunity to make sure their claims are paid. These creditors have a chance to protect themselves *before* the *seller* can transfer the assets to a bona fide purchaser and disappear with the sale proceeds.

It is important, particularly if you are a *buyer*, to make sure you comply with the law. The goods that are transferred—the "bulk sales items"—might be *tainted* with the seller's creditors' protective devices even if they are bought innocently. If you are buying a business and have not protected the *seller's creditors*, you might find yourself doing business with them in an unpleasant manner.

Here is the basic process for bulk transfers:

1. The new purchaser must obtain from the seller a *sworn list* (affidavit) of all of the seller's existing creditors.

2. The *purchaser* would then give *written notice* of the proposed sale to each creditor listed on that schedule, at least *10 days* before he takes possession of the goods or at least 10 days before he pays for such goods;

3. The purchaser must make sure that the sales proceeds are used to pay off the seller's debts that have been listed in the affidavit.

Because of the critical nature of the Bulk Sales Act, it is important for the purchaser to make sure these requirements are met.

Under certain conditions, these bulk sales rules do not apply.

Here are some of those conditions:

1. If the transfer is really made for finance and security purposes.

2. If the transfer is a general *assignment* for the benefit of the creditors of the seller.

3. If the transfer is made in settlement or realization of any *lien* or *security interest* of the seller's creditors.

4. If the sale is made by executors, administrators, receivers, trustees in bankruptcy or any other public officer under judicial process which has control of the bulk items.

5. Sales made in the ordinary course of judicial or administrative proceedings or in the dissolution or reorganization of a corporation.

6. Transfers to a transferee who assumes the debts of the transferor and gives notice of that fact and is solvent after becoming so bound.

7. Transfers to a new business entity organized to take over and *continue* the business of the transferor, if public notice of transfer is given and the new entity assumes the debts of the transferor.

8. Transfers of property that are exempt from execution as stated in the law itself.

## BUYERS NOTICE TO CREDITORS

The *buyer* is obligated to give notice to each of the *seller's creditors*. It is important for the buyer to make sure he consciously follows the list. The *buyer* must send the notice by registered or certified mail or deliver it personally to every creditor on the seller's list, or to any person who the buyer thinks might be a creditor.

What is important to include in the notice is the potential sale, the *location* and *general description* of the *property* involved in the bulk transfer, the estimated total of the transferor's debts, the location of the property listed in the sale where the list of the creditors may be inspected, and whether the transfer is intended to pay existing debts or involves new consideration.

## PURCHASER'S DUTIES

The potential purchaser must be sure the proceeds from the bulk sale are used to pay the creditors of the transferor (seller). This duty is enforceable by the seller's creditors.

If there is not enough money to go around to *all* the creditors, the purchaser has to distribute the funds on a *pro rata* basis. This requirement that the purchaser must assure the application of the proceeds is an *optional* provision in approximately 18 states.

If you are buying or selling your business, be sure to check with your business lawyer.

## FAILURE TO COMPLY

What happens if the parties do not comply with the Bulk Sales Act? The general rule is that a bulk sale made in violation of the Bulk Sales Transfer Act is ineffective and voidable by creditors of the seller. The seller's creditors have a right to *follow* their *goods* around under the UCC or the state law.

The creditors may be in a position of pursuing the goods by *attachment* or *levy*, or *garnishment* at law, or by a creditors *bill in equity*. This could obviously be disturbing to any buyer.

In some states the creditors have a lien on the goods in which they can claim an interest.

In a word, if you are keen on either buying or selling a business or buying or selling the assets of a business, you should be aware of the requirements of the bulk sales law. The process might entail notice not only to creditors, but possibly to *third parties*, such as taxing authorities.

# CHAPTER 6

## FRANCHISING

# CHAPTER 6

# FRANCHISING

Franchising can be an important choice if you are interested in *starting* a *business* with a higher probability of success than starting a business as an independent.

If you are an entrepreneur with a *going business*, you may be interested in using the franchise approach to expand your business, to increase your market presence or to expand the success of your business if it can be repeated by your training other individuals. There are certain essentials to franchising a business which would require a cookie-cutter approach. So there are two ways of viewing franchising, depending on whether your business horse is in the starting gate or at a gallop.

## WHAT IS FRANCHISING?

Franchising is a system of distributing a product or delivering a service in return for a franchise fee or some other consideration. The franchisee is allowed the right to market goods and services according to the franchisor's established practices and hopefully with the assistance of the franchisor. It involves a trademark or service mark or protected intellectual property which is part of helping to create a national image and a clean image. This image involves good will.

## TYPES OF FRANCHISES

There are several different ways of defining franchises. The following approach is used most often and is helpful in fitting them into two "clean" categories.

## PRODUCT FRANCHISE

This approach is one where a franchisor sells a product through franchised dealers. An example of this might be automobile dealerships, where you see the manufacturer's name attached to the business. Here someone is authorized to sell the product, but there also is a *close tie* or *relationship* between the manufacturer of the product and the retailer. This can also be done on a wholesale level, where the name is attached on the wholesale level. Generally there is no royalty remitted to the franchisor here. The franchisor makes its money through the product it sells to the dealer.

## BUSINESS FORMAT FRANCHISE

In this approach to franchising, there is not necessarily a product to which a name is attached, but a *method* of *doing business*. It may be a service business, such as in printing or selling hamburgers. Here there is a name that has good will attached. The franchisee can use the benefits created by a larger organization (the franchisor).

In both examples, the franchisee generally pays an up-front fee (a franchise fee). Generally there are ongoing royalties which are separate from "advertising fees." There are often two types of ongoing fees which accrue to the benefit of the franchiser.

There is also another type of relationship which is related to the franchise. It is called the *business opportunity venture*. For this particular relationship generally there are three elements:

1. The buyer, for instance, will sell goods and services which are typically supplied by the franchisor or a related person.

2. The franchisor assists the franchisee in *securing accounts* or *locations* for vending machines or rack displays or in supplying the services of a person able to do this.

3. The franchisee is required to make payments of $500 or more to the franchisor or to some affiliated person within six months after opening the business. In many states this business opportunity venture is less burdensome from a compliance viewpoint. There are generally less paperwork and fewer restrictions.

## ADVANTAGES OF BUYING A FRANCHISE

Certainly the fact that a franchisee has a ready-made package to start his own business is a benefit for someone who wants to be in his own business. Some of the advantages are:

1. Independence. There is a certain degree of independence, though it is not the same as an independent start-up, but with an increased success ratio.

2. Recognition of the Franchise Name. Part of the value received by the franchisee is the good will and trusted nature of the franchise product, service, name, good will, trademark, copyrights and related items.

3. An Established Business. One of the benefits of purchasing a franchise is that the business has run through some testing in another marketplace or possibly several marketplaces. At least to the extent of those markets, it has been shown to work with some degree of confidence.

4. Available Training. Another benefit of the franchise approach is that the franchisor feels fairly confident it can duplicate the training and abilities that it has shown, in its own prototype franchises. This is one of the strong elements that franchisors push.

5. National Advertising. Franchisors often sell as a benefit, and sometimes actually deliver, a national sales and promotion package, including tested advertising. This is not always the case, but can be one of the benefits gained by a franchisee

who does *not* have *expertise* in advertising and promotion.

6. Purchasing Economies. Many franchisors are able to purchase products at a significantly lower cost than franchisees would be able to do. In a number of franchises, the savings gained by the group purchases more than offset the cost of the franchise. Again, that is not always the case.

7. Innovation. Franchisors, if properly managed, are able to experiment and do product and service testing that would be too expensive for an individual franchisee. Thus, if conscientious research and development is done, the franchisor can provide a method of innovation to keep the franchisee ahead of his competition. Unfortunately, this is not always the case.

## DISADVANTAGES OF BUYING A FRANCHISE

1. Lack of Total Freedom. A franchisee is controlled by a very lengthy *agreement* that defines "quality standards," possibly opening and closing times, number of days per week to be open, product standards, service standards, warranty standards, lack of assignability or salability of the franchise (without the consent of the franchisor) territorial restrictions and many other restrictions. The idea of a franchisee being in business for himself or herself is inaccurate. The franchisee has more freedom than a corporate employee, but is under very serious restraints within the context of the franchise agreement and the franchisor's standards.

2. Personal Involvement Required. Many franchisors will not allow a franchisee to be an *absentee* owner. Franchisors often require personal involvement of an owner or a part-owner. Part of the reason for franchising is that some franchisors believe a franchisee will run the business better and more profitably than a company-owned business is run—that franchise will generate more profit for the franchisor than a company-owned business. That is not always the case.

3. Dependence on Franchisor's Judgment. Often when individuals purchase a franchise, they do it because they *lack experience* in running that

particular type of business. They are dependent on the franchisor for their lifeblood. Unfortunately, franchisors do not have access to Mount Olympus. They do not always make good decisions. Sometimes they make *terrible* decisions, and most franchisees are not sophisticated enough to know when that is the case. Even if a franchisee is sophisticated enough to tell when the franchisor has blown it, the franchisee is usually not in a posture of bailing out. It is often too late. So it often works like a ratchet: You can get in fairly easily but you cannot get out easily. By the time the franchisee learns the ropes and can recognize good judgment, he is generally stuck for a number of years in a long-term franchise agreement.

4. Restriction on the Sale of the Business. Franchisors keep a pretty tight rein on the ability of the franchisee to resell the business. Usually the franchisee cannot sell the business without a long, burdensome process. The theoretical reason is that the franchisor wants someone just as responsible and capable as the current franchisee. This control also allows some franchisors to extract more fees.

## REQUIRED DISCLOSURES

What is important here, from either viewpoint, is a discussion of the types of disclosures that have to be made before a franchise can be offered or sold. The legally required disclosures also describe what potential buyers can and should expect from the franchisor. If you are thinking about franchising, you will need to seek out a lawyer who is a *franchise specialist*. A general lawyer cannot handle the *special areas* of law that are involved. There are two disclosure approaches to franchising. The U.S. Federal Trade Commission dictates one.

The other was developed by the Midwest Securities Commissioners Association. It's disclosures are equal to or greater than those required by the FTC. It is known as the Uniform Franchise Offering Circular.

## INFORMATION ABOUT THE FRANCHISOR

The franchisor must disclose some of the following information about the franchisor's business:

1. The business history of the company, giving the reader some idea of the type of business and when it began, etc.

2. Employment history of the officers and directors of the company, giving some idea of their relevant background.

3. A description of any litigation incurred by the company or the officers or directors that might be considered important to a potential purchaser.

4. Any history of bankruptcy proceedings of the company and of certain of the individuals.

5. A financial statement of the franchisor.

## THE FRANCHISE BUSINESS

1. The franchisor has to give a sufficient description of the franchise business that the reader can understand the nature of it.

2. The franchisee's initial investment must be disclosed and stated. If there is some variety or variability depending on market levels or different sizes of stores, for instance, then those varieties must be disclosed in dollar amounts.

3. Required purchases of required supplies or any required standards which have to be met must be disclosed.

4. Any financing provided, directly or indirectly (with an affiliated person), and a minimal description of the type of financing.

5. The types of services provided by the franchisor. This is a mushy area, because the *extent* of providing services is difficult to *quantify*. Nevertheless, a description of the types of services supplied.

6. Any *trademarks* which may be licensed and part of the good will which the franchisee is licensing.

7. Any patents and copyrights that are part of the body of value the franchisee is licensing.

8. A description of the restrictions on sales of the business by the franchisee.

9. Any arrangements that are made with public figures (e.g. for endorsement purposes).

10. The number of existing and terminated franchisees.

11. Any aid the franchiser provides for site selection.

12. The type and extent of training the franchisor provides.

## FRANCHISE AGREEMENT

1. A description of what fees are stated in the franchise agreement that must be paid, when they must be paid, and the different types of fees and any different payment schedules.

2. A description of any exclusive area, how it's defined, or at least a blank space for stating an exclusive area.

3. Any requirement for active franchisee participation. This is where the franchisor may allow or not allow *absentee* ownership.

4. Conditions for renewal. It might be for one term or the length of term after the *first term* and the number of days or months *in advance* that notice of renewal must be given by either party.

5. Termination conditions. This must also be stated in some detail. This is one of the major areas of litigation. Many agreements list these conditions in some detail. Some listings are meticulous and picky.

6. Repurchase rights. Most franchisors, if not all, want a right to *repurchase* the franchise under certain circumstances. Some at least want to have the right of *first refusal* on any attempt to resell the franchise.

7. Modification conditions. The agreement should state under what conditions the agreement can be modified. Typically it would state that any modification must be in writing and by persons having authority to do so for each of the parties.

8. Transfer provisions. This would include provisions in the agreement which would list what is required for the franchisee to sell or transfer the franchise to another person. These usually contain some onerous provisions and relate to the franchisor's repurchase rights.

9. Death or disability of franchisee. What happens on the death or disability of the franchisee? The agreement typically points out the conditions or enforcing provisions that give the franchisor's or franchisee's representatives certain rights. These provisions also contain certain limitations generally on the franchisee or franchisee's representatives.

10. The *term* (length) of the agreement. This may state the initial term and the conditions of any potential renewal. It is not unusual for the initial term and the renewal term to be of the same duration. Sometimes there is no renewal or option term. Sometimes a renewal is allowed, but under the royalty and advertising fee rates that exist at the time of renewal.

11. Restrictive covenants on competition. Most franchise agreements, if not all, restrict the

---

## *POWER POINTS* _____

▶ Franchising is a complex approach to doing business. It can be very effective but is not best suited for the start-up business.

▶ Franchising can be most beneficial for a "proven" business that can be easily taught to another person. This is the cookie-cutter approach.

▶ Franchising involves lots of paperwork and filings for the franchisor.

▶ Potential franchisees need to do some heavyweight homework before buying one. It is a game with serious war-risk from superior warriors.

franchisee's ability to compete with any other franchisee in the system or with the franchisor.

## EARNINGS CLAIMS

Franchisors are not required to make any earnings claims. Typically it is the strongest selling point, or one of the strongest, that will hook a franchisee into the system. There are certain requirements under the Federal Trade Commission Rule and also under the Uniform Franchise Offering Circular format, which affect, how a franchisor may make any earnings claims. If you are offering franchises, this may be your strong suit. If it is overstated, such overstatement could result in some future restrictions on your pocketbook. In other words, one "good" lawsuit could bankrupt you.

## POSSIBLE FRAUD PROBLEMS

Despite all the information required by the FTC or the UFOC rules, there is no way of defining all of what must be disclosed. So franchisors and franchisees must be aware that there are state contract requirements, common-law theories of fraud, and the application of many state franchise laws that would bring the disclosures we discussed under anti-fraud requirements. If any statement of fact in an offering circular is incomplete or is a half-truth and does not contain *all* of the *important* or *material* information a typical investor/franchisee would need, the law may have been violated.

What all this means is that you may *nominally* meet the rules of the UFOC or the FTC and still be violating contract law or common-law fraud standards or in some cases statutory fraud requirements.

Franchising is a game—if the franchisee wins, the franchisor also wins. But if the franchisee *loses*, the franchisor still *wins*.

This writer has published a book called *Franchise Selection: Separating Fact From Fiction*. It is a guidebook for a *potential franchisee* in looking not for the tip of the iceberg, but for the nine-tenths of the iceberg that is *submerged*. It has received excellent reviews. Any potential franchise investor should purchase it. An order form is in the back of this book.

# CHAPTER 7

## UNFAIR BUSINESS PRACTICES

# CHAPTER 7

## UNFAIR BUSINESS PRACTICES

The success of businesses, and the economic system of our country, are primarily based on fair competition. Competition helps create a whole body of law, a more efficient system, which was derived from the common law and also supplemented by current statutes to protect free and fair competition. These laws essentially prohibit any business, large or small, from taking unfair advantage of any of its competitors businesses or of their customers.

First, let's examine the common law. Then we will take a look at the statutory guidelines at both the state and federal levels.

### UNFAIR COMPETITION

Unfair competition includes business *torts* through which one business may interfere with the contractual relationships of another business. You might see it as product and service defamation, disparagement, taking credit for the work and time and effort from another business as your own, or misrepresentation of your product or of the other person's products. It can also include patent or trademark or copyright infringements. It can include commercial bribery.

What may be obvious at first blush may not be obvious in some complex situation. There are times when either you or your salespeople may be bordering on something that may be dangerous, although not intentional. It is the type of thing that would cost

---

**POWER POINTS** _____

▶ The criteria for this problem area are worth noting:
  a. There must be an existing, valid contract (even if it has no specific term, e.g., one month or one year).

  b. The interfering party must be aware of this contract.

  c. The interfering party must intentionally cause one of the parties to breach the contract.

▶ If you are looking to get your product into a retail store or to hire away a competitor's employee, use caution.

▶ Enhancing total competition is beneficial to customers.

▶ Destroying competition or a competitor may not be beneficial, especially if the means are unfair.

---

you dearly in terms of your reputation or possibly in terms of the negative publicity from being a defendant in a lawsuit.

Another reason to discuss this is so you will know or have some idea of acceptable behavior for your competitors, suppliers or customers.

What we are saying is that nuances can mean a lot if you or your employees are nudging that *line*.

## INTERFERENCE WITH CONTRACTUAL RELATIONS

What are we talking about here? We are talking about illegal interference with an ongoing relationship between a customer and a supplier. Assume there is an ongoing relationship between Business *A* and Business *B*. You happen to be Business *C*. If you do something that would adversely effect a business relationship between Business *A* and Business *B*, you may be on solid ground if it occurs because you have legitimately lowered prices and Business A now buys from your company. On the other hand, if you have used any unfair methods of competition, you may have committed a *business tort*. This is generally called interfering with ongoing contractual relations.

This tort may occur when someone induces or causes a third party not to perform a contract. You will have to act with diligence, for instance, even if the other parties do not have a long-term contract. You have to be careful when approaching this situation even if both parties have no ongoing contract. In a word, you must watch your P's and Q's when wedging in between some existing relationship. Even if they, the other parties, are on a handshake basis, be careful.

Although small businesses do not have the same problems, Texaco paid about $3,000,000,000 to learn this lesson. I still wonder what Texaco's lawyers told it before it approached Getty Oil.

There are legitimate ways of getting your product into a new location. There are also illegitimate ways of doing it. The concept of "anything goes" if there is no signed contract is incorrect. There are times when larger companies have taken unfair advantage of smaller competitors by utilizing their *muscle* or their *size*. That's the time

for the small business owner or manager to know what is legitimate and what is not. What are unfair methods? If you happen to be the person who comes out second in this two-horse race as a result of unfair business practices, you certainly should seek to protect your rights.

This has happened in many fields. Let's assume that Mr. *A* starts a new stock brokerage firm and he would like to get the employees and the customers from Brokerage House *X*. He approaches the employees of Brokerage House *X* and seeks to give them better compensation. He also wants them to bring over their customers. He hires half of an entire branch office from that large brokerage house. Now Mr. *A* has captured the assets of a competitor. Probably the lawsuits will fly—and they should.

This particular transaction in may look innocent and legitimate in one respect. On the other hand, it probably involves interference with contractual relationships that are ongoing. It is not that he could not end up with the same result. Mr. *A*'s approach might end up being a business tort (wrong). Now Mr. *A* might be liable for money damages and an injunction to stop the exodus at least of Broker *X*'s customer lists.

Let's assume you are a distributor of canned vegetables. You are trying to penetrate a new supermarket chain that is just coming to your area. If you do *not* employ proper competition means, you could become one of their new suppliers.

How can you get into trouble? You can do it by falsely disparaging your competitor's products. You can do it by paying off someone. You can do it by violating a protected trademark. You can do it by having a large percentage of the market and selling a product at prices that could drive your competitors out of that market. If you happen to be a minor factor in the market, you probably can sell at a loss to penetrate the market. On the other hand, if you happen to be in control of 50, 60 or 70 percent of the entire canned vegetable market there, you may have a problem selling at a loss.

Obviously, these prohibitions also involve the antitrust laws. By ignoring *fair* competition practices, an illegal player could be guilty of this illegal interference with an ongoing contractual relationship and be guilty of violating the antitrust laws. You might view this as using an economy of scale by violating several laws at the same time. The violator's defense lawyer should love it!

## DEFAMATION

Defamation occurs in the business context when one party communicates to third parties a false written or oral statement that injures another party's reputation or product. The offender does this by disgracing the person or diminishing the public perception or respect for a product or a service or a person (company).

If the defamation is handwritten, typewritten, printed or pictorial in nature, it is generally considered *libel*. If it is spoken or oral, it is generally designated *slander*. Sometimes it is called *trade libel*. In any event, the key is the publication of defamatory statements that get customers to cease purchasing a product or distorts its public image.

Are there any defenses to accusations of defamation? Truth is a defense. There are also privileges that might protect an individual. Privileges allow some leeway in communicating ideas that might be defamatory if in good faith and in a protected arena.

There are generally three categories of privilege:

1. Absolute privilege.
2. Conditional privilege.
3. Constitutional privilege.

### Absolute Privilege

An absolute privilege, though very narrow, would include:

1. Statements made in a judicial proceeding.
2. Statements made by members of the Congress on the floor of Congress.
3. Statements made by certain executive officers after leaving their governmental duty.
4. Statements made between spouses when no one else is present.

### Conditional Privilege

A conditional or qualified privilege is *conditioned* on the proper use of such privilege. An example of this can sometimes involve a protection, where there is potential defamatory material, when a person is acting to protect his or her own legitimate interest. An example sometimes includes comments made in response to reference requests about former employees. This qualified privilege might also involve a potential new customer of a company asking you about that company.

The conditional privilege is *ineffective* for legal purposes if the publisher of the defamatory comments acts in an excessive manner and without probable cause or for an improper purpose. So watch what you say and write about business competitors or suppliers.

### Constitutional Privilege

Constitutional privileges exist essentially under the First Amendment of the U.S. Constitution. This Amendment guarantees freedom of speech and freedom of press. The courts have interpreted this with a number of facets to protect this Amendment but allow some "joint flexing."

There is a distinction between public figures, public officials and individuals who are not in this category (the rest of us). Comments against public officials are generally constitutionally privileged unless the publisher or communicator of the statements made them *knowing* they were *false* and made them with *malice* or with *reckless disregard* of what the truth might be.

Trade libel may occur when false statements disparaging a product, a service or an individual come into play in the conduct of a business or trade or profession. If this type of communication is inaccurate or made in violation of the standards of fair comment, then there is potential liability for the person making the statements.

The potential damages can be significant. Assume that business is ruined because of some false comments. The plaintiff (injured party) may recover *damages* as a result of the defamation, sometimes without having to prove the exact dollar loss. The plaintiff calculates the specific and projected losses and then adds to the damages. If a business was producing profits of $50,000 a year, damages could include a multiple of $50,000 to cover future losses. The awards can be very large.

## DISPARAGEMENT

Disparagement is similar to libel. It can be defined as a falsehood which creates liability as a result of its publication of something that harms another party's interest. If the publisher of the disparaging statements knows the statements are false or makes them with reckless disregard for their veracity, illegal disparagement might be the result.

Defamation and disparagement overlap, but they are not necessarily identical. Some similarities include the fact that the defense of truth works for both of them. Also, the different types of privileges, including absolute, conditional and constitutional privilege, may apply.

Defamation is primarily geared toward the *reputation* of the injured party. If there has been defamation of a business person in a business context, she or he may be able to collect damages for emotional distress alone. If the injured party lost no money, she or he may still collect for the emotional strain she or he has. On the other hand, disparagement as a tort protects primarily the *economic interests* of the plaintiff.

If you have been a victim of one of these torts, the potential losses can extend not only to direct losses (lost sales or fees), but also to reasonably foreseeable future losses.

If a person makes a statement over the loudspeaker to a stadium full of people, it is reasonable to assume that the crowd of people hear it and that each may go and tell someone else. In effect, someone's reputation could be ruined by one simple public statement. On the other hand, if it is made to *one* person, the damages would extend to each person who would hear it. The judge or jury would determine what is reasonably foreseeable under the circumstances.

## APPROPRIATION

Appropriation occurs when an individual takes over somebody else's name or appearance to benefit themselves. The type of thing we occasionally see is when someone uses the image of a well-known person without authority. If you were to use the likeness of someone well known in sports without authority, to back your diet foods or vitamins, you might be liable for appropriation.

## MISREPRESENTATION

Misrepresentation could occur when Mr. Omega fraudulently makes a misstatement or misrepresentation of an important fact about a product, service or business person for the purpose of inducing someone else to act or to refrain from acting. This individual would act in *reliance* on the misstatements made. This creates liability for the victim (reliant person). The basis of it is deceit. If there is a pecuniary loss caused by this justifiable reliance, then there can be a cause of action based on misrepresentation. This is very important if we have salesmen or if we are relying on what a salesman says. Salespeople are generally the communicators of the business world. They are the ones who make the wheels of business turn.

On the other hand, your company or another company may not have any "salesmen." The president or the vice president of the company may be the salespeople. Your engineers may be the salespeople. They may make statements about the quality of your products or the quality of their construction expertise. This can result in a business tort.

The key is to know what to look for and to know what *not to do*. It is not always that simple.

---

The elements for misrepresentation are:

1. False representation.
2. Of a fact.
3. Which is *material* (significant or important).
4. With *knowledge* of its falsity or *reckless disregard* of its accuracy and
5. With *intent* to *deceive*.
6. Which is *justifiably* relied upon and
7. The communicator knows or is aware of

---

One thing that is very important for any business person to realize is that stating a half-truth or making a statement which in and of itself is accurate, but is incomplete, still involves misrepresentation.

Many times I have heard people say, "I told them the truth, but I did not tell the *whole* truth." If what Mr. *A* has omitted is important and significant or Mr. *B* acts without having complete information, we have the potential business tort of *misrepresentation*.

A party who has been induced to enter into a contract based upon a misrepresentation may be able to recover two types of damages. One is called "out-of-pocket damages." This amounts to the difference between the market value of what you received and the value paid for it. In other words, if you received $100 worth of goods or services, but spent $200 on it thinking you were getting $200 of value, then your out-of-pocket loss would be $100. This result is the difference between the fair market value ($100) of what you actually received versus what you gave up ($200).

On the other hand, there is another approach, known as "benefit-of-the-bargain rule." The way this one works is that you would be allowed damages based on the value of what you received versus the value you were *told* you were *going to receive*. For example, you may have spent $200 on a product, but the communicator or miscommunicator may have told you you were getting a $300 value. Thus, even though you gave up $100, your loss would be the difference between the $100 "discount" you received and the $300 that you were told you were getting.

There are other forms of unfair competition that crop up. You as a business person must be vigilant for additional approaches to unfair business competition. They include not only appropriation of another's name but also appropriation of another's trademark or service mark. An example of this would include an unrelated company using the logo of the Xerox Corporation or the logo of the IBM Corporation. These torts also include the hiring of employees to get trade secrets or confidential information.

There have been cases involving threats of patent infringement suits which are made in *bad faith* against a person just to stop him from using a competitor's product.

Another example is intentional harassment of a competitor's customers or employees done in bad faith.

Another approach includes potential commercial bribery. Sometimes we have seen this bribery when a company is attempting to get its product into a new supply chain or into a new outlet. It is usually illegal, but even if it is not, this tort might make a contract unenforceable.

The remedies for any of the above generally include or can include these: (1) direct and foreseeable damages; (2) injunctive relief, whereby a court can order an offender not to perform or stop performing some offensive behavior; and (3) an *accounting* for any *profits* made illegally. Assume that a defendant has used the logo of another party and in the process has made money. The bad guy may have to give back all the profits he made by appropriating someone else's logo.

## UNFAIR AND DECEPTIVE PRACTICES

This category of unfair business practices arises out of state and federal statutes. There is a Uniform Deceptive Trade Practices Act has been enacted in a number of states.

This Uniform Act includes the following as *unfair trade practices*, when in the course of an individual's business, vocation or occupation he does any of the following:

1. Passes off goods or services as those of another.

2. Causes likelihood of confusion or misunderstanding as to the source, sponsorship, approval or certification of goods or services.

3. Causes likelihood of confusion or misunderstanding as to the affiliation, connection or association with, or certification by, another.

4. Uses deceptive representations or designations of geographic origin in connection with goods or services.

5. Represents that goods or services have sponsorship, approval, characteristics, ingredients, uses, benefits or qualities they do not have, or that a person has a sponsorship or approval, status, affiliation or connection that he does not in fact have

6. Represents that goods are original or new, if they are deteriorated, altered, reconditioned, reclaimed, used or secondhand.

7. Represents that goods or services are of a particular standard, quality or grade or that goods are of a particular style or model, if they are of another.

8. Disparages the goods, services or business of another by false or misleading representations of fact.

9. Advertises goods or services with intent not to sell them as advertised.

10. Advertises goods or services with intent not to supply reasonably expectable public demand, unless the advertisement discloses limitation of quantity.

11. Makes false or misleading statements concerning the reasons for, existence of, or amounts of price reductions.

12. Engages in any other conduct that creates a likelihood of confusion or of misunderstanding.

This law is not to be taken lightly. Many states have enacted it. It gives teeth to many consumer lawsuits that did not exist before. The prevailing consumer can generally collect attorney's fees, which is not true for "older" statutes.

## UNREASONABLE RESTRAINTS OF TRADE AND MONOPOLIES AT COMMON LAW

First, what we are looking at are laws that involve *unreasonable* restraints of trade, but not specifically those statutes that most of us know of as the *antitrust laws*. Here we are talking about the body of law that was built up *prior to* the Sherman Act of 1890. They still come into play in most jurisdictions because the common law attempted to *encourage trade* and *competition*. This encouragement was in the form of fair trade and fair competition.

As we will discuss later, vertical and horizontal price fixing and certain types of agreements or combinations to limit or control production or manufacturing of commodities have been held illegal even under the common law, prior to the antitrust laws as we know them.

## AGREEMENTS NOT TO COMPETE

I would like to distinguish two areas that we will examine. They are treated slightly differently under the law. One involves the sale, lease or transfer of a *business* or *profession*, whereby an agreement not to compete is ancillary or essentially a sideline to the main agreement not primary to it. These agreements are to be distinguished from an agreement not to compete that is part of a termination provision of an *employment contract*.

## HOW TO DECIDE IF THE AGREEMENTS ARE VALID

An individual might want to sell her pharmacy, which she had owned for a number of years and built up. She would probably want to sell it with a restrictive non-compete provision. What are the factors we must look at to decide whether or not the restrictions are enforceable?

What type of restrictive covenant would we see in such a sale? Assume our pharmacist had built up this pharmacy and now has a respectable following of customers. Ms. *X* is very well known. She has this pharmacy for 15 years. She sells it to Mr. *Y.* Mr. *Y* certainly would not want Ms. *X* to wait six weeks and start another nearby pharmacy with Ms. *X*'s name prominently displayed on the front. Ms. *X* would be able to take back all of the customers who were part of the sale. Part of what Mr. *Y* was buying was the following of customers.

What is reasonable? We would examine what is reasonable as to *time.* We would also examine what is reasonable as to *territory* and what would be reasonably necessary to protect the sale of the business or to protect the previous employer.

In the sale of a business, the purchase price may be far in excess of the value of the building and the inventory (hard assets). Here Ms. *X* sold "good will."

Sometimes a business may be sold at several times the current earnings. That is the sale of "good will." That is the piece that the buyer (Mr. *Y*) does not want to purchase only to have it taken away. Otherwise, why buy it?

Sometimes other items sold may include trade secrets. Therefore, the buyer may also want protection for trade secrets or any other confidential information he purchases. Trade secrets can be the cornerstone of a business, including customers' lists, methods of doing business, routes or other types of information which are unique to that business entity.

## FACTORS USED IN DETERMINING WHETHER THESE COVENANTS ARE VALID IN EMPLOYMENT CONTRACTS

As we have mentioned previously, the courts take a slightly different view in employment arguments in reviewing restrictions on competing with a *former employer.* The courts look at reasonableness. But the standards for reasonableness for employment contracts are much more stringent than for the sale of a business. We will look at the same type of bases, including reasonable time and territory, but several other factors come into play.

These restrictions can take away an individual's (complete or partial) basis for his

livelihood. This is much more critical. So the courts do not like this approach very much. The results vary in many states. Courts often look for ways around these restrictive covenants.

## REASONABLENESS

We are talking about an agreement, for example, which restricts a computer salesman from competing with his former employer for two years in the entire City of Z and the three contiguous counties. The time can be longer or shorter and the territory can be larger (*e.g.,* the entire U.S.) or smaller.

Some states have specific laws and specific maximums. General guidelines revolve around several requirements. If an employer is going to invest significant amounts of money into educating an employee or making this employee visible, the employer may want to protect his or her investment. A typical example might involve an automobile salesman. You are the dealer and advertise this individual in the newspaper and on television. Assume he becomes very visible locally. You also send this person to several education courses. You as an automobile dealer may want to restrict the ability of this employee to compete with you if he quits working for your dealership.

The courts would probably look at factors such as what is your geographical area (your area of influence). If your area of influence is one or two counties in the state, you probably could not restrict the individual from competing with you in every other county in your state. So there are reasonable limits as to territory.

The courts do not like these types of restrictions. The courts would look stringently at the *time* and geographic limitation involved. The courts might enforce the same provisions incidental to the sale of a business and refuse to enforce them in an employment non-compete provision.

## RESTRICTIVE COVENANTS NOT TO COMPETE IN A FRANCHISE AGREEMENT

Many new businesses in this time and age are being developed under a franchise agreement for-

---

## POWER POINTS _____

▶ Reasonable restrictions can be enforced.

▶ The factors that are examined include:
   a. Protected territory versus the actual territory previously serviced.

   b. Time period.

   c. Need of the business for this protection.

   d. Balancing of business need against the burden on the individual.

▶ The results may differ when examining the sale of a business versus the termination of employment.

---

mula. Part of the benefit that is often sold to a franchisee is a restriction on the territorial area. In addition, we see a restriction on that franchisee being able to compete with that company, should the franchisee *get out* of the business or *terminate* the agreement. The courts interpret this as the sale of a business. The courts generally examine time and territory restrictions similar to those in the sale of a business.

In the franchise arena, some courts have allowed broader restrictions than we would see in an employment situation. We would have to look at the effective territory for the original business. If it operated in only one or two counties for 95 percent of its business, the franchisor could not restrict the *employee* from future employment with another competitor from the *entire state*. In the sale of the franchise business, the courts might enforce a broader restrictive territory.

## COVENANTS NOT TO COMPETE IN SHOPPING CENTER LEASES

On occasion, businesses will enter into a lease in a shopping center and at the same time not want the center owner to lease space to another similar business. There can be arguments pro and con. It may be possible for a lessor to agree not to lease other premises to potential competition. An example would be that if you happen to have a store that sells scents, fragrances and wax products, it may be possible that the lessor can legally agree not to lease to a competitor. It appears that on occasion this type of clause has been enforced.

Now, what can the first lessee do if the center owner violates this non-compete covenant? It can seek money damages against the lessor for violating the agreement. It might also seek injunctive relief against the lessor for violating this non-compete provision in the lease.

# CHAPTER 8

## UNFAIR AND
## DECEPTIVE PROMOTIONAL PRACTICES

# CHAPTER 8

# UNFAIR AND DECEPTIVE PROMOTIONAL PRACTICES

One of the most important aspects of any business is getting business. We can use many fancy terms, and there are many pieces to what is generally termed marketing.

It obviously includes sales, but it also includes promotion, advertising, sales brochures, distribution, pricing, company policy, service policy, warranty policy and many other aspects that define what it is the customer receives.

In addition to this, there are numerous laws on the books that attempt to dictate a level playing field. They are designed to promote competition, and not allow any one or more competitors to hurt competition and they are also designed to prohibit deceptive acts and practices in which any company might engage.

On a national basis the Federal Trade Commission is the primary enforcement vehicle for the prohibitions against these practices. On the state level there are many trade commissions, called by various names.

There is also a Federal Trade Commission Act and its various amendments which help to define things that are unfair methods of competition and deceptive acts and practices.

On the state level there are similar laws that track the Federal Trade Commission Act or that develop their own approaches to fair competition and responsible business practices.

## DECEPTIVE ACTS AND PRACTICES

We will focus on the Federal Trade Commission Act because it acts as a model for many of the state acts. It also applies across state lines.

What types of activities are deceptive and therefore prohibited? They include some of the following:

1. Unfair and deceptive prices including bait-and-switch type advertising and offers of "free" products and services that aren't really free.

2. Failure to disclose important aspects of a product or service in advertising or promotions.

3. Illegally using someone else's well-known name or logo as the name of one's own business or product.

4. False criticism or characterizations of products or services of competitors.

5. False or deceptive representations that another individual or organization approves or sponsors your product or services.

6. Deceptive guarantees;

7. False or deceptive representations about the quality, composition, character or source of your product or services.

8. False or deceptive demonstrations of your product or services or mock-ups of your products or of your services.

9. Ambiguous and confusing statements that ultimately deceive purchasers.

10. False or deceptive implications about the qualities of your products or services.

These are certainly not all of the potential deceptive acts and practices, but they will give you some guidelines on what to avoid. Clearly, it is easier to state with some accuracy the qualities of your products or services, and the above can be used as a checklist to make sure you avoid any offensive or potentially offensive representations of product qualities. In addition, they may also give you some tools with which to gauge not only your own promotional practices, but also the practices of your competitors.

## IDENTIFYING DECEPTIVE ACTS AND PRACTICES

The primary criterion for identifying deceptive acts and practices is the capacity of an ad to deceive. You should be very well aware of the fact that consumers need not be actually deceived or damaged for there to be a violation of the law in a promotion. The Federal Trade Commission can seek a cease-and-desist order against a business practice or act even though no one has ever been damaged by the practice or act.

Another significant characteristic feature of deception might involve the type of information which the Federal Trade Commission would consider important in a particular case. In other words, it is not what type of information you might believe is important but what type of information the Federal Trade Commission (or effectively a third party looking at your promotional practices) would conclude. Another very important factor is that the FTC does not have to look any further than the advertisement itself to interpret its meaning. It is fairly easy to get cutesy at times, and we have all seen ads that do so. The ad may leave out certain very important information but say "More information upon request." Unfortunately, if the ad itself is seriously deficient or basically deceptive, you lose. The fact that you may have expert testimony to swear to any other thing that may support or buttress your argument is irrelevant. The FTC does not have to accept your version or your expert's version of what is reasonable in the ad.

A very important factor is that if your ads are ambiguous or your promotional practices contain ambiguous information and any one possible interpretation can be false, the entire ad can be considered false.

The principal factors for you to be aware of can be summarized as follows:

1. The practice or ad has any capacity to deceive the reader or potential buyer.

2. The ad speaks for itself and a business has no defense by claiming that it will link up some additional information.

3. If the ad can have multiple meanings, any one of which is false or deceptive, the entire ad can be considered illegal.

4. An ad can be deceptive if all the statements taken together create a false impression or are subject to a false interpretation.

5. The ad can be deceptive even if only the implications of the statements made in the ad or promotional literature are deceptive. The misstatement need not be explicit.

6. Even though an ad is generally interpreted correctly by consumers, if it may be read in any false or deceptive manner, the ad may be considered illegal.

## YOU NEED A REASONABLE BASIS FOR MAKING A CLAIM

There are many ads that probably violate the federal and state acts. But this does not mean that someone will take the business to court as a result of the unfair deceptive practices.

## PRIOR PROOF IS REQUIRED

If any claim is made in one of your ads, you must have sufficient, scientific or evidentiary proof of the validity of any claim that is made. You cannot get the proof after the fact. If you did not have the proof before you placed the ad, you may have committed an irresponsible act.

Advertising and promotion are essential to any business, but what you as a small business owner or manager must realize is that you cannot transfer that risk to the public. If you intend to make a claim in an ad or promotional literature, it must be based on evidence that exists in your files before you make such statement. The Act intends to require individuals to act responsibly *before* they develop a promotion for a product or service.

## COMPARISON ADVERTISING

All of us have seen comparison ads on television or in the print media. They generally involve comparing "two or more specifically—

named or recognizably—presented brands of the same generic product or service class in terms of one or more specific product or service attributes." We have all seen the ads comparing Pepsi and Coke; these are obviously comparison ads.

There is nothing wrong with comparison advertising as long as it is based on accurate description and non-deceptive behavior.

The American Association of Advertising Agencies and the major television networks have developed some guidelines, which could be helpful should you ever consider doing comparison advertising.

These guidelines include these factors:

1. The ad should be used to educate consumers and not primarily to discredit the competitive product.

2. The ad should be directed to significant competitors as opposed to minor players in the market.

3. The competitive product or service should be fairly and clearly identified.

4. The advertising should be comparing the same quality of the products or, as we say, comparing apples with apples and oranges with oranges.

5. The comparison should involve just that—a legitimate comparison—and not be used to associate the two products as in effect being in the same class or category. This could involve bringing out a luxury car next to one of the cheapest cars on the market. Certainly each one has four wheels and an engine, but very little else would be in common.

6. Independent third party objective testing procedures should be followed.

7. The testing must be the basis for any claims made.

8. Insignificant differences or partial results should not be part of any claims made.

9. Whatever characteristics the business claims should be significant in terms of being useful or valuable to the product purchaser.

10. Any personal testimonials should clearly reflect that one person's opinion, and not be considered or claimed as some representative opinion of, for instance, all baseball players.

Following these particular guidelines should help to keep you on the road to legitimate and accurate advertising.

## BAIT-AND-SWITCH ADVERTISING

Bait-and-switch advertising is "an alluring but insincere offer to sell a product or service which the advertiser in truth does not intend nor want to sell." The Federal Trade Commission has issued a rule which essentially states that any advertisement which is not truly a bona fide offer to sell and cannot be fulfilled is potentially illegal.

Here are some of the types of bait-and-switch practices that have been considered illegal or prohibited:

1. A business use of compensation practices which discourage its salespeople from selling the advertised product or service in favor of another product or service.

2. Showing a demonstration of a product which is defective, obviously to discourage its purchase.

3. Refusing to take orders for an advertised product which can be delivered in a reasonable period of time. In other words, if the only orders which the business will take require an unreasonable time to wait for delivery, it would be a bait-and-switch tactic.

4. Failure to maintain a reasonably adequate inventory to meet potential demand. This is not a precise requirement but one of general knowledge of the buying patterns of the consumers.

5. Downplaying the features of the advertised product or service in favor of an alternate product or service.

6. Refusing to demonstrate the product or to sell the product as it is advertised.

7. After the sale, practices that would encourage the consumer to cancel the sale and possibly purchase another product or service.

## ENDORSEMENTS AND TESTIMONIALS

We have all seen on television and heard on radio glowing testimonials about the qualities of products or services. They often come from well-known public or professional figures. Sports figures often make more money from their endorsements than they do from the actual sport in which they engage.

### Endorsement or Not?

It is important to distinguish what would be an endorsement from just a plug. If the average consumer can easily determine that the message in the advertisement is not necessarily the opinion of the announcer, then the message is not considered an endorsement. We see dramatizations on television where an individual wears a lab coat to represent a doctor or someone who fits a particular credible role. That is not necessarily considered an endorsement.

On the other hand, if the person making the endorsement does not appear to be an expert, then we end up with a different result.

If the ad is an actual endorsement from an expert, this endorsement must be supported by the expert using his talents in his skilled area in determining the product's characteristics. The Federal Trade Commission has several rules which if followed should answer your endorsement questions:

1. The endorser did actually use the product or service.

2. Endorser must be an expert or eminently qualified to make judgments about the product.

3. The endorser must actually make an extensive examination of the product or service in order to make his or her conclusions.

4. Endorser can compare products and make statements regarding comparisons, but the endorser must actually examine the competitive brands on which he or she focuses.

5. An endorsement from an organization can be effective and acceptable as long as it reflects the collective judgment of all the members or a governing body of the membership.

6. Dramatizations or announcements are not considered to be endorsements, but in addition they should be titled as such in any advertising.

## FREE AND SPECIAL BARGAINS

We often see the use of the term "free," but how can we use the word and still fit the Federal Trade Commission guidelines? "Free" essentially means that the purchaser does not have to pay anything for the item or service. If the free item can be received as free only if another item is purchased, then "the other item" must be offered at its regular price and no more; and again, as a small business owner or manager you have to be able to prove that the price is the same as it was previously. Thus, the "regular price" becomes critical.

If you are going to offer any "free" products you should consider the following guidelines:

1. Are there any contingencies or wheres, ifs or buts. You must be sure they are clearly visible, not only acceptable, but easily located in the literature and on the product.

2. If you are a supplier and there is printed special bargain information on the product, you as the supplier must make sure the retailer carries out the bargain. There is no passing the buck here.

3. If there is some limitation to the "free" promotion or some methods of distribution in which it is not available, you must state that in the advertising.

4. A "free" offer is not free if it is made for more than six months in any 12-month period. In other words, if it is always "free" or substantially always free, it is obviously part of the product and intended to be sold that way. The Federal Trade Commission says that at least 50 days should elapse between free offers and that no more than three free offers can be made in any year.

If you follow these guidelines, you should be able to avoid the ire of either the Federal Trade Commission or your state version of the Federal Trade Commission. You should also be able to avoid the distaste of any of your competitors.

## REMEDIES

You should be aware of the basic remedies that either the Federal Trade Commission or consumers can seek if a business engages in deceptive acts and practices:

1. Requirement that the business engage in corrective advertising. There are several significant cases whereby the Federal Trade Commission has

required that the businesses not only stop the deceptive acts and practices, but also admit to the public in their advertising that their product or service does not perform in the manner in which it was advertised. In effect, they must admit that they lied.

2. Requirement for substantiation of any advertising claims. The Federal Trade Commission can, as it has in the past, require a company to show that it has a "reasonable basis" for making a claim or series of claims. The Federal Trade Commission has gone after huge companies and has required small companies to meet this standard. It is advisable that you keep any substantiation for at least three years after an ad or promotional campaign has ended.

## REQUIRED DISCLOSURE

The Federal Trade Commission has under certain programs, and with regard to certain types of advertising, required an advertiser to disclose information which it might not want to disclose. This includes both positive or affirmative disclosures as well as disclosures about negative features of a product.

## COOLING-OFF PERIOD

On occasion the Federal Trade Commission has required that a company offer a 10-day cooling-off period before any contract became final. An example might be giving a customer three days to cancel a contract for purchasing a particular product or service.

## CONSUMER ACTION

At least with regard to the warranty rules, the federal Act gives the consumer a legal cause of action. Unfortunately for most of the rules we discussed above, the consumer cannot sue the business based upon the Federal Trade Commission Act. One of the exceptions is the Magnuson-Moss Warranty Act. On the other hand, many states allow the consumer or a competitive business the right to sue under a state version of the Federal Trade Commission Act.

## INJUNCTIVE RELIEF AND FINES AGAINST THE OFFENDER

The Federal Trade Commission can issue cease-and-desist orders and require that offending businesses or individuals pay fines of $5,000 to $10,000. The commission can also seek temporary injunctions for certain violations.

Once the FTC has issued a cease-and-desist order against some prohibited practice, then it may utilize its authority to fine a business or individual. That is, only if a business violates the cease-and-desist order can the Federal Trade Commission fine a particular business. On the other hand, if the cease-and-desist order is violated, a fine of up to $10,000 a day can be levied against any business for disregarding the cease-and-desist order.

The above categories can be used as a checklist for testing your advertising. One of the most important things to remember is that not your version of the facts or my version of the facts controls. What controls is the regulated version of what is important, meaning you have to look at the regulations for those things that are required or prohibited; and you must also realize that third parties may view our advertising in a totally different way than we do.

# CHAPTER 9

## PRODUCT WARRANTIES AND PRODUCT LIABILITY

# CHAPTER 9

## PRODUCT WARRANTIES AND PRODUCT LIABILITY

One way a business does well is by projecting and delivering quality and service.

Many businesses develop loyal followings (customers) and record profits by producing quality *products* and by standing behind their assurances of quality.

Excellence is a benchmark. If you advertise and promote the excellence of your products, this chapter will give you some guidance on the legal requirements you will face.

Generally, the UCC discusses two basic kinds of warranties, implied warranties and express warranties.

These involve the seller's backing up representation about product's "clear" title, quality or performance.

### IMPLIED WARRANTIES

Implied warranties are those that are not specifically mentioned. These may be expressed in a document. These may be implied or sometimes discussed orally by salespeople. They are, however, created by state law.

Implied warranties are generally based upon the common-law principle of fair value for the money a purchaser has spent.

There are two types of implied warranties that we generally come into contact with in consumer product sales. They are (a) the implied warranty of merchantability and (b) the implied warranty of fitness for a particular purpose

### IMPLIED WARRANTY OF MERCHANTABILITY

This applies only to a merchant. A merchant is someone who holds himself out as selling a particular product. It is a basic promise that the goods he sells you will do what they are supposed to do and that there is nothing significantly wrong with the goods. This promise is implied and warrants that the goods can be sold and are fit to be sold. The law requires that merchants make this promise every time they sell a product as long as they are in the business of selling such products.

Thus, someone who sells television sets warrants that the sets are "merchantable" and work in an average fashion and can be counted on for a reasonable amount of time. In a case where the product does not meet these standards, the law requires that the seller provide a remedy so the buyer can get a good, working television set.

### IMPLIED WARRANTY OF FITNESS FOR A PARTICULAR PURPOSE

The implied warranty of fitness for a particular purpose is not limited to merchants. The law requires that the seller stand behind its product in a very specific way. Assume a seller has discussed the needs of the buyer and understands what the buyer is trying to accomplish. When the seller knows that the customer is relying on the *seller's advice* that this particular product can be used for a *specific purpose* that the *buyer has*, then the seller must stand behind this "fitness for a particular purpose."

An example might be if a buyer is purchasing a lawnmower that is supposed to be able to cut grass down to a certain number of inches. The discussion focuses on this particular purpose. The seller is, in effect, stating that this product will meet those standards as they are discussed. If the particular mower which this retailer recommended proves unable to cut down to this level, the warranty of fitness for a particular purpose has not been met. The seller is obligated to make good on the warranty of fitness for a particular purpose.

## IMPLIED WARRANTIES IN GENERAL

Implied warranties are promises about the condition of the product at the time it is sold. They do not necessarily guarantee that these conditions are going to last forever. Nor does the seller guarantee that they are going to last any particular time. Products are sold based on "This is a reasonable time period given all of the facts and circumstances." Implied warranties also exclude certain things that would be *reasonably excluded*. For instance, selling a lawnmower that may cut down to the right level does not imply that the lawnmower has to last through misuse and abusive behavior, like riding it in subdivision drag races.

There are statutes of limitation which limit the maximum period during which a buyer can seek recourse against a seller. There are no specific periods that these warranties last. State law would apply a maximum time during which one could

seek a remedy. Buyers cannot sit on their rights forever.

## SELLING "AS IS" OR SELLING WITHOUT IMPLIED WARRANTIES

A merchant or any other individual may sell a product or provide a service and state that there is *no warranty* and that the product is sold "as is." In addition, there can be implied warranties on *used* products; these typically apply only when the product is sold by a *merchant*. Often when products are sold, the "as is" language will be and should only be applied by merchants when there is *justification* for it. Sometimes some merchants slip the "as is" language into *every contract*, in which case a buyer should refuse to sign such an agreement.

Also, "as is" language must be *very conspicuous*. It must be *clear* and of such a *nature* that no one could miss it. It has to be clear to any *purchaser* that the *entire product risk* will fall on the *purchaser*. Therefore "merchantability" must be *specifically excluded*, or words such as "with all faults" or "as is" must be *prominently displayed* and possibly initialed by the purchaser. Some states—though certainly not the majority of states—do not allow consumer products to be sold "as is."

In addition, if there are express warranties, which we will discuss, federal law makes illegal any attempt to *disclaim implied warranties*. In other

---

## POWER POINTS _____

▶ Service and quality may be the lifeblood of your company's future.

▶ Warranties and the diligent protection of your product or service quality are synonymous with your business.

▶ These legal rules on warranties should be a minimum which you would strive to exceed.

▶ Customers are loyal when service is paramount.

▶ Profits may grow with customer loyalty.

words, you cannot make some specific express warranties and in the next sentence disclaim any implied warranties.

## EXPRESS WARRANTIES

Sales literature is full of the wonderful qualities of various products. Often these representations become warranties. Let's examine some of the legal rules:

Express warranties are specific representations made to a customer in the course of a sales transaction. They are promises or statements that the seller will voluntarily make about the product or about the seller's commitment to remedy any defects or malfunctions that any of the customers may experience.

Express warranties take a number of forms including advertising claims, claims in brochures, booklets or newspaper ads; some even include formal certificates. Express warranties can be made *orally* or in *writing*. With regard to written warranties on consumer products, we will briefly take a look at the Magnuson-Moss Warranty Act to see what requirements a small business has to meet if there are any *written* warranties.

The Magnuson-Moss Warranty Act is a federal law that governs *written warranties* on *consumer products*. It was passed in Congress in 1975, and requires that manufacturers and sellers of consumer products provide consumers with detailed information about any warranty coverage. Additionally, it also affects both the *rights* of *consumers* and the *obligations* of the *warrantors* under these written warranties.

Any business must be protective of its good will. Though it may sound as if warranties are created in a vacuum, they obviously are not. The success of many businesses is based on how they take care of the customers' interests. These warranties leave customers with the feeling that they have gotten a good deal, even if not the cheapest deal.

If the seller or manufacturer stands behind the product, the customer can buy with greater assurance of protection. Nobody wants to buy a lemon. If someone does buy a lemon, they are likely to shout it from the rooftops if they have been *stiffed* by some retailer or manufacturer.

## "NON-REQUIREMENTS" OF MAGNUSON-MOSS WARRANTY ACT

There are some misunderstandings at times as to what this Act may require. There are several things it does *not* require. These include the following:

1. This Act does *not require* any business to provide a written warranty. If you have a product that you do not feel should include a warranty, you do not have to include one.

2. The Act does *not* apply to *oral* warranties.

3. The Act does *not* apply to warranties on *services*, but only on goods.

4. The Act does *not* apply to warranties on products sold for *resale* or for *commercial purposes*. It applies only to consumer products that are to be consumed by the purchaser.

The covered warranties apply only to *tangible* goods and only those used for personal, family or household purposes.

The Federal Trade Commission has issued rules to bring about these warranties. The rules passed by the Federal Trade Commission include the following:

1. As a warrantor, the business person or manufacturer must designate or title any written warranty as either "*full*" or "*limited.*"

2. The warrantor must state certain specified information about the coverage of the warranty in a *single, clear* and *easy-to-read document*.

3. The warrantor/seller must ensure that *warranties* are available where the warranted customer products are sold, so the consumers can read them *before buying*. The titling requirement (the proper titling of the warranty information) applies to all written warranties on consumer products costing more than $10. However, the disclosure with presale availability of the warranty information as applies to all written warranties on consumer products costing more than $15.

## TIE-IN SALES PROHIBITION

As a result of this Act, warrantors or sellers are generally prohibited from requiring tie-in sales for any written warranties to be effective. An example might be a seller's requirement that the purchaser must buy an additional item or service from a particular company to use *with* the *warranted product* to receive a *remedy* under the warranty. If you have to use Brand *X* oil in your lawnmower to have the two-year limited warranty effective, you are the victim of a tie-in sale. The seller may require that an appropriate replacement oil be used. The seller cannot require that a brand-name product be used.

Though a business cannot generally require tie-in sales, the warranty may exclude certain replacement parts, repairs or maintenance that are inappropriate for the product. The manufacturer may recommend that you utilize his dealers, for instance, for maintenance. He may state that improper or incorrectly performed repairs may void the warranty. He *can* state that if you utilize a non-authorized service dealer for warranty service, you lose your warranty automatically. For a limited warranty which covers replacement of defective parts only, the manufacturer cannot specify a dealer. If the warranty covers labor and parts, he can require an authorized dealer.

## DECEPTIVE WARRANTY TERMS

Warranties cannot contain *deceptive* or *misleading* terms. For instance, you cannot offer a warranty that gives *apparent* coverage but *no actual* coverage. An amusing example has been given of warranting all of the *mechanical* parts in an electronic calculator that has *no moving parts*. This would be considered deceptive and unlawful. Another example would be offering a warranty providing service that is totally unavailable. This could occur if there are no service centers nearby to work on a heavy bulldozer. That would obviously be deceptive.

## ADDITIONAL FEATURES OF THE MAGNUSON-MOSS ACT

There are two features in the Act that are important. First, the Act makes it easier for purchasers to sue for breach of warranty, by making breach of warranty a violation of federal law. Also, it allows consumers to recover court costs and reasonable attorney's fees. This means that if the warrantor or retailer loses the lawsuit for breach of a written or implied warranty, the warrantor (seller) may have to pay the customer's costs of bringing the lawsuit, including attorney's fees.

---

### *POWER POINTS*_____

▶ *Only* the Federal Trade Commission can sue offenders based upon the Federal Trade Commission Act, which defines many unfair business practices.

▶ May states have "little FTC" acts through which individuals and competitors can seek relief.

▶ The federal trademark protection act now allows competitors to sue offenders who unfairly disparage or harm another party's trademark or service mark.

▶ Spend some time learning from your trade association what types of practices are legally fair.

▶ This area is extremely important to know. A successful lawsuit based on unfair trade practices can evaporate a business.

## ALTERNATIVE DISPUTE MECHANISMS

The Act encourages manufacturers, warrantors and retailers to develop *informal processes* for *settling* any legal disputes or disputes involving a warranty. The Act allows any warrantors to include a provision in the warranty that requires customers to try to resolve warranty disputes by means of an *informal dispute resolution mechanism* before going to court. It is an attempt to get the parties together before there is any litigation.

Certainly from the viewpoint of customer good will, it may be good to attempt to get the parties together. A retailer who is attempting to build for the long term should take heed of this particular mechanism.

The Federal Trade Commission has issued rules on this informal dispute settlement procedure. Several of the features are worth noting:

1. The mechanism must be adequately funded and staffed to resolve disputes quickly.

2. A procedure must be available *free of charge* to consumers.

3. The staff must be able to settle disputes *independently* without influence from the parties involved.

4. The resolution procedure must be *written*.

5. Both parties must be aware of the *notice* of any dispute and of the *facts* alleged by each of the parties.

6. The mechanism must provide a means of *gathering, investigating* and *organizing* all of the information necessary for each dispute to be decided fairly and quickly.

7. The mechanism must provide *each party* an opportunity to present its *statement* of the facts, submit *supporting material*, and rebut points made by the other party. The mechanism can allow, but is not required to allow, oral presentations.

8. The mechanism must inform *both parties* of the decision and the reasons supporting it within 40 days of receiving notice of a dispute.

9. The mechanism must provide that its decisions are *not binding*. This fact should be made known to the parties. In addition, either party must be free to take the dispute to court if dissatisfied with the decisions.

10. The dispute mechanism must provide for keeping records of *all disputes*.

11. The mechanism must provide a method for auditing the company's compliance with the rule on an annual basis.

## PROPERLY TITLING WRITTEN WARRANTIES—FULL OR LIMITED

The Magnuson-Moss Act requires that every written warranty on a consumer product costing more than $10 be properly titled, with a "full" or "limited" added to the title. The intent here is to allow the customer at a glance to get some idea of whether they are getting the "expensive spread" or the cheap imitation spread.

The title "full warranty" gives a clear message to consumers that the coverage meets standards for *comprehensive* warranty coverage. On the other hand, the term "limited warranty" alerts consumers that the coverage does not meet the standards for full coverage under the Act.

## FULL WARRANTY

A full warranty must meet these requirements:

1. It is *not limited* as to *duration* with regard to any implied warranties.

2. The warranty service is provided to *anyone* who *owns* the product during the warranty period. Coverage is not limited to first purchasers.

3. The warranty service is provided *free of charge*, including such costs as returning the product or removing and reinstalling a product when necessary.

4. The retailer or warrantor provides at the *consumer's choice* either a *replacement* or a *full refund* if after a reasonable number of tries the warrantor is unable to properly repair the product.

5. The warrantor did *not* require the customer to perform any duty as a *precondition* for receiving service except notifying the seller that the service is needed. An exception exists if you can demonstrate that the *duty is reasonable*.

If *any* of these five statements are not true, then the warranty is *limited*. No company is required to make an entire warranty full or limited. If the statements above are true about coverage on some parts of the product, or if the statements are true about the coverage during only one part of the warranty period, then your warranty is a *multiple* warranty that is part full and part limited.

The wording for warranties is not cast in stone. As long as there is a fair or reasonable standard applied to the description or the wording of the warranty, the warranty may pass muster. The FTC's rules do not specify the form or the wordage.

## DISCLOSING TERMS AND CONDITIONS OF YOUR WRITTEN WARRANTY

The FTC has promulgated rules that are separate from the titling rules. These involve the *method* of *disclosure* of the written consumer product warranty and its *terms* and *conditions*.

This rule requires that the written warranty on a consumer product that costs more than $15 be *clear*, *easy to read* and contain specified items of information about its coverage.

## BASIC INFORMATION REQUIRED FOR ALL WARRANTIES

Under the FTC's disclosure rules, there are five basic requirements of coverage that your warranty must describe:

1. *Warranty Coverage* or lack of coverage. Your warranty should describe every type of malfunction or defect that may appear in all parts of the product.

2. *Period of Coverage.* If the coverage begins at some point in time *other than* the *purchase date*, the warranty must state the time or event that *begins the coverage*. In addition, the warrantor must make clear when the coverage *ends*, if some particular event would terminate coverage.

3. *Extent of Problem Correction.* This part of the FTC disclosure provision requires that the warrantor provide an *explanation* of whatever remedy the seller intends to offer under the warranty. This may be *repairing* the product, *replacing* the product or providing a *refund* of the purchase price, or providing a *credit* toward any subsequent purchase, or any combination of these. It may also include a description that one condition applies initially and another one may apply subsequently.

If necessary, the FTC Rule requires that the warrantor explain what it is the seller will *not* do. This requires a description of any types of *expenses*, if any, that the warrantor won't cover. It may exclude, for instance, labor charges or consequential damages. It may exclude the cost of repairing or replacing *another* product that has been damaged when the warranted product fails. It may exclude any incidental damages, which could include the cost that a consumer incurs to obtain warranty service, such as towing an automobile or a long-distance telephone call or the time lost from work or transportation costs or the cost of renting a product temporarily to replace the warranted product.

4. *Requirements for Warranty Service.* The warrantor must tell customers where they can go for any warranty service and how to reach these persons or companies. Thus, the warranty must include the *names* and *addresses* of the company and any person or office that customers should contact. It is important to note that they can call *locally* or *toll-free*; then the warrantor can give the *telephone number* instead of the address. If the warrantor wants customers to contact local or regional centers first, the warranty must explain how this can be done.

5. *Customer's Rights Under State Law.* The FTC Rule requires that the warrantor answer the question of how a state law will affect a customer's rights under the warranty. Implied warranty rights and certain other warranty rights may vary from state to state. To solve this disclosure problem, the FTC has adopted the following statement which, at least temporarily, addresses the issue. It must be included in every consumer product warranty: This warranty gives you specific legal rights, and you may also have other rights which vary from state to state.

## INFORMATION REQUIREMENTS — OPTIONAL TERMS AND CONDITIONS

Generally, if the warrantor intends to impose on customers any additional obligations (other than just notifying warrantor that the customer needs service), the warrantor must state in the warranty what these obligations are. Also, if the warrantor intends to establish any other conditions, limitations or terms that the warrantor intends to enforce, the warrantor must state them in the warranty. There cannot be *hidden* requirements or "around the corner" requirements that are not obvious. An example of such a prohibited condition or limitation would be a provision voiding the warranty if the serial number on the product is defaced.

## RESTRICTED DURATION OF IMPLIED WARRANTIES

If the warranty contains a provision that restricts the duration of implied warranties, the FTC rule requires that the warrantor include a statement that *state law* may override such restriction. This statement is required because *some states* prohibit any restrictions on implied warranties. The requirement only applies to limited warranties, because only in a limited warranty can you *restrict* the *duration* of implied warranty.

## POTENTIAL LIMITATIONS OF LIABILITY

If the warranty contains a provision intended to restrict or eliminate the warrantor's potential liability for consequential or incidental damages, the warrantor must include a statement that state law may not allow such a provision. The FTC Rule requires that if there is an attempt to do such in the warranty, the following statement is required:

Some states do not allow the exclusion or limitation of incidental or consequential damages, so the above limitation or exclusion may not apply to you.

## RESTRICTION ON WHO HAS WARRANTY RIGHTS

If the warranty contains a provision that attempts to restrict who has rights under the warranty, the warrantor must include a statement explaining specifically *who is covered.* If the warranty is restricted to the initial owner or the initial purchaser, then the warranty must say so.

## REQUIREMENT FOR CUSTOMER TO USE DISPUTE RESOLUTION MECHANISM BEFORE SUING

If the warrantor intends to *require* the customer to use a dispute resolution mechanism prior to suing under the federal Magnuson-Moss Act for breach of warranty, the FTC Disclosure Rule requires that the following be included:

1. A statement informing the consumer that she can sue under *state law without* first using the mechanism, but that before suing under the federal law the customer *must first* try to resolve the dispute through the dispute mechanism.

2. Information and materials about the dispute mechanism, including the name and address or toll-free telephone number or a form for filing a claim. Obviously if the dispute resolution requirement is not contained in the warranty, then the informal dispute resolution mechanism must comply with the FTC dispute resolution rule, which we mentioned above.

## AVAILABILITY OF WARRANTIES PRIOR TO SALE

As we have mentioned previously, the FTC rule on products costing more than $15 requires that there be *pre-sale availability* of the written warranty terms on consumer products. The rule has provisions that specify what retailers, including mail or catalog and door-to-door sellers, must do to comply with the pre-sale availability of the warranty information. The rule also specifies what the manufacturer must do so that sellers can meet their obligations under the Rule.

## RETAILERS OBLIGATION

When the retailer sells directly to consumers who come to the retailer's place of business to purchase products, the retailer must make written warranties available at the point of sale. You must do this with all written warranties on products you sell, including warranties from manufacturers as well as written warranties that the retailer extends.

The seller must make the warranty readily available to prospective buyers by displaying them in close proximity to the warranted product or by furnishing them upon request prior to sale. The seller must post a sign, which is *prominently* displayed, to let customers know that warranties can be examined upon request. There is no one set way of fulfilling these requirements. There are actually a variety of ways where the consumer can easily read and learn what the warranties say. For instance, a retailer of small products such as watches and electric razors might keep the warranty readily available behind the counter or indexed in a binder near the warranted products. The retailer must post signs that these warranties are available nearby.

## MAIL-ORDER COMPANY REQUIREMENTS

If the retailer accepts orders for warranted consumer products through the mail or by telephone, the mail-order retailer must include in any catalog either the warranty or a statement telling consumers how to get a copy of the warranty. This information should be near the product description or clearly noted on a separate page. If the mail-order dealer chooses the approach of using a separate page, the mail-order dealer must provide a page reference to the warranty statement near the product description.

## DOOR-TO-DOOR SALES COMPANIES

If your company sells warranted products to consumers in their homes or in some place other than your place of business, you must offer the customer copies of the written warranties *before the sale is completed.*

## MANUFACTURER'S REQUIREMENTS

If the manufacturer is making the warranty, the manufacturer must provide retailers of the product with written warranty materials that they will need to meet their requirements as described. There are a number of ways that manufacturers can comply with this and provide the necessary copies. The manufacturer can provide copies of the warranty to be placed in a *binder.* Another manufacturer may provide warranty *stickers, tags, signs* or *posters.* In addition, the manufacturer may print the warranty on the *product's packaging.*

As long as the manufacturer can prove that it has supplied the retailer with the warranty materials, the retailer needs to comply with the rule. Under these conditions, the manufacturer is not legally responsible under the federal Act, if the retailer fails to make the warranties available.

## ADVERTISING WARRANTIES

The federal warranty law that we have been discussing does *not* cover *advertising* warranties. On the other hand, the FTC Act, which generally prohibits "unfair or deceptive acts or practices in or affecting commerce," does cover *warranty advertising.* Therefore, it is a violation of the FTC rule to advertise a warranty *deceptively.*

The FTC does provide a guide known as the *"Guides for Advertising Warranties and Guarantees."* These guides, however, do not cover every aspect of warranty advertising and cannot substitute for consultation with a lawyer who is knowledgeable in warranty advertising matters.

## ADVERTISING WARRANTIES AND PRE-SALE AVAILABILITY

In general, the FTC's Guide advises that if a printed or broadcast ad for a consumer product mentions a warranty and the advertised product is covered by the pre-sale availability rule ($15 Rule), the ad should inform consumers that a copy of the warranty is available for consumers' education *prior* to sale, at the place where the product is sold. Print or broadcast advertisements that mention a warranty on a consumer product that can be purchased through the mail or by telephone should inform the consumer how to get a copy of the warranty prior to sale.

For advertisements on consumer products costing less than $15, the FTC guide does not require any pre-sale availability of such disclosure. Nevertheless, the FTC Act still *prohibits unfair* or *deceptive* acts or practices. So you should be aware of the broad applicability of the general requirement that you tell it straight.

## "SATISFACTION GUARANTEED" ADVERTISEMENTS

The FTC guide advises warrantors that regardless of the price of the product, advertising terms such as "satisfaction guaranteed" or "money-back guarantee" should be used only if the advertiser is willing to provide full refunds to customers when, for any reason, customers return the merchandise.

Furthermore, the guide advises that an ad mentioning a "satisfaction guarantee" or similar offer should inform consumers of any material conditions or limitations on this particular offer. For example, a restriction on the offer to a specified time period, such as 30 days, is a *material condition* that should be *disclosed*.

## LIFETIME WARRANTY ADVERTISING

"Lifetime" warranties or guarantees can be confusing depending on the language used. This occurs because sometimes it is difficult to tell just *whose life* measures the period of coverage. Lifetime could be, for instance, the lifetime of the external product. A muffler in an automobile might be warranted for the lifetime of your automobile. The lifetime might be a life intended to last only as long as the vehicle does not change owners, in the case of the muffler. Thus, in order to avoid any such confusion, if there is any such advertising of "lifetime," the lifetime should be specified (e.g., "as long as you own your car" sez Midas.)

## SERVICE CONTRACTS

A service contract sold or offered in conjunction with the sale of a consumer product is an optional agreement for product service that customers can sometimes buy. These contracts provide additional protection beyond what the warranty offers on the product. "Extended warranties" are what we typically hear when we discuss these types of contracts. There are some differences between *warranties* and *extended service contracts*.

Warranties come with the product and are included in the purchase price. On the other hand, service contracts are agreements that are separate from the purchase contract. They are separate in several ways. They are separate because these service contracts are offered and made *after* the sale of a product or because they cost the customer a *fee* in *addition* to the purchase price of the product.

## SERVICE CONTRACT—TERMS AND CONDITIONS

If a warrantor offers an extended service contract, the Act requires that the seller list conspicuously *all* the terms and conditions in simple and readily understood language. On the other hand, unlike warranties, these service contracts are not required to be titled "*full*" or "*limited*", but must contain the special standard disclosures.

The company that makes the service contract is responsible for ensuring that the terms and conditions are disclosed as required by law. It is not necessarily the responsibility of the seller of the service contract, unless the seller and the maker of the contract are the same company.

## LIMITATIONS OF IMPLIED WARRANTIES—SERVICE CONTRACTS

Sellers of consumer products who offer and make service contracts on their products are prohibited under the Act from disclaiming any implied warranties. However, sellers of consumer products that merely sell service contracts as *agents of service contract companies* (third parties), and who do not themselves extend written warranties, can *disclaim* implied warranties on the products they sell.

## PRODUCT LIABILITY—TORT BASES

We have been emphasizing the advertising and delivery of product quality. This is the high side of the quality picture.

There is also a problem side. It is the liability that erupts when someone gets injured as a result of a defective product.

In the beginning of this we discussed a business's potential liability based upon express warranty, implied warranty of merchantability, implied warranty of fitness for a particular purpose, and the Magnuson-Moss Warranty Act.

Tort liability for product liability can arise from additional bases such as these:

1. Intentional acts.
2. Negligent acts.
3. Strict liability.

Intentional torts include acts such as assault or battery. These types of torts are not generally seen in the product area, though there is such a potential. If an individual intentionally made a product defective, the intentional nature would clearly arise.

Negligent manufacturing, inspecting and handling of products does arise from time to time.

## Duty To Warn

A manufacturer or merchant may have a duty to warn potential buyers of reasonable foreseeable dangers given the use of the product.

## Improper Design

Product liability may arise if there are avoidable design defects. A product may pose an unreasonable risk of harm because of an improper design.

These are defenses to these tort bases for liability from product injury: Negligence must involve behavior below the reasonable person level. Also the damage must be proximately caused by the negligent behavior.

There may be *no duty to warn* if there is no reason to foresee that a likely user would be unaware of the danger. If there is an obvious danger, the user might be expected to avoid the danger.

Improper *design* may *not* create product liability if there is no reasonable method of making the product safe and if the product creates some benefit for users. There may be no liability if the manufacturer has met current state-of-the-art standards. Also, some courts will quash liability if the benefits to society outweigh the risks from the product.

Strict *liability* is liability regardless of the fault of the actor. This type of liability can arise when a merchant sells a product that is defective yet is sold to a user. Usually the product must be unreasonably dangerous and must be the proximate (foreseeable) cause of the damage.

## LEGAL REQUIREMENTS

Just as it is important to keep up customer good will, it is also important to know the legal requirements to meet the Magnuson-Moss Warranty Act. It is ultimately best for any warrantor or retailer to avoid potential litigation. A number of recent best- sellers on successful companies point toward providing exceptional service or going the extra mile and a half. The theme of these books is that quality and service are these companies.

Although this chapter is pointing out the "don'ts" as much as the "dos," the best "do" is to attempt to provide the best service you can for your customers without going broke doing it. Many times, providing the best service may actually produce greater sales and leave more money for the bottom line than might be the result of providing less service.

# CHAPTER 10

## ANTITRUST LAWS

# CHAPTER 10

# ANTITRUST LAWS

Most of us are aware of the implications of the types of serious antitrust behavior which have made the newspapers. There are, however, many types of specific instances of antitrust behavior that are much more subtle. A discussion of such behavior is beneficial to any business owner.

It is ironic that the grandiose forms of antitrust behavior are not generally within the power of the small business owner or manager to *undertake*. The small business owner or manager cannot usually monopolize or even attempt to monopolize a particular market. Nevertheless, many other types of anti-competitive behavior come within the scope of these laws. You could be a victim. Know the law.

The *common law* had, as part of its tradition, the goal to protect *competition* and to prohibit *unreasonable restraints* of *trade*. It even prohibited monopolies.

Most of us have heard of the Sherman Antitrust Act passed in 1890. This law has been one of the most important forces in our government's attempt to maintain competition. It also allows individuals to act to protect against anti-competitive behavior. The Sherman Act was enacted to supplement the remedies provided by the common law.

In addition to the Sherman Act, the Clayton Act (1914) was passed because of perceived failings and deficiencies of the Sherman Act. Because business was growing larger and larger in size and in proportion to the entire economy, Congress passed the Clayton Act in 1914. Later, in 1936, Congress enacted the Robinson-Patman Act, which focuses more specifically on price discrimination and also on mergers and acquisitions.

The Federal Trade Commission Act of 1914 not only created the Federal Trade Commission, but also gave it its mandate to protect competition, to prevent unfair competition and also for deny businesses the ability to use unfair trade methods and unfair and deceptive acts in doing business.

## SHERMAN ANTITRUST ACT

The Sherman Antitrust Act contains *criminal* (as well as civil) penalties for individuals or entities who violate it. For individuals who violate the Act, the maximum imprisonment is up to three years, and fines range up to $100,000. For corporations, there are fines of up to $1 million. New federal sentencing guidelines will apply to corporations and other legal entities for antitrust violations.

One of the most intimidating features is the *trebling* of damages in civil suits under this Act. Therefore, by law, there is a punitive effect via damages if an individual or entity has violated this law.

Assume a company is responsible for price-fixing and the amount of overcharges was $1 million. The plaintiff(s) who prove in the antitrust suit that they paid the $1 million in overcharges can collect $3 million plus reasonable attorney's fees and court costs.

An additional item you should note is the distance a potential claimant can be from the transaction. A plaintiff can collect overcharges only if the plaintiff is a direct purchaser who paid the overcharges, even if the overcharge was passed on to an indirect purchaser. However, a number of states have passed laws allowing indirect purchasers to bring suit for overcharges.

## RESTRAINTS OF TRADE

The Sherman Act provides that "every contract, combination in the form of trust or otherwise, or conspiracy, in restraint of trade or commerce among the several states, or with foreign nations, is declared to be illegal . . . ."

There are several important features of the restraint of trade prohibition and the Sherman Act. First, the courts essentially look to invalidate those types of restraints of trade that are *unreasonable*. There are essentially two areas of unreasonable behavior. One type of behavior the courts have declared to be illegal *per se*. Any type of behavior that has a definite, "pernicious" anti-competitive effect is considered to be *illegal per se*. A defendant will not be allowed to defend its practice as "reasonable" no matter what the particular circumstances happen to be. These behaviors only hinder or stifle competition.

## PER *SE* TYPES OF VIOLATIONS

These particular types of restraints in general fit into the following categories:

1. Price-fixing, whether it be done "vertically," by a manufacturer all the way downstream to the retailer (generally referred to as "resale price maintenance") or "horizontally," meaning among competitors at the same level of competition.

2. Tie-in arrangements. This is a condition imposed by a seller whereby, for an individual to buy *one product*, he or she *must buy* a *related* or *unrelated* product which the individual does not want to buy. It sounds like "I have the only decent 45-inch TVs in town, and if you want to buy my 45-inch TVs, you must also buy some of my unpopular rabbit-ear antennas." There is a definite element of *coercion* involved;

3. Boycotts (refusals to deal). These can be vertical— where the manufacturer is attempting to restrict one or more of its distributors from dealing with a particular business—or horizontal—where potential competitors in the same market are boycotting a certain manufacturer. There are exceptions to court application of this "per se" rule. Some courts restrict the use of this rule to some horizontal group boycotts.

4. Horizontal or territorial market division. This is a condition whereby potential competitors are splitting up markets.

There are other types of competitive behavior which the courts analyze on the basis of their being *reasonable* versus *unreasonable* and are not illegal per se. Here, the courts use the *"rule of reason"*; that is, is the challenged activity actually pro-competition and therefore "reasonable"?

The "rule of reason" is applied to deem illegal those restraints of trade that injure the public interest by unduly restricting competition or by unduly obstructing trade. The rule can be applied not only to ban a detrimental effect, but also to ban an "evil" purpose.

The "rule of reason" is applied to exclusive dealing arrangements, requirements contracts and vertical territorial or customer selection. Exclusive dealing agreements generally require a buyer or

---

## *POWER POINTS* _____

▶ Small businesses are not generally able to monopolize a market. Small businesses may be victims of such practices, however.

▶ Small businesses are capable of restraints of trade, including price-fixing, market division and boycotts. Restraints of trade range from the obvious to the sublime, and come in innumerable shapes and flavors.

seller to deal only with the other party on an exclusive basis. These particular arrangements are generally subjected to the "rule of reason" test by the courts, and are not automatically forbidden.

Requirements contracts exist where an individual supplies *all* of the requirements of a particular user of their product or service on an exclusive basis. The courts usually use the rule of reason to determine the legality of these arrangements. Vertical territorial agreements might involve allocating territories to distributors, which must be reasonable. Allocating or selecting customers in a vertical situation must also meet the *rule of reason*.

## CONSCIOUS PARALLELISM

Behavior that is possibly legal, but is subjected to severe scrutiny, is called *conscious parallelism*. This exists where there is no express agreement among the parties to fix prices, but the parties seem to be acting in concert. If a party initiates a price change and the other competing entities follow suit by changing their prices to the same competitive level, there might be no antitrust violation. But you never know if there is some connection that is not obvious. It is not illegal to follow a price leader, but you must do everything possible to ensure that your activities are unilateral responses to competitive situations.

## MONOPOLIES

The Sherman Act makes it illegal for any person or corporation to monopolize or attempt to monopolize or combine or conspire with any other person or persons to monopolize any part of the trade or commerce among the several states or with foreign nations. Although small business owners are not typically in a position of monopolizing any particular market, they certainly can be the victim of someone else's monopolization of a market.

There are a couple of additional factors that come into play in determining whether there is a violation. First, the Sherman Act requires that there be some *intent* to monopolize or create monopoly power. In addition there must also be an attempt to

acquire or maintain or *exercise* that monopoly power. A violation cannot happen by accident or by vigorous competition. It takes something *in addition to* monopoly power to violate the law. There must be some evil attempt to create or expand an existing monopoly.

What do we mean by monopoly power? Generally it means the power to control prices or exclude competition. Anyone can raise prices to artificially high levels. However, the business owner might go bankrupt as a result of it because no one buys the product. But if someone is in a position of raising prices to such high levels and *getting* the price without lowering his market share very much, then he may be in a position of having monopoly power. Also, an entity can *exclude* competition because it takes an awful lot of money to enter that particular business. An entity might be able to shut a competitor down as a result of a multitude of techniques. Under these circumstances, the entity may qualify for having *monopoly power*.

It is also important to determine what is the *relevant market*. By market we mean the geographical area of sales of a certain product (and that product's possible substitutes). We also examine the types of products that compete with this product. Here's an example of the latter. Silver may be ideal for certain types of products in electronics. But the price of silver might become so exorbitant that there are competing metals which can be substituted for it at some price. Therefore, we must look at whatever types of products could be substituted for this product at certain price levels. The analysis is certainly much more complex than most of us can deal with on a day-to-day basis.

## ATTEMPTS TO MONOPOLIZE

Anyone, including an 8-year old lemonade entrepreneur, can attempt to monopolize a particular market. What the courts generally look at is not only specific intent to monopolize, but also the probability that the person or persons are capable of doing it. In other words, the 8-year old lemonade entrepreneur who controls only one city block probably would not fit any category. This young tiger would not run the risk of violating the monopoly provisions of the antitrust laws.

## MERGERS AND INTERLOCKING DIRECTORATES

*Mergers.* The Clayton Act was passed to strengthen the Sherman Antitrust Act, as we said. As time goes by, Congress has a chance to evaluate the weaknesses of particular statutes. When continued abuses occur, we sometimes see new legislation to close another loophole or abuse.

The Clayton Act outlawed tie-in, contracts and also certain exclusive dealing agreements (related to tie-in). Exclusive dealing exists when someone is required to buy a particular product(s) exclusively from the seller. If the buyer cannot deal in competitive products or services, the agreement may be illegal.

The Clayton Act also attempted to protect competition that might be lessened by *mergers* and *acquisitions* (a corporation purchasing stock of another company). It is certainly one way of lessening competition: Buy out your competition. Essentially there are three types of mergers that the law would examine. One is a horizontal merger. A *horizontal* merger is the purchase of a *competitor*. A *vertical* merger would be where an entity, for instance a manufacturer, might purchase one of its distributors. It might also involve purchasing the manufacturer, and so forth.

A *conglomerate* merger exists when an entity purchases a *non-competitor*. The Clayton Act examines these also. An automobile manufacturer might purchase an unrelated business such as a computing firm. The resulting octopus may be able to control capital sources. This gargantuan beast might be able to lessen competition for capital. So conglomerate mergers can display anti-competitive behavior. The law is essentially aimed at preventing a company from lessening competition by purchasing a competitor or other companies, which can jointly hurt competition.

*Interlocking Directorates.* It is amazing that Congress was able to see the potential problems long before our society became as complex as it is: It passed a law prohibiting (under certain circumstances) a person from being a director on the board of competing corporations.

If an individual were to sit on the boards of two potentially competing companies, even if the companies might not purchase each other, they could be combined indirectly. With a unified board of directors, the two or more corporations could act in coordination to lessen competition. So the law prohibits this.

## PRICING PROBLEMS

Congress concluded that certain pricing schemes could damage competition. Such schemes could also help create or enhance monopolies. Let's examine some of the problems the Robinson-Patman Act addresses.

*Predatory Pricing.* As a general rule, it is illegal for a seller to sell his products at lower prices in one area than he sells those same goods in other areas to eliminate competition. It is also illegal for a seller to sell goods at a price that is below cost (determined in various ways) for the purpose of destroying competition.

*Price Discrimination.* It is amazing to see the ways individuals have dreamed up to take advantage of our economy and of particular competitors. The Robinson-Patman Act, passed in 1936, was designed to strengthen the laws that then existed to reach certain types of price discrimination then practiced by large companies to the detriment of smaller purchasers, which did not seem to be covered by any of the previous Acts. Certain types of price discrimination clearly created unfair competition. Thus, the Robinson-Patman Act made it unlawful for any seller of goods to *discriminate* in price between different purchasers who were purchasing similar quantities of goods of like grade and quality. There must be more than one sale to two competing buyers in interstate commerce, or at least having a substantial effect on interstate commerce.

Also, the Act applies only to transactions involving goods, not services.

Where the effect of this price discrimination would *substantially lessen competition* or might end up tending to create a monopoly or would hurt competition, the behavior would be potentially illegal. Thus, the courts generally look for injury to competition as a result of price discrimination, although a few situations of obvious discrimination may rise almost to the level of *per se* illegality.

One of the types of behavior that are prohibited is the discriminating granting of a commission, brokerage fee, or any other type of compensation or allowance or discount, *except for services* that were *actually rendered* in connection with the sale or purchase of goods. This can be likened to commercial bribery, which may be prohibited by the Robinson-Patman Act.

An example of this might involve competing supermarkets. The produce department might be of such a size that it could extract *more than normal discounts* from a distributor. Or the offending supermarket might be able to force a manufacturer to give abnormal discounts or be shut out of a significant piece of a market. If this chain market could extract greater-than-normal discounts (in excess of what economy of scale would yield), there is a potential violation of the Robinson-Patman Act. This behavior could also include subterfuges.

Let's look at an example. Suppose two different retailers can purchase a certain grade of garden hoses for $7 per hose in lots of 25. Further assume that the wholesaler gives only one of the two retailers an advertising rebate of $1 per hose. The nominal price for 25 hoses is the same, but the actual price for the two retailers might be different. If the advertising allowance was a sham, then the price discrimination might be illegal.

A seller cannot discriminate in pricing. Assume there are two supermarket chains in one market. The seller must generally offer the goods for the same price based on comparable volume.

A manufacturer which sells to only one particular market can generally set the price at anything he or she wants. On the other hand, if the manufacturer has two or more customers, similarly situated, in the same market or different markets, then the customers must pay the same price for the same quantity (in general). Remember, prices can be different if there are cost savings as a result of economic factors.

## DEFENSES

There are several defenses to price discrimination allegations and behavior. We have referred above to two of the most important ones. Let's summarize these two:

1. *The Cost Justification Defense*

It is difficult to determine "cost," since it involves direct and indirect costs as well as the many methods of determining these. In a word, proving "cost" justification for pricing practices may safeguard these practices, but this is no mean task.

2. *Meeting Competition*

If a seller acts in good faith (like a prudent business person) in meeting competition by matching the competitor's low price or service, the seller can act safely.

## REMEDIES

The previous Acts allow any business that has been injured to sue under these particular Acts. The types of remedies available and the parties to whom they are available are important.

### PROPER PARTY TO SUE

Not anyone can sue under the antitrust acts. The courts have taken a position that a person must be *directly* offended by illegal behavior to have *standing to sue*. Thus, for a party to seek treble damages, injunctive relief or other remedies provided under the antitrust laws, the party must be directly affected by the illegal behavior.

If you perceive that you have been injured as a result of a violation, ask a couple of questions. Are you in the target area and have you received a "direct injury" as a result of any of the behavior? Part of the problem is that an individual may be *injured* but be *two* or *three* layers *down the line* from the illegal behavior. That individual might not be able to *sue* the party who is violating the law. Also, a *competitor* does not have standing to sue for a price-fixing conspiracy, horizontal or vertical (even if it is a *per se* violation), unless the price fixed pursuant to the conspiracy is predatory.

## CLASS ACTIONS

One of the additional remedies under federal antitrust law includes the class action. This is certainly a means of maximizing the effect of the antitrust laws. If a company is fixing prices on widgets, plywood, shoestrings or any other type of product, the idea of 10 persons suing may not be a threat. The amount of dollars involved may not be great. But if *all* the potential victims can be included in one lawsuit, the deterrent effect becomes much greater. The class action is an additional threat to keep the marketplace competitive.

## STATUTE OF LIMITATIONS

With regard to the federal acts, the statute of limitations is generally four years. In other words, an individual has approximately four years from the time of the offending behavior to file suit. A cause of action generally arises at the time that an individual is *first injured* as a result of a violation of the federal antitrust laws.

Under the federal laws, this four-year period can be tolled, or in effect stopped. If the Department of Justice or the Federal Trade Commission has proceeded civilly or criminally against any particular party, the statute of limitations can be frozen at that time.

There are several remedies that come into play in the antitrust arena:

1. *Treble Damages.* These laws generally provide for tripling damages that a court or a jury has determined. For example, if there has been some illegal price-fixing which has raised the cost of widgets a total of $500,000, the courts triple this amount. The amount of damages becomes $1.5 million. The trebling is not something the jury does. The court will automatically treble damages, along with costs and reasonable attorney's fees to the prevailing plaintiff.

2. *Injunctive Relief.* The courts also allow the plaintiffs to be able to restrict the defendant's illegal behavior in the future. The court can say, "Thou shalt not do this anymore. If you do it again, you will be violating a court order, and that would be a potential criminal act."

3. *Divestiture.* In the case of mergers or acquisitions that will substantially lessen competition or tend to create a monopoly, the courts can require that any assets or businesses or stock which the offending party has acquired be given up.

4. *Additional Items.* Attorney's fees and court costs can also be granted under these laws to the prevailing party.

5. *Criminal Liability.* As we have mentioned, there are also criminal liabilities that can attach to behavior which violates the antitrust laws.

*Exemptions From the Federal Antitrust Laws.* Though this is not terribly important to the small business owner or manager, it would not hurt to be aware of some exemptions from the antitrust laws. You will get some idea of politics. They include:

1. *Professional Sports.* There is an exception for professional baseball and two narrowly defined statutory exemptions from the antitrust laws. Generally, however, the antitrust laws apply to all professional sports.

2. *Organized Labor.* The Clayton Act contains a specific exemption for labor organizations from the antitrust laws. This exemption can be lost if the labor union acts in conjunction with a non-labor organization to violate the antitrust laws.

3. *Insurance Companies.* In 1945 Congress passed the McCarran-Ferguson Act, which grants a limited antitrust exemption to the business of insurance. This was a federal attempt to defer to the states. Congress wanted to let the states regulate insurance, and they have essentially done so since then. Of course, the way the "business of insurance" is defined is not quite as broad as it might seem. The courts look at specific factors to decide what is the "business of insurance." Not everything involving insurance is exempt.

4. *Limited Exemption for Agricultural and Fishing Cooperatives.* Agricultural and fishing cooperatives have been given limited statutory ex-

emptions. Thus, producers of agricultural products or catchers and processors of fishing products are given a limited exemption to organize and operate cooperatives. The purposes of the cooperatives may involve jointly processing, handling or marketing the product. This allows them to exchange among cooperative members information, product and marketing data. This exemption can be lost by over stepping its bounds.

5. *Soft-Drink Limited Exemption.* There is a soft-drink exemption. It is very limited in fashion. It does, however, allow soft-drink manufacturers to have certain vertical territorial restraints in their industry. The act which is called the "Soft Drink Inter-Brand Competition Act," permits soft-drink bottlers through vertical territorial restraints to limit the right of licensees to sell particular soft-drink products in a defined geographical area. It allows soft-drink manufacturers to limit what would be considered interbrand competition. Thus, two bottlers of the same soft drink may not compete with each other. Courts apply the "rule of reason" to this act.

6. *Learned Professions.* Actually, the courts have over the past few years left very little of an exemption for any learned profession from the antitrust laws. In other words, doctors, lawyers, dentists, engineers, opticians, pharmacists, architects are not exempt from the antitrust laws. I believe the public has benefitted from this new competition. Several studies, including one by the Federal Trade Competition, seem to indicate that competition among "learned professions" is healthy for the buying public.

7. *Government-Regulated Industries.* Some of the activities, but not necessarily every activity of regulated industries, may be exempt from the antitrust laws. The antitrust laws may be restrained from application under some regulated conditions, but only to the minimum extent necessary, where the laws and any needed governmental purposes are in conflict. Thus, an electric power company may have no antitrust exemption from its practices when selling appliances. On the other hand, it is usually protected from the antitrust laws when it charges its customers utility rates approved by the regulatory body that, oversees and approves such rates.

## FEDERAL TRADE COMMISSION

In 1914 Congress created the Federal Trade Commission (FTC) by means of the Federal Trade Commission Act. One of the essential provisions of this Act was for the FTC to prevent "unfair methods of competition in commerce and unfair or deceptive acts or practices in commerce."

Along with this charge, the FTC was given the power to investigate potential violations, hold hearings, and establish certain industrywide rules and regulations. The FTC has the power to issue "cease-and-desist orders," which are enforceable in the federal courts. It also has the power to issue regulations in conjunction with broad based studies of the practices in an industry. The FTC can also proceed to federal court to stop particular behaviors that are considered offensive to its charge. It can stop acts that result in unfair methods of competition which are unfair or deceptive acts or practices.

The consumer does *not* have a right to sue a defendant based upon the FTC Act. The FTC Act gives the power to the Commission itself to enforce it. The FTC may promulgate rules and regulations requiring certain practices. An example involves "rain checks" in retail stores. If an offender is caught by a private individual, this individual does *not* have a cause of action against that violator, the FTC alone can act upon it. Needless to say, the FTC's resources are limited. It is unable to act on most of the complaints it receives. An individual may have a cause of action under a state unfair trade practice act.

In summary, the Federal Trade Commission has examined and issued statements and sometimes regulations on false and misleading advertising, on passing or pawning off goods, on lotteries, gambling schemes, false or misleading labeling of products, false or misleading comments about competitors' goods, false or misleading descriptive names, false or misleading testimonials, and many other unfair trade practices. It has coordinated power in a number of areas with the Department of Justice.

## THE UNITED STATES DEPARTMENT OF JUSTICE

The U.S. Department of Justice (DOJ), as well as the FTC, can move civilly against particular violators of the antitrust laws. There is some overlapping of jurisdiction when considering *civil* antitrust suits. The DOJ, however, has sole jurisdiction when federal *criminal* actions are taken against alleged violators.

The antitrust laws, at least in the area of unfair trade practices and restraint of trade, can affect the small business person directly. A small business can be a victim or an offender. A small business can occasionally have problems with pricing and advertising. If you have any questions, contact the FTC for its guidelines in these areas.

# CHAPTER 11

COMMERCIAL PAPER

# CHAPTER 11

# COMMERCIAL PAPER

Part and parcel of doing business is borrowing or lending money. It may be from a bank or to a customer. There is a large market in commercial paper. There are certain fairly strict requirements that have to be met. The reason you must know these is to allow you to take advantage of the favorable provisions of the rules of commercial paper.

We are not going to look into the UCC provisions in detail. Most small business owners and managers sign promissory notes from time to time. You will have checking accounts or possibly issue drafts. Three of the four forms of commercial paper (notes, checks and drafts) come into play often. Even the fourth (certificates of deposit) is used in business. Let's take a look at some of the general requirements.

## DIFFERENT TYPES OF INSTRUMENTS

It is important for you to know the different types of instruments. They are: Bank checks, promissory notes, drafts and certificates of deposit.

In one sense the types may be fairly familiar to you and in another sense they may not be. Common sense will not suffice when dealing with UCC endorsement requirements. So take heed.

## BANK CHECK

In any checking transaction, we are typically dealing with three parties. That is why a check is sometimes called a *three-party instrument*. Who are the three parties and what is the effect of it?

First, your company is the account holder. If your company is going to pay the rent for this month, you make out a check payable to the

## BANK CHECK

| | |
|---|---|
| Bradley C. Drawer | No. 323 |
| | December 3, 1990 |

PAY TO THE ORDER OF  Payee Credit Company*********************** $ 259.00****

*Two hundred fifty nine and no/100********************  dollars

Drawee National Bank

*Bradley C. Drawer*

landlord. Your company is the *drawer* of the check. The landlord becomes the *payee*, and you draw it on your bank. Your bank is known as the *drawee*.

Your company is ordering the bank (although it is not a true legal order) to pay your landlord a certain sum of money to the "order of" this particular person or entity.

Typically a check is not supposed to be a *time* negotiable instrument. It is supposed to be payable on *demand*. But a check can in effect be turned into a time instrument.

How do you do this? You can *post-date* the check, meaning put a date, for instance, of one month from now. If today is July 1, you might put August 1. Theoretically the check is not payable until that particular date.

The bank is your agent. The bank is not necessarily obligated to pay the *payee* (landlord), despite the fact that we assume the bank will pay it. This might shock you, but the bank has a contract with you but not with your landlord. So it can snub your landlord, though it may be violating its contract with you.

What happens if the bank does not pay one of your company's checks. Assume your check is made out properly and your account has sufficient funds to pay it. The bank might be liable to your company for damages for not paying the check. The bank is not liable for damages to the third party (landlord).

## STOP PAYMENT ORDER

It is possible to stop payment on a check, but if the bank does not do so, your company may still lose. First, an oral stop payment is good for *14 business* days. A written stop payment is good for *six months*, but each of these must be *renewed* for it to continue. Never assume, if the check is still outstanding, that you can rest on one stop payment to solve the problem.

In addition, you have to give the bank *sufficient time* to disseminate the information among its branches or within the bank itself. You may actually beat a check to your bank to issue a stop payment, but the bank may not be responsible for having paid it if you have not given it enough time to disseminate the stop payment information. Also if the bank ignores your stop payment, the UCC might still shield the bank from your company's loss if your company had to pay the debt anyway.

## Check Certification

A check can be certified at the request of one or two parties. You as the *drawer* can request certification. A *holder*, including a payee, can also so request.

On many occasions a supplier or property seller may require that you pay them with a *certified* check. For this check to be certified at your request, you (drawer of check) take it to your bank. A bank official will note that on your account and immediately pull the money out of your account. A bank official will note on the check that it has been *certified*. This adds the bank as an additional party along with you. A Holder's Request is one who is liable for paying this check.

A check can also be certified by a *payee* or other holder of the check. Let's assume your landlord did

---

## *POWER POINTS*

▶ An oral stop payment order is effective for 14 days.

▶ A written stop payment order is effective for six months.

▶ Remember to *renew* when appropriate.

## PROMISSORY NOTE - BEARER PAPER

$ 500.00                              Citytown, PA                    December 3, 1990

**Sixty days** after date, for value received, the undersigned promises to pay BEARER,
**Five Hundred Dollars** with interest from date at the rate of **12** percent per annum
(computed on 360-day year and actual days) with interest payable at maturity.

*Mike Maker*

not want to cash the check yet, but wanted to make sure there was sufficient money in the account. He or she could go to the bank and pay a fee to have the bank *certify* that the funds are available. In this case, if the third party or the payee requests certification, your company will no longer be liable. Of course, the money is taken out of your company's account immediately. Nevertheless, your company is no longer liable on that instrument unless there has been some fraud or other irregularity.

### Cashier's Check

This is a check which is drawn by a bank on itself. It differs from a certified check that is accepted by the bank, but drawn on your account.

## PROMISSORY NOTE

The most common form of negotiable instrument is the promissory note. A promissory note is generally referred to as a two-party instrument because the creation of it involves only two parties. One party is the maker, the one who will owe the money. The *maker* is the one who is legally obligated to pay the amount due on the note. The other party is the payee—the person who will receive the money. The *payee* is at least the person who is the first-named individual or bearer who has received the instrument when it is issued.

This promissory note is payable to bearer. Thus, anyone has possession of it is the "bearer."

The following promissory note is payable to the *order* of particular payee. This is the type of note you should note (to be a bit redundant).

## PROMISSORY NOTE - ORDER PAPER

$ 500.00                              Citytown, PA                    December 3, 1990

**Sixty days** after date, for value received, the undersigned promises to pay
to the order of   **T. E. Smith**
**Five Hundred Dollars** with interest from date at the rate of **12** percent per annum
(computed on 360-day year and actual days) with interest payable at maturity.

*Mike Maker*

## DRAFT OR BILL OF EXCHANGE

$ __700.00__    _____Los Angeles, CA_____    _____December 3, 1990_____

__Sixty days after date_____

Pay to the order of Payee __Payee Whole Suppliers__

__Seven hundred and no/100_____ dollars

For value received and account of_____

Accepted at _____ on _____, 19_____

Payable at __Bank of Drawee__    __Wholesale Corporation_____

Acceptor is __*Tom Banker, V-P*__    By: __*C.E.O. Smith*_____

## DRAFT OR BILL OF EXCHANGE

A draft or bill of exchange is a three-party instrument that contains an unconditional order to pay. The drawer (who has the money or the credit) orders a second person (the drawee, e.g., a bank) to pay a definite (certain) sum of money to a third person (payee, e.g., a supplier). This draft can be payable upon demand or at a particular future date.

## CERTIFICATE OF DEPOSIT

A certificate of deposit (CD) is a two-party instrument. It is between a financial institution and the registered owner at a determinable future date.

CD's are sold by banks, savings banks and savings & loans. Large CD's may be negotiable.

## CERTIFICATE OF DEPOSIT

FIRST SOLID NATIONAL BANK    NUMBER 8726

_____Washington, D.C._____    _____December 3, 1990_____

This is to certify that __M.Y. Account_____

has deposited in this bank $__500.00____.

__Five hundred and no/100_____

Payable to __Mr. M.Y. Account_____

or order __3 months_____ after date above with interest

at the rate of ___ percent per annum from date above.

Due __March 1, 1991_____

*I.M. Cautious*
President
First Solid National Bank

## LETTER OF CREDIT

This is not a note or a draft but is noteworthy. It is a written instrument that is often issued by a bank for a customer's benefit. The issuer promises to honor drafts or other instruments written against the customer's credit amount of this letter of credit.

## REQUIREMENTS FOR COMMERCIAL PAPER

For commercial paper to be negotiable (different from a contract) there are certain requirements it must meet. Commercial paper can give to the holder or bearer enforcement rights that are greater than you would have under a contract. I'd like you to pay attention since this could affect your bottom line.

Negotiable commercial paper must meet the following conditions:

1. It must be written in permanent form and movable.

2. It must be signed by the maker for a note or the drawer of a draft. This condition can also be met by a facsimile or stamped signature. It can be signed by an agent but make sure the company is named and the agent's title or position is clear.

3. It must contain an unconditional promise or order to pay. It cannot be contingent upon some event or an outside document. If payment is to be made only from a particular personal bank account, it is non-negotiable.

4. It must be payable in a sum certain. The amount must be calculable from the face of the instrument.

5. It must be payable in money. Bushels of wheat or illegal currencies will not suffice.

6. It must be payable upon demand or at some future definite time.

7. It must be payable to the *order of* an entity or person or it must be payable to the *bearer* (holder) of the document.

## NEGOTIABILITY

It is important to understand the concept of negotiability as it pertains to commercial paper. It does *not* mean negotiating as we typically think of it. We do not mean bargaining or haggling with give and take. Negotiability means meeting certain requirements of the UCC so that a holder of commercial paper has a greater likelihood of being paid. If a person has negotiated commercial paper, his recipient is *more* than an assignee (as under a contract). An assignee *only* has somebody else's rights assigned to him or her under a contract. Am assignee gets no *greater* rights than the party who assigns (assignor) her rights to the recipient (assignor).

A recipient of commercial paper through negotiation can be a "holder in due course" (HDC). An HDC may have *greater* rights than would an *assignee* or mere holder who gets rights from another person under a contract.

## NEGOTIATION VERSUS ASSIGNMENT

One of the important things we mentioned previously is that commercial paper (given the proper provisions in creating it) can attain special status. If commercial paper contains the right stuff, it can be transferred by "negotiation." This method transfers both the *title* and the *ownership*. The question is, what does it take to do this? Remember, an *assignee* has more stumbling blocks on the road to payment than someone who gets a note by *negotiation*.

Let's look at what you need to get that favored status under commercial paper.

## HOLDER IN DUE COURSE

One of our goals in this chapter is to get you to focus on the special status of a holder in due course (HDC). If you are a holder in due course as opposed to an ordinary holder, you are more likely to get paid on the commercial instrument you are holding. Your bottom line is your focus here.

A HDC can get paid regardless of the maker or drawer contractual claims or defenses. If one party does not perform under a contract, the other party might be relieved of having to pay under the contract.

Assume Part *A* has agreed to paint Party *B*'s house for $1,000. If Party *A* fails to paint the house, then Party *B* does not have to pay Party *A*. Thus if Party *A* has *assigned* to Party *C* his right to payment from Party *B* for a reasonable amount, Party *B* still does not have to pay Party *C*. Why? Since Party *A* failed to paint the house, Party *B* has a *defense* which is also effective against Party *C*.

Now let's bring in a HDC. Assume Party *B* signs a promissory note payable to the *order* of Party *A* for the $1,000 at the time of closing the deal with Party *B*. Now Party *A* negotiates this note to Party *C* by selling her (Party *C*) the note for a reasonable amount. One week later, Party *A* fails to paint Party *B*'s house.

Party *C* now calls upon Party *B* to get paid. Guess what? Party *B* has to pay Party *C* if Party *C* is a HDC.

Now that I've gotten your interest, let's look at the requirements for a HDC. To be holder in due course, you must meet these provisions:

1. You must give value.

2. You must take the instrument in good faith.

3. You must take the instrument without knowing or being on notice that it is overdue, or has been dishonored or that anyone has a claim or defense against payment.

## PERSONAL DEFENSES

A HDC will get paid despite the following potential defenses; which are often called personal defenses:

1. Failure of or failure to pay consideration (e.g., failure to paint *B*'s house).

2. Breach of contract.

3. Breach of warranty (e.g., failure of the goods to be of reasonable quality).

4. Fraud in the inducement (e.g., salesman's misrepresentation).

5. Ordinary duress which is not a serious, bodily threat.

6. Undue influence exercised against a person who is subservient or dependent economically or psychologically.

7. Failure to consent to deliver the instrument.

## REAL DEFENSES

On the other hand, there are some defenses which are effective even against a HDC. Watch out for these. These defenses are:

1. Forgery of the signature of makers, drawers or endorsers.

2. Material alterations of the instrument, including the amount, date, parties or any information which form part of its terms or conditions. The instrument can be enforced to the extent of its pre-alteration state for a HDC.

3. Fraud in the execution. This involves fraudulently misrepresenting the nature of the instrument such as getting someone to sign a note while hiding part of its provisions. This rare, but happens occasionally.

4. Void (attempted) transactions, including illegality (e.g., part of a drug deal) or extreme duress.

5. Lack of capacity which results in a disaffirmance (e.g., a minor who disaffirms a contract under state law).

6. Discharge in bankruptcy.

### Holder Through a Holder in Due Course

There is another way for you to get the benefits of a HDC even if you cannot meet all of the requirements for a HDC. This is sometimes called a *shelter* provision since you can be sheltered from some defenses because you have gotten the instrument through a HDC.

To qualify you must trace your ownership to a HDC (e.g., a HDC gave you the note). In addition, if you previously held this note, you were not a tainted holder. If you were on notice of a potential defense or claim at the time you initially acquired the note, you could not subsequently clear up your problem by coming back into the title chain.

## FTC MODIFIES HOLDER IN DUE COURSE PROTECTION

The U.S. Federal Trade Commission (FTC) has modified the HDC rules which involve the sale or lease of goods or services to *consumers*.

If the consumer is the maker of any note or drawer of any draft issued to purchase consumer goods or services, the HDC "special status" is severely cut back if not eliminated. The HDC reverts practically to the position of an *assignee*. The FTC rule requires a statement in any consumer commercial paper to contain language preserving the consumer's claims and defenses.

This rule requires this language:

---

NOTICE

ANY HOLDER OF THIS CONSUMER CREDIT CONTRACT IS SUBJECT TO ALL CLAIMS AND DEFENSES THAT THE DEBTOR COULD ASSERT AGAINST THE SELLER OF GOODS OR SERVICES OB-TAINED PURSUANT HERETO OR WITH THE PROCEEDS HEREOF. RECOVERY HEREUNDER BY THE DEBTOR SHALL NOT EXCEED AMOUNT. PAID BY THE DEBTOR HEREUNDER. IF THE SELLER REFERS CONSUMERS TO A CREDITOR OR IS AFFILIATED WITH THE SELLER, THEN THE SAME NOTICE BUT WITH THE WORDS "OBTAINED PURSUANT HERETO OR" MUST BE USED BY THE SELLER.

---

## SOME STATE LAWS PROTECT CONSUMERS

Several states have passed laws to protect consumers in a manner similar to the FTC rule. Several of these laws eliminate a holder in due course's superior posture when faced with personal defenses available to the consumer (maker of a note.) Usually these laws relate to consumer promissory notes and drafts, but not to checks.

In addition many courts deny finance companies HDC status if these are closely affiliated to the retailers who see the consumer goods.

## PROMISES TO PAY

Promissory notes and certificates of deposit (CD) are considered in the same vein as promises to pay. These need involve only *two parties*. If Party B has borrowed money from Party A, Party B can sign a *promissory note* and say, "I promise to pay *to the order of* Party A a certain number of dollars on a certain date at a certain annual interest rate." The analogy is the same for a CD.

## ORDERS TO PAY

First let's take a look at drafts and checks. They are considered *orders to pay*. In a draft or a check, Party A is owed some money by Party B. Party A owes money to Party C. Therefore, Party A would like Party B to transfer the money to Party C. Though it is called an order to pay, there is really no legal command to do such by Party B.

In a check, for instance, the bank (Party B) holds money for Party A, therefore Party A can write a check to Party C to pay a debt. Party C brings the check to the bank (Party B) and the bank pays the check. Here we have three parties involved in the payment of a debt.

Certificates of deposit are essentially promises to pay, but issued by a bank.

## TRANSFERRING COMMERCIAL PAPER

There are two ways of transferring your interest in commercial paper. One way to transfer your interest is by *assignment*, and the other is by *negotiation*.

Negotiation is the important concept that can give commercial paper a *higher level* of enforceability in one sense, or can make it a special version of a *contract*. You are able to transfer rights that contract holders cannot.

*Bearer Paper.* It is easy to transfer bearer paper (which is payable to the bearer). The bearer is the *holder* of the commercial paper. All that is necessary is to transfer *physical possession* of it to another holder. Viola! it is transferred.

*Order Paper.* Order paper, on the other hand, means commercial paper that is payable to the *order of* an individual or person. There are two require-

## PROMISSORY NOTE - ORDER PAPER

$ 500.00          Citytown, PA          December 3, 1990

**Sixty days** after date, for value received, the undersigned promises to pay BEARER, **Five Hundred Dollars** with interest from date at the rate of **12** percent per annum (computed on 360-day year and actual days) with interest payable at maturity.

To pay to ORDER of____T. E. Smith____

*Mike Maker*

*Back of Instrument*

ments for transferring or *negotiating* it to another holder. First, it must contain all of the necessary *endorsements*. If it is payable to the order of Mr. *X*, to transfer it he must *endorse* it properly. Then Mr. *X* must also transfer *physical possession* of it to the new holder.

Typically, in any negotiable instrument the information includes the amount of money, the payee, the time of repayment (upon demand or over a certain time period), and any interest rate payable. In commercial paper the usury laws come into play. These laws involve a maximum interest rate that can be charged for certain types of loans. Before you arbitrarily put an interest rate on a promissory note, you should check with your banker, lawyer or accountant to see what is the maximum interest rate allowed.

### TYPES OF ENDORSEMENTS

In any business you must be familiar with the different types of endorsements. You will not always have an expert on hand. Again, endorsements are necessary for transferring *order paper* (i.e., payable to the order of . . .)

The types of endorsements are: (1) blank; (2) special; (3) qualified; (4) restrictive.

### Blank Endorsements

A blank endorsement is the equivalent of having bearer paper. It is the transferor's signature without any other words. It results in a transfer similar to currency or paper money. If you lose a

note with a blank endorsement, it is possible for the locating party (even a thief) to become a legitimate owner of it. It becomes the same as finding a $100 bill in the street. (Finders keepers...) So it is preferable to avoid blank endorsements, even if you endorse it in your bank. In other words, it is perfectly legal and legitimate to transfer commercial paper this way but it can be dangerous.

It is possible to *convert* a *blank endorsement* on the back of commercial paper. You can convert it back into commercial paper where you become the named, specific transferee. In a word, you can change a blank endorsement into a special endorsement<$Ispecial endorsement$Iendorsement. Just insert "Pay to Mr. *X*" above the signature of Mike Maker. Read on for the advantage.

### Special Endorsement

A special endorsement is one that *names a particular person* or *entity* (called an endorsee) to whom, or to whose order the instrument must be paid or transferred. Thus, not anyone who finds the instrument or not any thief can get any *legitimate rights* to that particular instrument. That is why the special endorsement is so important. This is the type of endorsement with which you ought to become familiar. The special endorsement—for instance, "Pay to Mr. X, or Pay to X Corporation" then protects the holder from its transfer to *any other entity* or *person*.

Special Endorsement
*Back of Instrument*

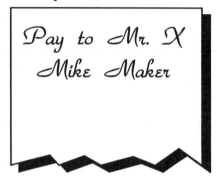

An endorsement on the back of a check or promissory note does not have to contain the words "Pay to the *order of*," though those words may be necessary on the *front* of the negotiable instrument. It does not hurt to include them in an endorsement, however. If you happen to be the *payee* on a check, you can endorse the back, "Pay to the order of" your bank if you are depositing it in your bank. As a matter of fact, it is best to put on your bank deposit stamp the following: (1) "pay to the order of your

*Back of Instrument*

bank"; (2) your bank account number; (3) your company name; and (4) "for deposit only."

## Qualified Endorsement

A qualified endorsement is one we do not commonly see. It occurs when one party wants to specify the types of guarantees he is making on an instrument. A qualified endorsement potentially limits or disclaims liability if the instrument is dishonored.

A most common qualified endorsement is

Qualified Endorsement
*Back of Instrument*

"Without recourse," or some similar wording, which *disclaims* particular types of liability on the instrument.

Why would someone endorse the instrument by using a qualified endorsement? A qualified endorser is making a disclaimer. He is saying that he or she will assume *no responsibility* to pay the instrument if the maker or the drawer of the note *will not pay.*

If you have endorsed an instrument that way, you are saying, "If the *maker does not pay*, do not come back and look at me. I am not going to pay it either." You can do that legally. If you omit these words, and the maker does not pay, then you as an endorser must pay.

A qualified endorser is not getting out of certain assurances that are implied under the UCC. There are certain things an endorser is still guaranteeing as a *qualified endorser*. It is possible for you to negate all of your guarantees, but you would have to disclaim them *specifically*. A qualified endorser is not necessarily getting off the hook, unless he or she makes specific disclaimers. The UCC can require some picky language to escape liability.

The qualified endorser is still guaranteeing: (1) that he or she has *good title* to the instrument or is *authorized* to obtain payment or acceptance on behalf of someone who does have good title, and that the transfer to him is rightful; (2) that all signatures *prior* to his and including his are *genuine* or are *authorized* by the appropriate persons; (3) that the instrument has *not* been *materially altered*; (4) that he has no knowledge that there is any good *defense* against any party which would stop the person receiving the negotiable instrument from getting payment; again, he is saying only that he has *no knowledge* of it; and (5) that he or she has *no knowledge* of any insolvency proceedings against the maker or the acceptor, or the drawer, in the case of an unaccepted instrument.

### Restrictive Endorsement

We see restrictive endorsements from time to time. These are used to accomplish a specific purpose. These endorsements essentially restrict payment. Restrictive endorsements include the following:

1. When there is any *condition* placed on the endorsement as *pay to Company X if they complete building the road per our agreement*. If this condition were placed on the *face* of the *note*, the note would be non-negotiable; it would become a plain old contract. But if such an endorsement is a *condition* of *transferring* it from the second party who received the note, to a third party, then this condition is enforceable and valid. Thus, the note would *not be payable unless the conditions* were met.

2. The instrument may attempt to *restrict* or *prohibit* any further *transfer* of the instrument. The endorsement might say that it is transferable to Mr. *X* and *cannot be transferred* any further. (As an aside,

this restriction will probably *not* restrict or kill the *negotiability* of the instrument.)

3. Words including "For collection only" or "For deposit only" or "pay any bank" are considered *restrictive* endorsements.

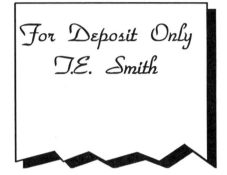

Restrictive Endorsement
*Back of Instrument*

For Deposit Only
J.E. Smith

4. An endorsement stating that it is for the benefit of or in trust for a *particular person*.

These are all restrictive endorsements, that will not kill the negotiability of the note.

Illustrative but not suggested. See Bank Deposit Endorsement above.

A restrictive endorsement sometimes acts as *notice* to the *first* party receiving it (transferee). But subsequent holders are able to ignore the restrictive endorsement. An example of this may be when you are depositing a check made payable to you. You put "For deposit only." Assume that this check is written on a bank 1,000 miles away. You deposit it into your checking account and your bank puts it in the bank collection system. *Only your bank* must make it a *deposit* to *your account*. The other banks do not have *your account*. They are not depositing it into your account. They have nothing to do with your account. So the restrictive endorsement does not adversely effect those subsequent banks.

---

## *POWER POINT* _____

▶ You must put endorsers on notice of a dishonor to hold them secondarily liable.

The same type of restrictive endorsement may affect a payment to a person as *trustee* for a minor. The initial bank should know that the trustee has an account on behalf of or as *trustee* for the *minor*. Thus, only the bank in which the trustee has an account is obligated to make sure there is such a trustee account, not the subsequent banks in the system.

There are a few other conditions that can affect your rights or anyone else's rights. These apply to all commercial paper unless there are specific laws to the contrary.

## PRESENTMENT

If you are the holder of commercial paper, you will have to make demand on it eventually. If it is *demand* paper, you make demand at any time after you become the holder.

If the paper is time paper, you can and should make demand for payment after its due date.

### Promissory Notes or Certificates of Deposit

For these types of commercial paper, the only presentment you can make is for *payment*.

#### Order Paper—Drafts or Checks

For these types of commercial paper, you can make a presentment for *acceptance* or for *payment*, or both. Obviously in order to get paid, you must present it for *payment*.

## DISHONOR AND NOTICE

Assume you are the *holder* of a negotiable instrument. You present it for acceptance (draft) or payment and it is refused. It is most important that you *put any other endorsers on notice in writing*. Often we see in negotiable instruments a provision that *no written notice* is required. The safest approach for the holder is to put everyone on notice *even if you don't have to*. If a negotiable instrument has been dishonored, it is best to put *all* of the other potentially responsible parties to the instrument on notice. If they are endorsers, you are *required* to do this to have a cause of action against each of them.

*Protest.* If a negotiable instrument is *dishonored* (will not be accepted, if a draft, or will not be paid, if any type of commercial paper), the UCC does not require that you use a *formal* notarized statement of dishonor to send to any of the *potentially liable* parties.

Nevertheless, this form meets the highest level of notice, which you might want to use to put anyone on notice. It is generally a *formal* notice which would be *notarized* by a notary public or certified by a U.S. consul or vice consul. This written *protest* or notice of protest must specify, as any other notice of dishonor (a) the negotiable instrument, (b) the holder, (c) that due presentment was made or that there was no reason to make such presentment (excused by law or by the document itself), and (d) that it was in fact dishonored by *non-payment*. It is also best for this written protest to certify that notice of dishonor has been given to all parties or to specific parties.

In a written *dishonor* (which is not a protest), you do not have to specify that you have already placed individuals on notice. The notice of dishonor itself is sent to the specific parties and need not be a two-step process stating that you have already done that.

A formal *protest* is required on notes that are *international* in nature.

## LIABILITY OF THE PARTIES

Though most of us would understand where the buck stops in any negotiable instrument, we will discuss this specifically. We will look at primary and secondary liability.

### Two-Party Instruments - Promissory Note or Certificates of Deposit

In a promissory note, we are usually talking about only two parties. The *maker* of the note (the person who owes the money) is the *primarily liable party*. The maker is the party who in effect cannot go anywhere. The buck stops here even if that party does not have the buck to pay it off. The holder is the unlucky other party.

This process works the same way for a Certificate of Deposit. If the bank does not pay, the bank is the *maker* of that particular certificate of deposit and is always *primarily liable*.

Endorsers are *secondarily* liable after any primary parties.

## Three-Party Instruments— Drafts or Checks

In drafts or bills of exchange, if the *drawee*, the bank for instance, has *accepted* the draft or the bill of exchange, then the bank or any other party who is the *acceptor* on that three-party instrument becomes *primarily liable*. If there is no party who *accepts*, then there is *no party* who is *primarily liable* on that instrument.

There can be *secondarily liable* parties. These include the *drawer* and any *endorsers*. The object is to put all of these persons on notice if you are the holder who is left holding the bag. Thus, if you are not going to get paid by the *primarily liable* person, you must sound the alarm.

Note that to make endorsers secondarily liable you must put them on notice.

You might note that the *instrument* and the *debt* in this particular case are *separate*. If you owe your supplier money under a contract and "pay" him with a draft, you may be secondarily liable on the draft even though you are the only party liable on your purchase contract.

## DISCHARGE

A commercial instrument can be discharged in one of several ways.

## DISCHARGE BY PAYMENT

When the primarily liable party pays the amount due in full, an instrument is discharged.

If a person obtained the instrument by theft, the note will not be discharges. In a word, there are some limitations on an instrument's discharge by payment.

## DISCHARGE BY CANCELLATION

An instrument is discharged if it has been canceled in a manner which is obvious from its face (e.g., stamped "paid"). It can be canceled even without consideration or payment.

## DISCHARGE BY REACQUISITION

You can discharge a commercial instrument by acquiring it again. This act would discharge all endorses between your previous ownership and your current purchase.

## DISCHARGE BY IMPAIRMENT

If a holder were to give back the collateral securing payment on a note, the holder would be discharging any prior endorsers. If a holder limited the legal recourse available to any secondarily liable party, this secondary party would be discharged.

## PROMISSORY NOTE CHECKLIST

I would like to go through the elements necessary for drafting a promissory note. Let's examine what it is you are agreeing to if you sign one. Some of the basic elements include the following:

1. The name and address of the maker. Sometimes you will not necessarily see this. Sometimes the name on a note may be virtually illegible. Certainly if someone is going to owe you money, it is best to type/print onto the instrument the name and address of the maker and have him sign it. You should not need a hieroglyphics translator to determine who the maker is.

2. A recital that there has been sufficient consideration given. It is not uncommon to see such wording. It means that there has been something received in return for someone signing this note.

3. A promise to pay *to the order* of a *particular payee*. It can instead be payable to *bearer*. It may be unwise to do so, but on occasion it is done. (The strongest protection for you if you are going to owe money, or if you are going to create a note, is to have a *specific named* and *knowable payee* (the person who is going to receive the money).

4. The place of payment. Individuals move, but it is best to specify the place of payment. If you

## *POWER POINTS* _____

▶ If you sign a note or draft as an agent for your company, make sure your company is named, your title is clear and the fact that you are signing as an agent is without doubt.

▶ A note has a maker and a payee.

▶ A draft or bill of exchange has a drawer, a drawee and a payee.

▶ Drafts and notes may also have endorsers.

▶ You must be a valid holder before you can be a holder in due course.

▶ In order to receive the benefits of the law of commercial paper, the instrument must meet the elements of negotiability.

▶ If commercial paper is not negotiable it may still be enforceable as an ordinary contract.

▶ Try to never leave an instrument blank or partially blank. If you must leave the amount field open, at least print on the check some amount and time limit on the face of the check.

▶ If you have a check amount imprinter in your company, guard it like the crown jewels. Unauthorized use of it can destroy your company.

▶ Consider fidelity bonds for any employee with access to your company's "jewels."

are the holder, you will certainly want to notify the maker of your change of address, if any.

5. The principal sum payable. It is best to specify that it be paid in currency of the United States unless you intend to make some other arrangements. You also want to be very specific and exact as to the *amount* of the *sum* that will be *payable*.

6. The method of payment: (a) single payment—if it is the intent of the parties to create a lump-sum payment, then state it exactly that way; (b) installments—if that is the case, then you will want to state exactly the month, day, date and year of the first installment, the number of subsequent installments, specifically when each payment is due (monthly, quarterly, annually) and when the last installment is due. Sometimes in amortization schedules, the last payment may not in fact be *equal*

to the other payments. So state any difference or the exact amount of this payment. If there is any variability in any payment the only safe way is to specify it in a note.

7. Interest rate. Are you going to calculate a yearly rate? Is the rate going to be computed against an unpaid balance, meaning that the interest will vary? How is the interest going to be calculated? Is it going to be calculated on a daily, monthly, quarterly, semi-annual basis? All of these can have an effect on the exact calculation of interest. There may be some compounding of interest; and you would want to know if the interest is going to be calculated in advance or in arrears. You would also want to know if it is going to be calculated as of the payment date.

8. The makers. There are several approaches to an *individual* or *several individuals* being responsible or legally liable on the note. Are there going to be two or more makers of the note (*joint obligors*) (each liable for the entire debt)? Or are the obligors on the note going to be *several* (each liable for a part of the total debt)? I will give you an example. When two parties sign a note and they are jointly liable, they are each liable for the *entire amount*. On the other hand, if they are "*severally liable*," then it is specified that each party is responsible for only a *particular portion* of the note. So most of the time you will see joint and several liability in a note. Thus, each of the parties is responsible for the entire amount. Only one of the parties, in effect, has to be found to enforce a judgment against that particular party.

You might also see joint and several liability for which each obligor can be held liable either together or separately.

9. Acceleration of payment if any installment is in default. You will usually see this in installment notes. If the maker (borrower) of the note is a certain number of *payments behind* or a certain number of *days behind* in making the particular payments, the entire debt becomes due.

10. Acceleration for other reasons. Some promissory notes provide that if the maker is involved in any type of legal action started by his or her creditors, including an assignment for the benefit of creditors, insolvency, any failure to pay other debts, or bankruptcy, the *entire balance* becomes due immediately. This may be the case even if the payment was initially due under installments.

11. Security for the note. It is not uncommon for some promissory notes to refer to a separate *security agreement*. In that security agreement, you would generally see the name of the secured party and the name of the maker of the note, the date, the description of the collateral, and any filing or recording data or other details of the transaction.

12. The collateral in the note. Sometimes a note itself will contain the information describing the collateral. In that case, you insert a description of the collateral. You might include the value of the collateral. You might also state that the holder of

the note has a right to *demand more collateral* if he or she feels insecure. This is allowable as long as the holder is acting in *good faith*. The note might contain a definition of events that create a default or put someone in default. Sometimes you will see the right to sell the collateral by either public or private sale. Sometimes it can be done with or without advertisement or notice to the maker of the note. There might be some statements on how the sale proceeds have to be applied. Sometimes proceeds are applied first to principal, sometimes to interest, and sometimes first to the cost of *enforcement*. Next, there might be a statement that any excess monies from selling collateral must be returned to the *maker* of the note. Sometimes you may see a statement involving the right of the *payee* (lender) to purchase the property in satisfaction of the note amount (debt).

13. Guarantor or endorser. Sometimes lenders, as a result of concerns they may have in lending money to the maker, may require that there be a *guarantor* or that there be some *endorser*. This is a backup to payment. Some of the types of provisions in the promissory note that you may see will include:

a. Some guarantee of principal or interest or of costs, which could include court costs or attorney's fees.

b. Certain waivers. In some notes even without a guarantor, the maker agrees to *waive* any *notice*, or acceptance of the note or any *protest* of the note or any demand on the note, or notice of demand or non-payment. This can adversely effect the maker of the note. If you are signing a note and you can negotiate these waivers out of the note, it might be worth a try. On the other hand, most lending institutions would make these a *condition* of your borrowing money.

c. Waiver of defenses. This makes the note more *enforceable* by the holder. You are agreeing to give up any defenses you may have to paying on the instrument.

d. A statement that any *extensions* of *time* to pay the note, or *waiver* of a *particular installment*, will not affect the *guarantor's liability*.

e. Statements to the effect that the principal obligation of the party that is guaranteeing the note is set even if the maker has not been put on notice.

All of these are "fun" provisions if you are signing such a note.

### Miscellaneous Provisions

In addition you will occasionally see other types of provisions, including:

a. That any unpaid principal will be charged with *interest* at some *increased rate* from the date payment was due until it is actually paid. Thus, there may be a step rate. Interest might be payable at 10 percent on the normal payment time. If, payment was due by the first of the month, but is not paid until the 15th, the additional 15 days would be payable at 12 percent annual interest rate.

b. The *state law* which will control the transaction sometimes is stated in the negotiable instrument.

c. Sometimes there is a *description* of the *transaction* out of which the note arose. It is important to note that if there is another contract that is *included* by *reference*, you may be destroying the negotiability of the note. It is OK to *refer* to another contract (*e.g.,* "as per contract"). It would be dangerous, however, to include specifically all of the wording of the contract *by reference* into this promissory note. You will lose the negotiability of the note.

d. Any *attorney's fees* that may be payable if the action requires the services of an attorney. Sometimes you will see the statement of "reasonable attorney's fees," or sometimes you will see a specific percentage. In many states the courts oversee the determination of attorneys' fees even if they are stated as a percentage. In a word, the percentage may be too high, and some courts might cut the percentage based upon the time and effort involved. Sometimes the time required to enforce the note may be minimal. Some courts may not allow 25 percent on a $1 million note, if it took an attorney only two hours to enforce the note. That may not be the case in every state. Depending on which side of the transaction you are on, you might want to watch this and negotiate it.

e. *Confession of Judgment.* A provision that you will commonly see in promissory notes or any other negotiable instrument is known as a "confession of judgment." It is common in business transactions.

Some of the provisions that you will see in confessions of judgment include:

1. The right of any attorney to file a confession of judgment against the maker. When does this come up? Assume the maker cannot pay the note and so states. The holder then gets his or her attorney and files the note with the confession of judgment in the original document. The confession of judgment can be triggered by the failure of the maker to pay any installment of principal or interest or to pay the entire amount if it is all due.

2. Typically in confessions of judgment, the maker also waives the issuance and service of process. In effect he is agreeing that even if he or she does not learn of the suit or get "put on notice," it is OK because he agreed to it in advance.

3. Often in the confession of judgment, the maker is confessing the *amount* of the *note*, meaning the original amount, the balance due, the interest due. He is also confessing or agreeing to whatever the *costs* of *filing* the *suit* are and any reasonable attorney's fees that may be stated or may be reasonably proved by the holder of the note.

4. The confession of judgment may result in the maker or drawer agreeing to release other parties from any errors and waive his or her right of *appeal* against the *holder* or any *other party* enforcing their rights.

In a word, you give up a ton of your rights when you sign a confession of judgment.

## TRUTH-IN-LENDING REQUIREMENTS

If you are a party to a note, there are certain legally required "truth-in-lending" provisions that have to be met. These are important provisions, because if they are not followed the entire transaction may be *illegal* and hence *unenforceable*. Some of the items include:

1. A clear statement of any additional fees or charges.

2. The specific *financing charges* that are made over the entire period of the loan.

3. The *annual interest rate*.

4. The number, the amount and the dates of payments.

5. The total amount of the payments to be made. This is the gross amount including principal and interest.

6. Charges for late payment or payment after default. Late payments cannot be unreasonable. They have to be related to the loss or use of money for that time period. Charges for this cannot be punitive.

7. A statement of the method of computing any unearned finance charges. You will generally end up having to look to state law to see what is *allowed* and what is *not allowed*. You ought to be aware of the "Rule of 78." It is generally more punitive to the borrower. If you have a balance to pay off, it would cost *more* under the Rule of 78 than if the payoff were based on the *unpaid balance* approach.

8. Any other legal requirements of the transaction. You might see, for instance, prepayment penalties. You might be prohibited from making early payments. Or there might be a certain additional interest charge if you pay off the note early. Sometimes there are maximum amounts which you are allowed to pay on the outstanding balance (*e.g.*, 25 percent in any year).

## MISCELLANY

Before you sign a promissory note on behalf of your company, you have to be sure you know what wording to insert and sign. You cannot protect yourself after your creditors have brought you to the financial gallows. And if you think your banker is going to protect you, I have some oil interests on Venus I would like to sell you. I got them cheap in an S & L collapse.

# CHAPTER 12

## INSURANCE

# CHAPTER 12

## INSURANCE

The concept of insurance is vitally important to any business person. Certainly the small business owner or manager must seriously consider the need of any business to be able to *transfer risk* for a fee. That is the concept of insurance.

Insurance has been around for a long time. There is some indication that there was even some kind of insurance in the ancient societies of the Greeks, Romans, Chinese, Teutons, Hebrews and early Christians for mutual benefit and assistance.

Of more recent vintage, the development and basis for insurance arose out of shipping and merchant trading. Merchant traders for a fee essentially from the 14th through 16th centuries A.D. developed the idea of risk transfer.

There are many types of insurance and many contracts and specific forms of coverage that exist as a result of different needs.

The types or kinds of insurance include: (1) accident insurance; (2) airplane insurance; (3) annuities; (4) assessment insurance; (5) assigned risk and plans; (6) automobile insurance; (7) bank deposit bond and securities guarantee; (8) boiler insurance; (9) bridge insurance; (10) burglary, robbery, theft and larceny insurance; (11) business interruption insurance; (12) carriers and railroad insurance; (13) casualty insurance; (14) commercial insurance; (15) concurrent and co-insurance; (16) confiscation insurance; (17) contract guarantee; (18) contracts liability insurance; (19) credit guarantee; (20) credit life or health insurance; (21) criminal liability insurance; (22) crop revenue guarantee; (23) elevator insurance; (24) embargo insurance; (25) employer's liability insurance; (26) endowment insurance; (27) family income insurance; (28) family insurance; (29) fidelity guarantee; (30) fire insurance; (31) floater and blanket policies; (32) flood insurance; (33) garage liability insurance; (34) group insurance; (35) guarantee insurance; (36) hail insurance; (37) health or sickness insurance; (38) homeowners insurance; (39) hospitalization and medical expense insurance; (40) industrial and burial insurance; (41) inland marine insurance; (42) mutual indemnity or reciprocal insurance; (43) jeweler's block insurance; (44) land value insurance; (45) liability insurance; (46) life insurance; (47) lightning insurance; (48) live-stock insurance; (49) machinery breakage insurance; (50) marine insurance; (51) marriage insurance; (52) mutual insurance; (53) patent infringement insurance; (54) physicians', dentists', druggists' and hospital liability indemnity; (55) plate glass insurance; (56) products liability insurance; (57) professional insurance; (58) property damage liability insurance; (59) public liability insurance; (60) rain insurance; (61) reinsurance; (62) rent insurance; (63) repurchase guarantee; (64) riot and civil commotion insurance; (65) sprinkler leakage insurance; (66) strike insurance; (67) title insurance; (68) tornado, cyclone and hurricane insurance; (69) transportation insurance; (70) unemployment insurance; (71) use and occupancy insurance; (72) voyage insurance; (73) war risk insurance; (74) water damage insurance; and (75) weather insurance (are you tired yet?).

These do not constitute every conceivable type of risk transference. Nevertheless, if you run through the list, you may get a better idea of the types that might help your business. You can then ask your insurance agent to give you some information on the several types that may cover portions of your business. Obviously, purchasing insurance is part of the number of complex decisions you will have to make in a business.

Now it is appropriate to examine some of the legal factors that apply and some of the basic kinds of insurance.

## STATE REGULATION

The business of insurance is essentially regulated by the states. There are a number of lengthy explanations involving both U.S. Supreme Court cases and laws enacted by Congress and by the states. Nevertheless, the basic point is that the states generally exercise the heavy hand in regulating the insurance business.

This type of regulation generally takes the form of state insurance codes and state departments of insurance. These departments oversee the forms of insurance offered, the contract forms and the types of information that must be requested from an applicant. These departments oversee the insuring provisions that are required to be placed into standard policies. State departments of insurance often oversee premium rate structures and liquidations of policies. They also are prominent in issuing regulations to carry out their charge.

## STANDARD INSURANCE POLICIES

Part of the states' Standard Insurance Policies effort to regulate the issuance of insurance and the transference of risk involves a trend toward standardizing policies. It is very common in specific areas of insurance to see the state attempt to require that there be standard forms which cover standard risks. The attempt is to create some minimum standards.

It is very important for you to realize that policies may state in general what types of risk they cover. You must read the *details* in any particular contract to pick out the specific types of risk that are actually transferred. For example, an all-risk form policy does not cover all risks. Beware!

One of the forms of progress that have occurred in the past few years is the requirement that consumer policies must be translated into plain English and not insurance jargon. This evolution has been a tremendous benefit for the consuming public, even if the consumer is a business person who has some degree of sophistication. Being able to read a policy that uses plain language allows you to get a better handle on what is covered. Again, the caveat is: Do not assume from the *title* that a coverage is as *broad* or *comprehensive* as it may appear.

## THE NATURE OF THE INSURANCE CONTRACT

The basic relationship between the parties, as stipulated in a contract, is that one person remits a *premium* to another person and the latter person undertakes to indemnify the premium payer against certain specific losses. These losses are generally contingent on circumstances that are beyond the control of the premium payer. These contingencies, perils or hazards are called *risks*.

The basic concept is that one party pays a premium to another party who then assumes a certain level or type of risk of loss. The risk taker agrees to pay up to certain amounts to the *premium payer* in the event of any specific type of loss.

Sometimes in insurance policies, there is a third person who may receive a benefit under the policy. In these particular instances, the contract may be called a third-party beneficiary contract.

## GENERAL INTERPRETATION OF INSURANCE CONTRACTS

The general rules of contract law, just as we see in most other types of contracts, are generally applicable to insurance contracts.

One additional item comes into play, however. Because insurance contracts in substantially all cases are written by the insurance company, these contracts are generally considered to be "contracts of adhesion." Thus, if there is any ambiguous language, the courts will interpret it in favor of the premium payer (insured). An unreasonable interpretation is unacceptable in deciding what these contracts say. Thus even in such a contract, the insured premium payer must generally have a reasonable interpretation that also favors him or her to prevail.

## ORAL VERSUS WRITTEN CONTRACTS OF INSURANCE

Unless it is specifically prohibited by statute, it is possible to have an oral contract of insurance as long as it has the necessary elements required for a contract.

It would be extremely unusual for an insurer to attempt to establish an insurance contract orally. Nevertheless, an oral contract of insurance can be legal (but dangerous for all parties).

## BINDERS OF INSURANCE

It is extremely important for you to be aware of the concept of insurance *binders*. This is especially true for business owners and managers.

An insurance binder, especially in business insurance, can be useful especially when opening or starting a business or when attempting to buy new types of coverage.

A binder is a contractually valid and enforceable *receipt* or *evidence* of *insurance* given to the *premium payer* (the insured) even if he or she has not paid a premium to the agent for the insurance company. This receipt binds the insurance company. What does it bind the insurance company to? It binds the insurance company to protect against the loss as stated in the contract or as understood. In other words, the policy of insurance may not have been issued yet. Nevertheless, given the proper circumstances, the premium payer (the insured) is *covered* for the *losses* that are agreed to.

The insurance binder temporarily creates a binding insurance contract between the two parties. The binding can be extremely important if a small business owner is attempting to insure his business against fire, theft, burglary or business interruption.

Sometimes binders are subject to certain conditions or limitations not contained in the policy. An example might be a life insurance contract. The company may be bound, but subject to the individual passing a particular level of medical examination. Thus, if the individual *fails* that examination or fails to meet the standards which the insurance company requires the individual to meet, then with proper wording in the binder the insurance company is not bound.

In order for anyone to purchase insurance the law requires that that person have an insurable interest in the subject matter.

What is an insurable interest? An insurable interest means that the insured has a financial or economic stake in the subject matter of the policy, be it a house, a business or a life.

The courts and laws require an insurable interest. Otherwise the contract is considered a wagering contract. In a wagering contract, the individual who is putting up the premium has nothing to lose but the premium and hopes to earn winnings. This is the equivalent of placing a bet on a roulette wheel. The amount of money placed is the maximum amount of loss that the person could incur. In addition, there is a potential for extraordinary gains on top of that.

There are different types of insurable interests. This depends on the type of insurance. Property or casualty insurance has a different version of insurable interest from life insurance.

## PROPERTY INSURANCE AND INSURABLE INTEREST

If an individual has property whereby she can expect to receive some monetary or financial gain, profit or benefit from the continued existence of the property, she has some interest in protecting the property. She would suffer some financial or monetary loss or disadvantage by its destruction. She has an insurable interest in the property. The insurable interest must exist at the *time* of any *loss*.

## LIFE INSURANCE AND INSURABLE INTEREST

An individual has an insurable interest in the life of a person if he has the reasonable expectation of receiving some financial or economic gain from the *continued living* of the insured. The insured is the person who is the subject of the policy. Insurable interest exists if this individual would suffer some financial loss if the insured died. The insurable interest must exist at the *time* the policy is *issued*.

## LIABILITY INSURANCE

A person has an insurable interest if the person has an interest in protecting himself or herself from legal liability from the particular risk or perils for which he is being insured. For instance, an individual may buy automobile liability insurance to protect his or her estate from the potential ravages of a lawsuit that could arise out of driving negligently.

For life insurance, as we said, an insurable interest must exist at the time of the purchase of the insurance. Therefore, if an individual purchases insurance himself and names someone else as the beneficiary, the insured clearly has an insurable interest in his own life at that time. If a beneficiary were to purchase insurance on another person (the insured), at that point in time the beneficiary must have something to gain as a result of the person's continued living.

With regard to property insurance, an individual must have an insurable interest at the time of a loss, not necessarily at the time of purchasing the insurance.

## INCONTESTABILITY CLAUSE

An important concept in insurance involves a certain element of protection for the insured that we do not normally see in a non-insurance ordinary contract.

A number of states require as a standard provision in a life insurance policy a provision that makes the policy *incontestable* for certain reasons after a certain time—generally one to two years.

This provision is intended to give the insurance purchaser a greater assurance that the insurance company will perform under the contract and *not contest its provisions*. This provision is not an absolute assurance for the policy owner, but it increases significantly the burden on any contestant (insurance company).

The idea is to force the insurance company to act promptly to flush out any irregularities in the contract. If the company does not act within the contestable period, it may be stuck even if the insured is guilty of behavior that could allow a contract rescission.

Therefore, as a gesture to quiet anxiety with regard to issuing primarily life insurance policies, most states require that the incontestability clauses be put into the policies.

Most states allow some types of limitations, but the types of limitations are too complex to be the subject of a short discussion.

## GRACE PERIOD FOR PREMIUM PAYMENTS

This is another item that is important. It is required in most if not all life, health and accident insurance policies, for the benefit of the *insured*. It is a minor problem many times. There appeared to be a need to protect the insured from losing coverage as a result of a short-term lapse between getting premium notices and remitting premiums.

Therefore life, health and accident policies contain a *grace period* which allows up to 30 days after the premium due date for the insurance company to receive the premium.

During this grace period, the policy is in force and coverage is in effect. Any claims that arise during that grace period are covered.

## CO-INSURANCE CLAUSES, OR THE OTHER PART YOU PAY (IN ADDITION TO THE PREMIUM)

This concept is important because it is used more in casualty and property insurance. It can also involve health insurance.

What is co-insurance? This is a certain type of *division* of the *risk* between the *insurer* (company) and the individual insured in the event that there is a loss.

One of the purposes of this co-insurance clause is to require that the insured pay for some of a covered loss. It gives the insured a financial stake in any loss. It is also an attempt to keep the insured from under-insuring a property.

Thus, it is possible with a co-insurance clause that if the person gets too little insurance, he or she may lose in more than one way.

Assume that a property insurance policy contains an 80 percent co-insurance clause. If you insure your business property for at least 80 percent, then claims for *less* than that amount are generally fully covered. Assume the value of the building is $200,000. Eighty percent of fair market value is $160,000. Assume you have a fire that causes $25,000 of damage.

---

1. Value of Building = $200,000
2. Co-insurance Maximum Calculation:
   $200,000 x 80% = $160,000.
3. Since loss is less than $160,000, then
   insurance will cover entire $25,000.

---

Now assume that you have purchased *less* than the 80 percent of the co-insurance amount. Assume you had purchased only 50 percent of the amount, or $100,000 of coverage.

---

1. Value of Building = $200,000
2. Co-Insurance Maximum Calculation:
   $200,000 x 50% = $100,000.
3. Since Insured purchased only 50%,
   only 5/8 of loss is covered.
4. Insurance covers
   5/8 of $25,000 = $15,625.

---

Here is the way you calculate this. If you purchase only 50 percent of the coverage ($100,000) and 80 percent ($160,000) is the co-insurance amount stated in the policy, then for partial losses you would receive 50 divided by 80, or 5/8 of the amount of the *partial loss*.

It is called co-insurance because the insured will pay some of any loss. So you are co-insuring to the extent of the proportion of the 80 percent value that is required to be purchased to the 50 percent you actually purchased.

## NAMED PERIL VERSUS ALL RISK

With regard to property and casualty insurance, there are often two approaches to the insuring agreement or the substance of the coverage. One is generally considered a "named peril" approach. This exists where each specific named potential type of risk is *enumerated*. You end up with a lengthy list defining each potential specified loss that is covered.

The other approach is the "all risk approach." This means the policy covers everything *except* those things that are specifically *excluded*.

For those of you who are computerists, there are different default positions in different types of policies. In one case, the default position might be that it covers certain losses specifically unless they are *not specified*. On the other hand, one of the default positions is that it covers everything unless it is specifically excluded.

However, if you see the term "all risk," you have to read the rest of the contract to see which risks have been excluded.

## EXCLUDED RISKS

It is important to know that there are several different ways whereby risk can be excluded. There are generally considered to be three:

1. Some types of risks or perils are excluded because they are basically uninsurable. An example of this might be a war exclusion clause for losses as a result of insurrection or rebellion. These types of things are rather difficult to predict.

2. Some types of risks are excluded because they are *not* the *subject matter* of this type of contract. These are generally considered to be covered under another, more appropriate contract. An example might be an automobile insurance policy on your personal car. It probably excludes commercial use of the vehicle, because this heavier usage is covered by a specific commercial policy.

3. Some types of specific risks are excluded but can be covered for an *extra charge*. This is generally done by adding an endorsement. It generally involves a piece of paper attached to the policy with additional provisions for an additional premium.

## EXCLUDED LOSSES

You must read these documents with a cautious eye (It's too bad they don't contain pretty pictures and animated graphs).

Most insurance contracts have provisions that exclude certain types of losses even though the policy may cover the particular type of peril that causes these losses. An example might involve a fire insurance policy on your business. It might cover the *direct losses* to your business resulting in damage to machinery. This particular policy probably would not cover the losses to your *ongoing business*. That might be covered by business interruption insurance.

Hopefully, this will give you some incentive for reading your insurance contract with a keen eye, a sharp pencil and maybe lots of coffee.

## EXCLUDED PROPERTY

Often most obvious property is included in coverage, but there might be specific exclusions. Fire policies, for instance, might exclude the loss of *deeds* to property, *bills* or *invoices*, *manuscripts*, or *money*.

The fire insurance policy is generally intended to cover the *building* itself. Now, again, there can be additions in the form of riders (additional coverage). These can be added for extra premiums. Again, the intent of the fire insurance policy is to cover the physical structure as opposed to *all* of the *contents*.

## EXCLUDED LOCATIONS

An insurance policy focuses on specific types of losses and also *specific locations*. Assume you have two pieces of property, one of which you live in, in this state, and one of which is in some resort area. The insurance policy is intended to focus on your residence. If your residence is covered by a policy, your summer home is not included by presumption

or assumption or otherwise. Each location must be addressed specifically.

## ACTUAL VALUE VERSUS REPLACEMENT VALUE

Another important item involves the different methods of calculating the loss. There are several different ways of a policy's provisions paying for any loss. How much money are you going to get back if there is a loss?

One of the approaches is considered actual cash value of a loss. This is often the *depreciated replacement* value. Assume that you bought a backhoe for $20,000 and have used it for a year and a half. The actual cash value might be the cost of it less the *depreciation* that typically occurs on any vehicle. It would not involve replacing it with a *new one*.

On the other hand, a *replacement* cost policy (more expensive) would allow a new replacement. (This type of policy does not apply to automobiles.) This could apply to machinery or office equipment.

## CLAUSES LIMITING THE AMOUNTS PAYABLE

In many types of insurance, the contracts require that the insured also have something to lose from each dollar of actual loss. In this approach, the insurance company will not cover the *entire loss* so there is a strong incentive for the insured to avoid the loss. We see these in the form of *deductibles*. An example involves a health insurance policy, whereby the first $200 of any medical costs each year must be covered by the insured. So you pay the first $200 and the health insurer pays amounts above this $200.

## DISAPPEARING DEDUCTIBLES

Some policies have a concept that is a little different, in that there is a deductible used to discourage the insured from going to the doctor needlessly. But should the total amount of medical benefits paid exceed a certain amount (*e.g.*, $200), the *deductible* is then *waived* because in this particular circumstance the reasoning would be that the person would not needlessly incur large amounts when he is at risk himself. Co-insurance, as we mentioned previously, is the concept whereby the individual also incurs a certain percentage of the cost. The insured can lose money as a result of incurring medical expenses. Sometimes the co-insurance portion can disappear.

## TIME LIMITATIONS

We have all heard that time is money. It can also work for or against a particular loss. If you incur a loss, it is incumbent on, you to *act promptly* to assure that you not lose out on any time limitations.

Many policies contain provisions that *require* the insured to *notify* the insurance company if there has been a loss. The insured might have to notify the insurer that claims should be paid. Or the insured might have to submit proof that there has been a loss. Typically you have to submit specific types of information. Be vigilant . . . then . . . don't worry, as the song goes.

In some policies there are also provisions for requiring a certain waiting period *before* you can recover. An example in certain disability policies involves an elimination period. No benefits are payable for the first 90 days of any disability. If the individual is still disabled after 90 days, then the individual can collect under the policy. Elimination periods vary, and obviously affect the premium.

## DOLLAR LIMITATIONS

It is common for insurance contracts to contain dollar limits (maximum) for certain types of coverage. Most insurance policies speak of certain types of limits. There are generally two types. They are *specific* limits and *aggregate* limits. Specific dollar limitations restrict payment to a certain ceiling amount if there is one specific loss, or to a specific piece of property or to a named peril.

Aggregate dollar limitations involve a ceiling on *all* the *losses* covered under a particular policy. A policy may pay up to $100,000 for losses you have caused to another single person. But should there be five individuals injured, the policy may have an aggregate limit of $500,000.

You may have heard someone describe an automobile insurance policy as 10/20/5. This refers to the limits of (a) $10,000 for a single personal injury loss, (b) $20,000 for an aggregate personal injury loss, and (c) $5,000 for any property damage loss.

## APPORTIONMENT OR COORDINATION OF BENEFITS CLAUSES

Some policies contain certain additional types of limitations. A disability policy may provide payment to an individual if he or she is disabled. It may provide for $800 per month as an example. This policy may provide that the policy will pay an amount less any amount paid by Social Security. We see this in *group* policies but not often in individual policies. In effect one policy gets credit for the benefits received under another policy.

## PRO RATA CLAUSES

Another version of apportionment appears in property insurance contracts.

This type of provision will provide that if more than one policy of insurance covers the loss on a particular piece of property, each policy will pay in the proportion of its face value to the total amount of insurance in force. Assume that you have one policy for $50,000 on the same piece of property and one for $100,000 on a piece of property. The smaller policy would then pay $50,000 over $150,000 or one-third of any loss, and the larger policy would pay $100,000 over $150,000, or two-thirds of any loss.

## KINDS OF INSURANCE

We have listed numerous kinds of insurance, but we would like to examine a few specific types of insurance.

## LIFE INSURANCE

We are all aware of life insurance. Certainly no one is actually guaranteeing that someone will live. Insurance is only providing that an insurance company will pay a certain dollar amount to a beneficiary if the insured person dies during a certain time.

Payments on life insurance are based upon a policy owner having paid a premium to the insurance company. The payment to the beneficiary is made upon the insured's death.

Naming a *beneficiary* is generally a *privilege* of the owner of the policy and not necessarily of the *insured*. It is also possible for the owner of a life insurance policy to *give up this right* to be able to name or rename a *beneficiary*. This concept exists when the insured names an "irrevocable beneficiary." The insured may relinquish her right to change a beneficiary. This can be done for numerous reasons, especially for estate taxation reasons.

Generally the owner of the policy reserves the right to change the beneficiary.

## ORDINARY LIFE INSURANCE

The term *ordinary life* insurance contains a blending of two different financial pieces. One piece is the *pure insurance portion*. The other is the *investment* or *savings* portion.

Ordinary life insurance assumes that a group of individuals will live to a maximum age. It assumes that these individuals die at various ages, and the insurance companies use statistics to help predict how many per year will die. The actuaries (higher math types who live in numerical ecstasy) for the insurance company attempt to decide how *many* will still be left each particular year. They then determine what cash value should be accumulated to pay off these death amounts when they occur. The actuaries can then calculate a level premium (like a mortgage) that an insured pays. This approach assures us the insurance company will be solvent during the entire period that each individual has insurance coverage. Since the actuaries use the mathematical laws involving large numbers and various statistical methods, they are able to produce an amazing "product" called *ordinary life* insurance.

There are numerous variations of this product. You may have heard of *whole life* insurance. This insurance is designed to run for the entire life of the insured.

Limited *payment life* is a form under which the individual will pay for a *limited time*. The payment period may be for 10, 15 or 20 years. The cash reserve amount builds up during this period, so that no more premiums are due. If the insured dies, the insurance amount and possibly more is paid. *Single premium* life insurance is also a useful financial planning vehicle. An individual pays one lump sum to the insurance company, and no more. In return for this the insured receives full coverage for the face amount of the policy.

## TERM LIFE INSURANCE

Term *life* insurance involves *pure* life insurance protection. It can be for a level amount, an increasing amount or a decreasing amount. There is no cash value buildup. At the end of the term, if the individual is still alive, there is nothing payable.

## UNIVERSAL LIFE INSURANCE

This type of life insurance contains the elements of both ordinary life and term life insurance which we have mentioned. It exists in a more competitive environment. Some of the features of universal life include the ability to change the amounts of the insurance. Typically, under an ordinary life policy, the insured cannot change the life amount. Nevertheless, in a universal life policy it is possible. An individual might want to raise the amount of insurance from $100,000 to $150,000 because there is some additional need for a certain period. Therefore, without having to get approval the individual may be allowed to just raise the amount of insurance. The insured need only send in a form and pay an additional premium. Nevertheless, a feature of the policy is flexibility. In addition, universal life generally allows the insured to place some money with the insurance company. With it the insurance company will also pay a competitive rate of interest. The insurance company competes now with the other financial institutions for these funds. Therefore, the concept of universal life has some new, *improved* features. The features are often, however, extensions of the provisions of previous contracts.

## ENDOWMENT AND ANNUITY CONTRACTS

Endowment contracts are generally contracts in which the insurance company may agrees to pay to the insured a lump sum of money when the insured reaches a certain age. This contract will pay, if the insured dies, an amount of money to a beneficiary. An example of this is an endowment policy that has been used to fund a child's future college costs.

Annuity contracts are contracts that focus on the payout feature. Individuals often purchase annuity contracts to cover their retirement. One of the unique features of annuity contracts, which does not exist in a non-insurance context, is that an insurance company may guarantee for the *life* of an individual a certain monthly dollar amount. Here an insurance company gets its actuaries to examine mortality rates and determine how much the company needs to guarantee payments for *life*. This is a valuable consideration if you are looking to protect your retirement income.

## ACCIDENT INSURANCE

Accident insurance requires that the insurance company pay certain dollar amounts to an individual if that individual loses the use of a hand or a leg, or certain specific dollar amounts for specific named losses. This insurance sometimes pays a death benefit, but only if the death or loss has been accidental.

## HEALTH AND SICKNESS INSURANCE

This type of insurance covers the individual for sickness or illness that results in hospital or other medical expenses. These policies may specify the daily room rates it will pay at a hospital with deductibles, co-insurance features and so forth. The covered losses must arise out of an illness or accident. Sometimes accident and health insurance policies are combined. Sometimes they are separate. Sometimes they include only medical bills. Sometimes they include more. Sometimes the reimbursement amount is fixed for a certain type of medical procedure. This type of coverage can be expensive. The small business owner or manager may have to look hard for coverage if there are only two or three employees. It is possible to get this type of insurance for a reasonable cost so employees can have some coverage.

There are a few companies that cover the small employer. The risks are high since the number of employees is low. The companies need large numbers to better predict their potential claim payments.

## FIRE INSURANCE

Fire insurance, as most of us know, protects the person who has an insurable interest in the property. The person is protected from loss or destruction to the property caused by fire or certain types of related perils.

There are certain standard types of fire policies containing standard provisions that are dictated by state insurance departments. There still can be numerous provisions, endorsements or riders that can be added to these policies to broaden the coverage.

We referred previously to co-insurance provisions. Fire insurance policies are the type of policies where you see co-insurance clauses where the typical *minimum* percentages (*e.g.*, 80 percent) are stated.

## CASUALTY INSURANCE

This type of insurance is important for business owners and managers. We live in an age of potential risk, and damaging and costly accidents.

This insurance generally covers losses that arise out of damage or destruction to (business) property by various causes, *other* than *fire* or the types of perils protected by fire insurance policies.

Sometimes the losses that are covered apply to personal injury or sometimes to death and physical property loss due to a covered accident. Any small business owner or manager must examine this type of insurance as part of risk management.

## COLLISION INSURANCE

When new automobiles are purchased with borrowed money, the lender requires that the automobile itself be covered with collision insurance and not just third-party liability insurance.

Collision insurance protects the owner or the mortgagee of an automobile against the risk of loss or damage that may occur as a result of named causes or any cause generally. Often there is a deductible amount that is, in effect, not covered. The first $250 or $500 might not be covered. If damages exceed that amount, the insurance company picks up the tab.

## LIABILITY INSURANCE

Liability insurance is a contract under which the insurance company agrees to indemnify or pay the person who has incurred any loss as a result of the covered party's fault. This may occur as a result of an employee negligently injuring another person in the company's vehicle. A business owner or manager should have liability insurance. It can cover liabilities arising from movable property as well as real property. What happens if a roof shingle or part of a building falls and injures someone? If you are a business owner, you may want to transfer this risk to an insurance company.

## CREDIT INSURANCE

Credit insurance can protect individuals who lend money against a loss from the non-repayment of that money which might occur as a result of the *insolvency* of the debtors.

Credit *life* insurance, for instance, protects a creditor and a debtor by providing for repayment of the amount owed in the event the insured dies.

If you have a large *number* of accounts receivable or a large one that is material (could bankrupt you) to your business, check out this form of insurance.

## FIDELITY INSURANCE

Fidelity insurance can protect the insured from the dishonest acts of employees. This can include not only loss or theft of *money*, but also theft or loss of *other property* including movable property other than money.

## GROUP INSURANCE

This area is very important for employees. Any business owner must be aware of the various types of group insurance, especially for creating good employee morale.

Group insurance is intended to cover large numbers of individuals. The cost of group insurance is often less than an individual version of the same coverage. Group insurance allows the insurance company to make better predictions, because there are larger numbers involved.

The types of insurance that can be included in group insurance include life insurance, accident and health, medical insurance, hospital indemnity (a policy may pay $100 a day for each day that an individual is in a hospital), and disability insurance.

Group insurance can also include other types of insurance that individuals may purchase. There are numerous tax benefits for both the employer and the employee with group insurance coverage. An employer should seriously consider this insurance as a fringe benefit.

## MARINE INSURANCE

Marine insurance has a long history in insurance annals. It is responsible for the development of the concept of insurance.

Marine insurance originally covered only destruction of vessels or cargoes as a result of perils that befell vessels or cargo at sea. Now there are broader forms of insurance coverage for ships and cargoes. These forms have expanded just as other forms of insurance have expanded.

At one time the distinctions involving marine insurance split up the types of policies into ocean going marine coverage and inland marine coverage. It appears that this distinction is less and less now.

If you have risks of loss for any marine property or from transportation of goods by water, dig into this area. It is a specialty area you will have to examine.

## TITLE INSURANCE

Title insurance is a form of insurance that will pay for losses incurred as a result of a defect in the title to real estate the insured individual or entity has purchased. The losses can result from defects in the title. They can result from encumbrances (liens) that were *unknown* to the parties to a real estate transaction.

There are essentially two types of policies. Often when a business purchases a particular piece of real estate, the business buyer can purchase title insurance to cover the *mortgage amount*. Sometimes this purchase is required. The business owner may also be able to purchase insurance to cover difference between the *mortgage* amount and the *purchase price* at the time of purchase. The new owner can get *additional* insurance to cover what might be the *down payment* in addition to the mortgage amount. Generally, the amount of title insurance is frozen as of the date of the act of sale. The title insurance would not cover the *increase* (if any) in fair market value. It would also not be affected by decreases in fair market value.

These policies, again, are geared to protect the *mortgagor* (the creditor). They can also be modified to protect the business buyer.

## DEFENSES OF THE INSURER

If we purchase insurance, we want to be paid in accordance with the contract. Let's examine some of the defenses that insurers have utilized to *deny payment*. Some of these defenses include misrepresentation, breach of warranty and concealment.

Generally an insurance company will ask certain questions of an individual or business applying for insurance coverage. These representations are generally made by the applicant to persuade the insurance company to undertake the risk for the premium.

Sometimes the representations made are specifically stated to be *part* of the insurance contract. If the representations made become a part of the contract, they are considered to be *warranties*. These are guarantees that such statements are in fact true. If the representations are part of the contract, and a warranty is breached, then there was in fact no contract to begin with.

If a warranty is breached, it may be possible for the insurance company to *rescind* the contract. The company will return the premiums and get back the policy or be freed from the risk. This occurrence is not common, but it is important to keep in mind.

We have mentioned the incontestability clause in many policies. This may be where an insurance company may have its hands tied if it has not acted *within* a *certain time*. The company must act promptly.

Certain types of representations result in premium adjustments. Assume that a person misstates his or her age, or maybe it is miscalculated and put on an application. Later the individual dies, and as a result of some research the insurance company finds out that the person was in fact older than what was placed on the application.

---

### POWER POINTS _____

- ▸ There are numerous new forms of insurance to minimize casualty and other risks to your business.

- ▸ There are numerous forms of protecting you and your business from risks you cannot control.

- ▸ Business insurance allows you to transfer much of these risks to an insurance carrier.

- ▸ If you are not an insurance expert, contact one or more (preferably) knowledgeable insurance professionals.

This means that the person did not pay sufficient premiums. In life insurance, older insureds pay higher premiums, since mortality is higher. In our case of age understatement, there might be an adjustment in the amount *payable*. The insurance company calculates how much insurance the insured would have in force, given the *correct age* and the actual premium paid. Then that amount would be sent to the beneficiary.

States vary in the remedies available. They also vary regarding the time periods within which each party must act. We are not stating any hard and fast *rules* as to how to interpret whether or not a misrepresentation is a *warranty* versus a *misrepresentation*.

## CONCEALMENT

On occasion an individual intentionally conceals some *material* (important) fact. The failure to reveal that fact has resulted in a loss to the insurance company. It is possible that the insurance company might have refused to insure the person or the business or the peril, had it known the truth. The insurance company may have been duped. This might be considered fraud. If this occurs, the insured may *not* receive the policy proceeds or may not receive coverage as initially contemplated.

## WAIVER AND ESTOPPEL

Waiver generally means giving up a right. It is an intentional giving up of a particular right that an individual has. Estoppel exists when a person as a result of his own fraud or unfair behavior will not be allowed to take advantage of his or her own conduct.

Assume that an insurance company has a condition precedent to its policy. It may require that an individual have a certain income to receive a certain minimum policy level. Assume that the agent overlooks this and takes an application from an individual who doesn't qualify, even though the incorrect information is stated on the face of the application. Assume that the insurance company then overlooks it or sees the application and decides that in this particular case it will accept this individual. The insurance company could be waiving its rights under these circumstances. If it knows that it has a right to decline this

particular applicant, but decides to accept this individual on the risk anyway, the company has changed its requirements, at least for this policy.

Estoppel may come into play in a slightly different circumstance. Courts apply estoppel where it might be unfair for an individual to present the actual facts. The two concepts of waiver and estoppel are essentially used interchangeably, although they are not always the same.

Here is an estoppel example. The agent might make some misrepresentation about the policy with regard to its coverage. Assume that the insurance company generally accepts the behavior of this agent, knowing that the agent often exaggerates the policy coverage despite what is written in the policy. The courts may say that even though the agent is exaggerating or somewhat misleading the other individual, the insurance company is estopped (prevented) from denying this particular coverage. The insurance company here might be unaware of what the agent actually says, so there is no waiver. But if it disregards the agent's reckless sales practices over time, the company may be estopped from denying coverage that the agent verbalized contrary to the written policy.

## CANCELLATION

Cancellation sometimes takes place, but the reasons can be myriad. There are several ways of *terminating* policies. Cancellation is one of the several ways. Sometimes an insurance company is allowed to cancel a policy during a certain time period. Automobile insurance policies at one time were for one-year time periods and could not be canceled during that year. Some states began allowing shorter time periods. Generally these policies are not cancelable. But even that has been changing, so that sometimes policies can be canceled during the term of the policy.

## TERMINATION

Generally insurance policies terminate as of the end of the term for which they are written. There is often a grace period of 30 to 31 days, during which an insured is covered for an additional period. Often this is because the legislature wanted to allow a period for paying premiums and catching up the coverage.

# CHAPTER 13

## SECURITIES LAW

# CHAPTER 13

## SECURITIES LAW

One of the most essential sections of law comes into play when any business attempts to raise money. It involves the securities laws. The area of securities laws or securities regulations affects the investment of money in any corporation and in limited partnerships. These laws cover any size and kind of investment.

Unfortunately, not many individuals are aware of it. Often, promoters or small business people who are starting up with an idea need capital. These promoters begin touting how valuable their ideas are and also the need for *investors*. They need individuals to lend them money on their new and speculative project or even on an old, seemingly non-speculative business.

One of the essential focuses of this chapter is to make you aware of the *strict requirements* of telling the truth and the whole truth. Any time you or anyone else is seeking investment funds for any of your projects, take heed of a whole new world of openness you have not experienced otherwise. In a nutshell, the day of telling the *half*-truth or not telling all of the gory, bloody facts that may affect an investment are *gone*. Many of us may think that the only dishonest thing under the law that we have to be concerned about is affirmative lies. That is not true. If I do anything in this entire book to dispel a myth, this is one of them.

If you or anyone is attempting to offer securities or asking other individuals to invest in your business, you have an obligation to tell not only the good, but all of the bad. If not you may be damned or ruined as a result of not doing so. It is unfortunate that many professionals, including lawyers, seem to think that if the business is *small* none of these laws apply.

We are going to review some of the basic requirements. The most poignant feature is that you cannot get around these laws applying to your deal. It is rare, and even if you are the one case in a million that gets around all of the federal securities laws when selling investments, the state law may get you, because it generally picks up all of the *remains* of those two or three microbes that get around the federal law. The securities laws' stringent requirements place a heavy burden on anyone offering securities.

Let's take a survey approach. Most states have laws called "blue sky laws." They often parallel the federal laws. There is no way for us to cover all of the nuances of state law, nor for that matter all of the nuances of federal law. But if you get comfortable with these concepts, you should be in good shape in understanding your state laws.

The federal securities laws in which we are interested here consist of two statutes. They affect most businesses. The Securities Act of 1933 contains provisions that generally dictate the *types* of *disclosures* which must be made when a company is offering securities to the public. It also dictates some of the consequences or provides remedies if an offering *should* be registered or should contain all of the disclosures but *does not*.

In addition, the Securities Exchange Act of 1934 provides a number of additional features. It expanded the protections far beyond the 1933 Act. It created the Securities and Exchange Commission. It also allowed for regulation of the stock exchanges and regulation of brokers. It also dictated the type of disclosures required of those companies that must report on an *ongoing* basis. It dictated certain types of *reports* that must be filed by *brokers*. Its most prominent provision prohibits misrepresentation, deceit and other fraudulent acts and practices in connection with the sale of securities even if the securities were *not registered* or did not have to be registered.

If you are starting up a corporation and intend to look for investors, you should seek a qualified securities lawyer who can tell you what steps you must take to comply with the Act, or whether there are any available exemptions from the registration requirements of the Act. As we said, it is very difficult to get around the full disclosure requirements of the Act. It is conceivable, though highly unlikely.

## SALE OF SECURITIES TO THE PUBLIC

The Securities Act of 1933 attempted to bring some antiseptic provisions to the offering of securities to the public.

There are several important questions we should ask: First, what is a security? Second, are there any exemptions from registration? Third, what is the process for registering securities so that there is compliance?

## SECURITY

A security means any note, stock, treasury stock, bond, debenture, evidence of indebtedness, certificate of interest or participation in any profit-sharing agreement, collateral trust certificate, pre-organization certificate or subscription, transferable share, investment contract, voting trust certificate, certificate of deposit for a security, fractional undivided interest in oil, gas or other mineral rights, any put, call, straddle, option or privilege on any security, or in general, any interest or instrument commonly known as a "security," or any certificate of interest or participation in, temporary or interim certificate for receipt for guarantee of or warrant or right to subscribe to or purchase any of the foregoing. It is intended to cover at least three elements. These are (1) it involves an investment in some common venture; (2) the investment is premised on some *reasonable expectation* of *profit* or at least a minimizing of loss; and (3) the profit has to be derived from the managerial efforts of other individuals. Courts have examined this definition and excluded certain types of investments, including investments in cooperative housing.

## EXEMPTIONS FROM REGISTRATION

There are certain exemptions from registration that can be beneficial to us. I would like to emphasize one extremely important fact. Even if our offering fits an exemption from *registration*, we do not necessarily have an exemption from the *fraud requirements* or the full disclosure requirements of the securities laws.

Registration entails filing a *lengthy disclosure document* with the SEC or the state government, or both. This is an expensive, timely process that involves audited financial statements, which can be expensive, especially for a new business. It involves disclosure of a management's background, of *all* of the *risks* involving the business. It involves disclosing the substance of the business and some description of the potential competitive environment in which the business operates. In other words, everything that would be considered *material* or important, that a reasonable investor in making a decision, must be disclosed. *Material* does not mean disclosing only that factor which would *turn* a *person's decision around*. It includes any and all factors that would be considered *important*, cumulatively, in making a decision.

The SEC does not verify the information in a registration statement. If there are some obvious *deficiencies* on the face of the registration, the SEC may comment on it. The fact that a registration statement clears the SEC does not mean it is OK. The SEC's reviewers do not have kryptonite vision.

### EXEMPT SECURITIES

These are types of securities for which Congress has determined that there is a lesser need to oversee as heavily. The exemptions contained in the federal law sought to minimize SEC responsibility when the states or other federal agencies already had oversight responsibility for certain types of entities. Thus, there is a rational basis for designating these exemptions.

### INTRASTATE ISSUES

If an offering is essentially issued within a particular state and sold only to persons living in that particular state, the security issued may not have to be registered with the SEC. It is, again, defined such that the monies and the stockholders are strictly within the state. The issuer must have its principal place of doing business in the state, it must be organized in the state, it must get 80 percent of its revenue from the state, at least 80 percent of its assets must be located in the state, and at least 80 percent of the net proceeds must *come to rest* and be used in that particular state. In addition, all of the offerees and the purchasers must be residents of the state, and the purchase or sale of securities must be restricted for at least nine months to that particular state. Any resales after that period can be made to out-of-state residents.

The federal securities laws look to the *substance* of a transaction. Therefore, do not think *technically*, because you will end up losing if you do. In other words, if you are trying to utilize the intrastate exemption, make sure you exceed the minimums in the rule.

### SHORT-TERM COMMERCIAL PAPER

The Securities Act of 1933 exempts from registration any note, draft, banker's acceptance or acceptance issued for working capital that has a maturity from the time of issuance of not more than nine months. This exempts most of the short-term financing where companies and individuals invest their temporary excess cash.

### REGULATION A

Regulation A is an exemption of sorts. It may save a company or an issuer of stock from having to file a lengthy registration statement. On the other hand, the disclosure document that is utilized under Regulation A for offerings of up to $5 million requires that the issuer file a notification and an offering circular with the SEC regional office prior to the sale of securities. The difference between the disclosure here and a full-blown registration is not monumental. This "exemption" from registration may save you some money. Certainly when a business is starting up money is a scarce feature, but you still have to make similar disclosures.

### OTHER EXEMPT SECURITIES

There are other types of securities that are exempt from registration. Though they do not typically apply or affect the typical business, I would like to list a few of them:

1. Debt securities issued by domestic governments.

2. Securities of domestic banks and savings and loans and pension and profit-sharing plans (the reasoning there is that they are highly regulated—which is questionable—by the states or the federal government so there is no need to have a duplication of oversight.

3. Securities of not-for-profit charitable organizations. It is important to realize this is only from filing the lengthy registration statements and not necessarily from the types of disclosures that are necessary.

4. Securities of issuers where the issuance is regulated by the Interstate Commerce Commission.

5. Certificates issued by a receiver or trustee in bankruptcy with the court's approval of the issuance of the certificate.

6. Insurance policies and annuity contracts issued by regulated insurance companies.

7. Securities issued solely for exchange by an issuer with its existing securities holders where no commission is paid.

8. Reorganization securities issued in exchange with court or other government approval.

In addition to these exempt securities, which means that the insurance process is exempt, there are also certain types of *transactions* that may be exempt from filing a registration statement. Here the focus is on the *transaction*. The securities themselves may or may not qualify for an exemption.

## EXEMPT TRANSACTIONS

In the past decade the SEC has eased the burden of having to file a registration statement. These transaction exemptions essentially involve what are called "private placements" where the offer is limited to either $5 million or $500,000 or limited to a special category of "accredited investors." Let's take a look at these.

## PRIVATE PLACEMENTS

The concept of private placement includes the sale or offering of securities when it is not done publicly. There can be no newspaper advertising or no general advertising. The offer may be by word of mouth, or by some limited solicitation, but it cannot be a general solicitation.

There is a category of investor called an accredited investor, someone or some entity that is fairly sophisticated or able to protect itself, where the common investor may not be. Accredited investors might include banks, insurance companies, investment companies, executive officers or directors of the issuer, or any person who is able to purchase at least $150,000 of the securities being offered, as long as the total purchase price does not exceed 20 percent of the investor's net worth. It includes persons whose net worth exceeds $1 million and persons with an income over $200,000 during the past two years who reasonably expect an income over $200,000 in the current year. The reason is that with sophisticated investors, a company may seek capital in virtually unlimited amounts as long as they are all accredited investors. There is a limitation on the number of *non-accredited* investors. Therefore, this accredited investors concept can be important to someone seeking investors in a business.

## PRIVATE OFFERS NOT EXCEEDING $5 MILLION

The SEC has issued a rule whereby an issuer can offer securities not to exceed $5 million in any 12-month period. The issuer can have no more than 35 unsophisticated or non-accredited investors, but can have an unlimited number of accredited investors. If the sale involves any *non-accredited* investors,

*all* of the purchasers must, prior to the sale, be provided information that is considered important or material to an understanding of the issuer, its business and the securities being offered. The rule says that if they are *all* sophisticated investors (accredited investors) this type of information need *not* be furnished. It is difficult, even with sophisticated investors, for the issuer to be protected without submitting all of this information to the investors. My caveat is to make the effort of getting out *all* of the material information necessary, no matter who the investors are.

In this particular case, the rule attempts to make it easier on the issuer if there are only accredited investors. The issuer must also have reason to believe that each non-accredited investor has such knowledge and experience in financial and business matters that he is capable of evaluating the merits and risks of this potential investment.

## UNLIMITED PRIVATE PLACEMENT OFFERS

If an issuer restricts his offers, sales and purchases to accredited investors, the issuer may seek unlimited amounts of money. The burden is upon the issuer to guarantee that all of the offerees are in fact accredited investors. There is a heavy burden on the issuer to verify the degree of sophistication of the offeree.

## PRIVATE OFFERS NOT EXCEEDING $500,000

The SEC makes another provision for a "small private offering" where the securities are offered and sold without general advertising. The amount that can be offered within a 12-month period (both before and after the offering) cannot exceed $500,000. The issuer must take precautions to restrict any non-exempt unregistered resales.

Certain states require *registration* of this offering before it can be made in that state. The rule might also allow general advertising.

Offers Solely to Accredited Investors. Section 4(6) of the 1933 Act allows an issuer to offer and sell up to $5 million of securities if the offer and sales are made solely to accredited investors. No information is required to be furnished to the purchasers.

These investors can fend for themselves. This offer is restricted to accredited investors.

## RESALE OF RESTRICTED SECURITIES

These exemptions that look toward any *transaction* exemption contain some additional burdens. There is some restriction of the *resale* of these securities in a subsequent transaction. One of the rules, under the Securities Act of 1933, contains conditions that, if met by a person selling the securities covered by a *transaction-based* exemption, allow the resale of these securities. There must be some *adequate current public* information about the issuer. The issuer might be a current reporting company under the 1934 Act, or there can be some public dissemination of important information about the company. The person who is selling the securities must wait at least two years. Also, the seller may sell them only in limited amounts through brokers and must put the SEC on notice of the sale.

If you are holding any restricted securities or are interested in issuing any under a "private placement," I suggest you consult a securities lawyer who can lay down in detail the rules you will have to follow. A securities lawyer is one who spends a significant amount of time practicing in the business and corporate securities areas. The general legal practitioner cannot spend the time learning this specialty area.

## LIABILITY

There is a potential for liability for failure to comply with these laws. The Securities Act of 1933 contains a number of sanctions for *failure* to comply with its provisions. They can include administrative remedies initiated by the SEC, civil liability initiated by investors, and criminal liabilities.

## LIABILITIES FOR UNREGISTERED SALES

The 1933 Act imposes very strong civil liability for the sale of unregistered securities that should have been registered. In other words, if there is no exemption for the security and no exemption for the transaction, the *issuer* and *associated persons* may be responsible or liable for failure to register them. This liability is virtually absolute, and there are no defenses to it. The potential plaintiff has a right to tender the securities back to the seller and recover the purchase price.

If the buyer no longer even owns the securities, he or she may still recover monetary damages from the seller.

## LIABILITY FOR INACCURATE REGISTRATION STATEMENT

In addition to the potential liability for failure to register when required, an issuer may also be liable for issuing securities pursuant to a *materially deficient* registration statement. This liability results from a registration statement that contains an untrue statement or an omission of the complete facts, with regard to any material facts that should have been disclosed. It is important to note what the courts generally mean by "material." It means any of those matters or items of information which would have a substantial likelihood that a reasonable investor would *consider* them *important* in determining whether to purchase the securities. It does not mean an item of such importance that it would have *changed* the *investor's mind*. It need only be one of the cumulative set of facts any reasonable investors would consider important.

It is not only the issuer who has to be concerned about potential liability. Others include (a) any persons who signed the registration statement; (b) every person who was a director or partner; (c) the accountant, engineer, appraiser or expert who prepared or certified any part of the registration statement and, (d) all the underwriters. These persons are jointly and severally liable for any of misrepresentations or omissions of fact.

What is their liability? Their potential liability is the amount paid for the security less either its value at the time of suit or the price for which it was sold. Some of you may be aware of the concept of "due diligence" which is required of experts and others preparing an offering for market. It is possible for a defendant, other than the issuer, to use as a defense their using due diligence in preparation. Thus, if they have exerted an effort that is reasonably sufficient under the circumstances, they may be safe from liability. In other words, there is a potential defense to this liability.

The standard that the courts will use is the standard of *reasonableness* required of a prudent person in the management of his or her own property. That is not necessarily an easy standard to meet. This standard points out the level of burden placed on any of the parties associated with the issuance of a registration statement.

Anti-fraud Requirements. The Securities Act of 1933 has two provisions that essentially impose liability based on violations of the anti-fraud standards in the Act. The most important definition of a violation of the anti-fraud provisions is stated in Section 17(a). It is unlawful for any person (1) to offer or sell securities in interstate commerce who uses, directly or indirectly, any device, scheme or artifice to defraud; or (2) to obtain money or property by means of any untrue statement of a *material* fact or to omit to state a material fact which would be necessary to make the statements already made *not misleading;* or (3) to engage in any transaction, practice or course of business that operates or would operate as a *fraud* or *deceit* upon the purchaser. This definition is generally used for the purposes of the Securities Act of 1933. Virtually the sale provisions are carried over into the 1934 Act, which gives *private individuals* a cause of action against violators of these standards.

## CRIMINAL SANCTIONS

The 1933 Act contains criminal provisions for willful violations of its provisions. A conviction can carry a fine of $5,000 but not more than $10,000, or imprisonment of not more than five years, or both.

## THE SECURITIES ACT OF 1934

For most small business owners or managers, the 1934 Act may not have particular relevance, but with some hard work and good luck you could fit into that unfortunate category. It is not wise to issue securities to the public unless you believe it is neces-

sary. Knowing the scope of this Act can be of some benefit to you.

This particular Act applies more particularly to companies that have assets exceeding $3 million and have a class of equity securities with *500* or more shareholders. If this fits your company, then your company must register with the Securities and Exchange Commission and must comply with the registration and periodic reporting requirements. There are also other requirements that will apply to your company, including penalties if there are short-swing profits, the tender offer provisions, proxy provisions and the internal control and record-keeping provisions of the Federal Corrupt Practices Act. Let's take a look at some of the specific requirements.

## REGISTRATION AND PERIODIC REPORTING

Under this 1934 Act, all covered publicly held companies must *register* with the SEC. This requires quarterly and annual reporting. The registration requirements here are somewhat different from those in the Securities Act of 1933. Much of the same information must be reported, however. There are also *exempt types* of *securities*, which you need not register. Many of them correspond to the exemptions of the 1933 Act.

This 1934 Act requires *disclosure* of *information* involving (a) the organization, (b) its financial structure, (c) the nature of its business, (d) a description of the various types of securities outstanding, (e) the names of the directors, officers and underwriters, (f) any security holder owning more than 10% of each class of non-exempt security, (g) description of the bonus and profit-sharing arrangements, and (h) balance sheet and profit and loss statements for the three preceding fiscal years. The company must keep this up on a continual basis. There are reports called 100s, which are quarterly reports, and 10Ks, which are annual reports. There are other reports.

In addition, the Act requires that each director, officer or any person who owns 10 percent or more of the registered equity security file *monthly* SEC reports if there are any *changes* in the ownership of this individual or entity. In other words, the owners do not have to file every month if there is *no* change. They must file this report if their ownership changes or they trade in the company's shares.

This 1934 Act imposes penalties on the company or other person filing false statements and reports. These persons may have potential liability to investors who suffer losses when they purchase or sell such securities in reliance on such information. The potential criminal liability can carry a fine of not more than $100,000, or imprisonment of not more than five years, or both. There is a defense to this criminal liability from imprisonment if the person can prove that he had no knowledge of the rule or regulation.

## ANTI-FRAUD PROVISIONS

The 1934 Act contains one of the most important sections of the Securities Laws, known as Section 10(b) of the 1934 Act, and Rule 10b-5, which was promulgated by the SEC to bring this section alive. This law applies to virtually *any securities purchased* or *sold* in interstate commerce. It makes illegal the following:

1. Employing any device, scheme or artifice to defraud.

2. Making any untrue statements of a material fact.

3. Omitting to state a material fact necessary in order to make the statements not misleading.

4. Engaging in any act, practice or course of business which operates or would operate as a fraud or deceit upon any person.

Note that this is strikingly similar to the requirements of the 1933 Act. One of the essential differences is that this Act applies to *purchases and sales* and is *not* limited to non-exempt securities. It applies virtually across the board. It applies to securities of companies that do not have to register under this Act.

## BREADTH OF SECTION 10(b)

It is important to realize that this Act has a significantly broad range and breadth. There are a number of factors you ought to be aware of so you know it is *virtually inescapable.*

First, it covers not only *purchases* but *sales*. Second, it covers not only common stocks, but virtually *all securities*. Essentially there is no escape from it. Third, it covers securities whether or not they have to be registered under the 1933 Act or the 1934 Act. Fourth, it covers securities whether they are public traded or closely held. Fifth, it covers securities whether they are listed on an exchange or sold over the counter. Sixth, it covers securities whether bought at initial issuance (from the company) or at secondary distribution (from a person other than the company). So large and small, wide and tall, or any color, shade or shape, securities are covered by this anti-fraud section.

## MEETING THE REQUIREMENTS OF SECTION 10(b) AND RULE 10b-5

In order to recover damages under these Rules, the plaintiff is required to prove the following: (1) a misstatement or an omission, (2) of a material fact, (3) made with knowledge of its falsity, (4) which was relied upon, (5) in connection with the purchase or sale of a security. Not many individuals are aware of the breadth of this rule. If you are offering securities to the public, if you are looking for investors in your business, you will have this heavy obligation of disclosing everything. The skeletons, the good parts, the bad parts, the heavy risks must all hang out. Furthermore, you have to be able to *prove* that you *disclosed all* of this *information.*

## INSIDER TRADING

Section 10(b) and Rule 10b-5 also cover the insider trading prohibitions that we have been reading about lately in all of the newspapers and business journals, including the Wall Street Journal. Insiders include directors, officers, employees, agents of the company, underwriters, accountants, lawyers and consultants. Insiders also include tippees (people who receive illicit information) or individuals who have received information from one of these inside persons. So you include *outside* employees who somehow get information as a result of being exposed to *inside* information, which even includes employees of printers employed by or under contract to the underwriters.

## SHORT-SWING PROFITS

One section of the 1934 Act focuses on the potential for directors, officers or 10 percent shareholders being able to trade on *inside information*. Therefore, this provision contains a *blanket prohibition* against any of these persons buying or selling stock within a six-month period from the date of its purchase. The six-month period can be calculated before or after a sale or purchase. You do not necessarily have to *buy* it *first* and *sell* it *later*. You can sell it first and buy it back later, for instance as on a short sale, and still be violating the act. Any *profit* must be returned to the company.

## INSIDER TRADING SANCTIONS ACT

As a result of the tremendous number of abuses discovered within the last few years, Congress passed the Insider Trading Act of 1984. It allows the SEC to impose penalties upon any person caught trading on inside information. The liability under this Act also extends to *any person* who *aids* or *abets* a violation by such person. So it is not only the person who *makes* the *money* off the information who *has* the inside information, but also includes any additional person who helps in bringing about the violation of the Act.

The transaction must utilize the facilities of a National Securities Exchange or must go through a broker or a dealer.

The Act applies to purchases as issuance or public offering made by the issuer of the securities. There is a limitation on the civil penalty. It cannot exceed *three* times the *profit* gained or lost or loss avoided as the result of the purchase or sale based on such *inside information.*

## PROXY SOLICITATION

These provisions focus on the requirement that when a company solicits proxies (powers to vote in a shareholder's absence) from its shareholders, it delivers *complete* information in its request for such authority. A proxy allows management to vote your shares unless you intend to go to the meeting to vote the shares. Most proxies allow you to vote *for* or *against* or *abstain* from voting on a specific issue. Normally you know that management would like you to vote *for* their proposals. Nevertheless, the requirement under the Act and SEC rule is that *all material information* be disclosed so you can make an informed decision.

The 1934 Act makes it unlawful for any person to solicit a proxy for a covered company that does *not* meet the requirements of the rules and regulations of the SEC. Again, these rules require that management describe all *material* facts the shareholder would need to make an intelligent decision. An additional item is that any security holder who is entitled to vote has the opportunity to communicate with other security holders. There are some limitations on this right, because any kook could force some crazy, irrelevant idea to be disseminated to all shareholders. If any shareholder owns at least 1% or $1,000 in market value of the security and has held it for at least a year, this

---

## *POWER POINTS* _____

▶ This is one area of the law that takes an "emotional" conversion.

▶ It applies expansive concepts, since it is intended to cure fraudulent acts in the purchase or sale of securities.

▶ Securities laws look to the *substance* of a transaction and not to the way it looks.

▶ Tell the truth and the whole truth if you want to keep the securities doctor away.

individual may be able to require management to submit his proposal for a vote. It can be no longer than 500 words, and a security holder is limited to submitting one proposal to an issuer each year.

Management is *not* required to submit this proposal to shareholders (1) if under state law it is *not* a *proper subject* for shareholder action or (2) if it is *not significantly related* to the issuer's business or beyond the issuer's power to effectuate or (3) if it relates to conduct in the ordinary course of business operation of the issuer, where it is not a subject that the shareholders would typically vote on.

## TENDER OFFERS

The 1934 Act also extends certain reporting and disclosure requirements to tender offers and other block or group purchases of the securities of a reporting company. For instance, a tender offer is an invitation to shareholders of a company by an entity that wishes to purchase those shares at a specific price.

Any person or group of individuals who acquire or make a tender offer that could result in the acquisition of more than 5% of any specific class of registered equity securities must file a statement with the SEC. This statement must contain: (1) the person's background; (2) the source of funds used to acquire the securities; (3) the purpose of the acquisition; (4) the number of shares owned; and (5) any relevant contracts, arrangements or understandings with the company or with any other person.

This person must submit this statement to each offeree, and must also send it to the issuer (company). Again, it is unlawful for any person who is making this statement to make any untrue statements of material facts or omit to state any material facts or engage in any fraudulent, deceptive or manipulative practices in connection with the offer.

The Act also attempts to protect shareholders from being pushed around in the marketplace by fear or by lack of information. The Act allows shareholders who have tendered their shares to withdraw them unconditionally during the first seven days of any tender offer. If the offeror has not yet purchased the shares, even though they had been submitted, or the offer has been accepted within 60 days after that time period, the shareholders can withdraw their shares from the tender offer.

A general requirement for the person making the tender offer is that all shares tendered must be purchased for the same price. If the offered price has increased, those who have already tendered their shares must receive the benefit of this increase. There is much litigation as to how these two are tied together and how long it takes for an offer to die, so that a new price can be offered for other individual shares. In a word, it is not a settled area and there are many difficulties with it; and really both sides, both offerors and offerees, have complained about the rules that pertain to tender offers.

Another condition that exists sometimes is when more shares are offered than the purchaser intends to purchase. The shares are taken on a pro rata basis. This means that all of the shares which are offered must be purchased on a percentage basis so that the total dollar amount that the offeror intends to offer is distributed proportionately to the persons who offered their shares.

## FOREIGN CORRUPT PRACTICES ACT

Though this Act pertains primarily to companies that are required to report under the 1934 Act, it is broader than that. It requires certain internal controls to be placed on reporting companies. It also, in general, prohibits all domestic companies from bribing foreign government or political officials.

It contains certain accounting requirements which pertain to company issuers that have a registered class of equity securities. Some of the antibribery features also apply to other companies that do business in the international arena.

Violations of this Act can result in fines of up to $1 million for companies and up to $10,000 for individuals. In addition, individuals can be imprisoned for up to five years. Additionally, as a little kicker, these fines are imposed upon individuals; they may not be paid, directly or indirectly, by the issuer.

Securities laws are really *insecurities laws*. The legal obligation to spill your guts to the public about the bad things in your company can lead to heart attacks, lumbago and the heartbreak of psoriasis.

# CHAPTER 14

## INTELLECTUAL PROPERTY

# CHAPTER 14

# INTELLECTUAL PROPERTY

## PROTECTING TRADEMARKS, SERVICE MARKS, COPYRIGHTS AND PATENTS

When we discuss intellectual property, we are generally referring to a number of things. We include trade secrets, trademarks, service marks, copyrights and patents.

All of these types of property may be essential to a business. Sometimes individuals create unique approaches to doing business and want to protect them. The business may have a well-known logo. Most of us are aware of the trademarks connected to products. Some of the examples involved are the sale of drinks, photographic film and clothing. The number of examples is endless.

We will take a look at the general rules that apply to these areas. You can then get some idea of what is necessary to protect some types of intellectual property for your business. It will also give you some idea of the potential problems involved in violating someone else's rights.

## TRADE SECRETS

By trade secrets, we are generally talking about confidential information. This might include some formula for creating a product, or some process for creating a product, or a pattern, or some compilation program, devices, approaches or techniques to creating a product or performing some particular service where there is an *actual* or *potential* financial or economic value. The owner wants to keep the secret and not have it disclosed to any competitors or potential competitors. How is it done?

Under the Uniform Trade Secrets Act, a trade secret has been defined as meaning information, including a formula, pattern, compilation, program, device, method, technique or process, that:

1. Derives independent economic value, actual or potential, for not being generally known to and not being readily ascertainable by proper means by other persons who can obtain economic value from its disclosure or use.

2. Is the subject of efforts that are reasonable under the circumstances to maintain its secrecy.

Now, what is protected? What the law and the cases seek to protect is someone *misappropriating* (taking) someone else's trade secret. What do we mean by "misappropriating"? How can someone take it or use it? If it is being used by someone other than the business of a person who has created it or has ownership of it, we have a problem.

A misappropriation can include someone else's acquiring it or having it disclosed to another person by *improper means*.

Many individuals are aware of the secrecy surrounding, for instance, the formulas of certain soft drinks or the secret formulas for fragrances. It is possible with chemistry to determine or analyze products from a chemical viewpoint, but not always the exact proportions. There are legitimate methods that sometimes yield accurate results for duplicating a product. What we are examining are the illicit approaches.

Obviously, from what we just mentioned, an employer must have a process or something of value to protect. He or she must also make some *reasonable efforts* to protect it. That does not necessarily mean that he has to keep everyone in the business under chains and plug up their ears so they cannot hear and cover their eyes so they cannot see.

If you happen to have a business with some need to protect any of your valuable trade secrets, you should address the need for a specific agreement for each employee to sign. With this approach, you have made an effort to protect your trade secrets. You do not have to completely define every trade secret. There may be important items of information you have which are not copyrightable or patentable or do not fit in the trademark protection area, which you can still protect.

## ABANDONMENT AND LOSS OF TRADE SECRECY STATUS

Any businessman who wants to protect any of his trade secrets must be vigilant in *keeping* such trade information secret. Some court decisions have decided that certain trade secrets have been lost. On occasion, individuals have *inadvertently* disclosed some trade secret information. In some cases, the courts may interpret this as being an abandonment. Then anybody who can get their hands on it legitimately has a right to use it.

There are ways of having individuals legitimately ascertain your information. These ways include the following:

1. If it has been discovered *independently* or by an *independent development*.

2. If it has been discovered by *reverse engineering*. Individuals may take a look at the end product and work their way back to the trade secret.

3. If it has been discovered by *independent legitimate observation* in public use or in public display. This might not include flying or even around a new plant to observe what types of processes are visible.

4. If others have obtained the information legitimately and have published it in literature.

Sometimes there has been litigation involving the ownership of a trade secret. Obviously the judge and jury may have to get all the facts. Nevertheless, it may be possible to have a trade secret disclosed just to the judge or the jury yet still be kept as a trade secret. Courts often allow a "protective order" to keep these secrets under cover.

## DISCLOSURE OF TRADE SECRETS DURING UNSUCCESSFUL NEGOTIATIONS

What happens if you have a trade secret you will be willing to license? Or what if you are negotiating with someone who may want to license your secret? The general guideline for such negotiations is that the types of information may have to be disclosed for the potential buyer to determine value. Very few people are willing to buy a pig in a poke. Under these circumstances, you need not abandon your trade secret. Make sure you have the potential buyer sign an agreement so that the other party understands that whatever may be disclosed is *still subject* to *protection*. You could also add that the remedies include injunctive relief, money damages, attorney's fees and court costs. That is one method of protecting such secrets.

## PROTECTING CUSTOMER INFORMATION, INCLUDING ROUTE INFORMATION

There have been occasions where an individual such as a route salesman leave a company to work for a competitor. Generally his route information does not fit into the category of a trade secret. It may be easy for anybody, other route salesmen for instance, to reconstruct his route without even having a list. It's easy to use directories that might include all of the potential customers. Therefore, at certain times, an employer may want to keep certain information secret but it may not fall into a category where it is easy to protect. Sometimes it is difficult to protect these things. *C'est la guerre, mon petit cher.*

## REMEDIES FOR TRADE SECRET VIOLATIONS

The remedies for such a violation involving a misappropriation of a trade secret, where the owner has taken those reasonable efforts we discussed, include injunctive relief and monetary relief. These are the typical remedies.

Injunctive relief involves a *court order* to the bad guy to cease disseminating or using such information. The court might order this person to return the information from any potential recipient. The court might also enjoin any third party who has the trade secret.

Monetary relief can include not only the direct damages that may be lost, but also the *profits* that may have been made by the third party. In some states it can involve *punitive* damages (sometimes in huge numbers). Relief can also involve an *accounting*. If that third party has made money off the product or trade secret, he or she may have to trace every dollar earned and return any profits to the legitimate owner of the trade secret.

## TRADE SYMBOLS

Trade symbols are an important category, because most of us are aware of the efforts it takes to develop a good public image of your product or service. Any company that has spent considerable effort developing a quality product has an interest in preventing its *misuse* or any mis-association of its product with some *unrelated* company. We see this in the form of what is known as "pawning off" or "passing off" a product as being related to a well-known product.

There are several ways of protecting against this type of infringement. Again, we see these in the form of trademarks, service marks, certification marks, collective marks and trade names. Let's take a look at these.

## TRADEMARKS

A trademark is defined as being a distinctive mark, word, letter, number, design, picture, or combination of any of these forms, which is affixed to a specific good and is adopted or used by a person in distinguishing his goods from those manufactured or sold by another person.

A *commonly used* word which is only descriptive of your product cannot be used as a trademark. Trademarks may be registered with the U.S. Patent Office. They may also be registered in most, if not all, states. Thus you can protect your trademark with both a state and federal level of protection. The remedy for violations of these is generally similar to the violations we mentioned for trade secret protection, meaning injunctive relief and monetary damages.

## SERVICE MARKS

Service marks are similar to trademarks. Trademarks identify tangible goods, whereas service marks essentially identify services. A finance company does not sell a good, but sells a service. An insurance company does not sell a good, it sells a service. Thus, a finance company and an insurance company do not sell you a thing. So those entities cannot get trademarks. They can get service mark protection for the positive associations created around their names.

---

## *POWER POINTS* _____

▶ Trademarks and service marks can be protected on three different levels:

1. **Local or county**—Fictitious name or business name protection.

2. **State**—Trademark/service mark or corporate name protection; trade names under unfair competition laws.

3. **Federal**—Trademark protection or possibly trade name.

## TERM

The federal registration period for a trademark or service mark lasts for 20 years. It can be renewed for subsequent 20-year periods.

## CERTIFICATION MARKS

Certification marks are used in connection with goods or services of any person who is not the mark owner. They are used to certify that goods or services have material of a particular origin and method of manufacture, quality, accuracy or other characteristics. In addition, they may be used to show that the work or labor used in producing the goods or providing the services comes from a labor union or other organization. We have seen products with the "union bug" on them. The shape of certification mark shows that this product was union made.

## COLLECTIVE MARKS

A collective mark is another one of those identifiable marks or symbols which indicate membership in a trade union or trade association, fraternal organization or some other organization to indicate that the goods were made by some collective group. The mark is owned by the collective group and not by the user. If the mark is owned by the user, then it is a trademark or service mark.

## TRADE NAMES

A trade name is like a trademark. It creates the identification of a product with a particular manufacturer or distributor. Trade names generally have broader coverage or implication than trademarks. Trademarks are identified only with specific goods. Trade names that are not *also* trademarks or service marks do not generally enjoy federal protection. State common law and unfair competition laws often prevail in protecting them.

Trade names, for instance, may not be descriptive or generic terms. Some types of names may not qualify as trademarks or service marks. It is possible that they may be protected as trade names.

Therefore, trying to palm a product off as being of the same quality or as being made by the same company as a protected trade name may be violating the law. The type of damages that may be due, though not derived from federal law, might also include monetary damages and injunctive relief.

## COPYRIGHT

Copyrights are in a slightly different category from trade names or trademarks. Copyright generally involves a lower level of protection. Copyright is an exclusive right given under statutory or common law to an author or creator of a work to reproduce, perform, publish or display his or her work. Copyright protection can aid the person who has created literary works, musical works, dramatic works, pantomimes, choreographic works, pictorial, graphic and sculptural works, motion pictures and other audio/visual works and sound recordings. This list is not intended to give every possible category of protection, but nevertheless may be helpful. If you are in a business that is directly related to creating work such as a music recording studio that creates its own records, or a poster company, obtaining copyrights should be part and parcel of your daily business.

Excerpting material from a protected owner's work sometimes comes into play in a commercial atmosphere. We have seen this when a magazine gives a glowing product report and a seller of this product wants to use the entire report.

The federal copyright law contains a "fair use" provision that allows some limited use of someone else's material when it is not a substitute for the entire material. The entire work obviously costs money. That is what the author owns. Ideas in general, even if they are unique or titles of works, are not copyrightable. There is no copyright protection for ideas, for plots, for themes or for dramatic situations and events.

What is essentially copyrighted is the *form* of *expression* in that particular work. Someone may reproduce a scene through a photograph. Someone else can photograph the same scene with another camera. Each photographer can copyright his own particular photographic rendering of the scene. Thus even if the pictures were taken at the same place and same time and look identical, they are different works and can each be copyright protected. I would love to become the owner of the City of New York because I took a picture of it.

Private utterances are not copyrightable. You can have copyright protection available for your speeches, addresses, monologues, panel discussions that you have delivered publicly.

Generally, works produced for the U.S. Government are not copyrightable. It is possible, however, for the U.S. Government to receive and hold copyrights transferred to it by assignment or otherwise.

Copyrights can include such things as advertising materials, maps and charts. It can also include a fabric and dress designs. It can include architectural plans, architectural drawings and many other types of things that have not yet been dreamed of. However, forms are difficult to copyright.

The "fair use" doctrine, as we have mentioned previously, creates a privilege for persons other than the copyright owner. It allows them to use the copyrighted material in a reasonable manner and without having to get consent from the owner.

The law looks at the following factors for "fair use":

1. The purpose and character of the use of what is in focus, including whether it is done for a commercial purpose or for non-profit educational purposes.

2. The nature of the copyrighted work.

3. The amount and substantiality of the portion being used in relation to the size of the entire copyrighted work.

4. The effect of the use upon the potential market for and value of the copyrighted work.

In effect, if someone is quoting a limited number of words from a work which in no way reflects the entire work, it is unlikely the person is stealing the market for the entire work. If someone has written a play which is 50 pages long and an individual is quoting 20, 30, 40 or 50 words from the play, no one is likely to substitute those few words being quoted for reading the entire play. That is a general idea of what "fair use" is looking toward.

The owner of a copyright is the author of the copyrighted work. It can be bought and sold, and an individual can be hired to create it. The employer of the individual can be the owner, but there has to be some express written agreement to that effect. Otherwise, the creator is the owner.

TERM

How long is a copyright good for? A currently attained copyright lasts during the life of the author plus 50 years. It is not necessarily identified with the publisher.

In a case where there is a work that is created by two or more authors who do not work for hire, the duration of the copyright is for the life of the last surviving author plus 50 years.

If the work was created anonymously or with a pseudonym or as a work for hire, the duration of the copyright is for a term ending with the earlier of (a) 75 years from the date of its first publication or (b) 150 years from the year of its creation.

ADDITIONAL PROTECTION

If you wish to have copyright protection on any work, the notice of copyright must be visually perceptible. You must generally use the letter "c" in a circle or the word "Copyright" or the abbreviation "Copr." The year of first publication of the work (though there are some exceptions) and the name of the owner of the copyright of the work or an abbreviation by which the name can be recognized or any generally known alternative designation of the owner must be placed next to the symbol and the year.

Adding "all rights reserved" can add the protection of a number of additional countries under an international agreement called the Buenos Aires Convention

For phonograph records, the letter "p" is the symbol that must be used.

What happens if the notice of copyright has been omitted? The law allows some curing of this if any of the following has occurred:

1. Notice has been omitted for no more than a small number of copies.

2. The registration for the work has been made or is made within five years after the publication without notice that it has been made and the copyright owner makes a reasonable effort to add the notice to all of the copies outstanding.

3. The notice has been omitted in violation of an express agreement in writing that copies or phonograph records bear that prescribed notice.

## REMEDIES

Remedies for infringing copyrights include injunctive relief, impounding and disposing of the articles, recovery of monetary damages and recovery of costs and reasonable attorney's fees. In addition, there can be criminal liability under U.S. criminal statutes.

## PATENTS

A patent is a grant of authority by the federal government to a monopoly right to an inventor to make, use or sell an invention to the absolute exclusion of others for the period of the patent. Currently, that is 17 years.

The basic requirement is that the subject matter of the patent must be patentable. In addition, the invention sought to be patented must possess the statutory requirements of *novelty, utility* and *non-obviousness.*

The subject matter that the law requires can be a *process*, a *machine*, a *manufacture*, a *composition* of *matter*, or any new or useful *improvement* on an existing subject matter.

Services cannot be patented. However, processes, including mechanical, chemical, electrical, biological and many other processes, can be patented.

As common as computer programs are these days, we find that methods of expressing mathematical formulas cannot by themselves be the subject of a patent. It does appear, however, that the application of a *law of nature* or a mathematical formula written in a computer program to solve a specific problem or problems might be a legitimate subject matter of a patent.

A number of states have passed laws allowing protection of computer programs. Sometimes these protections are in the nature of copyright protection. Computer programs can be important assets for a corporation. You, as a business person, might be interested in protecting such assets. Ask the geniuses who developed the well-known computer spreadsheets and database programs.

What happens if there is a violation of a patent? Anyone who makes, uses or sells a patented invention without permission can be violating someone's property rights. He may also be violating criminal statutes.

## REMEDIES

The civil remedies available include (1) injunctive relief; (2) damages, which can include a reasonable royalty for the use; (3) triple damages (three times the actual damages); plus (4) attorney's fees in certain cases.

# CHAPTER 15

LEASING COMMERCIAL SPACE
FOR YOUR BUSINESS

# CHAPTER 15

## LEASING COMMERCIAL SPACE FOR YOUR BUSINESS

Almost all businesses end up needing space to locate in, and most businesses lease that space.

It is not always necessary for the small business owner and manager to have knowledge of all the nuances of real estate law with regard to leases. On the other hand, since so many small businesses sign leases, I would like to review some of the general features of the lease and then go into an effective checklist of the type of provisions that you may see in a lease—some of which you may want to omit, some of which you may want to make sure are included in your lease.

Let's take a look at some of the essential features of the lease or tenancy.

### REAL ESTATE LEASE VERSUS PERSONAL PROPERTY LEASE

One of the things I would like to distinguish is that there are significantly different features to consider when you are leasing space for a business, in effect space involving real property. This is to be distinguished from leasing personal property, such as an automobile. The statutes are almost totally different, or at least significantly different, to the extent that you cannot consider the same principles to apply in all cases.

A lease of personal property is called a bailment. On the other hand, there can be a mixing of these two, for instance when a small business or any business may be leasing real property which includes personal property and they include equipment and furniture and so forth. So there can be a blending of the two. Sometimes this creates quite a complication.

### TYPES OF GENERAL CONDITIONS OF A TENANCY

There are several types of tenancies, as they are called, meaning different term relationships, and they can also involve when a lease might end or what is the term of such a lease.

There can be a term for years, where you have agreed to a year or 18 months or 24 months and one week or 15 years and so forth. This is known as a term for years.

A second type of tenancy is called a tenancy at will, which means that the lease is terminable at any time.

A third type of tenancy is a tenancy from period to period, which could result from there being an end of an initial lease with no statement as to any carryover, but where the tenant stays in the space for whatever is the normal period in that state or any normal period stated in the lease. The lease would be carried over for this particular time period.

A fourth type is called a tenancy at sufferance, which means as long as the landlord or the owner is willing to allow the tenant to remain.

A fifth type of tenancy is called a tenancy for life, which is obvious: The tenancy lasts as long as the tenant lives.

The sixth type is called a tenancy in fee.

### WHAT HAPPENS IF A MORTGAGE IS INVOLVED

A lease can be made on premises that are mortgaged. One of the essential caveats is that the mortgagor (debtor) (lessor) cannot make a lease that would adversely affect the creditor, meaning the lender, who has a security interest in the real property. It has happened in the past, and will happen in the future, that on occasion leases are made where the creditor has agreed to certain terms and conditions of the lease. So sometimes creditors come into the picture when establishing the lease.

## NECESSITY TO HAVE THE LEASE IN WRITING

Considering that location is essential for most businesses, it is important for any business person to put the lease in writing. There can be the clearest of understandings made orally, but this is extremely dangerous. There are enough court cases that I have conveyed the message to get it in writing. In some states, any lease of a year or longer must be in writing. The statute of frauds requires that any relationship that would take more than a year from the date of signing the agreement to perform must be in writing. In addition, the statute of frauds also pertains to interest in real property having to be in writing. Again, it depends on the state, but certainly it would be wise to always get your leases in writing.

## MINIMUM REQUIREMENTS OF THE LEASE

The basic necessities of a lease would include:

1. The names of the parties such that they could be identified as lessor and lessee.

2. A statement of the lessor that he is going to let the lessee occupy the property which is being leased.

3. A description of the property being leased.

4. A statement of the amount of the rent.

5. Typically, a term. Virtually all leases have a term, but that is not always a basic necessity in many states.

## ADDITIONAL PROVISIONS

Certainly most leases of business property, for that matter even residential property, contain a number of clauses in addition to the bare-bones clauses we just mentioned.

In modern relationships, especially involving leasing of business or office property, each person should expect to see detailed provisions, which involve not only a terminal in the lease (which is not necessary), but might involve statements as to the payment of taxes, the purchase of insurance, the amount and type of insurance, who handles what repairs, and the categories of repairs that are the burden of the lessor and those that are the obligation of the lessee. Leases also contain clauses as to the types of alterations that can be made and those that are prohibited, or as to the allowance of any assignment of the lease or of any subletting.

## CONDITIONS VERSUS COVENANTS

Let's look at this important distinction.

It is extremely important for you as a potential lessor or lessee to understand the distinction between what are called covenants as distinguished from conditions.

If there is a condition or some particular provision which says that this lease or the continuation of this lease is conditioned explicitly on some behavior or act or occurrence of something, it must be clear from the context that it is a condition of the lease. If a condition is not met or if a condition is broken, the other party is in a position of terminating the lease totally, because there has been a failure of this particular condition. In that case, the party who has the right to rely on this particular condition can get out of the lease and also sue for damages.

On the other hand, a covenant may be only a representation— for instance, a statement that the premises may be used only for a particular purpose—or there can be other representations. If the representation is that the property will be used for a particular premise or if there is the representation that looks like a covenant, meaning it is not a condition, then the non-offending party, the party who has a right to rely on that covenant, cannot terminate the lease and can only sue for damages because he or she has not gotten their money's worth under the lease provisions.

Again, the results can be very different, and that is why it is important to pay attention to the distinction between a condition or covenant.

What would give you some indication that something is a condition? The use of the words "on condition that" or "provided that." On the other hand, just seeing these words may not be a guarantee that such will be a condition.

You as a potential lessee or tenant of the property may want to make sure that the landlord will put in two or three walls. Maybe he has agreed to such a thing. It would be extremely important for your document to contain the words "our company will lease this on condition that" those particular walls be put in at your particular specifications on which you agreed. Again, it is better to state it even more strongly so that if the condition fails or is not met the lessee will be in a position of terminating the lease immediately.

One thing to watch out for is that sometimes the words are used, but if the rest of the document uses words that cut against it being a condition or seem to imply that it is really a covenant—meaning it is not an absolute guarantee upon which you can get out of the lease—then the contradictory language changes the nature of what is an obvious condition into a covenant.

## RECORDING
It is important to realize that lessees may be in a position to protect themselves over the long term by recording the lease at some public registry.

Different states have different requirements for recordation, but a typical example would be the following: If the lessee were to sign a five-year lease, in some states if the lessor sold the property to another person after a year, two years or later the lessee would not have an agreement with the new owners unless he or she signed a lease with the new owners. On the other hand, if the lessee had recorded that lease, any new owner would be put on notice that the lease is good for five years, and the lessee would be protected for the term of that lease and also for the conditions of that lease.

## RENT PROVISIONS
Leases, especially long-term leases, can provide for some of the following types of rents:

1. Flat rent for the entire term.
2. Rents providing for periodical increases based on some formula or a fixed percentage.

3. Rents calculated to be a certain percentage of the value of the property, which can be periodically appraised and result in a change of the rent.

4. Rents calculated as a fixed base amount, but in addition a percentage of gross sales if in excess of a particular amount, which can also be variable based on different triggering points.

## DEATH OF THE LESSEE
Leases generally do not terminate on the death of the lessee, but there can be certain conditions where they would. The lease may state that or, on the other hand, a lease can be so personal that most parties would understand that if the lessee dies the lease itself would terminate automatically.

## SECURITY DEPOSITS
Security deposits are generally for security either for damage or for non-payment of rent, but do not result in automatic forfeiture.

It is possible for a lease to have what is known as a liquidated damages clause where the damages are calculated in advance and as long as they are reasonable there will be no further damages due on the lease, but any fixed amount which meets the legal requirements for a liquidated damage amount would be automatically taken care of or provided by the deposit. The lease would have to be specific and explicit in stating that the security deposit is the liquidated damage amount. In a word, this is generally not the case, meaning that security deposits generally are security for either damage or the rents, but are not automatically forfeited.

## CONDITION OF THE PREMISES
Generally if you were to lease premises for use in your business, possibly with some office space and storage space, it would be stated that the premises are fit for that particular use. Thinking you could use it for that is the main reason you are leasing the property.

## INSURANCE
Most commercial business leases require that the tenant have a certain level and type of insurance, including general liability insurance, to act as a

cover for any potential liability the lessor might have.

If the agreement does not require insurance, then the lessee would have no obligation. The fact that you rent property does not mean you are required to have insurance. There is no doubt that even if the lease does not mention it, you as a tenant should seriously consider getting insurance. The cost of it is generally nominal in comparison with the coverage you can receive.

## LIABILITY FOR INJURIES

In many states the landlord and tenant can negotiate for particular liability for injuries which occur under certain circumstances. Generally neither party can exempt himself or herself from liability for things that party causes.

In other words, you cannot be absolved from liability for something you do personally. On the other hand, if there are some things the lessor may be liable for just because he or she owns the property, it is possible in the lease to transfer this potential liability to the lessee under certain circumstances. Not all states are uniform, but at least you ought to know that this in particular comes out of the rent. The rent can include dollars, and it also can include transfer of liability. You ought to be aware of the fact that this is sometimes a part of the bargain or agreement.

## EXCULPATORY PROVISIONS

Often you will see, in conjunction with the potential for liability, a party's attempt to shift the liability to someone else. As I just mentioned, though, a party will be liable for his or her own behavior but can exculpate or free himself or herself from a potential liability for things you might normally be liable for, by using particular provisions in the agreement.

Certain types of exculpatory provisions are clearly against public policy, and even if they are in a lease they would be unenforceable.

## THE LESSOR'S LIEN

In most states a lessor has a lien in the leased premises, and possibly in the personal property of the lessee, if the lessee fails to perform under the lease. For instance, let's assume the lessee fails to pay rent for one month; it is possible for the lessor to actually seize or have an interest in the personal property of the tenant and get a court order to protect and hold or seize his property so the landlord can guarantee payment of the rental amount.

In other words, the lessor would be able to seize the lessee's movable personal property on those premises as security for the rent or lease amount.

You will see this on occasion done by judicial sale. If there is sufficient property to cover the debt, then any excess goes back to the lessee.

In many states the parties can create a lien on the lessee's property in favor of the lessor specifically.

## RENEWAL OR EXTINCTION

Just as any lease will have an initial term typically, it is also possible they will also put in there the right to have an optional term or a renewal term. The initial term may be for five years and the lessor may be willing to allow the lessee to have an option for another two years and then possibly will renew for another two-year term. These are not suggested terms; it is just that the new terms may be at different lengths and different rental rates or, may be the same.

## REPAIRS

Generally repairs to major portions of property or to structural types of things are the obligation of the lessor. On the other hand, the lease may transfer this obligation. Especially in commercial leases, you may see the transferring of obligations to fix things or to repair things that may be part of the structure.

It is not uncommon in the leasing of office space to see that the tenant is obligated to fix virtually everything on the property that may be damaged. I have seen leases where the tenant was obligated to fix the roof and the air conditioning and lots of other things that might typically be considered structural.

By agreement the parties can transfer the financial obligation to fix almost any part of the leased premises, including the structure.

## SIGNS AND ADVERTISEMENTS

Another important aspect, in this day of technical zoning laws, may be provisions involving the types of signs that may be put up or the types of advertisement that can be placed on the premises.

Sometime there may be one place and one place alone where the tenant is allowed to place a sign, and by law or by provisions or covenants that go with the land, the tenant may be allowed only so many square feet for a sign area. It is important to ask these questions, and it is important to make sure these provisions are covered in the lease.

## TAXES AND ASSESSMENTS

In most business leases as opposed to residential leases, you will see the pass-through of taxes and other expenses. It is fairly common to pass through taxes to the tenant so that each tenant pays his or her proportion or share of the total tax bill for the property.

In addition there are sometimes common areas, common costs, such as in a strip shopping center where there are lights that go on at dark. The electrical expenses and cleanup expenses may be split up on a proportionate basis and assessed to each of the tenants. A lease should contain these particular provisions.

Obviously maintenance, water, gas, electricity can also be included in these types of assessments.

## TERMINATION OF THE LEASE PRIOR TO THE END OF THE LEASE TERM

Leases may contain provisions including conditions where the lessee may be able to terminate the lease prior to the end of the term.

Certainly the parties jointly have the power to terminate at any time by agreement.

Nevertheless, you should pay attention to any lease provisions which discuss this matter particularly.

## LEASE CHECKLIST

Let's discuss a short checklist of lease provisions you may see, may want or may want to exclude. They may include:

1. *The Parties*. Typically you want to have the landlord define the name and address of the landlord, and the state of incorporation if it happens to be a corporation.

In addition the tenants should be named. You would want the name of the tenants and the state of incorporation, if the tenant is a corporation.

2. *Description of the Premises*. We should have the municipal address, otherwise known as the street address, the city, the county, and the state of the premises. These are not to be assumed. We would also want a legal description of the property. This may be lengthy, but nevertheless a legal description may be more important than the municipal address. You want the size of the area that is being leased, whether or not it includes any parking area, how many parking spaces and the location of the parking spaces. If possible you want to attach plaques to the parking spaces.

3. *Lease Term or Length of the Lease*. The information should include the number of years, the months or precise method of calculating it, the exact date of commencement and the exact ending date. Do not assume, just because you are talking about 12 months, that it means a particular date. You want the precise ending date.

4. *Renewal Options*. You would want to include any renewal options and the concise conditions for the renewal, including whether or not the landlord has the option of renewing, whether or not the tenant has the right to renew, and whether or not the tenant must be in total compliance in order to exercise such renewal. You want the precise term of the renewal. It may not be the same length as the term of the original lease. You would want to state the number of renewals that can be exercised and the requirements for exercising them. For instance, you may want to require that certified mail be used or some form of express mail whereby there is a receipt. You would also want to address whether or

not there would be any change in the rent during that time.

5. *The Rent.* There are several ways of stating what the rent will be; let's look at some:

a. Fixed. You might want to state that the rent is a fixed monthly fee. You would also want to note when the first payment is due and when each subsequent payment must be received by a particular date.

b. Advance Rent.On occasion you will see in commercial leases that the lessee must pay in advance the first and last months or the first and last two months of rent. It does not act necessarily as a security deposit, but only as a payment in advance.

c. Percentage Rent. Often in shopping malls, shopping centers or strip shopping centers you will see rent as a percentage of gross sales or a percentage of sales less refunds, allowances and taxes. You may see a definition of whether interstore transfers are included or excluded. If this store transfers merchandise to another store, is that included as part of the sales? It may go on the books, but there are other purposes for sales. On the other hand, is it to be included in the rental calculation? You would obviously want a statement of what the precise percentage is and under what conditions it applies. You also might want to address whether or not the landlord has a right to inspect the books and records of the tenant. You might want some statement of the exact books and records the tenant must keep. You might want to include some provision for submitting monthly statements of the sales. The lease might state the conditions whereby the tenant may have to pay the auditing firm if there is some discrepancy—more than 5%, for instance.

There might also be some minimum rent, even though there is some percentage rent that could apply, but the base amount should be specifically stated.

6. *Place of Payment.* It is very important to state exactly where the tenant has to send payment.

7. *Deposit.* We want to state the amount of any deposit, whether there is any interest payable, whether it can be used by the landlord, and whether it can be applicable to the last rent.

8. *Tenant Alterations.* If a tenant is allowed or required to make certain alterations, the lease provisions should specify it. Particularly, a lease might state that it has to be done in workmanlike condition and specify that any of the changes can be specified, such as building plans.

9. *Tenant's Obligations.* Most leases would state what the tenant's obligations are in terms of the type of business in which they may engage, the obligation to maintain orderly and clean premises, other types of signs (which we mentioned above) and statements that the tenant will operate the business in the confines of the legal statutes applying to that business and also the zoning statutes and any safety statutes that may apply. In addition there may be some statement in the lease that the tenant will get all the required licenses and will pay taxes and utility bills timely.

You may see some statement about indemnifying the landlord for any injuries occurring on the premises.

10. *Landlord's Obligations.* Again, just as the tenant has taken on certain obligations, the landlord's obligations may be specified.

The landlord obviously has to deliver premises that can be used for the purposes of the tenant—certainly the ones that are stated in the lease. There is some statement about the space that is available; there may be some statement that the landlord will pay certain types of taxes or will take care of certain types of repairs. There may be some obligation that the landlord has to furnish water, gas, electricity and other facilities, and there may be some particular ones that are peculiar to your type of business.

For instance, a dentist needs certain types of plumbing facilities that a typical business may not need.

11. *Insurance.*

a. Tenant's Obligation. Typically a landlord would have insurance on the building, including general liability insurance and other commercial types of insurance. On the other hand, it is fairly typical for landlords to require that the tenant also purchase certain types of insurance, such as comprehensive general liability at a minimal amount of

$300,000 per incident or a minimum of $500,000 as a cap. There may be higher amounts or different types of coverage that may be peculiar to that type of business and required.

Certain types include fire and extended coverage, public liability insurance and workers' compensation; and the landlord may want to see a copy of the policy, may require a statement of the amount of the insurance and the name of the insurance carrier, along with the address in the lease provisions; and a lease may require that the landlord be listed as an additional named insured. A lease may also include a requirement that the landlord be notified of any change of coverage or termination of coverage.

You may also see an optional provision that allows the landlord to purchase such insurance if it is not purchased by the tenant, with the charge back to the tenant.

b. Landlord's Obligation. The lease may include the landlord's obligation to also get certain types of insurance including fire and extended coverage, public liability for the open areas or common areas, and may also state the requirement that the landlord give the name and address of the carrier and the amounts that the landlord will cover.

12. *Damage To Premises.* A lease for commercial property may include who is going to be obligated to make repairs for certain types of damage. It may be stated in terms of a percentage of the frontage involved or a percentage of the premises that are damaged or the time period in which they must be fixed or certain percentages of the parking area. The tenant may be able to terminate the lease if the parking is eliminated or if it is unusable for a certain period.

The tenant may be able to cut back on the rent if less than all of the premises are available.

13. *Expropriation or Appropriation of Property*

## Tenant's Right to Terminate

There are certain conditions where the tenant may want to be able to terminate without default if a state or federal government takes certain portions of the premises. Even if there is the possibility of being recompensed for the loss of the business, then the tenant may want to get out of this particular lease and go somewhere else—not necessarily where the landlord goes.

In any case, it can be stated as an expropriation or an appropriation by a public authority, which would create grounds for the tenant to terminate the lease; or, for that matter, the landlord may want to do so.

14. *Defaults.* Most leases would state what would constitute a default and what are the time periods for acting under that default, what time period the tenant has to receive notice of the default so that he or she can cure it. What constitutes a default? Is it using the premises for an unlisted business or for unlisted conditions, or tenants having financial problems including bankruptcy or insolvency?

15. *Assignment.* We would address the possibility of the tenant being able to assign or sublease the premises to someone else. The lease may contain a statement that even though there may be an assignment the assignor is still continually liable. The lease would not have to necessarily say this, but if it does it makes it more difficult for the initial lessee to deny that he has a continuing obligation even though the entire lease has been assigned to someone else.

16. *Other Types of Provisions.* Some of the types of provisions that you will see can include a statement that the lease contains all of the provisions which apply to the relationship between the parties and that no other agreement shall apply, and that if there are going to be any changes they must be in writing.

17. *Notices.* It would be wise in any lease to state specifically where notice should be sent to either of the parties. In other words, specify the name, address, preferably a municipal or street address as opposed to a post office box, where either of the parties can let the other communicate for specific official purposes.

18. *Other Landlord Rights.* You may also see provisions allowing the landlord the right to enter the property or to place signs to rent the property under certain circumstances when the lessee is not going to stay.

19. *Broker's Fees*. Sometimes there is going to be a real estate broker involved who is going to receive a percentage of the fee, which may be stated in the lease itself.

20. *Applicable Law*. Sometimes you may see a statement of the particular state law that is going to apply to this agreement.

21. *Parties Who Would Guarantee the Lease*. It is not uncommon, with new incorporated businesses, to see individuals having to guarantee the lease. Typically you will see their name, their address and some description of the party who is guaranteeing it. Then you will also see particular provisions that apply to the guarantee. In other words, when does it work, or what are the conditions where the guarantor has to get notice before he or she is liable, or whether the guarantor is liable regardless of notice.

Sometimes you will see specific waivers of any notice.

We have discussed many provisions that may or may not be seen in a lease. Again, as we have said, you may want them included. If you are a lessor you will certainly want to specify those things that cut down on your liability and increase your ability to get your rent.

On the other hand, if you are the lessee, leasing commercial or office space, you will want to make sure you can guarantee that the premises will be available as you understand them and that the landlord will provide you services that are expected.

In any event, the above can be used as a checklist to discuss with the other party as it pertains to any potential lease.

# CHAPTER 16

## SECURED TRANSACTIONS
## IN PERSONAL PROPERTY

# CHAPTER 16

# SECURED TRANSACTIONS IN PERSONAL PROPERTY

The sale of personal property often involves a security interest which the seller may take in the goods sold. Assume you, as a retailer, sell a television set to one of your customers. The payments are in installments. There are certain wrinkles in that transaction that can be important and also can adversely affect you.

Assume that the individual does not continue to make the payments. You may not, with anything else other than that sale, be able to *seize* that *television set*. Now, most of us would understand that as a retailer, we should have a "seizable" interest in that television set. The UCC requires that there be something *more* than *just a sale* of that particular product for us to have an interest in that particular television set. There is a device that creates such an interest. It is fairly common. But it takes a little effort and additional provisions in any sales agreement or in any related agreement to create such interest in that particular good or product.

What do we mean by *secured transaction?* What does it include? There are generally two pieces to it:

(1) There must be a *debt* or some *obligation* to repay *money*; and

(2) The creditor intends and the debtor intends that the *creditor* will have a partial ownership *interest* in the specific property which the debtor is using to secure the payment of that debtor's obligation.

In the case that we have given, it has to be specifically agreed to for you, the retailer, to have an interest in that television set which the debtor is purchasing over time. It is not necessary to create a *debt* to have an *interest* in that television set. This interest adds security for you, as a retailer, in collecting the debt if the buyer defaults.

Several elements are required for the lender to have an interest in the specific goods. What we are dealing with involves Article 9 of the UCC. It applies to circumstances whereby the *debtor* is *consenting* or *agreeing* to allow the *creditor* (the seller of the goods, or someone else who is lending money to buy the goods) to have a security interest in those specific goods. This interest is often known as a security lien.

In any of these secured transactions (by agreement) there are always the debtor, the secured party (the seller), and the collateral, meaning the goods in which the interest arises. There must be a written security agreement between the debtor and the seller, and there must be a specific security interest that is "brought alive" in the collateral.

The debtor is the person who owes the money or has incurred the debt. The secured party is generally the creditor or the lender. Sometimes the secured party can be the seller or sometimes it can be another person who already has an existing security interest in the goods. The collateral is the property that is the focus of the security interest.

The security agreement is the agreement that creates the security interest or brings it alive for our purposes. The security interest is the interest that the owner of the property, the buyer, is *giving up* in favor of the *creditor* to secure the debt. Of course, to modify the ownership concept, you need not own something in order to give a security interest in whatever usage you may have. For instance, you may have the right to use an automobile that you have leased over a certain time period. You could give someone a security interest, not in the car itself, but in the *use* of the automobile over time.

## CREATING OF THE SECURITY INTEREST

How is the security interest created? It can be created when an individual goes to buy that television set. The television set is delivered to the buyer, who becomes the debtor. At the time of the sale, the buyer can sign a retail installment contract, which can create the security interest with the proper language. This agreement will give the retailer, who becomes the secured party, a security interest, meaning a right to seize the product up to the secured amount, in the television set. The TV becomes the collateral.

## TYPES OF COLLATERAL

Under the UCC, many different types of collateral have been analyzed. The UCC attempts to deal with the differing nature of various types of collateral. The Code has separate categories for different types of covered personal property, because there are different types of problems that arise from it. What are the types that are considered goods? The general classes of collateral are goods, collateral involving what is known as "indispensable paper," whereby it is essential to have a *document* to evidence a debt or a form of ownership, and intangibles.

## GOODS

Goods are *tangible personal property* that is essentially movable at the time the security interest becomes alive or arises out of the security agreement.

Goods are further subdivided into five categories.

1. Consumer Goods.
2. Equipment.
3. Farm Products.
4. Inventory.
5. Fixtures.

The same item of personal property could fit into several categories. It depends on the *use* by the *debtor*. Where a couch or sofa could be inventory for a retail furniture dealer, it might be considered equipment in a doctor's office. It could also be considered a consumer good if used in someone's home.

### Consumer Goods

Consumer goods are generally defined as those used or bought for use primarily in someone's home. The use can be for personal, family or household purposes.

### Equipment

Equipment is tangible personal property used, or purchased for use, primarily in a business. It can also include a farming business or professional business, provided it is not specifically included as *inventory* or as a *farm product*, or as a *consumer good*. As we mentioned before, a couch in a doctor's office would be considered equipment.

### Farm Products

Farm products generally include crops, livestock, or supplies used or produced in farming operations. In addition, it can include crops, livestock or supplies that are *products* of *crops* or *livestock* in their unmanufactured states. Thus, farm products could include corn, which is grown on a farm, and could include animals on a farm and the horses, cows, hens. It can also include the eggs.

Now, it is important to realize that when these goods are possessed by someone who is not involved in the farming operation, then they are *no longer* considered farm products.

### Inventory

Inventory generally includes tangible personal property. This would be goods held for sale or lease, as well as goods in process. Raw materials, work-in-progress or materials used or consumed in a business are also considered inventory. If, at a plant which manufactures furniture, the wood used has not yet been converted into finished furniture, it is still included in inventory.

### Fixtures

By fixtures we generally mean personal property or goods that are so closely identified with a particular piece of real estate that a security interest in them may arise under your state's *real estate* (real property) *law*. In other words, the law of the state where the property is located may control, not the UCC.

To determine if these items are *goods* or *fixtures*, we generally have to look to not only the UCC, but also state real estate law. Its definition can control when a security interest arises and who wins. Could the secured party be the *mortgage holder* on the real estate or the lender on the movable home?

Some examples include sprinkler systems, air-conditioning units, heating units, plumbing units, furnaces and other similar types of equipment. There is no simple answer all of the time. But who wins in a court battle is what is at stake.

INDISPENSABLE PAPER

There are essentially three kinds of collateral that involve what we called "indispensable paper." They are: (1) chattel paper, (2) instruments, and (3) documents. What is the difference between these?

1. *Chattel Paper*. Chattel paper is something we see on occasion. It is not quite as esoteric as it might seem. It is generally a writing that creates a *debt* and also creates a *security interest* or lease of specific goods. An example might arise when a business person wants to buy an automobile for business purposes. The auto dealer may sell the automobile on what could be called a purchase money security interest or a conditional sales contract.

Assume the purchase price is $15,000 and the purchaser signs a conditional sales contract to pay money in 36 installments. This conditional sales contract also creates a security interest in favor of the automobile dealer. Thus, if the business defaults on its monthly payments, that automobile dealership can seize its interest in the automobile and possibly sell it to recover the amounts that are left unpaid. This instrument is called "chattel paper." The chattel paper does not have to be owned or held by the dealership. It can be held by a bank.

2. *Instruments*. Instruments include negotiable instruments, promissory notes, stocks, including common stocks and preferred stocks, bonds and other investment securities. Instruments include any writing that evidences an obligation to repay money. The instrument can be transferable by endorsement or assignment. There is *one proviso*. The instrument itself *does not create* a *security interest* or constitute a lease. Instruments are different from chattel paper by definition.

3. *Documents*. The term "documents" can be very broad. There are millions and millions of different documents. Documents include documents of title, such as bills of lading or warehouse receipts. These may be negotiable or non-negotiable. By negotiable we mean that we can actually transfer it to someone with *better legal rights* than we have in the document. When a document is non-negotiable, we may transfer only the legal rights in it that we have. Typically in a contract, for instance, we can assign our rights to another individual. When we assign our rights we are only transferring to this individual the rights we have. If the *other person* has some legal defense against us, our assignee is stuck with that. On the other hand if we *negotiate* a bill of lading to someone (as opposed to *assigning* it), the transferee may not have to worry about the *other person's* legal defense. A document of title is another category for secured transaction purposes.

INTANGIBLES

This is the third general category which the UCC puts in a unique position. It includes accounts and general intangibles.

1. *Accounts*. This generally refers to the right to payment that a business has for goods which have been sold or leased, or for services rendered. Everyone has heard of accounts receivable. *Voila!*

In this particular case, there is no *specific promissory note*. Or there is no *chattel paper*, so we are *excluding* those categories. Essentially it includes what we might call a *contract right*, but it is *not limited* to contract rights.

2. *General Intangibles*. This category includes any personal property other than goods, accounts, chattel paper, documents, instruments and money. It is a kind of garbage-can approach: It picks up everything else that does not fit into another category. Thus, it creates or leaves an opening for other types of new instruments or new kinds of

collateral. It can include a collateral interest in good will, patents, trademarks, copyrights or literary rights.

## ATTACHMENT

How does the creditor or the entity lending the money have an interest attach to a particular good? A security interest has to *attach* for it to be *enforceable* against the good or personal property. The security interest becomes effective once three events have taken place:

1. The secured party or the creditor must give value. He must give up something of *value*.

2. The *debtor* must have *rights in* the collateral. In other words, there can be no secured transaction if the debtor has no rights in the personal property.

3. There are several conditions that have to be met for the secured interest to arise. They include one of the following:

a. The collateral or personal property must be in the *possession* of the *secured party* pursuant to some agreement which gives that party a security interest in it.

b. A security agreement, which is in writing, must contain a reasonable description of the collateral and must be signed by the debtor. If this agreement exists, the secured party (lender) need not possess the goods.

A typical example occurs in the leasing of an automobile. There might be no point to your business leasing an automobile if you do not have possession of the automobile. How could you use it?

1. *Value*. By value we generally are talking about consideration. Value can mean not only consideration as we generally understand it under contract law. It can also include a binding obligation to extend credit, and can also include an already existing debt.

2. *Debtor's Rights in Collateral*. A *debtor* will have rights in collateral if he owns it, or if he has legal possession of it. For some matters, he may have rights in collateral even if he is *going* to *acquire* certain rights in the goods.

3. *Security agreement*. The lender will have an *interest* in the *specific* property only (a) if there is an agreement between the debtor and creditor (b) which grants, creates or provides for the creditor, (c) getting a security interest in this particular good.

Generally, there are two options for the creditor. He or she can have *physical possession* of the goods *or* must have a *written agreement* which is signed by the debtor and which contains a reasonable description we mentioned. In the second case, the creditor need not have possession of the goods to have a security interest in the particular goods. The debtor can have possession.

It is important to realize that due to the complexities of business, sometimes agreements have to be flexible. One of the concepts that come into play involves what is known as "after acquired property." This means property acquired after the date of the security interest. It may be an additional way to encourage the creditor to lend money, because it gives the creditor a security interest in *additional personal property* or *additional inventory* or *additional farm products* that may come into the possession of the debtor after the debt was incurred.

## AFTER ACQUIRED PROPERTY

If you are the lender, you may be able to have a security agreement to state that you will have a security interest in *any property acquired* by the debtor *after today's date* or the *date* of the *agreement*. In other words, any additional items acquired by the borrower/debtor might be subject to your security interest. The new property might also become collateral.

This does not happen automatically. A particular item under which it arises is often inventory, which fluctuates. Some lenders may be willing to lend money on inventory as long as they can have a security interest in the *new inventory* that is purchased. Often the borrower is selling the current inventory and replenishing it.

We see why this involves a "floating lien" or a "continuing general lien."

It is, however, important to know that a current secured lender (new lender) may get a security interest in inventory even ahead of someone who has a floating lien on existing inventory (old lender).

The current or new lender must meet certain stringent requirements.

If there is a *new* loan of purchase money to buy new inventory, that new lender may have the first rank on the *new inventory*. If the new lender secures his or her interest in the new inventory within ten (10) days after lending the money, then he may prevail over a lender who had a floating lien on newly acquired inventory. The new lender may have to make sure that the agreements are signed and perfected within ten (10) days after giving the value (money).

## PROCEEDS

A secured party can be further protected from potential competing creditors by having an interest in the *proceeds* from the sale of the collateral. Sometimes collateral can be sold by agreement, for instance, when it is inventory. On the other hand, sometimes it may be sold inadvertently or intentionally by the *debtor*. If the creditor finds out about it, the creditor may still have an interest in the *proceeds* of such sale.

Thus the secured party (the lender) may have an interest in the proceeds from the sale, exchange, collection or other disposition of the collateral. It does not necessarily have to be cash, but it may be money or checks. It could be deposit accounts or promissory notes, or an exchange for other types of personal property. It is possible for rights in proceeds to be excluded, but this must be stated in the security agreement.

## Future Advances

Just as we talked about the floating lien, it is possible for a lender or the secured party to sign an agreement with the debtor that creates a current lien for future loans (advances). In other words, the lender may lend someone $25,000 now, subject to a security agreement, but then may lend *additional* amounts of money, possibly $15,000, some time during the next six months. That additional loan can be covered by the same security agreement. It is in effect a *secured line* of *credit*.

## PERFECTION

It is important to realize that attachment is a basic requirement for creating the security interest in a particular good.

There is a concept called "perfection," which raises it to its highest level that is required by law. This involves the secured party (lender) having done everything required by the law. This makes the secured interest effective against other potential lien creditors of the borrower. It may not always guarantee that the lender gets paid. In effect, it is meeting the minimum standards for having it enforceable against a particular good.

The requirement for any security interest to be good against third parties including competing creditors is that the security interest must be perfected. What is required for perfection? There are essentially three approaches to it, any one of which, if met properly, can perfect the interest:

1. An interest is perfected by *filing* a *financing statement* which states the security interest in the

---

## *POWER POINTS* _____

▶ The financing statement is different from the security agreement.

▶ The financing statement is filed and becomes a public record.

▶ The security agreement is usually not filed.

---

| Classification | Probable Filing Location |
|---|---|
| Fixtures | County (same place as real estate mortgages) |
| Consumer Goods | County where located |
| Agricultural Transactions | County where located |
| Other Collateral | Secretary of State |

particular personal property. It must be signed by the debtor.

2. The secured party can take *physical possession* of the collateral.

3. Certain types of security interests arise *automatically* upon the attachment of the security interest. This is generally considered to be an area of purchase money security interests. That is, however, not the only meaning. A purchase money transaction involves a *sale* of goods. Not all financing transactions involve the sale of goods.

We will see that purchase money security interests can attach automatically.

## FIRST METHOD OF PERFECTION

### FILING A FINANCING STATEMENT

One of the essential methods of perfecting a security interest is filing a financing statement. The financing statement does not have to contain all the details of the lending agreement or the security agreement. It must contain some specifics.

The financing statement is used to put the public on *notice* that there is a security interest in a particular piece of *personal property*. It describes the property, identifies the debtor and the creditor, and generally gives the names and addresses of both the secured party creditor and the debtor. It includes a reasonable description of the collateral so the public is aware of what the collateral is.

Under the UCC, the maximum effective period for a secured financing statement is five years. It is possible to continue this by filing a *continuation statement*. This must be filed by the secured party within six months before the existing financing statement expires. Thus, the financing statement can be extended for another five years.

A security interest in motor vehicles involves different laws from other goods. In many states there are specific financing statutes relating to motor vehicles and obtaining and securing security interest in motor vehicles.

*Where to File the Financing Statement.* The general rule is that in order to *perfect* a security interest (with certain exceptions) you must *file* the financing statement.

The *place* depends on the category or classification of the collateral. We would also examine state law, because there are several alternatives.

We will try to give you some idea of the general approach, but not necessarily the one that is specific to your state. The proper filing place for a security interest in *fixtures* would normally be the place where you would file *mortgages* for the real estate. This would generally be the county (or parish) where the real estate is located.

Often filings for consumer goods or for agricultural transactions are generally considered local and would be filed where the farm or owner of the consumer goods is located. This would usually be in the recorder's office of the county or township. Generally all other transactions are filed with the Secretary of State. Again, look to your state law for specifics in filing for particular goods.

### IMPROPER FILING

Sometimes the secured party fails to file the financial statement in the proper location or fails to file it in all of the several required locations. Then what happens? Generally the filing is ineffective if it is filed in the wrong place. However, there are a few exceptions.

One of the exceptions involves a filing which, if it's made in good faith, will be effective when it pertains to any particular category of collateral for which the *other* filing requirements have been met.

Assume there are *several different* types of collateral to be included in the security agreement. With regard to certain of the collateral, the filing has been proper. With regard to those goods the filing would be effective, though it may *not* be effective for the other goods for which any filing is improper.

A second exception would apply to those individuals who are *on notice* that there is a security agreement. If a person has *actual* knowledge that a security interest has been created in these goods, no filing is necessary. Here even though the filing may be in the wrong place, it may be effective against any persons *on notice*.

### Changes of Information After the Filing

On occasion debtors may change their place of residence or their use of the collateral. In all of the UCC states, a change in the use of the collateral does not limit the effectiveness of the original financing statement. Thus the effectiveness continues despite any change in the location, as long as the goods are within the same state.

In *some states* if there is a change in the use or location of the collateral, the effectiveness of the filing is limited to a period of four months after the debtor has moved his residence or place of business. After the four months the financing statement is not effective.

### Collateral Moves

What happens if the collateral is moved *interstate*, meaning to another state? There are generally two situations which may require that a new financing statement be filed.

A first instance exists if the collateral involves *mobile* goods, accounts receivable or general receivables, and the debtor moves his residence or place of business to another state.

The second occasion arises if the *debtor* moves the collateral to another state. In these cases, the original filing is effective for up to four months or until the perfection would have terminated under the original financing statement if this occurs before four months. For instance, if the original financing

statement was to run out in one month and the debtor moves to another state, then it would be the earlier of the four months or the date when it would have expired under the original agreement (one month).

Therefore, if you are lending money or if you have a security interest in some goods that were sold, you might want to pay attention to where the collateral is used and how long it has been out of sight.

## SECOND METHOD OF PERFECTION

### POSSESSION

A form of *perfection* of a security interest includes a pledge or a "possessory security interest." This is the *actual delivery* or taking physical possession of the personal property by the creditor. It can also occur when the property or collateral is put in the hands of a *third* party who is acting as an *agent* for a secured party and such possession is security for the payment of the debtor's obligation. An example of this occurs in a bonded warehouse.

In a bonded warehouse, the warehouse operator becomes the custodian who takes control of the goods. The borrower can only get goods under limited conditions. The warehouse operator is responsible for policing the rules.

Therefore, this type of delivery or transferring of the collateral to the creditor or to the creditor's agent involves a delivery and would create a *perfected security interest without the need for filing*. A typical example is a pawnbroker.

Another example that could take place would be where the goods would have to be transferred to a field warehouse under the control of an agent for the creditor.

## THIRD METHOD OF PERFECTION

### AUTOMATIC PERFECTION

In many instances the UCC tries to solve practical problems by providing for automatic perfection of a security interest: for example, the sale of goods where the retailer lends the money to the buyer to buy the goods. This is like a Sears charge card. Or it could involve some entity that is lending money to the debtor to buy goods.

There are two situations that are most significant where automatic perfection takes place. These are:

1. Where there is a *purchase money security interest* created in consumer goods.

2. When there is a *temporary perfection* in instruments and documents.

Let's take a look at these two.

Purchase Money Security
Interest In Consumer Goods

Assume you are a retailer. You are selling a television set to a buyer. You have a simple way of securing your purchase money security interest. Or similarly, if a bank is lending the borrower money to buy the TV from you, the retailer, the bank will also be able to secure a purchase money security interest (PMSI). It is an automatic security interest that does not require the filing of a financing statement or possession. It is created in the agreement.

If the purchaser is buying a consumer good, then these sets of rules apply. It is simple to perfect a purchase money security interest, because it is automatic here. Except for motor vehicles, which may have a separate set of rules, it is perfected automatically. Perfection occurs as soon as the transaction is completed, without anyone having to file a financing statement. That is what makes PMSI different from what you may have conceived. Here the UCC eases one of the burdens for selling consumer goods and creating a security interest in the goods.

For the television set we talked about, it is easy to have the security interest attach and be perfected. If the television set is used for personal, family or household use, then as long as there is a written agreement stating that you, as a retailer, have a security interest in the television set, it is perfected automatically. This same thing could happen if a bank had lent money to the buyer to buy the television set and had a security agreement giving the bank a PMSI. A PMSI would arise automatically upon the sale of the television set.

## TEMPORARY PERFECTION

As we have mentioned, a temporary perfection of a security interest may arise in negotiable documents or instruments.

This security interest perfection can arise without filing or even taking possession of the goods. It only arises for 21 days from the time that it attaches to the extent that it arises for new value given under a written security agreement. This only arises if someone is giving value for a negotiable document or instrument. By negotiable documents, we generally mean negotiable instruments, stocks, bonds and other investment securities or instruments. By instruments mean bills of lading and warehouse receipts that are negotiable.

One of the problems here, however, is that the secured party (generally the lender of the money) can run the risk of losing the security interest during this 21 day period if a holder in due course of the negotiable instrument or the holder of a document receives the instrument properly according to the UCC. Then it is possible for even this temporary perfection to be preempted.

---

**SUMMARY OF PERFECTING SECURITY INTERESTS**

Goods
  Filing a Financing Statement on Possession
    • Consumer goods
    • Equipment
    • Farm products
    Inventory
  Automatic
    • Consumer goods only for a purchase
      money Security Intereest
Indispensable Paper
  Filing a Financing Statement on Possession
    • Chattel paper
    • Instruments
    • Documents
  Automatic (for 21 days)
    • Instruments
    • Documents
Intangibles
  Filing a Financing Statement
    • Accounts
    • General Intangibles
  Automatic
    • Accounts

## PRIORITIES

These rules of perfection do not always guarantee that the holder of a particular interest wins. There can be competing perfections (security interests). There are some rules that help to decide who wins in cases where two lenders have *competing security interests*. Sometimes when there are several creditors, and a debtor does not have enough money to go around or goes into bankruptcy, or a debtor has sold his or her interest, then we may have competing security interests.

```
GENERAL ORDER OF PRIORITIES

Competing Interests                          Priority
1. Unsecured versus Unsecured                First to Perfect

2. Unsecured versus Secured                  Secured

3. Secured versus Secured                    First to Perfect

4. Secured versus Secured                    (Formula for
   Commingled Goods                          Calculating Priority)
                                             Cost of Goods for a
                                             Particular Party
                                        =    ──────────────────
In 4, if Party A has 30% of all goods, Party A   Total Cost of
has a priority in 30% of total commingled goods. Commingled Goods
```

### AGAINST UNSECURED CREDITORS

Once a secured party has the benefit of a security interest *attaching*, then this secured party has a priority over claims of *unsecured* creditors. In the case of the retailer selling the television set, if there is a purchase money security interest in that television set, then that lender (retailer) has a priority over other interests in that television set ahead of all other *general creditors* who are unsecured.

### AGAINST PERFECTED SECURITY INTERESTS

Where there are two or more secured parties who have competing security interests, generally the first to perfect prevails.

### AGAINST COMPETING SECURITY INTERESTS IN COMMINGLED GOODS

When goods are commingled or processed into a mass, security interests attach in the proportion that the cost of the respective goods bears to the cost of the total mass of goods.

There are examples where an unperfected security interest would not win with regard to certain types of unsecured creditors. For instance, when there has been an assignment for the benefit of creditors or where the individual has entered bankruptcy or the courts have appointed a receiver in equity, a secured but unperfected interest may lose. So these are not absolute rules. These rules generally give you some idea that it is better to be a secured creditor even if the interest is *only attached* and has not been *perfected*. Assume you, as a retailer, have a security interest which has been perfected because it is a purchase money security interest. You would then be ahead of any lien unperfected creditors.

*Example of Lien Creditor.* Assume that an individual has not paid other debts to a third party and that third party has gotten a judgment against the individual. Then that judgment creditor has attempted to seize an interest in specific property. You as a *perfected creditor* would generally be ahead of that lien creditor, where the lien has arisen for other reasons. On the other hand, if you have an unperfected security interest, you may lose out to lien creditors who have *seized* the property.

# CHAPTER 17

EMPLOYMENT LAWS

# CHAPTER 17

# EMPLOYMENT LAWS

The tradition of an employer/employee relationship has evolved and expanded through the common law—primarily those areas involving contract law and also the area of tort law.

The relationship between employer and employee is created by contract, both express and implied. The employer generally controls, within limits, the employee's behavior, workplace and benefits. We see part of the law involving principals and agents coming into play.

If an employee is an agent of a principal (employer) it is possible for the agent to commit the employer (the boss) to liability. This can occur even if the employee did not have the authority to do so. In many cases the employee may have acted in a manner exactly contrary to what his or her duties were as defined by the employer.

When we are discussing employment law, we will generally be talking about federal statutes regarding labor and management. This can apply to unions interfacing with employers. In addition, federal law comes into play when we are discussing employment based on sex, race, creed, age, handicap or national origin.

Additionally, federal and state laws come into play when we are discussing employee safety. We would like to briefly discuss these areas so you will be moderately familiar with them and will know when to seek more sophisticated consultation.

## LABOR-MANAGEMENT LAW

There are several laws involved. Here are the most prominent federal laws covering labor-management relationships.

## NORRIS-LaGUARDIA ACT

This law was passed in 1932 and effectively governs management and labor disputes. It was intended to protect the status of unions as legitimate vehicles for employee concerns.

## NATIONAL LABOR RELATIONS ACT

The National Labor Relations Act was enacted in 1935 and was the next step in the federal government's affirmation of the concept of collective bargaining via unions. The law did not say that unions would be favored over management, but it gave legitimacy to unions.

This particular law defines certain things that are considered unfair for management to do. The law includes some of the following:

1. Attempts to interfere with employees' rights to unionize and use the collective bargaining mechanism. An example might be someone being fired for attempting to form a union.

2. Attempts to dominate or control a union.

3. Attempts to discriminate against union members.

4. Attempts to discriminate against an employee who has exercised his rights under a collective bargaining agreement, or under the National Labor Relations Act.

5. Attempts to refuse to bargain in good faith with a designated representative of a union.

## LABOR-MANAGEMENT RELATIONS ACT TAFT-HARTLEY ACT

This Act was passed in 1947. It amended the National Labor Relations Act by prohibiting secondary boycotts, jurisdictional strikes of work assignments, refusals to bargain in good faith, and forcing an employer to have to pay for work not actually performed. It also outlawed strikes to force an employer to discharge or discriminate against non-union employees.

It provided for the availability of civil injunctions in labor disputes. These could be used only against *unfair* labor practices and could be requested only by the National Labor Relations Board. This Act further refined some of the relationships and specified weapons which could be used against unfair behavior on the part of labor or management.

## LABOR-MANAGEMENT REPORTING AND DISCLOSURE ACT

This Act, passed in 1959, attempted to create a bill of rights for unions. It attempts to bring greater democracy to union meetings and requires that unions make greater disclosure of finances.

Congress had discovered that there had been numerous breaches of trust and much corruption in some labor unions. This Act attempted to further strengthen the antiseptic approach to the labor-management process.

## DISCRIMINATORY EMPLOYMENT PRACTICES

There are several areas of the law which have applied for a number of years to practices that affect your business or a business in which you might be an investor. These laws apply whether or not a union is present.

## EQUAL PAY ACT

Every employer who has two or more employees is prohibited from pay discrimination among employees on the basis of sex.

The Act prohibits this practice where two individuals might be performing the same task but are given different titles. Their tasks may overlap but one is paid significantly less. Typically, the female ends up with the lesser pay schedule, but that is not always the case.

In any sex-based suit on this particular Act, the employee carries the burden of showing that there is some discrimination. It would then be up to the employer to show that this difference is based on some factor other than sex.

Some of the defenses include the fact the difference is:

1. Based on a seniority system.
2. Based on a merit system.
3. Based on a system of "piecework" or earnings based on quantity or quality of production.
4. Based on some factor other than sex.

An employee who has been discriminated against may be able to seek back pay and also seek an injunction prohibiting further unlawful conduct by the employer. The Equal Employment Opportunity Commission has authority also to sue employers and seek remedies under this Act.

## CIVIL RIGHTS ACT OF 1964

The Civil Rights Act of 1964 prohibits discrimination in employment practices based on race, color, sex, religion or national origin. This behavior is prohibited in hiring, in firing, in compensating employees, in promoting employees, in training employees, or in any other act that shows an adverse impact based on one of the prohibited factors.

This Act applies to employers who have 15 or more employees. The Equal Pay Act is based on two or more employees, but the Civil Rights Act of 1964 (Title VII) applies to companies with 15 or more employees.

One of the things that are important for every employer to know is that even though behavior on its face *looks* neutral, if the net result is discrimination, then even a small business owner may have potential problems.

If an employer has what appears to be innocent practices, but they result in an under-hiring of a minority group or racial group, there is the *potential* for problems. If the employer has rules that appear "neutral" but have an adverse impact on a person in the protected group, the "neutral" behavior or practice may be illegal.

The Equal Employment Opportunity Commission is in a position of enforcing this Act, but individual employees can also do so. The Act acknowledges basic defenses. If there is a bona fide seniority or merit system or a professionally developed ability test or there are bona fide occupational qualifications (not based on sex, race, national origin, creed, color or religion or any protected categories), then the employer may justify the numerical results existing in his or her business.

## AFFIRMATIVE ACTION

Affirmative action can come in several forms. It generally means that a company may have an obligation to actively recruit minorities. Some courts have imposed quotas or ratios on employers. Other courts have utilized hiring goals. Courts swing back and forth from strict numbers to affirmative action.

## AGE DISCRIMINATION IN EMPLOYMENT ACT OF 1967

The Age Discrimination and Employment Act prohibits discrimination in hiring, firing, compensation or otherwise on the basis of age. Initially the age category was from 40 through 65. It is now, for most intents and purposes, without a cap.

If someone cannot do a job because they no longer have the ability, they may not in fact be protected. On the other hand, just using age as a criterion is illegal. Private employers having 20 or more employees are covered by this Act. It applies to all governmental units regardless of their size.

The Act basically prohibits the mandatory *retirement* of employees. At one time it was under the age of 70; now there is no age limit. Of course, if job performance is affected, that employee may not be protected. There are certain exemptions from the Act for executive types (not just higher-paid employees).

*Remedies Under This Act.* Remedies may include back pay lost if an employee has been fired. If an employee has not received a promotion for which he or she is qualified, back pay can include the differential that may have been deserved. Remedies can also include injunctive relief and the requirement of affirmative action. Therefore, if your company has 20 or more employees (including part-time employees) you may have to be concerned with this Act.

## REHABILITATION ACT OF 1973

The Rehabilitation Act of 1973 attempts to remedy discrimination against handicapped individuals who are able to perform a job. This Act requires employers to provide some rehabilitation training for employees, access to public facilities, and also employment. Essentially if an individual could perform job tasks but for some minor needs, the employer cannot discriminate against this individual. The employer may have to make changes in the physical facility or provide some minor retraining.

An example might be an individual who is in a wheelchair but can perform all of the job duties. Assume the job involves clerical work or computer-type work, where the individual can perform an adequate or even a better than adequate job in comparison with other employees. This Act prohibits such discrimination if an employer company has federal contracts or involves federal financing for its business.

## Executive Order Affecting Employment Discrimination

In 1965, President Lyndon Johnson issued an executive order prohibiting discrimination by any federal contractor on the basis of race, color, sex, religion or national origin in employment on any work performed by the contractor. It was not limited to just federal work the employee performed.

Within the Department of Labor, there is a specific Office for Federal Contract Compliance Programs (OFCCP). Any federal contractor that has performed work for the U.S. Government in excess of $10,000 must comply with OFCC programs.

Compliance with affirmative action dictates may be different if it is a construction type contract versus a non-construction type contract.

Non-construction contractors with 50 or more employees or with contracts for $50,000 or more are required to have a *written affirmative action plan* to comply with the Executive Order.

Some of these numbers get into *bigger* business, but apply to numerous businesses that may have at least 50 or more employees or have contracts of $50,000 or more with the federal government.

This Affirmative Action Plan (AAP) must include (a) a specific work force analysis, (b) a plan for any corrective action needed, (c) specific goals and timetables, and (d) procedures for auditing and reporting to the government.

The OFCCP office periodically audits and checks the goals and timetables for both the construction industry and non-construction contractors.

## EMPLOYEES AND PAYROLL

There are a number of laws that affect not only the labor area but also the taxation area. These come into play in the payroll practices of virtually all employers.

## FAIR LABOR STANDARDS ACT

The Fair Labor Standards Act (FLSA) covers workers in interstate commerce and workers providing goods in interstate commerce. It establishes minimum wage rates for regular time, overtime rates, equal pay, record-keeping rules and standards for child labor.

1. *Wage and Hour Controls.* The FLSA contains certain provisions that dictate certain requirements relating to wages and hours of an employee.

The specific ones involving the wage-hour provisions are twofold. They are:

a. An attempt at stopping companies from employing individuals at substandard rates of pay (minimum wage).

b. An attempt at increasing employment by increasing the cost of overtime, essentially in excess of 40 hours a week.

2. *Employers Effected.* The wage and hour law is enforced through the commerce power of the federal government. This law applies to any employer who affects interstate commerce or who is in interstate commerce.

This specific law, as we have mentioned, sets minimum rates of pay and determines when an employer must pay. It also restricts child labor and contains civil liabilities and criminal penalties for violations.

## Employer-Employee Relationship

First, this law functions only where the employer-employee relationship to exists. It generally does not apply to *independent contractors*.

How do we decide who is an employee? Generally the law looks to what is known as the common-law standards to decide who may be an *employee*. The common-law standards are not controlling, but they can be helpful in trying to decide who is an employee. The court might look at several different factors from several different viewpoints.

Let's take a look at one of them. The courts might look at what the "employer" is doing:

1. Does the employer have the authority to hire or fire this individual?

2. Is the employer supervising or controlling the work or the services being provided?

3. Has the employer incurred any obligation to pay for all of the work being performed? If there is a subcontractor involved, is the employer the individual who is also hiring the services of someone two steps removed from the "potential employee"?

4. Does the employer dictate how many hours are going to be worked, and what are the specific wage rates, or is there a package deal which the employer is purchasing?

All of these factors are part of the stew being cooked.

## Determining Coverage

There are two ways to view doing business in interstate commerce. It is very difficult for any business to escape the coverage. The two approaches are:

1. Whether or not the individual employee is performing services of such a nature that it is *in interstate commerce*. Thus, the employee would have to be engaged either in interstate commerce or in the production of goods for interstate commerce. There are some exemptions from this act; they include examples such as learners, apprentices, some handicapped workers, messengers, certain types of students in retail service establishments or in agriculture, students in institutions of higher learning, students working for schools, and workers in certain American territories. Also, certain types of

industries have certain types of exemptions: (a) employers with relatively small gross yearly sales or revenue, (b) employees of certain retail establishments, (c) employees of amusement or recreational establishments that are seasonal, (d) certain agricultural employees, (e) employees engaged in the fishing industry, (f) employees involved in certain types of small circulation newspapers and (g) several other types of industries. If you have any specific questions or doubts about your coverage, you would do well to seek advice either from your lawyer or from the U.S. Department of Labor. Do not assume that there are any exemptions.

2. In addition the Act covers an employer who is *involved* in interstate commerce or in the production of goods *for Interstate Commerce.*

If you put these two types of coverage together, you might get the idea that most businesses are covered. So if your company meets this commerce threshold, then the FLSA applies. There are *excluded* industries that are in interstate commerce.

If your type of work does not involve any of the *exemptions* from interstate commerce or from the specific Fair Labor Standards Act, it is best to assume that your business is controlled by this law.

### Minimum Wages

The FLSA requires that an employer pays his employee a minimum hourly wage, as long as the employee is covered under the Act. The minimum wage is raised periodically. You will have to check with the Department of Labor for the current rate.

There are several features of the Act that can be beneficial to our understanding of how to meet the minimum wage. What does the term "wage" include? It includes the "reasonable costs" to the company of furnishing an employee such things as board, lodging and other facilities. It can include dormitory rooms, tuition and meals furnished by the employer at company restaurants, cafeterias, hospitals, hotels and restaurants.

Wages can include housing furnished for residential purposes, general merchandise purchases at the company's stores (commissaries), fuel for the non-commercial or personal use of the employee, and transportation furnished to the employee between house and work (where the travel time is not included as compensated time and the transportation is not a necessary part of the job).

If you wanted to include some of these forms of compensation in your minimum wage calculation, there is a three-form test that the law requires. This test includes:

1. The facility or whatever has been additional must be furnished for the benefit of the employee.

2. It must be accepted voluntarily by the employee, not forced on him.

3. It must be of the kind that is customarily furnished by a company engaging in activities similar to your company's.

Previously, restaurants and lounges could include tips as part of the credit toward the minimum wage. Thus an employee might get only a percentage of the minimum wage, with the employer getting credit for tips the employee received.

*Overtime Pay.* One of the important features of the Wage and Hour Provision is that any non-exempt employee who is covered must receive overtime compensation at the rate of one and one-half times the employee's regular rate for any hours worked in excess of 40 hours a week.

This might mean that if your regular work week is 35 hours, and you worked 42 hours in any particular week, the employer could pay you straight time for the hours between 35 and 40 hours. For over 40 hours the employer must pay time and a half. It is also possible for commissions to be included in calculating overtime pay.

*Working Time.* It is difficult sometimes to determine what is working time. If you are having any problem in deciding, you may end up having to seek help from legal counsel or the Department of Labor. Sometimes it includes waiting time, make-ready time, other non-productive time, and time to get from the front gate to the workbench.

In general, *time* that occurs *before* an employee begins his productive working time or at the *end* of his productive working time is generally not included in calculating the *working time* that is applied under the Act.

*Computing Overtime.* As we mentioned, 40 hours is the *threshold*. Any time in excess of 40 hours must be paid at one and one-half times the regular rate. Even *piece rates* are subject to overtime requirements.

There are also payments which, though they may be included in the employee's W-2 wages, might *not* be considered part of the *regular rate.* Here are examples:

1. Gifts, including Christmas bonuses.

2. Idle-time payments.

3. Reimbursement for expenses.

4. Discretionary bonuses.

5. Pension and profit-sharing plan and savings plan payments.

6. Radio and television talent fees.

7. Several welfare benefit plan contributions.

8. Payments for daily or weekly overtime hours.

9. Premium pay for Saturdays, Sundays, holidays and days of rest are generally not part of the regular rate.

10. Premium pay of up to 150 percent for work outside regular eight-hour days or straight time work weeks that are not exceeding 40 hours. Any of the premium type payments in the last three can be included in overtime pay.

Our purpose is not to provide a mathematical formula for computing all of this. It is to give you enough information to spot the potholes in the road.

## CHILD LABOR

Our society has sought to protect its future generation from exploitation in several ways. At one time, the visible area of abuse involved oppressive child labor practices. Let's examine some of the provisions adopted in this area.

Children under the age of 14, subject to certain exemptions, may *not* be employed at any time in an occupation covered by the Act, or employed in an enterprise covered by the Act.

Children under 16 may not be employed generally. An exception exists if their parents or guardians employ them, as long as the job does not involve manufacturing or mining or any other category considered detrimental to the employee's health or well being. Some of the specific prohibited types of activities for children between 14 and 16 are:

1. Certain types of manufacturing, mining and processing occupations.

2. Public messenger services.

3. Operating and attending power-driven machinery, other than light office equipment.

4. Operating motor vehicles or serving as helpers on such vehicles.

5. Occupations in transportation, warehousing and storage, except for office and sales type work.

6. Communications and public utilities, except for office and sales type work.

7. Occupations in construction, demolition and repair work, also excluding sales and office type work.

In other words, you have to watch out during the ages of 14 to 16. You are allowed to hire them in retail type stores, food service and gasoline service establishments from ages 14 to 16.

Some of the acceptable categories may involve children being employed by their parents as long as it is not mining, manufacturing or anything hazardous. It may also involve working as an actor or where children do agriculture work outside school hours, with a parent or guardian, or with the consent of the parent or guardian. Also allowed are children delivering newspapers, children homeworkers, making "evergreen leaves" and types of employment where the employers have received a waiver of the child labor restrictions.

### Children Under Age 18 Years

No child under age of 18 can be employed in particularly hazardous jobs which involve commerce and the production of goods and services in commerce or any covered enterprises, or where the work is of such a nature that the Secretary of Labor has declared it to be specifically hazardous for minors.

Several types of occupations have already been labeled hazardous. They include:

1. Coal and other mining.

2. Plants manufacturing explosives, brick or tile or related items.

3. Power-driven hoisting machinery.

4. Logging and operation of sawmills.

5. Driving motor vehicles or acting as outside helpers, except for incidental work involving school bus driving.

6. Exposure to radioactive substances.

7. Operation of power-driven woodworking, metal forming, punching, shearing, bakery or paper products machinery;

8. Employment in slaughter or meat-packing plants.

9. Operation and maintenance of circular saws, band saws and guillotine shears.

10. Shipwrecking and wrecking or demolishing buildings.

11. Roofing operations.

12. Excavation type work.

This Act basically prohibits onerous child labor. It is aimed at preventing outrageous practices that preceded its enactment. Generally children under 16 are protected by the Act from employment except by a parent, and then under certain circumstances.

Children 16 to 18 cannot be employed in certain hazardous jobs or those types of jobs that might be detrimental to their health and well-being.

Children 14 and 15 can be employed outside of school hours in some non-manufacturing industries. There are certain conditions:

1. Maximum of three hours on a school days.

2. Maximum of 18 hours in a school week.

3. Maximum of eight hours on a non-school day.

4. Maximum of 40 hours in a non-school week.

(School co-op students can work up to 23 hours in a school week and three hours on school days during school hours.)

A minor's workday may begin at 7 a.m. and must end no later than 7 p.m. (except from June 1 to Labor Day, when quitting time can be 9 p.m.). There are exceptions to the above.

You should note the coverage of the Fair Labor Standards Act:

a. Minimum wage.

b. Payment of "time and a half" for work over 40 hours.

c. Exempts certain categories of employment including executives, sales personnel and professionals.

d. Generally children under 14 are forbidden employment.

## HANDICAPPED WORKERS

The Rehabilitation Act of 1973 and the Vietnam Era Veterans Readjustment Assistance Act of 1974 prohibit covered employers with federal contracts from discriminating against handicapped workers.

Certain states have laws protecting handicapped workers from employment discrimination.

Congress has also passed the Americans with Disabilities Act of 1990 (ADA), which bars employment discrimination against people with physical or mental disabilities.

An individual with a disability "is one having a disability, having a record of a disability, or being regarded as having a physical or mental impairment that greatly limits a major life activity."

This 1990 Act covers employers with as few as 15 employees.

It requires employers to make "reasonable accommodations," including furnishing accessible facilities, qualified readers, altering work schedules or restructuring jobs.

The EEOC has jurisdiction over initial charges of ADA violations. If it cannot generate a conciliation, it can, issue a "right to sue" letter. The employee or potential employee then has, 90 days to file suit.

Employers with 25 or more employees have two years to comply with the employment aspects of the Act. Employers of 15 to 24 employees have up to four years to comply with these aspects of the Act.

The types of discrimination prohibited by employers or unions with 15 or more employees are:

a. Race.

b. Sex (equal pay applies only if tow or more employees).

c. Religious.

d. National origin.

e. Age (40 and over).

f. Handicap.

## Penalties for Disregarding This Law

What liabilities are created if any of these child labor laws are violated? Violators may be subject both to criminal prosecution and to injunctive restraint against the employer. The Department of Labor in conjunction with the Attorney General may seek injunctive relief and any lost wages if there has been a wrongful discharge. Only the Attorney General can bring direct criminal charges against a violator.

## RECORD-KEEPING

Some of the best advice that any commentator can give in carrying out the wage-hour law is that keeping adequate records has been called an additional form of business insurance. Adequate and well-kept records may end up being the employer's best shield, because the burden is on the employer to prove that he or she has complied with the law. A company covered by the Fair Labor Standards Act may have to keep records for all its employees, even for those who are not tied to interstate commerce.

What types of information do you need in your records? What information is required under these laws? They include:

1. The full name of your employee, including identifying information.

2. The home address, including ZIP code.

3. The date of birth if the employee is under age 19.

4. Sex, and occupation in which the employee is engaged.

5. The time of day and the day of week in which the employee's work week begins.

6. Regular hourly rate of pay, basis on which wages are paid, and those things that are excluded from the regular rate.

7. Hours worked each workday and the total hours worked each work week.

8. The total daily or weekly straight-time earnings or wages.

9. Total weekly overtime excess compensation.

10. Total additions to or deductions from wages paid each pay period.

11. Total wages paid each pay period.

12. Date of payment and pay period covered by payment.

13. Any retroactive wage payment under government supervision.

There are some exemptions from several of these items with regard to exempt executive, administrative and professional employees and outside salespersons. For safety's sake, it would behoove the employer to keep all of the information for these exempt employees on the same basis as for any other employee.

## PRESERVATION OF RECORDS

*Three-Year Requirement.* Basic payroll records must be kept for at least three years from the time they should be originated. The records should be kept at the place of employment or places of employment or at a central record-keeping place where such records are customarily maintained. If there are any collective bargaining agreements or employment contracts guaranteeing wages or profit-sharing plans and trusts, the employer must keep these for three years.

*Two-Year Requirement.* The law also requires that certain "supplementary basic records" be kept for at least two years. They include:

1. The basic data used in computing hours worked and computing the amounts that were due.

2. Wage rate tables, if your company has them.

3. Work time schedules, order, shipping and billing records, and supplementary records of additions to or deductions from wages paid.

These come within the two-year requirement.

It is important to note that, regardless of the time period of this record-keeping obligation, the employer *cannot delegate* this task to anyone else, be it an accountant or bookkeeper or data processing service. If the employer does not have the records, the employer is liable! There is no passing the buck—or the computer.

## INSPECTION OF RECORDS

The Wage and Hour Division of the Department of Labor has authority to inspect these records and can enforce its rights by subpoena (present yourself to give testimony) and by subpoena *duces tecum* (you present the records demanded.)

Employees can also inspect an employer's records under federal and state procedural rules to secure such information necessary to prove any wage suits they may have.

## ENFORCEMENT-PENALTY

The law provides plenty of fire-power; please take careful note. The enforcement tools include:

1. Criminal prosecution, including fine and imprisonment.

2. Injunctive proceedings, in which the Secretary of Labor may also seek unpaid wages.

3. Wage damage suits by which employees may be able to collect double unpaid wages, plus costs and attorney's fees.

4. Wage suits by the Secretary of Labor on behalf of the employee.

5. Supervision by the Wage-Hour Administrator of payment of past due wages. The Administrator is the officer empowered by the law who can prescribe recordkeeping.

We have been looking at the federal labor provisions. Let's take a look at state law provisions.

## STATE WAGE-HOUR LAWS

Many states, in addition to the federal government, have enacted legislation on minimum wages, maximum hours and child labor. In this area, the states are not pre-empted from enacting legislation with higher standards than the federal government's. As a matter of fact, most states actually had legislation in these areas before the federal government did.

Suits under a state law generally are not removable to the federal courts.

## FAIR EMPLOYMENT PRACTICES

The fair employment practices that we discussed initially cover not only private employers, but also federal and state governments, unions and employment agencies. These entities would not be able to discriminate on any of the bases we have discussed (age, sex, race, *et cetera*).

We have also mentioned that companies with certain government contracts become subject to these laws.

Another question is, what employment practices are affected? These laws cover recruitment and hiring including racial discrimination, religious discrimination, sexual discrimination, national origin discrimination and age discrimination.

*Advertising.* None of the covered employers or entities can advertise or list job notices that state or imply a maximum age or a particular race or sex.

## ABILITY AND EXPERIENCE

Title VII of the Civil Rights Act of 1964 and the Age Discrimination in Employment Act prohibit discrimination in hiring on the basis of race, color, religion, sex, national origin or age. An employer can refuse to hire an applicant if his decision is based on some *other valid business criterion or criteria*. However, this criterion or criteria cannot be a mere subterfuge to deny or get around equal employment opportunity.

It is possible for an employer to refuse to hire an individual if he/she does not have the basic ability or experience needed to perform the job. The employer can establish his or her own standards as long as the standards can be justified by the requirements of the job.

Nevertheless, placing restrictions in one form or another that result in the failure to hire individuals in the protected age group (over 40) or sex can result in potential discrimination, in violation of the Acts covered.

It might also be possible for an employer to refuse to hire an individual who does not meet certain physical requirements of the job. This choice must certainly be able to withstand an objective test requirement.

## OCCUPATIONAL QUALIFICATION

The law does allow bona fide occupational qualification (BFOQ) to be the basis for hiring. But this BFOQ, as it is called, is and has been interpreted very narrowly by the courts.

Thus, employers cannot refuse to hire applicants on the basis of some of the following:

1. Stereotyped characterization of the sexes.

2. Assumptions of comparative employment characteristics of the sexes.

3. Preferences of the employer, co-workers, customers or clients for employees of a particular sex.

4. Reluctance to provide separate company facilities such as restrooms.

An employer can prove that bona fide occupational qualifications are met by proving both of the following:

1. That it is highly impractical to deal with each person over a maximum age on an individual basis to determine his or her particular ability to perform a job safely, effectively and efficiently.

2. That some of the individuals in that age group have traits which would generally preclude them from being able to perform the job or task safely and efficiently.

These two conditions are difficult to meet. Courts often see through smoke screen arguments that really do not meet these tests.

## PREHIRE INQUIRIES

All of the details of the anti-discrimination statutes apply to inquiries that any employer would make before hiring an individual. This includes inquiries about race, sex, color, religion, national origin or age. The pre-hire queries include questions on application forms. It includes questions asked in employment interviews about arrest records and inquiries about resumes of experience or any educational requirements, or any kind of written testing.

Questions regarding an applicant's race, color, religion, sex, national origin or age are generally looked upon *unfavorably* by the Equal Employment Opportunity Commission, which enforces the Title VII of the Civil Rights Act and the Age Discrimination in Employment Act.

The laws do not prohibit asking these questions. However, it seems to create an inference that an employer asking them cannot easily overcome. If you ask them, the odds are much greater than even money that you will be looked upon in a negative light and lose any potential case based on discrimination. So don't ask, my friend.

It is possible to ask whether or not a potential hiree is male, female, Mr., Mrs., Miss, or Ms.?

Certain local, state or federal agencies may require that you keep track of certain inquiries ethnic and minorities, e.g. in order to administer their fair employment practices laws. Sometimes you may end up having to ask questions that would normally not be allowable under other circumstances, to meet other laws.

Employers have particular problems asking for age on an application, and also asking for such things as arrest records. It has been shown that minority groups generally are more likely to have arrest records. Therefore, basing any decision on arrest records or asking for such information is generally considered discriminatory unless there is some very strong business reason. Inquiries about honorable discharge from military service may be a problem.

## Testing

At one time the idea of measuring and testing work potential of employees was not considered discriminatory. However, some court cases and studies found that some tests ended up resulting in racial and other biases.

Professionally developed tests can aid an employer in making a selection. It is possible for a test to measure general intelligence, learning abilities, specific intellectual abilities, accumulated knowledge and proficiency, certain attitudes, personality or temperament; mechanical, clerical and other similar types of aptitudes; and also dexterity and coordination, especially for physical tasks. Many of these can be acceptable.

## Validity

Some testing has had a negative effect on some of the protected categories. What do we look for in valid tests?

Initially, in evaluating a test we ask whether the test unfairly disqualifies minority groups including women, older persons or other protected groups at a substantially higher rate than other individuals. What the courts would look for is the validity of the test or screening methods. The test must be able to predict job performance with what is considered some high level of confidence. This means that there is a high correlation between the test results and the method used. The test must be predictive of the actual results as discovered later on.

If the relationship between the test scores and job performance has resulted from chance more than one time out of 20, the validity of the test may remain in question. Some courts have ordered a ban on certain tests. As a result of cumulative courtroom experience and some studies, a number of tests result in a higher rejection rate for persons in the protected category and have resulted in the invalidation of these tests. Hence, these tests cannot be used.

Even some of the language used on a test, which might include trade jargon or slang or inside terms, might adversely effect individuals who could be qualified for the job. These types of tests have been held to be invalid.

## Practices That Are Discriminatory in Effect

You as a small business owner, a manager, must be aware of the fact that Title VII of the Civil Rights Act of 1964 prohibits not only *obvious* discrimination, but also practices that *appear* to be *fair* in form, but end up being *discriminatory* in *fact*.

Some of these include requiring minimum height and weight standards (often excluding women), requiring information on arrest records, excluding certain minority groups, requiring certain educational levels (discriminating against certain minority groups), and using paper and pencil tests who often discriminate against those groups which had been discriminated against in the past because they are not familiar with that particular job.

## EMPLOYMENT STATUS

These laws focus on several employment factors that affect an employee on the job. By employment status, we are talking about denying a covered individual money, working or other conditions, and privileges of employment. In addition,

we are referring to an employer's activities that might directly or indirectly deprive a person of employment opportunities.

### Compensation

Discrimination in pay on the basis of race, color, religion, sex, national origin or age is also obviously covered by the federal law. This can result from indirect activities or classification including:

1. Job classifications or titles.

2. Minor differences or unsubstantial differences in the degree of skill required that would adversely result in discrimination.

3. Possession of a skill not even necessary for the job; in other words, stating that you have to have a particular skill so you can put a particular person in that job and pay that person higher, even though the skill is not required, can result in discrimination.

4. Occasional sporadic form of activity that may require extra physical or mental exertion, which could include once-a-year lifting of a weight that is heavier than most women can lift, so that an employer can justify having a male for the job.

5. The mere fact that jobs are in different departments of an establishment, when in fact they are no different in substance, could be used as a discriminatory basis for pay.

### Merit, Incentives And Seniority Plans

The acts we are discussing generally allow some differences in pay based upon the quality of performance (merit) or incentive performances, for instance piecework. Piecework would involve a person receiving pay based upon so much pay for each shirt sewed. This approach can be justified in a defense to claims of Title VII discrimination.

In addition, seniority plans are considered legitimate where someone who has been in the ranks for a longer time receives more pay than someone who has not been in the ranks as long. The courts have, however, modified a number of these plans, because seniority may result in the minority group being discriminated against continuously. The younger workers on the job would also end up, if there is any cutback on the job, being the *first ones fired.* Here you witness a perpetuation of the old discriminating pattern.

### Insurance, Retirement and Welfare Plans

Title VII covers discrimination or potential discrimination in direct benefits. It also covers indirect or fringe-type benefits. Obviously when we are talking about employee welfare benefits plans or employee pension or profit-sharing plans, there can be no discrimination based on the protected categories.

*Age Discrimination.* Generally, individuals age 40 or over cannot be discriminated against in the area of insurance, retirement or welfare plans. An example of this may be the types of health and accident benefits that you have for your employees.

Certainly the cost of health coverage increases as a worker gets older. Group life insurance companies price their insurance based upon increases in mortality with age. Therefore, as an employee gets older the cost of benefits generally increases. The Age Discrimination Employment Act now requires that an employer must spend essentially the same amount of dollars for a worker over 65 as he does for a worker under 65. The law allows a five-year band or average. The employer takes the amount of money he or she spends for welfare benefits on employees from age 60 to 64 and spends the same amount of money, for instance on employees 65 to 69 or 70 to 74 or 75 to 79, and so forth. It does mean that the benefits will decrease. The benefits can decrease as long as the overall amounts of money spent on health and welfare benefits are the same.

With regard to pension benefits or retirement benefits, the employee over age 40 must continue to receive any accumulation of benefits until she or he retires or is legally terminated (up to any plan maximum). Allocations to employee pension accounts cannot be discontinued or reduced for a worker simply because he reaches some specified age. Even if an employee is past the normal retirement age as defined in a plan, the employee or participant must continue to accumulate benefits under the plan if the younger person would be allowed to do that. Again, some limits. If a plan has a maximum benefit, this will apply to anyone who has reached it.

*Promotion and Seniority.* Promotion is a serious consideration in employee benefits. It certainly involves the morale of the company. Most individuals, as they progress and learn the job better, ultimately expect to be promoted. Therefore, the means of promoting individuals can be based on various factors. A promotion can be based on seniority, on testing, on the recommendations of supervisors.

In any event, promotions cannot be discriminatory. Again, there are many ways of having nominally fair procedures that result in keeping minorities and females away from the plum jobs.

Remedies for discrimination can include retroactive or constructive seniority. Thus, if someone has been given an unrealistic line of progression to follow, the courts might recognize this practice as resulting in discrimination.

Let's look at an example. Some senior jobs in a plant may *not involve physical labor*, but some companies might try to force each of their *promotable* individuals to do *hard physical labor* that is not necessary for those good senior jobs. This is one way to discriminate against women. If this discrimination is discovered and challenged in court, the courts may require that the individuals be given seniority, even if it's artificial, because they were artificially held down.

*Dress and Appearance.* Sometimes dress and appearance standards may adversely effect individuals. These standards can result in sexual, race, religious or other types of discrimination. In general there can be dress standards, but the courts have upheld different grooming standards for each sex. So, as long as they are reasonable and appropriate for the particular sex group, the courts will allow these appearance standards.

*Hair Length, Beards and Mustaches.* Generally males have complained about unreasonable standards on hair length, beards or mustaches, which may not apply to women. These are not a basis for discrimination claims. In general, male hair length does not fall within the protected category though it can result in adverse consequences.

*Manner of Dress.* Unless there is some good business reason, an employer cannot generally refuse to allow black employees to wear hair or dress styles symbolic of their heritage or refuse to allow head coverings or styles of dress required by religion.

*Leave of Absence Benefits.* In 1978 Congress passed a Pregnancy Discrimination Act. It provided that women unable to work for pregnancy-related reasons would be entitled to disability benefits or sick leave benefits on the same basis as any other sickness or disability for any other employee. This means basically that pregnancy would have to be put in the same category as any other physical disability that may occur to any employee. The employer should treat pregnancy the same as automobile accident injuries or broken bones resulting from recreational football.

*Holidays, Vacations and Free Time.* Employees must be given the same privileges regardless of their race, color, religion, sex, national origin or age. In addition, employers must make some allowances and exercise affirmative action to accommodate the religious needs of employees.

Once the employer has made some reasonable accommodations for the employee, the employer need do nothing further. Certainly religious dictates cannot control or totally disrupt the operation of a company. But based upon religious grounds, employers may have to bend and rearrange schedules.

*Retaliation and Harassment.* It is unlawful under the acts that we discussed (primarily Title VII and the Age Discrimination Act) to fire an employee who has attempted to exercise his or her rights. It is also illegal for the employer to harass an employee or to allow other individuals to harass employees or transfer an employee to a lower-paying job or to do anything that has an adverse impact on the employee.

## SEXUAL HARASSMENT

An illegal activity that occasionally occurs involves complaints of unlawful sexual harassment directed against female workers or job applicants. We see this in three forms:

1. Submission to sexual conduct is a condition for a female's employment.

2. There is retaliation against the female employee for resisting unwelcome sexual advances.

3. The employer or its employees create an offensive atmosphere interfering with job performance.

It is possible for the sexual harassment to adversely effect men.

*Discharge.* The federal law prohibits discharging individuals on the basis of any of the protected categories. As we have said, these categories include race, color, religion, sex, national origin, or age, 40 or older.

An employer is allowed to take appropriate disciplinary action against an individual, including discharging an employee. The action, however, must be done consistently and cannot be motivated by some discriminatory purpose.

It is incumbent upon the employer if he fires anyone to make sure that the factors include the inability of the individual to carry out his assigned duties effectively and efficiently. The action must also be based on non-discriminatory applied policy. The employer can discharge employees for excessive absenteeism, criminal convictions that cast doubt on the employee's ability to perform, business necessity, failure to meet a bona fide occupational qualification, or numerous other reasons the law has acknowledged.

*Union Membership and Representation of Members.* A union has the right to establish standards for its members. A union cannot evade prohibitions that apply to employer, such as creating false standards or standards that are neutral on their face but actually discriminate on the basis of race, color, creed, religion, national origin or age.

A union is obliged to represent all of its members in a bargaining unit fairly. The union itself must act in a non-discriminatory fashion when processing an employee's grievance under a collective bargaining agreement.

*Employment Agencies.* Employment agencies can also be the source of unlawful discrimination. Title VII and the Age Discrimination Employment Act prohibit employment agencies from discriminating by (1) failing or refusing to refer individuals for employment when they know there is a potential opening or (2) otherwise discriminating against a particular individual in the protected category. Employment agencies essentially cannot classify or refer individuals on the basis of race, color, religion, sex, national origin or age. An employment agency cannot advertise or publish discriminatory standards for potential job applicants.

*Record-Keeping and Reports.* General Requirements Under the Civil Rights Act of 1964 (Title VII).

It is very important for the small to medium-size employer to be aware of the potential reporting requirements. The EEOC requires that certain employers, unions, employment agencies and joint labor-management committees file reports with the EEOC. You must retain a copy of the latest report. You must produce it for the EEOC when and if it is requested.

The information you must keep includes records so the EEOC can determine if any unlawful employment practices have occurred. The employer must preserve those records for a period of time as the EEOC prescribes. Thus if any charges of discrimination have been filed, the covered party must keep the records at least until the final disposition of the case has occurred.

*Reports by Private Employers.* The magic number for triggering the reporting requirements is 100 or more employees. Any employer covered by Title VII who has 100 or more employees must file standard form 100-Employer Information Report EEO-1 each year with the EEOC. An employer who has fewer than 100 employees might also have to file with the EEOC.

There are no precise record-keeping time periods, but the EEOC has reserved the right to establish one.

*Age Discrimination in Employment Act.* Covered parties, including employers, are required to keep records under the ADEA for three years, including payroll and other records, containing the following information for each employee:

1. The name, address, date of birth, occupation, rate of pay and amount of pay earned each week. Assuming that the employer must keep such employment records, he must keep for a period of at least one year records relating to hiring, promotion, demotion, transfer, selection of training, lay off, recall, or discharge.

2. Job orders submitted to an employment agency or labor union or recruitment of personnel for a particular job opening.

3. Test papers completed by job applicants or candidates for promotion, transfer or training, if the papers are considered by the employer in connection with any personnel action.

4. The results of any physical exam, if the exam is considered by the employer in connection with any personnel action.

5. Any advertisement or notices to the public or to employees relating to job openings, promotions, training programs or opportunity for overtime.

Records regarding employee benefit plans must be kept by the employer for the full period in which the plan or system is in effect and for at least one year after the plan's termination.

If the job is of only a temporary nature, then the employer or covered person must keep the pre-employment records of applicants for 90 days from the date of the personnel action to which the records relate.

*Other Reporting.* Labor unions are covered by certain reporting requirements, and so are employment agencies. Employment agencies must keep particular information, including the following information, for at least one year from the date of the action to which the records relate:

1. Job placements.

2. Referrals where an individual is referred to an employer for a known or reasonably anticipated job opening.

3. Job orders from employers seeking individuals for job openings.

4. Job applications, resumes or any other form of employ-ment inquiry of any individual that identifies his job qualifications for present to future job openings.

5. Test papers completed by a job applicant or candidate for any position, when the test is considered by the agency in connection with any job referrals.

6. Advertisements or notices relative to job openings.

Again, even if a job is temporary in nature, any pre-employment record of applicants must be kept for 90 days from the making or obtaining of the particular record involved.

*Enforcement and Compliance.* The enforcement of the Civil Rights Act that we have discussed (primarily Title VII and the Age Discrimination in Employment Act) is the responsibility of the Equal Employment Opportunity Commission. Other agencies such as the Federal Power Commission, may consider the consequences of discriminatory employment practices when regulating their particular industries. The result is some overlapping at times.

## Criminal Penalties for Interference With Employment Rights

We should all take note of the potential stiff criminal penalties that can result from violations of the Civil Rights Act of 1967. The penalties extend not only to those who injure, intimidate or interfere with a person's civil rights, but also to those who attempt to do so.

Certainly very few employers or other persons covered by these acts engage in criminal behavior. But you certainly want to do your best to meet the many requirements that affect your business.

## FILING AN EEOC CHARGE

How does a charge of unlawful discrimination come about? The EEOC may accept a filing of a Title VII violation by one of the following:

1. Any person alleged to be injured by such a violation.

2. A member of the EEOC.

3. Persons acting on behalf of an aggrieved person.

The type of information that the EEOC needs includes:

1. The full name and address of the person making the charge.

2. The full name and address of the person against whom the charges are being made.

3. A clear and concise statement of the facts, including pertinent dates, making up the alleged unlawful employment practices.

4. The approximate number, if known, of employees or union members, if the party charged is an employer or labor union.

5. Information as to whether proceedings have been started before a state or local agency, and the date when such proceedings began.

## EXHAUST REMEDIES BY FIRST GOING TO STATE OR LOCAL AGENCIES

If there is a state or local law prohibiting the alleged discrimination and state law authorizes the state or local authority to grant or seek relief from discrimination or to institute criminal proceedings, the EEOC cannot immediately process that complaint.

Title VII provides that the complaining party must first seek out such state or local enforcement and that the state or local agency must be given at least 60 days to act upon the charge. This requirement that the initial complaint must be to state or local law does not deprive the EEOC of its jurisdiction over the case to the extent of delaying the EEOC's response.

Employers should note involvement of state and local agencies as well as the EEOC. In addition, we should be aware that the federal law seeks to require complainants to go to local agencies first.

## SUITS INSTITUTED BY INDIVIDUALS/PRIVATE EMPLOYEES

There are two prerequisites that are required before an individual can file suit and seek a judicial remedy. These are:

1. The filing of a charge with the EEOC.

2. The filing of suit in federal court within 90 days after receipt of an EEOC Right to Sue Notice.

In 1972 private individuals were given an additional right to initiate court action if (1) the EEOC has dismissed the charge or (2) 180 days have elapsed from the filing of the charge and neither the EEOC nor the U.S. Attorney General has filed a civil action or entered into conciliation agreement. An action under these conditions must be filed in court within 90 days of receipt of notice.

Therefore, there are some prerequisites to an individual filing an EEOC action, but they do not hamstring the individual.

## PUBLIC EMPLOYEES

Even public employees of state and local governments may bring court action under Title VII.

### Suit by EEOC or the Attorney General

The EEOC, under Title VII, has the authority to bring a civil action against an employer, union, employment agency or joint labor-management committee. This can occur if the EEOC has tried unsuccessfully to achieve an acceptable conciliation agreement. The Attorney General of the United States can also bring suits if the charges are brought against a public party, meaning a state, local or federal government. If a lawsuit is brought by a private individual, it is possible for the EEOC or the U.S. Attorney General to intervene in the suit upon a timely application and subject to the court's jurisdiction.

### New Proceedings

A suit brought by a private individual under Title VII is *not* a *review* of any action taken by the EEOC or by a state or local commission for that matter. The EEOC has no authority to make *legally binding* determinations of unlawful conduct. Therefore, a private individual is not relying on the findings of the EEOC.

The complaining party in any Title VII action has the burden of proving that the unlawful discrimination occurred. The defendant then has the opportunity to defend its position.

The following steps outline the procedure for an individual to follow before suing an employer under Title VII of the Civil Rights Act of 1964:

1. Employee must file a complaint with EEOC or with a state EEO agency within 180 days of illegal violation.

2. Within 10 days of receiving the complaint, the EEOC notifies the employer (EEOC works on conciliation among the parties).

3. After 180 days of filing complaint with EEOC or after 180 days of state EEO agency time to act, the employee can act on a "right to sue" letter or may sue.

An employee cannot sue until the above three time periods have elapsed. The employee must file suit within 90 days after number 3 above.

### FEDERAL EMPLOYEES

Federal employees also have a right to a complete new trial on whatever evidence they can present. Thus, even a federal employee does not get a mere review of any administrative record on any complaints of employment discrimination. She or he gets a new hearing with new evidence in federal court.

## Enforcement of Age Discrimination in Employment Act

The Equal Employment Opportunity Commission has primary responsibility as a government agency for enforcing the government's interest in ADEA violations. There can also be suits by individual employees.

*Suits by Employees.* Individual employees who believe they have been adversely effected by age discrimination can sue the individual employers and any other offenders, including employment agencies and unions. They can sue to recover unpaid wages, unpaid overtime and, in addition, liquidated damages. Individual employees, including more than one, can sue on your behalf, and they can also sue on behalf of themselves and any other similarly situated employees. Effectively, they can use a class action approach against potential defendants.

When they seek relief under the Fair Labor Standards Act, they may also recover, in addition to back wages, reasonable attorney's fees.

It is possible to seek a *jury trial* under the ADEA. If, however, the EEOC commences an action under the ADEA, the individual no longer has an *individual* right to pursue an individual remedy. The EEOC would pursue that individual's rights.

### Prerequisites to an Age Discrimination Suit

Most of the Title VII types of defenses are prerequisites to a suit. The ADEA requires that any potential plaintiff file a charge with any state or local government agency who may have such authority. The complainant must wait at least 60 days after the commencement of the state or local proceedings before initiating any individual court action, unless the state or local proceedings terminate at some earlier time.

However, commencement of proceedings in the state or local agency is only a minimum and is all that is required. State time limits or other requirements need not be met in order to file the federal action. Of course, if the state agency has no authority to proceed to grant relief, then the individual plaintiff need not wait. If a state agency cannot grant relief, there is no prerequisite to the lawsuit.

The individual not only must file with the state agency if such agency has authority, but also must file the charge with the EEOC to give federal officials the opportunity to settle the charges through conciliation. Filing with the EEOC must also take place within 180 days after the alleged unlawful practice has occurred or within 300 days after the unlawful practice has occurred, if first submitted to a state agency, or within 30 days after notice of termination of state or local proceedings, whichever of these three is earliest.

## TIME LIMIT ON SUITS

Suits by the EEOC or by individuals must be brought within two years after the cause of action has occurred unless the cause of action has been willful in nature. In such cases, suit may be brought within three years of the time when the cause of action occurred.

## GOVERNMENT WORKERS

The EEOC is also responsible for enforcing the ADEA with regard to state and local public employees. Federal employees must first notify the EEOC, and may not sue the federal government until at least 30 days after the EEOC has been notified of their intent to sue. The notice must be filed within 180 days of the occurrence of the alleged unfair discriminatory practice.

## RELIEF AND REMEDIES

There are various approaches for an individual to get relief for violations of the federal Equal Employment Opportunity laws. These include voluntary compliance and affirmative action programs.

The multitude of standards for affirmative action programs can be alarming. If you have any questions, I suggest you consult counsel who specializes in this area.

Even small businesses have to pay attention to numerous laws because they have employees. Almost every employer has spent several years trying to get straight with the IRS on payroll taxes. The fact that you send your taxes in on time does not mean that anyone at the IRS will know that. (Certainly you jest.)

# CHAPTER 18

EMPLOYEES AND
WORKING CONDITIONS—
OCCUPATIONAL
SAFETY AND HEALTH LAW

# CHAPTER 18

# EMPLOYEES AND WORKING CONDITIONS— OCCUPATIONAL SAFETY AND HEALTH LAW

## OCCUPATIONAL SAFETY AND HEALTH (PLANT AND JOB SAFETY LAWS)

There are now numerous statutes applying to businesses that have employees. Many states passed laws before the turn of the century to assure employee safety.

## OCCUPATIONAL SAFETY AND HEALTH ACT (OSHA)

The first federal safety statute that applied to most businesses was the Occupational Safety and Health Act. This Act was passed by Congress in 1970. It applies to all businesses that affect interstate commerce or are in interstate commerce. Thus, it affects virtually all businesses. There are minimum numbers of employees a business must have for OSHA to apply. It does not, however, create a private cause of action for an employee. This means an employee cannot sue the employer for non-compliance.

This particular Act is aimed at protecting the safety, health and welfare of employees in a couple of ways. It requires a certain minimal duty on any covered employer to prevent workplace hazards that may cause serious injury or death to its employees. OSHA also delegates to the Secretary of Labor authority to establish detailed health and safety standards in the form of regulations which must be complied with by covered employers.

Certain minimum levels of exposure to hazardous substances may be established. Some of these have included levels of asbestos, lead and other toxic chemicals.

One of the provisions of the OSHA Act established three new federal agencies: (1) the Occupational Safety and Health Administration, (2) the National Institute of Occupational Safety and Health, (3) the Occupational Safety and Health Review Commission. OSHA is the primary agency that was created by the Act, and this agency is within the Department of Labor.

## STANDARDS FOR ESTABLISHING REGULATIONS

Once OSHA has received sufficient information from all interested parties including employers and employees and health organizations, OSHA must publish any of its proposed or amended standards in the Federal Register. The public is then given at least 30 days to respond to the proposed standards.

Interested parties can request public hearings. OSHA can then schedule and publicize and hold a public hearing. After a public hearing is held, and within 60 days after the close of public comment and the hearing phase, OSHA is required to publish any new standards and the date that any new standards will become effective. The Secretary of Labor, however, has the power to delay the effective date of any new standards. The Secretary of Labor is also obligated to give reasons why any new standards are published.

## STANDARDS FOR APPEALING ANY OSHA DECISION

Any person adversely effected by an OSHA standard can file a petition challenging such standard, in the appropriate U.S. Court of Appeals, at any time prior to the 60th day after its issuance. Any effected party must act promptly to challenge this particular standard. The filing of such an appeal does not automatically stay the effectiveness of the standard unless the Court of Appeal decides to temporarily delay its effectiveness. Our attempt here is merely to expose you to some of the machinery that does apply to establishing the standards.

## Variances or Exemptions From OSHA Standards

Employers may seek exemptions or variances from standards they feel are inappropriate. It is impossible for any one person or group of individuals to know all the conditions or problems in a particular industry. OSHA, however, is charged with reducing risk to employees in particular areas. Sometimes there is a need for variances or exemptions from particular standards, because there is no one way to be all-knowing in such a complex task.

Temporary variances can be granted, as well as permanent variances. If you as an employer have a problem with a particular standard, you ought to be aware of this possibility. Obviously, you should seek counsel who is knowledgeable in OSHA matters so you may find a solution to the problem standards.

Seeking a variance from a temporary or permanent standard places a heavy burden on the employer. An employer is obligated to establish that all possible measures are being taken by the employer to protect its employees. The employer must also show that all the steps necessary to comply with any established standards are being taken. The employer is required to inform employees of any requested variances. Temporary variances can be granted for one year and are renewable twice, each time for six months.

Permanent variances can be granted to an employer who can prove, with substantial evidence, that his particular methods provide a safer workplace than the OSHA standard. The employer shows that its approach is different but provides the same or greater level of protection.

When permanent variances are requested, OSHA generally inspects the premises before granting such a variance. Here also, the employee must be informed of the application for the variance and must also be informed of the employee's right to request a hearing on such a matter. The employees may challenge any variance granted, if they act within six months after a permanent variance has been granted. The OSHA administration itself can take such an initiative.

## Employer Duties

Under OSHA, employers have three major responsibilities. The first is a general duty to protect the employee; the second is a specific obligation to comply with all OSHA standards, and the third involves record-keeping and reporting procedures to monitor occupational injuries and illnesses.

As we can easily see, the second obligation, which involves standards, can be lengthy and complex. This requires the employer to be aware of specific standards for specific types of businesses. Industry associations or groups often can be extremely helpful to you as an employer. The association may already have summaries of information that will let you know of any OSHA standards. If you are not fortunate enough to have access to an industry association that can help you in this aspect, consult an OSHA lawyer. Generally if you seek a lawyer knowledgeable in the labor and employment area, you will be able to get any OSHA standards.

## Record-Keeping and Reporting Requirements

For reporting and record-keeping, you ought to count employee noses. Small employers may be exempt from ongoing record-keeping. Employers who have 10 or more employees must maintain records of occupational injuries and illnesses.

An occupational injury is one that results from any work- related accident that involves at least a single incident, including a cut, fracture or sprain. An occupational illness is any condition resulting from exposure to any environmental or chemical or physical factors at a work site. Any occupational injuries and any occupational illnesses must be recorded by the employer if they result in death, loss of consciousness, a transfer to another job, medical treatment (other than mere first aid) or one or more lost workdays.

The employer must use specific OSHA forms and must present the records if an OSHA compliance officer requests them. Once a year these records must be posted to provide employees with the information that has been compiled for OSHA record-keeping.

Employers generally have 48 hours to submit these reports. Therefore, it is incumbent upon the employer to act promptly and to have the forms available and be aware of it.

## Inspection

As we have mentioned, the enforcement of this Act is primarily in the hands of the OSH Administration. It has inspectors. Inspectors may enter any workplace at any reasonable time without giving advance notice. However, if an *employer objects* to this inspection, meaning the employer does not voluntarily agree, the inspector can be *forced* to obtain a *search warrant* from a court of competent jurisdiction.

Inspectors usually check the workplaces, especially after fatalities have occurred, and often in response to complaints by workers. They also occasionally respond on a random basis. The inspectors may make observations of any of the conditions at the work site, take photographs, take instrument readings, take samples and also inspect records.

The inspectors are also authorized to question employers, their agents and their employees in private. Generally at the conclusion of an inspection, the compliance officer goes over his or her findings with the employer in what is called a "closing conference." At this time the employer can find out about any possible violations. This compliance officer then will report to an area director. The area director then decides if a citation is appropriate and if there should be a proposed penalty. The area director has a time within which to act. If the compliance officer becomes privy to any trade secrets, he is obligated to keep them confidential.

A compliance officer may issue a citation that carries a penalty of as much as $1,000 for each violation. A penalty is mandatory for any violation where the employer knew, or should have known, that there was substantial probability of death or serious harm. Willful or repeated violations can be subject to a civil penalty of up to $10,000. Criminal penalties can result in fines of up to $10,000 or six months imprisonment, or both, for willful violations that cause death.

---

## *POWER POINTS* _____

▶ OSHA's aim is to keep workplaces free from known hazards that injure or kill employees.

▶ Both employers and employees must follow OSHA regulations.

▶ OSHA has inspections and conducts investigations.

▶ OSHA requires certain reporting and record-keeping.

## CONTESTING A CITATION

There can be three levels of citations. They are the following:

1. De Minimis, a violation that has no immediate relationship to job safety, but on which a notice has been issued.

2. Non-serious, a violation that does have an immediate relationship to job safety, but probably would not cause physical harm or death.

3. Serious, a violation where there is a substantial likelihood that a serious physical harm or death could result. In this case proposed penalties of up to $1,000 are mandatory; in the non-serious category, they are discretionary.

## APPEALS FROM CITATIONS

If an employer decides to challenge a citation, he or she has 15 working days from the time of receipt of the citation to notify an area director in writing of such an appeal. This is generally known as a "Notice of Contest." This notice must also be posted to inform employees of what the employer is doing. In this case, the workers also have a right to participate in any procedures.

## AFFIRMATIVE DEFENSES FOR THE EMPLOYER

Several defenses, called affirmative defenses, are available to employers.

*Impossibility.* The defense of impossibility can be split up into three categories:

1. It is impossible to comply with this particular OSHA standard and still accomplish the job or task.

2. It is impossible to comply with the standard without damaging the work that has already been done.

3. It is impossible to comply with the OSHA standard due to the internal inadequacy of the building or the device itself to which the standard applies.

Many of these objections have been raised by employers in the construction area.

*Other Defenses.* There are other types of defenses employers have available. They include:

1. Procedural defenses, which challenge OSHA's inspection procedures, issuance of citations, hearing process and other processes.

2. Citing the wrong employer.

3. The defense of *res judicata*, which means OSHA has already ruled on the same facts in this citation.

4. The defense of using an improper method to create the regulations or standards.

5. The defense of vagueness of OSHA's standard.

6. The defense of unpreventable employee misconduct.

7. Several others.

## OVERLAPPING JURISDICTION

It is possible that another federal agency may have statutory authority over safety and health standards in a particular industry. In this case, if another federal agency has statutory authority, then it would pre-empt and OSHA would have no jurisdiction.

Several employers have claimed that there is such a conflict or that another agency has authority over the industry. This has been used as a defense to OSHA having any jurisdiction over a particular industry. OSHA has been successful where it has shown that its regulatory response affects the industry in a different way and involves different working conditions than are the field of the other agency that has some safety and health oversight.

Thus, if OSHA's regulations are of a different type and potentially non-conflicting, then OSHA is not pre-empted by the other federal agency.

If an employer contests a citation, the first contest is before an administrative law judge who is a member of the Occupational Safety and Health Review Commission. If the employer is dissatisfied with the decision of the administrative law judge, he or she may then appeal to the panel of the Commission itself. Then if the employer is still dissatisfied with the ruling, he or she may appeal to the U.S. Court of Appeals.

*State Programs.* OSHA permits states to develop and enforce their own health and safety programs. OSHA does have some temporary oversight and discretionary authority for three years over state programs. Nevertheless, states may establish *their own standards* which would probably be higher than the OSHA standards. There is some continuing oversight authority by the Secretary of Labor. It is possible, if state standards are insufficient, that federal enforcement could be reinstated. For that matter if the state programs are effective, the federal standards are curtailed.

# CHAPTER 19

EMPLOYER-PROVIDED BENEFITS

# CHAPTER 19

# EMPLOYER-PROVIDED BENEFITS

Employees should be keenly aware of the tax-favored benefits that can be provided to employees, including the management of a small business.

Employee welfare benefits and other fringe benefits can be provided without becoming taxable income for the employee who receives these benefits. Certain employee benefits can be excluded from the gross income of the employee.

Most medical care, including insured health benefits, is tax-exempt for the employee. In addition, pension or profit-sharing plans, cafeteria plans, group legal service plans and dependent care assistance can be provided with similar tax exemptions.

Also, many non-statutory fringe benefits have been provided without tax consequences for the employee.

Sometimes there are limits on the amount of benefits that certain shareholders and owner-employees can receive.

## TAX BENEFITS—SUMMARY

The employer can deduct as an expense many of the benefits we discuss below. In addition, the employer generally does not have to pay any FICA or FUTA taxes to provide the benefits. Lastly, the benefits generally are *not* taxable to the employee.

The following plans of deferred compensation are *tax-deferred* rather than tax-exempt.

## EMPLOYEE BENEFITS

1. *Tax-Qualified Plans of Deferred Compensation.* This includes stock bonus, pension or profit-sharing plans of the employer which are for the exclusive benefit of the employees and their beneficiaries. They must meet additional requirements of the Internal Revenue Code.

a. *Pension Plans.* This is specifically a plan that is established and maintained by the employer which is intended to provide a definitely determinable benefit to the employee over a period of years after retirement. It can also provide a fixed contribution each year on behalf of the employee. Pension plans may also provide disability and other incidental death benefits in addition to the retirement benefits.

b. *Annuity Plans.* Annuity plans are similar to pension plans except that benefits are paid out of annuity or insurance contracts.

c. *Profit-Sharing Plans.* These are plans established and maintained by an employer, provided from *profits* earned by the employer.

d. *Stock Bonus Plans.* Stock bonus plans, established and maintained by the employer, provide benefits similar to those of profit-sharing plans, except that the benefit and the contributions are not necessarily derived from the employer's profits.

e. Cash or deferred plans (Section 401(h) plans). These are plans that permit employees to have their salary reduced, with the reduction on a pre-tax basis invested in a profit sharing, fixed contribution or stock bonus plan.

2. *Medical Benefits for Employees, Retirees and Spouses.* It is possible for a pension or annuity plan to provide for the payment of benefits for sickness, accident, health and medical expenses of employees, retired employees, spouses and dependents, if certain conditions are met.

3. *Cafeteria Plans.* Cafeteria plans offer employees choices of two or more benefits that can consist of cash or other tax-qualified benefits. A plan may allow employees to place a certain amount of money into one or more medical plans, or a medical plan and a dental plan, or a medical plan, dental plan and employee dependent care coverage. It offers some variability in the employee's choice.

4. *Qualified Group Legal Service Plans.* Employers can contribute on behalf of an employee, his spouse or dependents to a qualified group legal services plan, when the value of such legal services will not be included in the income of the employee or the spouse or the employee's dependents. This benefit may not be available any longer unless re-enacted by Congress.

5. *Dependent Care Assistance Programs.* If properly structured, it is possible for the employee to exclude from his income amounts paid or incurred by the employer to provide for dependent care assistance. The tax law provides a maximum per year, which is currently $5,000, or $2,500 in the case of a separate return filer.

These plans provide among the best tax-favored benefits under the tax laws.

Every employer should seriously consider the long-term incentive these benefits can provide for employees.

## Fringe Benefits That Can Be Excluded From Gross Income

It is possible to have several additional types of fringe benefits that can be *excluded* from an employee's gross income. These can qualify if they fit the following definitions: (1) No additional cost services; (2) Qualified employee discounts; (3) Working condition fringes; (4) De minimis fringes.

1. *No-Additional-Cost Services.* No-additional-cost services are any services (a) provided by the employer to the employee for the employee's use (if such service is offered to customers in the *ordinary course* of the *employer's line* of *business* in which the *employee* is *rendering* a service) and (b) the employer incurs no additional cost, including forgoing revenue, in providing such service to the employee.

Now, this must be determined without regard to any amount paid to the employee for such service. For instance, tickets to a football game that is about to commence can be given to employees. Such tickets must be made available to the employees of the stadium or football team who are *not* engaged in the production or needed in the usual operating functions of the football game. In this case, the price of the ticket would *not* have to be included in the gross income of the employee.

2. *Qualified Employee Discounts.* Qualified employee discounts may include any discount, with respect to qualified property or services, to the extent that such discount does *not* exceed the following:

a. In the case of property, the gross profit percentage of the price at which the property is being offered by the employer to customers.

b. In the case of services, 20 percent of the price at which the services are being offered by the employer to customers.

The "employee discount" would be the customer price, less the price at which the property or service is provided to an employee for use by such employee. This difference equals the employee discount.

The "gross profit percentage" is the difference between the sales price to customers over the aggregate cost of such property to the employer. This gross profit percentage is calculated by looking at the basis of all property offered to customers in the ordinary course of business in which the employee is performing services. Also, this "gross profit percentage" can be calculated on a reasonable classification of property selected by the employer, and includes the employer's experience during the representative period.

"Qualified property or services" does not include real estate and personal property held for investment such as coins and securities, or services which are *not* offered for sale to customers in the ordinary course of the employer's business *in which the employee is performing services.*

3. *Working Condition Fringes.* A "working condition fringe" involves any property or services provided by the employer to the employee to the

extent that if the employee paid for such property or services, the *employee's payment* would be allowable as a *tax deduction*, as coming from a trade or business expense, or as an expense for the production of income.

4. *De Minimis Fringe Benefits*. This type of fringe benefit involves any property or service that is seldom provided and has such a small value that the accounting would be unreasonable or administratively impracticable. This fringe benefit is another which can be a legitimate expense for the employer, but is *not taxable* to the employee.

An example might be an eating facility for employees, which can be treated as a *de minimis* fringe if such facility is located *on* or *near* the business premises of the employer. In addition, if the revenue derived from such facility normally equals or exceeds the *direct operating cost* of such facility, the facility can meet this regulatory exclusion. On the other hand, there is a little hitch if such treatment applies only to highly compensated employees. Thus, the facility meets the *de minimis* rules only if *access* to the facility is available on *substantially* the *same terms* to each member of the group of employees under a *reasonable classification* set up by the employer. The facility cannot discriminate in favor of highly compensated employees. If the facility is provided on a non-discriminatory basis, employees can receive the benefit of this non-taxable benefit.

Other tax-advantaged fringe benefits can include airplanes, athletic facilities, automobiles, awards and prizes, bonuses, death benefits, dues and membership fees, education, gifts, stock options and jury duty pay. Additional tax-favored fringes can include lodging, maternity and paternity benefits, moving expenses, scholarships, sick pay, supper money, uniform, vacation, and wage continuation plans.

There are some benefits that provide current compensation.

## WORKERS' COMPENSATION

There were growing problems under common law which involved the right of an employee to *sue* his or her *employer* for injuries that occurred against him as a result of working there. Generally, under the common law, if the employee was not at fault, he or she might have a cause of action against an employer. He or she might also be able to sue other employees who may have been responsible for injuries. A real problem was created. Under these conditions, it was difficult for an employee to continue to work there if he had to sue his employer to get health benefits or compensation.

Also under common-law rules, there are defenses the employer might use to deny a worker recovery. If the employee contributed to his own accident or injury or knew there was a high degree of risk, the employee might not collect. Those circumstances were considered potential defenses.

In an attempt to lessen the level of litigation and also to lessen the hostility that may exist between employer and employee, all states have enacted Workers' Compensation Acts. What these statutes have attempted to do is to create commissions and boards to determine whether or not an injured employee is entitled to receive compensation. One of the benefits to the employee is that there are essentially no defenses to an employee's recovery for being injured on the job. Even if the employee or a fellow employee is responsible, the employee will be compensated in most circumstances. These acts in effect eliminated the typical common-law defenses.

As a trade-off, there is a limitation on the amount of compensation the employee will receive. It includes medical expenses reasonably related to the injury. The employee can receive compensation as long as he was injured in the course of normal employment activities. Generally, courts only enter the picture to review decisions of boards or commissions.

The amounts recoverable by an employee are generally fixed by statute for a particular type of injury. Injuries are generally placed on a compensation scale that is less than the common-law recovery would have been. Again, on the other hand, there are no defenses to it. So, in effect, there has been a trade-off. In this case, there is a no-fault approach, but there is protection for the employer also.

If, however, a third party (not the employer or fellow employees) is responsible for the injury, it is possible for the employee to bring a tort action against that third party.

Worker's Compensation laws provide income replacement, medical care and rehabilitation services for workers who have job-related injuries or sicknesses. They also provide income benefits for survivors of employees whose death was job-related.

## Social Security

Congress has in the past responded to the needs of workers for economic security. If a family loses earnings as a result of death, disability, retirement or medical expenses, Social Security may step in.

As most employers and employees know, Social Security is costly.

Social Security was legislated by Congress in 1935. Its initial intent was to provide limited retirement and death benefits for certain covered employees.

Additional features have been added to the original Social Security Act. The Social Security laws now include the following:

1. Old age and survivor's insurance.

2. Disability insurance.

3. Hospitalization insurance (Medicare).

4. Supplemental security income, which is based on need.

The Social Security system and funds are provided by contributions, essentially taxes, from employers and employees and from self-employed individuals. Typically, employees and employers pay matching contributions. Most of you are aware that the percentage changes on occasion, but not necessarily on an annual basis.

To date, Congress has put this on a basis of a base tax rate (percentage) with a maximum dollar amount. It is generally the employer's obligation to make sure the employee's portion of the taxes is withheld. The employer must remit these amounts, along with other taxes, to the Internal Revenue Service. The employee's contributions are not tax-deductible by the employer. However, amounts contributed by the employer are tax-deductible by the employer.

## UNEMPLOYMENT INSURANCE

The Federal Unemployment Insurance system was initially created as part of the Social Security Act in 1935. Subsequently, those particular provisions were supplemented by the Federal Unemployment Tax Act, as well as several other federal laws. These laws work in conjunction with numerous state laws to provide a method of covering unemployment.

Each state has a slightly different approach or different unemployment compensation level. We are not attempting to paint the entire picture in this area. Your accountant can give you a good idea of the cost of each of these programs.

Employer-paid benefits are one of the best forms of compensation. Your company gets a deduction, but the employee does not have to pay taxes on what he or she receives.

Under this joint federal and state program, workers discharged without being at fault can receive unemployment compensation. These laws require the employee have to worked a minimum period or a minimum wage amount to qualify. These periods or amounts vary by state.

The length of benefits varies by state. The unemployed worker must be ready and able to accept new employment.

# CHAPTER 20

## LOCATING A GOOD LAWYER

# CHAPTER 20

# LOCATING A GOOD LAWYER

## LOCATING A GOOD LAWYER

This area is most difficult to answer. But we will try. We will also examine how to get the best value for your dollars.

### CLIENT CONTROL

Before we get into the details of locating a good lawyer for a particular problem or for general problems, we must focus on one essential point. The lawyer is the individual who is most knowledgeable in his area of expertise. This goal clearly does not include *all of the law*. But THE CLIENT STILL CONTROLS THE LAWYER'S ACTIONS AND THE LAWYER'S EMPLOYMENT.

Many actions involved in resolving business problems or in preventing them do *not* necessarily involve *business judgment*. Nevertheless, the cost of legal services may be more expensive than the benefit received. It is always up to the *client* to determine this cost/benefit trade-off.

### LOCATING LAWYERS

I have read a number of books some of which describe how *easy* it is to locate lawyers in particular specialties. I have, in the last few years, managed litigation and hired lawyers across the nation. I have spent a lot of time trying to locate lawyers who are well versed in handling specific types of litigation and legal transactions. This task is very difficult. Furthermore, it is difficult to come up with a *formula* that works all of the time or even most of the time.

The small business owner or manager has to look at a few specific angles. First, it is best to attempt to locate lawyers who deal with *business*

problems on a *day-to-day basis*. For the most part, *your* lawyer is *not* the *correct person* to be guiding your business or to be giving you advice on *business-oriented legal* matters.

Most lawyers deal in general practice, litigation, personal injury and probate matters. Sometimes these lawyers even deal with criminal matters. Most civil-oriented lawyers do not have the time to learn the *specialties involved in business law*. If you heed no other advice in this chapter than that, you ought to be aware of the fact that most lawyers do not have the time and have not spent the time to become business-oriented. Unfortunately, not many of them will admit that.

## Methods of Locating Lawyers

1. What do you look for and where? Attempt to locate lawyers by their *specialty*. You can do that by looking for newspaper or journal articles written by lawyers. Even commercial section (Yellow Pages) of the telephone book can be helpful. The orientation you want is business law. The generalists will not be able to solve your problems.

2. *Personal Referral*. Quiz your friends on lawyers they have used. Do not take your friends' *recommendations* as being adequate, no matter how intelligent your friends are.

Your goal is to accumulate names and characteristics. Then put them in a list along with the other factors we look for in lawyers.

We live in a world where unfortunately most of us are blind, being in a different place. Each of us feels a different portion of the elephant and we all come to totally different conclusions. A person who feels the elephant's tail might believe that an elephant is small. Someone else, feeling an elephant's leg, would conclude that an elephant is much larger than the person feeling the trunk would think. The third person, who feels the elephant's stomach, may conclude that an elephant is a round animal. Some lawyers do not know what to look for because they do not pay attention to the requirements of the small business owner or manager.

3. *Bar Association Specialty Sections.* Most if not all bar associations, because of the need of specialization and special study, have *specialty divisions* or *sections.* Most bar associations have divisions that deal with business and corporations, personal injury, insurance, wills, trusts and estates, taxation, criminal law, financing law, securities laws, real estate, real property, trust law, and many other specialties. One way to get the names of lawyers who lean toward business is to check with your local bar association or the state bar association to see if they have a list of names of individuals who are members of a business-oriented section.

4. *Martindale-Hubbell Law Directory.* If you have access to the Martindale-Hubbell Directory, you may be able to find lawyers in your locality who have *representative clients* whose business is similar to yours. There are two sets of listings in this directory, by city and state. There is a free listing section in the front of the directory and a paid advertisement section in the back for each city. In the back portion, lawyers generally list some of their representative clients. You can find a copy of Martindale-Hubbell at a local law library.

5. *Large Law Firms.* Large law firms generally provide specialists in the areas in which most business people need help. Unfortunately, large law firms typically charge the highest fees. This solution is often an expensive solution. If you are going to utilize a large law firm, we suggest you try and focus on the young partner or senior associate who is in the business section. Most large law firms have a business section. If you focus on the young partner in that particular section, you will probably get more bang for your bucks. These firms know how to get the *bucks.* Your job is to concentrate on the *bang.*

Out of the first four above you may be able to locate a knowledgeable practitioner in a *smaller* firm. If you have a big business problem or a big bank account, the last solution will probably yield a well-versed business lawyer.

## INTERVIEWING THE LAWYER

The next important task after receiving the names of several potential attorneys is the *interviewing process.*

In this process, it is important that you ask questions without giving the lawyer a clue as to the answer you are looking for. Most lawyers can pick up quickly the trend of what you are looking for. If you signal it like the catcher in baseball, the lawyer will certainly be spouting back the answers you would like to hear. The interview should be a pop-quiz for the potential candidate.

It is also very important to interview several lawyers. If you want to help your own cause out significantly, you have to have a list of *several* lawyers. You must be willing to spend some time to find out which of those "candidates" will meet your needs. As part of any interview, it is often possible to discuss a matter with most lawyers without a fee. Usually the initial consultation is free. Verify this when you call to set up an appointment.

## BACKGROUND

One of the first things you should find out about any lawyer is a little bit about his or her background. Find out what bar association activities he or she is involved in. This may be a clue to his or her willingness to do a conscientious job.

### Areas Of Practice

After finding out something about a lawyer's background, you might ask whether he or she has published any articles. Find out his or her bar association memberships. You might also want to find out if your prospect has *categorized* his or her practice. Try to find out what percentage of his or her practice comes from the various areas.

Most lawyers in private practice have some idea what area of practice they derive most of their income from. If someone is a general practitioner, you will probably want to move on. Most family lawyers (generalists) have formed corporations and partnerships. Unfortunately, if this is *mixed* with many other types of practice, you do not have someone who has spent a lot of time learning the *business area*.

Here we are focusing on business problems. You are not looking for someone who has a smattering of knowledge in business problems. You are seeking someone who has been steeped in solving business problems. Again, general practitioners do not fit this category. The key is to try and determine what areas of knowledge this practitioner has developed. You want to get some idea of the lawyer's reputation with particular clients. Ask him for the names of business clients.

## MIND-SET

In any business, individuals develop skills or orientations for particular types of business. It is important for you to be aware of the different *mind-sets* that exist in practicing law.

Certain types of law involve shoot-from-the-hip types. Certain types involve concepts that are broad-based and not narrow. On the other hand, there are other areas of law that are very detail-oriented and involve "rifle thinking." An example might tax law. It is often detail-oriented. It is also form oriented as opposed to substance-oriented.

Securities law, on the other hand, looks to substance and virtually ignores what the surface looks like. I found, for instance, in those two particular areas that the mind-set of a securities lawyer is different from the mind-set of a tax-oriented lawyer.

Though there are some lawyers who can handle several areas of the law, there are very few who can do well in areas involving contradictory mind-sets. You may find a good securities lawyer, but go to someone else to do your tax work. If you find a good tax lawyer, by no means have him do your securities law. In either case you may end up paying for the rest of *your* life, not *their* lives (if you get the drift).

Another approach is to interview individuals at both large and small firms. There are also some benefits to *discussing* your potential representation with a generalists. If you know a general practice lawyer who is keen on getting the best representation by hiring specialists, speaking to the generalists may help your cause.

## SALESPERSONS

At many law firms there are some individuals who are known as "rain-makers." They are the ones that have the skill for drumming up business. They are the ones who will tell you virtually all of the good things about the firm (certainly not the bad). They are very pleasant and have the ideal personality for exuding confidence and for pleading *their firm's* case.

One of the things to find out is who might be handling *your work*. Is it going to be the "rain-maker" (probably not)? Or is there some firm *specialist* who will handle your business problems?

## CONFLICT OF INTEREST

This particular concept could be tied to mind-set, but in some ways it is different. Here is the way it works. Certain areas of the law require specialization. These areas require someone to spend an awful lot of time learning one particular area. In addition, most of the time firms specialize in *plaintiffs'* or in *defendants'* causes. Many small law firms specialize in personal injury law. Other firms, typically the larger firms, represent insurance companies or large trucking companies, and so forth. Thus, if you need an area of expertise, you will find sometimes that the only individuals around have the *wrong orientation for you*. For instance, if a firm typically represents automobile casualty insurance companies, it is difficult to have someone there who does lots of plaintiff personal injury work. Why is this such a problem? It creates a sort of legal schizophrenia.

Assume your state has no requirement that you wear seat belts. What is the effect of you not wearing a seat belt? A plaintiff attorney, if you were to get injured in an automobile accident, would contend that though you were not wearing your seat belt and should have, you would have gotten injured anyway.

On the other hand, an insurance defense attorney would have contended that, if you had been wearing your seat belt, you would not have gotten injured at all. This example illustrates why it is difficult for the same person or even the same law firm to contradict themselves over the same issues. It does happen, however. If you are looking for someone to represent your viewpoint, you have to be careful that you are not getting someone who is going to wear the *exact opposite* cap the *next day* in court, in contradicting his or her position from today. It is important to look out for potential conflicts of interest.

There are certain lawyers who represent *franchisors*. It is unlikely that they can do a decent job representing *franchisees*, because they would have to contradict the position that they took the day before—or even the same day, for that matter—in the same court.

### Bar Association Activities

Another helpful criterion, which we briefly mentioned in interviewing individuals, is to find out how involved they are in *bar association activities*. Look particularly for bar association activities pertaining to *business law*, corporation law, securities law, commercial law and those matters that a business-oriented lawyer should have. Find out what types of activities they get involved in in the bar associations, including the local, statewide and national ones.

## FEE ARRANGEMENTS

There are several types of fee arrangements. Let's examine the most likely approach for most business matters.

### FIXED FEE

A fixed fee matter is one where the lawyer agrees to handle a matter (through the trial level or through the completion) for a *fixed fee*. A lawyer may be willing to incorporate your company for a fixed number of dollars. He might handle a contract matter for a fixed number of dollars. This works well for some matters. On the other hand, the matter might be open-ended or involve some complica-

tions; then the *fixed-fee* approach may *not* be appropriate.

### CONTINGENT FEES

Contingent fees are those where an attorney will get paid a percentage or a fee *if there is a recovery*, or if a particular event occurs. Typically, this would involve a *plaintiff-type* case and is based on a *percentage* of the amount of money collected. Often in automobile lawsuits, the attorney might receive 25 to 50 percent of the entire amount. Some agreements have different percentages for settlements at different stages of completion and for trial.

### STAGE OF COMPLETION

Some lawyers, for instance, would agree to handle particular cases and receive a set payment based on how far into the case something has occurred. For instance, you might have three agreements necessary in a project. You might agree to pay your attorney a fee after completing the first agreement, and so forth.

### HOURLY RATES

The most common approach to business matters for business transactions or for defending business litigation is on an *hourly basis*. It is important to find out *up front* what the hourly basis. is. You should also get some estimate of *how many hours* it might take to complete the case. An estimate gives you some guideline from which to work.

Sometimes hourly fees are agreed to when business lawyers act for the plaintiff. Lawyers rarely charge hourly rates for personal injury recoveries. On the other hand, for business recoveries, the hourly approach is generally used.

It is important before selecting any lawyer to find out what rates he charges for *court* time, what rates (and minimum parts of an hour) for *office* time, what rates for *telephone calls*, and what rates for *research*. It is important to know how they charge for *going out of town*. You certainly should not have to pay for *unnecessary* travel. You certainly do not want to pay your attorney a high hourly fee just for *walking across the street* to do court filings when there may be delivery service that is much cheaper. You also do not want a high-priced lawyer digging out cases in a library when a paralegal or junior lawyer can do it for a lot less. Let your prospective counsel know this from the start. Set the ground rules and expectations right away.

### Photocopying and Fax Machines

You should find out the rate per copy the firm charges for *photocopying*. Tell them you expect the per-copy rate and total number of copies included in any bill. Find out how they charge for facsimile copies. Express mail can fall in the unnecessary category also.

These types of services are often profit-centers for law firms.

### OVERTIME

It is important when you are discussing potential fee arrangements with a lawyer, to let him know you will have to authorize any *overtime*. Most overtime is a result of *poor planning*, and not necessarily a result of some emergency. You should communicate that you do not want to pay extra for overtime when it is not absolutely necessary.

### ESTIMATES

It is important to get an estimate of the total projected time and expenses for a case or transaction. Certainly estimates change from time to time. Also, complexities of cases are not always obvious.

### MONTHLY BILLING

It is also important to get a monthly billing (if the lawyer bills on an hourly basis). It is too easy for lawyers to adjust bills to your detriment. If you are paying your attorney on an hourly plus expenses basis, get your bills as frequently as you can.

Another item of importance is to find out what fraction of an hour your potential counsel uses. Sometimes for a one- or two- minute telephone call, they may charge a minimum of one-tenth or two-tenths of an hour, or 25 percent of an hour, and so forth. Ask and ye may get some shocking news.

### ADVANCE RETAINER

Find out if the lawyer is looking for any advance retainer (money up front). This may be an advance against future billings. It may also be a non-refundable fee.

### COPIES OF ALL DOCUMENTS

Let your attorney know you want *advance* copies of any important documents. It is kind of unnerving to realize that many lawyers do not send clients copies even *after* these documents are filed, much less *before* they were filed.

You must remember that *you are the client* and *you control the case*. The lawyer may be knowledgeable in the law, but he is not always the one who should be making the decisions with regard your rights. What you need is a lawyer who gives you your alternatives along with his suggestions, but lets *you* ultimately *make* the *choice*. You cannot do this unless you preview court documents or unless you take a particular position on the law *before hand*. Lawyers often have an aversion to this, but you will be the one stuck with the results.

Sometimes documents contain inaccurate statements, for instance, which were unintended. You as the client can help your cause and your attorney by being able to *preview* documents. Be sure to let your attorney know you expect the opportunity to review documents prior to filing.

## Training Associates—WATCH OUT

If there is more than one lawyer in a firm who could effectively work on your case, you want the *cheapest* one. In addition, you want to make it plain to the lawyer that you do not intend to pay for *training* any of his *associates*. This process is expensive, and it is *unfair* to the client.

Unfortunately, having reviewed hundreds of bills from law firms across the country, I can tell you it happens. It happens to large clients and to smaller clients. The reason I mention this is that I have noticed that some firms *do not* charge clients to train their associates. Other firms try prestidigitation, if you get my drift.

In a nutshell, here are items you would want to communicate clearly to any lawyer you select:

1. If you are dealing with a larger firm, you want the young partner or senior associate to work on your case. If it is a smaller law firm, you want the lawyer who is most knowledgeable about your business law problem.

2. You want a monthly billing. You want it in a specific form where you can see *which lawyer* has done a task and the task has been defined. You also want a *summary* at the end which shows the following:

### Lawyer Classification

You should request the activity detail, with date, the lawyer, a designation of the activity and the time spent on each activity. Then with the summary above you would be able to see a listing of the lawyers, their ranking, the total hours that they put in for this month, their hourly rate, and the extension. Below that you want to see the *disbursements* that were made, the dates when the disbursements were made, photocopies at so much per page, telephone calls, fax calls, Federal Express and other specific costs. Request that any rates or expenses should be the lowest available to provide that particular service.

3. Let your counsel know you want to *preview* any important documents, especially for factual matters.

4. You want to know exactly *who* is responsible for the case, and you don't want to be shuffled around from counsel to counsel.

5. You want the lawyer to prepare an *estimate* or a *budget* of the case or transaction, even if it is redone occasionally.

6. You want to have any *legal research* done as *cheaply* as possible with someone who is knowledgeable. This often means using paralegals as opposed to lawyers.

Many lawyers utilize electronic research. Review these methods with the lawyer. Discuss this in advance. Often it is efficient, but it can be grossly expensive.

### MULTIPLE REPRESENTATION

You want to communicate to the lawyer that you think it is unfair for two or three lawyers representing you at the *same time* to be charging you for the *same time*. You want the leanest representation that is in keeping with good practice.

After taking all of these items into consideration, you will become a knowledgeable legal service buyer. Unfortunately, there is a steep and long learning curve involved which we all have to endure. After a while it gets easier, but it is not 100 percent certified. Most of us work like self-correcting guidance systems in rocket systems. We keep homing in on the optimum. Good luck on this difficult task.

Finding a business-oriented lawyer is as easy as writing a novel. You just get a telephone book, sit by the telephone and *open up a vein*.

| Person Performing Task | Position | Cumulative Time | Rate | Extension |
|---|---|---|---|---|
| R. Smith | Partner | 28.6 hours | 150 | 4290 |
| J. Jones | Paralegal | 17 hours | 65 | 1105 |
| | | | Total for month | 5395 |

**Absolute Privilege**—A protection that exists in the law of defamation which absolutely protects statements that are libelous or slanderous even though there is malice, therefore no remedy will be available in any civil action.

**Accord and Satisfaction**—This involves a two-step process. The accord is the agreement among parties to settle an agreement by taking less than or something different than what was originally agreed to, but the second requirement, satisfaction, must be met. If the party agrees to take less or something different than what is called for in the original agreement and does not receive the changed settlement figure amount or services, then the parties would revert to the original agreement.

**Accredited Investors**—A term that has risen under the securities laws stating a certain level of sophistication or financial stability in order for an issuer of securities to potentially be exempt from certain requirements of the securities laws.

**Affidavit**—A voluntary unilateral statement made by a party which has been reduced to writing and to which the party has sworn or affirmed its accuracy.

**Affirmative Action**—A process under the Civil Rights Laws by which an entity seeks to take positive action in order to seek out minorities or disadvantaged individuals covered by such laws in order to lessen the effects of any discrimination covered by such laws.

**After Acquired Property**—Property acquired subsequent to a loan and security agreement between two parties that will be covered by the security agreement. Thus, if an individual subsequently acquires another printing press the security agreement may also attach to the after acquired property.

**Age Discrimination in Employment Act of 1967**—This Act sought to reduce any potential discrimination against individuals age 40 to 65 in the employment arena.

**Agent**—An individual or entity who can act on behalf of another party, who is called the principal.

**Aggregate**—A mass or a joining together of the sum of all of the parts which would be taken together. An aggregate might be numerous family members who meet at a reunion; they are an aggregate, which is to be distinguished from an entity, such as a corporation, which is separate from its members.

**Alien Corporation**—A corporation formed outside the country. Thus, a Bahamian corporation, is an alien corporation for legal purposes, within the United States.

**Alimony or Alimony of Maintenance**—The allowance for support of one's spouse or divorced spouse as part of a marital or former marital obligation.

**Anticipatory Repudiation**—A concept whereby one of the parties to contract has put the other party on notice that he or she will not be able to perform the contract. In most jurisdictions the party who is willing to perform under the contract has several options.

**Antitrust Laws**—Federal and state laws which are intended to prohibit contracts, combinations or other arrangements such as trust pools, grouping of individuals, partnerships and so forth, which attempt to establish or maintain a monopoly in manufacturing or production of products or the sale of any commodities or perform any acts that might restrain trade.

**Apparent Authority**—Authority which, though not actually agreed upon between the principal and the agent, exists because the principal knowingly permits the agent to act as an agent or the condition whereby the principal allows the agent to hold himself out as having authority to act on behalf the principal.

**Appraisal Right**—In corporate law in certain states, a dissenting shareholder who objects to a merger or consolidation or an extraordinary corporate matter is given the right to have his or her shares appraised and purchased by the corporation. This is usually limited to shareholders of record who have the authority to vote on the matter in controversy at that time.

**Appropriation**—A taking of property or property rights to the exclusion of others. It is primarily used as indicating a public taking for public use of a private property usually under the power of eminent domain, which is available to public authorities.

**Arbitration**—A process whereby individuals give up their right to seek legal remedies and to apply legal due process in turn parties allow one or more individuals to determine a settlement for the matter in controversy.

**Assault and Battery**—Assault is the process whereby an individual knowingly attempts to physically injure another party. Battery is the process whereby they actually injure another party physically.

**Assignee**—The person or entity to whom rights or duties under a contract have been transferred. The assignee takes whatever rights there are, subject to any defenses that may have existed in the original contract, however.

**Assigning**—The process of transferring rights from a rightholder to someone who is seeking those rights.

**Assignment**—The process of transferring a right from a contract holder to someone who is seeking such rights. This is the transfer from the assignor, who has the contract rights, to the assignee, who will receive those contract rights or duties.

**Attachment**—A provisional judicial procedure whereby an individual receives an interest or physical possession of a property of a debtor. This is used to protect the creditor's right to collect a debt. The document is usually called a Writ, Summons or Judicial Order and allows the bringing of the property into the custody of the court.

**Automatic Perfection**—A process under the Uniform Commercial Code or security or lien laws whereby the creditor retains automatically an interest in the property on which the creditor has lent money.

**Bailment**—A process whereby temporary possession of personal property has been transferred to another individual. It is a lease of property on a temporary basis. It can also include the process whereby one party is storing the property of another but is obligated to use reasonable or sometimes extraordinary care to protect the property. Examples of bailments include leasing automobiles from a leasing company or storing one's furniture for a period of time.

**Bait and Switch**—A process whereby unethical merchants advertise a product at an extraordinary low price or advertise a product that is in high demand, when following the advertisement a customer either comes into the store or calls a mail-order merchant, then the sales individuals for the retailer attempt to switch the potential buyer to some other product—all with original intent to do so.

**Bearer Paper**—This exists in commercial paper or promissory notes whereby anyone who has physical possession of a promissory note or a bill of exchange becomes the legitimate holder of the note and therefore has the right to the proceeds. This can also include someone who has received physical possession from a thief.

**Bilateral Contracts**—These are contracts in which both the parties are obligated or have agreed to be bound by the agreement, as opposed to a condition whereby only one of the parties is bound to do something if the other party performs the other part of the contract.

**Bill of Exchange**—A three-party instrument in which one party is the drawer and draws an order for some definite amount on a second party and paying it to a third party, either at any time (meaning upon demand) or at some definite time in the future. A check is an example of a bill of exchange.

**Bill in Equity**—Though this term is not in common use, it essentially means a complaint by an individual under the equity side of the laws as opposed to the legal side. Bills in equity usually involve those areas under the old common law where there was no adequate remedy under the law. Therefore, the equity courts developed remedies; when an individual or person sought one of these remedies it would be through the process of filing a bill in equity.

**Blank Endorsement**—A process in commercial paper whereby an endorsement to a particular individual has been made and the individual endorses the document in his or her own name which now converts the entire document into bearer paper at least for the immediate future. This means that any individual who is the holder of the paper has legal title to it and can get paid on the document.

**Blue Sky Laws**—State securities laws which create certain requirements before an individual or entity or company or partnership or corporation can sell stocks to the public. It contains certain disclosure requirements or other stringent requirements in order to be exempt from having to file lengthy disclosure documents.

**Blue Laws**—Laws that prohibit certain commercial transactions or behavior on the Sabbath.

**Breach**—Breaking or violating an obligation or duty or contract.

**Bulk Sales**—Sale of goods or personal property in large lots usually without counting in small numbers. Usually it involves for state law purposes the sale of an entire inventory as opposed to the sale of inventory to single customers. There are laws in most states which allow buyers and sellers to protect each other if they meet certain procedures under the law. These are called bulk sales acts. The Uniform Commercial Code has a specific section covering this.

**Business Opportunity Venture**—A law which requires certain individual or entities offering business opportunities to other individuals as they meet certain criteria to disclose certain information, not only about the relationship but also about the entity offering this business opportunity. There are many states which have laws requiring certain disclosures and information about affiliates or certain affiliated transactions which most potential buyers of such an opportunity would want to know.

**Business Format Franchise**—A type of franchise or business relationship whereby a person would be buying or licensing or getting permission to use a method of doing business in a certain look or logo. If someone is cleaning carpets and wants to use a franchisor with a well-known name, the individual is purchasing a business format franchise. They may not be using a special process, but they are using the image of doing business in the format of that franchisor.

**Business Tort**—A violation of a business's civil rights or wrongful breach of the contract that injures a business. This right would injure the personal property rights, real property or intangible rights, including the reputation, of a business.

**Cafeteria Plans**—These are types of plans involving fringe benefits for employees by the employees permitted to select certain options, the same way an individual would walk down a cafeteria line and pick and choose what they want, given a certain number of dollars to spend. This is the nature of cafeteria plans. Thus, an individual might want to pick another week of vacation as opposed to dental plan coverage.

**Case Law**—The law derived from courts making decisions in particular conflict cases or controversy. Thus, the courts may interpret a particular statute or creative rule of law which can be used in determining the outcome of another similar case.

**Cease-and-Desist Order**—The process whereby a court or an administrative agency may tell a person or an entity to stop performing certain behavior that is violative of a law or someone else's rights.

**Certificate of Deposit**—A two-party instrument in commercial law where on person lends money to another party and expects the money back at a certain future time, usually with a stated interest rate added to the principal amount.

**Certification Marks**—Symbols attributable to a particular company stating that parts or services of the individuals which have these marks on them or are associated with them have a particular quality or derive from a particular region or area or state or have been manufactured using a particular method and typically have a certain quality of accuracy or other quality characteristics associated with them.

**Certified Check**—A check for which a bank has certified that the money it involves is set aside for the bearer.

**Chattel Paper**—A written instrument which gives evidence "of both the monetary obligation and the security interest in or at least of specific goods."

**Civil Rights Act of 1964**—Gives individuals certain enforcement methods in order to protect an individual's civil rights including race, color, creed, religion.

**Class Action**—A legal action whereby several individuals will be allowed to bring into a lawsuit all or most of the individuals who might have similar claims. The courts have created this action for individuals who all bought securities during a certain time period where there may have been some violation of the law adversely effecting them. The courts would allow them to take part in the action without actually having to hire their own attorney or to show up in court for every court hearing. The court appoints a class representative and also allows that class representative to appoint attorneys who look out for the rights of all of the similarly situated individuals. This can also take place for both plaintiffs (who would be the ones injured) and also for defendants who might be similarly situated.

**Clayton Act**—A federal statute enacted on Oct. 15, 1914, which is intended to protect the public against the lessening of competition. This Act prohibits certain practices in business which might reduce competition or create price discrimination which is not based on factors allowable under the law.

**Closely Held Corporation**—A corporation in which the officers or directors are actually the employees and also stockholders for most purposes they have the power to fill most of the officer positions and directorships without having the "public" at large or numerous stockholders involved. These are often family corporations.

**Collateral Estoppel**—A concept in the common law arising out of the equity courts, whereby the previous judgment on a given set of facts exists, and which would bar one of the parties to that previous action from raising that particular issue in a subsequent court challenge. This concept can involve litigation among the parties, even though there may be different claims involved in the second or subsequent action.

**Collateral**—This can be personal property including tangible or intangible personal property. It can also include real property used as security to guarantee a debt. This property can be seized to secure payment on a debt.

**Commercial Bribery**—Giving or receiving something of value for the purpose of receiving some commercial advantage. It is typically a payoff to an agent in order to receive some advantage such as a right to sell goods or service to an individual who is entrusted with the duty to look out for the interest of his employer, which may be adverse to the interest of the person offering the bribe.

**Commercial Paper**—Involves negotiable instruments, draft, certificates of deposit, checks and promissory notes. This is all further defined and explained in the Uniform Commercial Code.

**Common Law**—Law that should be distinguished from law created by statutes; these are laws created by the courts resolving disputes where there is no written law on which to base it. This is called the English Common Law, from which it is essentially derived. It is also over time included both the law courts in England and the equity courts, and also the merchant courts, which were used to resolve commercial disputes, all of which were brought together to create what we know as the "Common Law."

**Common Stock**—A representation of an ownership interest in a corporation or some similar entity. Usually common stock is the right to vote or to have some say-so on major changes to the entity, but this is not an absolute right. It usually gives the holder the right to residual assets: Should that entity be dissolved, after the payoff of all debts if there are any residual assets left, the common stockholders have rights to those assets.

**Compensatory Damages**—Damages in the form of a monetary recovery for loss or injury a person or an individual has sustained. This can include any damages or losses suffered, and it can include whatever it would take to fix the wrong; for instance, a fender-bender, compensatory damages would include the loss or damages in repairing the automobile, but also could include loss of wages, pain and suffering and other losses and injuries resulting from the wrongful behavior of another party.

**Conciliation**—The process of adjustment of disputed claims in some friendly or non-hostile manner. This typically results in a non-legalistic setting, meaning not in a courtroom.

**Concurrent Conditions**—This exists whereby two or more parties to an agreement are obligated to perform simultaneously or concurrently.

**Condition Precedent**—The circumstance whereby one party must perform or certain conditions must exist before there is a legal obligation or the other party to perform.

**Condition Subsequent**—This is the circumstance whereby parties are currently obligated to perform, but their relationship or the obligation may change if a subsequent condition occurs or does not occur by some specific point in time. An example might be that Party A will purchase property from Party B but this might be conditioned on a zoning change from residential to commercial within the following year.

**Conditional or Qualified Privilege**—In defamation actions, where one party has libeled or slandered another party, certain circumstances whereby there can be protection against the offending party if the offensive written or oral statements are made in a context that is given a conditional or qualified privilege. This means some good-faith statement by the offending party.

**Confession of Judgment**—This exists when the debtor, the individual borrowing money, has already admitted in writing that he or she has borrowed such money and will not contest such borrowing if he or she should default in repayment of the debt. Thus, the debtor would be waiving any rights to formal court hearings or to the time periods that might be extended, thereby allowing a swift court action to proceed against the debtor.

**Conflict of Laws**—A condition whereby two or more legal jurisdictions—which could be states, countries, nations have some interest in resolving a particular dispute—The laws of these jurisdictions may conflict but may have some bearing on the outcome of a case or controversy.

**Conglomerate Merger**—The process whereby a company purchases or merges with another company and there is no discernible relationship among the businesses. This means they would not be in the same industry or be able to share markets or control markets.

**Conscious Parallelism**—This term arises out of the antitrust area, whereby companies or entities theoretically do not communicate the raising of prices or any concerted action, but uniformity arises as the result of the parties consciously paralleling their company's behavior with the behavior of a competitor. This can include both price-fixing and other concerted anti-competitive behavior.

**Consequential Damages**—Damages which occur as a result of a breach of contract but not resulting from a direct loss. For instance, in an automobile accident, consequential damages would not involve the repair of the automobile directly but might involve the injuries which resulted as a consequence of the accident; in effect, one or more steps removed from the direct loss.

**Constitutional Privileges**—Those privileges which are granted under the U.S. Constitution and are guaranteed. This is included in the privileges and immunities provisions of the 14th Amendment to the U.S. Constitution.

**Consolidation**—The combination of two or more corporations or businesses into a new corporation or entity. It can also include the transfer of substantially or all of the assets in the same manner.

**Constructive Notice**—Information or knowledge of a fact imputed by law to a person, because he could have discovered the fact by proper diligence, and his situation was such as to cast upon him the duty of inquiring into it.

**Consumer Goods**—Goods as defined in the Uniform Commercial Code which "are used or bought primarily for personal, family or household purposes..."

**Contingent Fees**—Fees charges by an attorney which are contingent or dependent upon a favorable outcome. Typically an attorney may charge a contingent fee for a personal injury case, for instance often an automobile accident. The attorney will not charge the client if there is no favorable settlement or if the action is unsuccessful.

**Contract**—A set of promises for the breach of which the law gives a remedy, or the performance of which the law in some way recognizes as a duty. The contract may be bilateral, whereby both of the parties are concurrently obligated in the same agreement to perform, or unilateral, whereby only one of the parties is obligated to perform and the other party may or may not be obligated to perform. An example of this might be an insurance policy whereby the policy holder is not obligated to make the next premium payment, but if the premium payment is made the insurance company is obligated to provide the coverage.

**Convertible Bonds**—These are debt obligations of an organization or corporation which can be converted into another form of ownership in the organization or corporation. For example, convertible bonds may be convertible from bonds into preferred stock or into common stock.

**Copyright**—A right created under federal law to ownership of the work of an author that is fixed in some tangible medium such as books, photographs and so forth.

**Corporation**—An artificial entity created pursuant to the authority of some public authority or legislature. It has liability as an entity and is responsible for its own debts, which would generally not be passed through to any of the shareholders. Therefore, the corporation is artificial, created entity unto itself.

**Covenant Not to Sue**—The undertaking by a party not to sue or seek legal remedy against the other party. This generally arises out of the settlement of some matter whereby one of the parties is compensated for being prevented from ever suing the other party.

**Covenant**—An agreement or promise to undertake something.

**Creditor**—An individual or entity to whom money is owed.

**Cumulative Preferred Stock**—Preferred stock which is typically non-voting stock, but would pay a certain percentage or interest rate. An example might be a $100 par value six percent (6%) preferred stock. In the form of cumulative preferred stock the corporation or entity would have a cumulative obligation each year to pay the six percent (6%), and if the corporation had missed one year then in the following year it would be obligated to pay the current year's interest plus any prior years' missed, before the corporation could pay a dividend to the common stockholders.

**Cumulative Voting**—A system or method of voting for the directors of a corporation in which an individual is allowed to multiply its number of shares by the number of directors seeking election. It is a method of allowing minority shareholders the possibility of electing a director. In non-cumulative voting a minority shareholder would not be able to obtain any representation on a board of directors. On the other hand, if there were five director slots for election and an individual held twenty percent (20%) of the voting power under a cumulative setting, the individual would be able to elect one director; whereas in a non-cumulative setting a twenty percent (20%) shareholder individually would not be able to elect any directors.

**De Facto Corporation**—A condition whereby a corporation has been formed which has corporate attributes, but in the process of formation there has been some defect. If a corporation has been formed in good faith and the individuals forming it have made a reasonable attempt at complying with the corporate, laws and in fact used the corporation and its powers, then the association will be treated as a corporation in fact.

**De Jure Corporation**—A corporation that has been created in compliance with all the laws and is an entity in accordance with its full rights under the laws of that authority.

**De Minimis or De Minimis Non Curat Lex**—The law generally does not allow recovery or take notice of very small or insignificant matters.

**Debt Securities**—Securities of a corporation or entity which indicate that some money is owed to another entity or an individual.

**Debtor**—An entity or a person who owes money.

**Deceptive Acts and Practices**—Behaviors by individual businesses which are deceptive or create unfair results generally injuring a customer or another business entity.

**Defamation**—This involves libel or slander. This is the publication of information injurious to the good name or reputation of another entity or person which tends to bring that individual into disrepute with a third party.

**Defective Incorporation**—Creation of a corporation that is flawed. This might exist when there is some failure to meet one or more of the requirements for incorporating.

**Derivative Suit**—A lawsuit which is filed on behalf of a corporation but is a result of the corporation's failure to seek this civil remedy on its own.

**Detriment**—Consideration for a contract in the form of a forbearance or incurring some loss by an individual as his obligation under a contract. This involves the giving up of any legal right or the creation of any benefit for the other party.

**Direct Suit**—That condition whereby a party or person could sue the other party directly, as opposed to an indirect suit. An example might be if you were illegally injured in an automobile accident you would be able to sue the other party directly, but you would indirectly be able to bring the insurer into the suit. In some states the offended party can bring in the insurer directly.

**Discharge by Breach**—A condition whereby the innocent party in a contract which has been breached by the other party can treat the contract as being discharged. If you are the good guy in a contract and the other party breaches the contract, you may treat the contract as being breached and you may not have to perform under the contract. There are certain conditions that must be met before you can treat it as being discharged by breach.

**Dishonor**—A refusal by a party to a commercial instrument to honor or accept the document or instrument. An example of this might be where a bank refuses to accept or pay on a check.

**Disparagement**—Discrediting or detraction of anything of value owned by another person or an entity. An example might be the disparagement of your products by a competitor in an unfair or inaccurate statement by the competitor.

**Dispute Resolution Mechanism**—Some process whereby disputes that could result in court litigation not involving a formal court process or are somehow resolved in some alternative manner. This is often called an alternative dispute resolution mechanism.

**Dissenter's Right**—Are those defined under "appraisal right" above.

**Divestiture**—Remedy allowed in the antitrust laws—more specifically under the Clayton Act—whereby there has been a merger which has unfairly or illegally lessened competition. A remedy might be for the courts to require that the company which was illegally merged with another company must now be unmerged or divested; in effect, sold to an independent party.

**Documents**—Commercial documents or documents of title; generally these are instruments which show evidence of ownership by a party. They include bills of lading, warehouse receipts or dock receipts and similar documents.

**Domestic Corporation**—A corporation formed within a state.

**Dominant Party**—A party who has somehow either a psychological or legal superiority over an inferior party. An example might be an elderly aunt who is dependent upon her niece since the aunt is older and more fragile and is physically disabled. Therefore, you have a dominant party, the niece, and a subservient party, the aunt.

**Donee Beneficiary**—A third party who will receive the benefits of a contract but who has not paid for this benefit. They are the recipient as the result of a donor creating this benefit.

**Draft**—An order in writing by one person or entity to another to pay to a third party a particular sum of money. Though not the only example, a check is an example of a draft. This is also called a bill of exchange.

**Drawee**—The party on whom a draft has been drawn, who may have the obligation of making payment in accordance with the draft. Typically the drawee has no obligation to make such a payment until the drawee has accepted the obligation.

**Drawer**—The party who makes or draws a draft. It is as with your own checking account, you are the drawer and the bank is the drawee.

**Due Diligence**—An obligation to be thorough in making certain representations to the public. This arises prior to the public issuance of securities, but the term has been used more in other areas to show that those parties who make representations to third parties have some obligation to verify by using reasonable means, that the underlying statements are in fact true. Thus if an individual such as an accountant or a lawyer is making certain statements on which he is basing some opinion, then he may be obligated to verify some of the underlying facts.

**Duress**—A condition whereby one person compels another party to agree to a contract when in fact the person being forced would have not done so otherwise. An example might be to use the threat of physical force on a person unless he or she signs a contract.

**Emancipation**—A process which releases a minor from control of a parent. Thus, an individual who is under age but who can be emancipated in accordance with state law may be allowed to contract or to marry without parental consent.

**Endorsement**—A signature on the back of commercial paper or an instrument by the payee which indicates that the instrument is being transferred to another party or entity.

**Endorser**—One who signs on the back of a check in order to transfer ownership.

**Entity**—An actual or artificial existence or being.

**Equal Pay Act**—An act which requires that businesses covered by the act must pay most males and females on an equal basis. This federal law mandates the same pay for all persons who do similar work without regard to sex, age or other prohibited category or distinction.

**Equitable Remedy**—A method derived from the equity courts or the equity side of the common law in order to correct a wrong.

**Equity Securities**—A stock or similar security or any other security, which might be convertible, which evidences some ownership interest in an entity or corporation.

**Exclusive Dealing Agreements**—Agreements whereby a purchaser is obligated to purchase not only the products and services he or she intends to purchase but also additional products over a certain given period of time from the same supplier, to the exclusion of purchasing other similar products from competitors of this particular supplier.

**Exculpatory Provisions**—Provisions in an agreement which attempt to save one of the parties from his or her own illegal or errant behavior.

**Express Warranties**—A representation made by the seller of a good that it has certain qualities. This can also include the building of models or mockups of a product that become the basis for someone purchasing the product or utilizing the services.

**Expropriation**—The process of condemning a personal or real property for public use. This would exist when a public authority condemns an area for public use purposes.

**Extended Warranties**—Representations or guarantees which would safeguard the workings of a product beyond the existing warranty period. Many individuals purchase home appliances which come with one-year warranties, and then the purchaser may be able to purchase an additional extension of that warranty for some one year or five- year period.

**Extortion**—The process of forcing another to alter his or her behavior by the threat of violence or some economic form.

**Failure of Performance**—Failure to perform under a contract (also called failure of consideration) whereby one of the parties does not perform, thereby breaching the agreement.

**Fair Use**—This applies to copyrighted materials, whereby the law allows a certain type of use which would not be deemed to be infringement.

**Fair Labor Standards Act**—A federal law that regulates minimum wages and creates certain minimum requirements for other labor conditions.

**Fiduciary**—An individual who is a guardian, trustee, executor, administrator, receiver, conservator, or any person acting in a fiduciary capacity for any other person. A fiduciary is someone who must act with the highest and best intentions on behalf of the second party. This is a position of special confidence, whereby the fiduciary must act in the best interest of the second party.

**Fixture**—Personal property that has become attached to and become part of real property in such a way that it is now serving the interest of the real property.

**Floating Lien**—A security interest that attaches to personal property as it becomes part of the estate of a debtor by either purchase or inheritance. Thus the lien is considered floating, because it moves with the current property owned and nearly owned by the debtor.

**Force Majeure**—In the law of insurance and contracts, superior or irresistible force.

**Foreign Corporation**—A corporation formed within the United States but in some state other than the state of a domestic corporation. Thus, if you live in California, a Nevada corporation would be a foreign corporation.

**Foreseeable**—Capable of being anticipated. This is applied to the law by being able to anticipate the results of an individual's failure to perform under a contract. He or she or the entity may not know what would be the foreseeable consequences. It comes into play in the law by individuals generally only being held liable to what would be reasonably foreseeable.

**Franchising**—A process of a franchisor creating either a method of doing business or selling a product a franchisee would like to purchase. The franchisee would be granted the right to sell this product exclusively or to engage in business by utilizing the methods created by the franchisor. This involves the franchisor's trademark, service mark, trade name, logotype, advertising or other commercial symbols that represent the franchisor. The franchisee usually pays a fee, either directly or indirectly, for the rights which he or she is licensing under the agreement.

**Fraud**—Intentional misrepresentation of the truth in order to induce another party to some behavior by relying on the representations which the first party has made. The second party must incur some legal detriment or incur loss or damages in order for there to be fraud that is actionable in the courts.

**Fraud in the Execution**—Fraud whereby an individual has misrepresented what the document is, thereby inducing the innocent second party to sign or enter into such an agreement.

**Fraud in the Inducement**—Fraudulent or sales type behavior whereby there is material of misrepresentations in order to induce someone to enter into an agreement or sign instrument.

**Full Warranty**—This is defined under a federal law called the Magnuson-Moss Warranty Act. In order for a warranty to be considered "full" it must be written so that it meets the standards of this law. Such a warranty must provide a complete remedy for any defect in a product. This remedy cannot be limited as to time, and the warranty must be conspicuously visible and show any limitations on consequential damages. In addition, the warranty must provide for a complete replacement or refund of the product if the product cannot be repaired after a reasonable number of attempts.

**Garnishment**—A statutory proceeding whereby an individual's property, financial assets or credits in the possession of a third party can be secured by the creditor. An example might be garnishment of an individual's pay from his or her employer.

**General Partnership**—An association of individuals who are in business to make a profit. This partnership has partners who are all totally liable and have no limitation of liability.

**Good Will**—This is essentially the excess of the cost of acquiring a business over the sum of any net identifiable assets. This is the value of the business over the hard-and-fast assets which may be purchased. It can also be defined as the expectation of the public's future patronage of this particular business.

**Goods**—A tangible personal property.

**Guarantor**—A person who has agreed to incur obligations under a contract to guarantee to undertake the promise of another.

**Holder in Due Course**—A person who takes an instrument and has paid value for it and done so in good faith and has not been put on notice that the note is overdue or that there is any problem with its being honored or that there is any defense against it being honored. This gives that individual a favored status under the Uniform Commercial Code. This means that a holder in due course is more liable to get paid on the document than an ordinary holder.

**Horizontal Merger**—A merger between companies that generally compete in the same markets.

**Illegal Per Se**—This has also been called mala in se, which means that something is inherently wicked and for which there would be very little dispute or doubt. Murder and robbery would be examples of something which is illegal per se.

**Implied-in-Fact Conditions**—Those which a reasonable person would be able to ascertain from the intention of the parties. An example might include a restaurant owner's modifying or renovating his restaurant. The contract may have to be approved by the owner. This may be considered an implied-in-fact condition. In other words, not stated in the agreement but reasonable under the circumstances.

**Implied-in-Law Conditions**—Conditions which the law would require as a condition of completing a contract.

**Implied Warranties**—Warranties that have been defined by the Uniform Commercial Code. They include the sale of goods by a merchant, "merchantability." They could also include goods sold for a particular purpose whereby the person knows that the buyer is relying on his or her expertise in stating that this does fill a particular purpose.

**Incidental Beneficiary**—An individual or entity who may receive some benefit from a contract but was not intended to be the beneficiary under the agreement.

**Incidental Damages**—Damages which result from the breach of a contract. Other than the direct loss of value or cost of repairing the personal property these would be damages that would be incurred in any reasonable effort to avoid the loss or to recover the losses. These might include commercially reasonable charges, expenses or commission incurred in stopping delivery on the transportation care and custody of goods after the buyer's breach, or in connection with the return or resale of the goods, or otherwise resulting from the breach of the agreement.

**Income Bonds**—Bonds on which the interest rate is paid only when the corporation has earned the income in order to pay the interest.

**Indemnification**—A condition whereby one party agrees to save the other party from any loss or damages to create a condition of harmlessness which might result from any behavior the protected party may take. This is done pursuant to a contract.

**Indispensable Paper**—Any writing that evidences both a monetary obligation and a security interest (chattel paper), documents of title and instruments such as stock certificates and promissory notes.

**Injunction**—A remedy decreed by a court of equity to prohibit any party or enjoin a party from performing or continuing to perform a particular act the party may be disposed to do. The court may have concluded that this behavior is injurious to the complaining party and has fashioned this remedy to prevent the party from continuing or repeating any such behavior. The result would be known as injunctive relief.

**Insider Trading**—Selling or purchasing stocks or stock options as a result of an insider's gaining of material information prior to the public's awareness of such information.

**Instrument**—Generally, a negotiable instrument as defined under the Uniform Commercial Code: An instrument or any writing which evidences a right to the payment of money, of a type which is transferred in the ordinary course of business.

**Intangible Personal Property**—Things that one has a right to possess, but for which one must take legal action and not physical action to enjoy. Negotiable instruments, bank accounts, insurance policies and stock certificates are such properties.

**Interlocking Directorates**—This occurs when potentially competing corporations have one or more common directors or officers. Interlocking directorates between banks and competing corporations many be prohibited under the Clayton Act.

**Interstate Commerce**—Commerce or commercial transactions that affect commerce or trade between the states or the state and a foreign nation. Interstate commerce is under the control of the federal government.

**Jointly Liable**—A condition whereby two or more parties are each, together and separately, liable for the entire damages that may have been incurred by an innocent third party.

**Labor-Management Reporting and Disclosure Act**—A federal law which amends the National Labor Relations Act and imposes higher and more complete reporting requirements on labor organizations. In addition, it sought to make more stringent the organizational safeguards on the continued fairness of elections and managing of labor organizations.

**Lease**—An agreement between the owners of a property and a third party on the relationship and use of the property by the lessee. The lessor either owns or controls the property and the lessee is the party who is contracting for the use and habitation of the property.

**Levy**—Imposition of a tax or a right by a third party in a particular piece of property, be it personal property or real property. A secured creditor would have a right to seize such property until a debt is paid.

**Libel**—A malicious publication, in printing or writing or typewriting, which tends to damage or tarnish the reputation of an individual and expose him to public hate, contempt or ridicule. It is also the initial pleading of a suit in admiralty.

**Lien**—A charge against or an encumbrance on property to secure payment of a debt in performance of an obligation. Usually it is an interest in property which can be used to satisfy the payment of a debt.

**Limitation on Remedies**—Contractual limitations whereby one of the parties gives up his or her right to seek certain remedies if the other party breaches the contract.

**Limited Warranty**—Under the Magnuson-Moss Act, a limited warranty is any warranty which is not a "full warranty." These would be warranties that are limited as to time or as to the types of things the product seller will cure. An example of this might be 90 days on labor and one year on parts. Both of these types of warranties are limited as to their extent.

**Limited Liability**—Provisions in the law which allow a person or entity to limit its liability to a particular entity. It is also possible to limit your liability in a contractual setting between two or more parties to a contract. The law otherwise, even in the contractual setting, does not encourage or welcome with open arms limited liability provisions. It does, however, enforce them in the proper circumstances.

**Limited Partnership**—A partnership with one or more general partners and one or more limited partners. The limited partners, liability is limited to the extent of their financial obligation in the limited partnership. Thus, if a limited partner has agreed to invest $5,000 in a limited partnership, in general the limited partner will not be held personally liable for more than this $5,000. There are some limitations on the types of behavior that a limited partnership can engage in.

**Liquidated Damages**—Damage amounts which are agreed to among the parties to a contract as a definition of the damages that will be due under the contract. Liquidated damages must be reasonable in their amount and in their effect. They come into play only when it would be difficult for the parties to otherwise determine what types of damages may be due. If the liquidated damages are too high in relationship to what may be the actual damages, the courts may interpret this as being a penalty amount and hold that extraordinarily high amount to be unenforceable.

**Liquidation**—Erasure of a debt by payment. It can also mean the converting assets into cash in order to release the debts of an entity.

**Low-Balling**—A retailing technique whereby a retailer or merchant uses an artificially low price to lure customers to a store and then proceeds to add on many extras so the price then is no longer low—in fact, might be extraordinarily high. This is often used with bait and switch. If the retailer could not get the customer to switch to a more expensive product, they might use the technique of low-balling and then proceed to pile on expensive extras. Somewhat common in automobile dealerships.

**Magnuson-Moss Warranty Act**—An Act, passed in 1975, which included some provisions to protect the consumers from misrepresentation in product warranties.

**Force Majeure**—An irresistible force. This would involve an event that a person would be unable to correct, change or prevent by the exercise of any conscientious effort. This is a little broader than an act of God; it may also result from governmental intervention resulting from a war.

**Malicious Prosecution**—Civil or criminal litigation that is begun without probable cause or reasonable basis.

**Materiality**—The concept of materiality depends on the context in conjunction with the contracts. Misrepresentation would be considered material if it would be likely to induce a reasonable person to agree to the contract or if the maker knows that it would be likely to induce the recipient to agree to a contract. When used in the context of securities laws, the materiality of information or the misrepresentation of any information would depend on all the information that would be likely to affect the price of the stock or would be likely to be considered important in making a determination to either buy or sell a stock. It generally is not necessary that the fact be the factor that would change someone's mind; it would only be considered important in the total context of any decision that is made.

**Merchantability**—A concept utilizing the Uniform Commercial Code. Only a merchant—meaning someone who is knowledgeable in a particular business or has expertise at his fingertips or can hire experts—need be concerned about merchantability. Nevertheless, if a merchant sells goods, the goods carry an implied warranty as to the merchantability of the goods sold. The goods are of at least fair average quality and that they are fit for ordinary purposes for which these types of goods are used. This does not mean that the goods are perfect or will last forever, but that they fit the average of what those goods should be or could be.

**Merger**—A process whereby one entity absorbs another entity. One of the two or more corporations survives.

**Mirror Image Rule**—The process in common law contracts whereby an individual must accept the contract in terms that are identical to the offer. If someone wants $2,000 for their automobile, under the mirror image rule if there are any changes to the acceptance—that is, if the acceptance is not identical—then there probably has been a rejection or what is known as a counteroffer. The mirror image rule implies basically all or nothing.

**Misrepresentation**—Assertion or statement of fact which is inaccurate in the light of all facts, or omission of a material fact.

**Model Business Corporation Act**—A model drafted by the committee on corporate laws of the section of corporation banking and business law of the American Bar Association. While it per se was not a law when drafted, more than 30 states have either adopted it or use it as a basis for their corporation laws. This committee occasionally makes amendments to the model law from time to time, but it is up to the states to adopt any amendments.

**Monopolies**—When used in the context of the Sherman Act, monopolies involve those entities that have the "power to control market prices or exclude competition."

**Mutual Rescission**—Agreement by all the parties to an agreement to rescind or terminate the carrying out of the contract. Normally when there is a mutual rescission there are no damages due, since in effect the contract is erased.

**National Labor Relations Act of 1935**—This federal law was initially passed as the Wagner Act and subsequently was amended by the Taft-Hartley Act of 1947. This Act initiated the federal requirements to regulate labor-management relations and also collective bargaining agreements.

**Negligence**—Lack on the part of a person or entity to exercise due care or due diligence. This generally occurs when one party has injured another. The legal question is: Has there been negligence or has an individual violated a duty of care which is owed to the other person or entity? Negligence exists when an ordinary, reasonable person would foresee that such behavior would risk harming other persons.

**Negotiability**—The status of commercial paper whereby it is capable of being transferred either by endorsement or delivery so that the person who receives it, the new holder, the new transferee, acquires all the rights the transferring party had. This can include warehouse receipts, bills of lading or other similar documents that are negotiable.

**Negotiate**—Bargain for individual rights under a contract.

**Negotiation**—This is used in the particular framework of the Uniform Commercial Code to mean something different from "negotiate," the term that was just defined. Here negotiation is used with regard to a commercial instrument, and is the "transfer of an instrument in such form that the transferee becomes a holder." If the instrument is payable to order, it is negotiated by delivery with any necessary endorsement. On the other hand, if it is payable to bearer it can be negotiated by mere delivery; just handing it over to the other person would then result in a negotiation, which can only occur if we are discussing commercial paper, which is negotiable.

**Non-Accredited Investors**—Individuals who are not as financially secure or as sophisticated as an accredited investor.

**Non-Judicial Dissolution**—This occurs outside of the realm of judicial intervention or judicial oversight. It is a private dissolution of a corporation, for instance.

**Norris-LaGuardia Act**—A federal statute, passed by Congress in 1932, which essentially prohibits the courts, issuance of an injunction in cases involving or growing out of a labor dispute except under certain quite stringent circumstances. This was a federal statute; numerous states have enacted similar statutes.

**Novation**—Substituting a new contract that includes at least one of the parties to the existing contract, but also includes one new party who is never an obligor or an obligee under the original contract.

**Occupational Safety and Health Act**—A federal statute, passed by Congress in 1970, which makes provisions for certain safety standards in the workplace. It also resulted in the creation of the Occupational Safety and Health Administration, which is a branch of the Department of Labor that enforces the regulation which is the creed in setting standards and regulations under this Act.

**Offer**—The external showing of some willingness to enter into an agreement. This is done in such a manner that the other person would understand that the first person is agreeing to the bargain.

**Option Contract**—A contract which requires the party making the offer to keep the offer open for a certain precise limited time period. It is a promise which itself makes the requirements for a contract and which limits the power of the person making the offer to revoke it before the end of a set period.

**Order Paper**—Under the Uniform Commercial Code, order paper made payable to the order of a particular person or a particular entity. The outstanding feature of order paper is that in order for it to be negotiated there are two requirements: It must be endorsed by the person to whose order it has been made and it must be physically negotiated.

**Parole Evidence Rule**—A rule of contract law which holds that when a contract is formed all prior negotiation, pieces of paper, statements and other bargaining are merged into this particular contract. For most purposes, it all disappears. There are some exceptions where there has been fraud or ambiguity, but for most purposes the prior negotiations which may disagree with the current price disappear.

**Partnership**—An association of two or more persons who have agreed to carry on a business for profit as co-owners. All of those elements are necessary. If it is a non-profit combination or association it is not deemed to be a partnership for state or federal law purposes.

**Patent**—A right to "exclude others from making, using, or selling" a particular invention under the laws of the United States for 17 years.

**Payee**—A person to whom a payment on commercial paper is directed. The payee is the person to whom you make a check payable.

**Pecuniary**—Normally, involving money or worth; therefore, a financial or monetary term whereby something can be calculated or quantified.

**Pencil Whipping**—A sales technique often used by slick, fast operators to jack up prices and reap more benefits for themselves in heavy negotiations.

**Perfection**—A process under the Uniform Commercial Code in security laws whereby a person obtains priority over other conflicting claims collateral. For example, if you were to purchase an automobile and borrow the money from a bank, the bank would want to perfect its interest in the automobile ahead of any other potential creditor you might or might not have. On the other hand, just because an entity has a perfected security interest, this does not mean there are no circumstances under which it could lose its secure position.

**Plain Meaning Rule**—Holds that the courts will not look beyond the words in a statute if the court believes that the language is clear and that therefore the meaning of the statute is clear.

**Possessory Security Interest**—The lien or security interest that a creditor holds in property; but it is dependent upon the creditor having physical possession or control, either directly or indirectly, of the collateral. A pledge is included in this term. Under this pledge the creditor must have physical possession of the collateral.

**Pre-Emption of a Corporate Opportunity**—A provision under the corporate law whereby a director or officer or anyone who has a fiduciary or trust obligation to the corporation must defer personal gain to the corporation. Under these circumstances, if an individual were to come across some business opportunity or some financial opportunity which the corporation could handle, it is this person's obligation to present to the corporation this opportunity. If the corporation should reject such possibility, then the individual could pursue this corporate opportunity. The individual would be violating his or her duty to the corporation if he or she took the corporate opportunity prior to the corporation having an opportunity to reject it, being in possession of complete material information.

**Pre-Emptive Right**—Rights that begin under the common law which are generally provided for under state statutes. These rights allow a stockholder of a corporation to purchase any new issue or offerings of stock in the same corporation which would allow him or her to maintain the same proportion of the holdings as bear to the total outstanding stock in that corporation. In many, if not all states, the corporation can eliminate such pre-emptive rights.

**Preferred Stock**—This is stock that is preferred as to one of two categories. The stock can be preferred as to dividends over the common stockholders, or it can be preferred as to assets over other classes of stock. Usually it is not preferred as to both of these categories, but it could be.

**Price Discrimination**—A condition whereby a seller of goods of the same kind or quantity offers them to different purchasers at different prices, even though the delivered cost is identical for the seller of such goods or commodities. This type of behavior is often in violation of the Robinson-Patman Act.

**Price Fixing**—The unlawful joining or combining among competitors to fix prices or to specify prices under certain

circumstances. It is generally considered illegal per se under the federal antitrust laws.

**Principal**—Person or entity who employs an agent; under federal criminal law, the person who is primarily responsible for a criminal act.

**Private Placement**—Issuance of securities by an issuer meaning a corporation or a partnership, "not involving any public offering." Generally the issuer is relying on an exemption from registration under the federal or state laws. This is generally based upon the sophistication of the purchasers of such securities.

**Private Corporation**—A corporation which is not affected with the public interest. Thus, a large company which is publicly held and has millions of stockholders is considered a private corporation. On the other hand, a corporation created by the federal government or by a state for state or federal purposes would be considered a public corporation, as opposed to a private corporation. Private corporations can be very public and very huge.

**Product Franchise**—A relationship whereby a franchisor produces or licenses or has produced for it a product with its own name, which it then wholesales or retails to a franchisee. The franchisee would then have the rights to market the franchisor's product. This differs from doing business in a particular method as (defined above as the business format franchise).

**Promissory Estoppel**—A principle of law whereby an individual who has previously misrepresented the facts or misrepresented his or her own circumstances will not now be allowed to come into court and tell the truth. If the individual has defrauded people by lying to them before, he or she cannot defend himself or herself by saying what the truth is now because he or she took advantage of the individuals by lying. The third parties must have relied on the statements the individual made and acted on his or her statements.

**Promissory Note**—A written, unconditional promise by a person or entity to pay a definite sum either upon demand or at some definite time in the future to the holder or the holder's order. If a promissory note is a bearer note, it can be transferred by mere change of possession. If it is an order note, it must be properly endorsed and its possession must be properly transferred.

**Protest**—Under the Uniform Commercial Code, a certificate of dishonor made under the hand and seal of U.S. consul or vice consul or another Republic or other person authorized to certify the dishonor by the law of the place where the dishonor occurs. It is a formal document stating that the maker of the note will not pay it. It can also be a formal notice that the bank will not accept a particular check or the drawee of a particular bill of exchange will not accept it. For most purposes within the United States, we do not need a formal protest. On the other hand, when dealing in international finance it is common and may be required that a formal protest be utilized in an individual's notice of dishonor to the other parties.

**Proxy**—The authority a stockholder gives to another person or entity to vote his or her shares in a corporation or in any other circumstance. It is not limited to corporate law.

**Public Corporation**—A corporation formed for essentially governmental purposes. It should be distinguished from publicly held corporations—corporations which have sold their securities to the public.

**Puffing**—Exaggerating qualities of a product or the value of a service. Under the common law, puffing is generally considered OK, since it is not as bad as fraud or misrepresentation; it is the process whereby the seller tells a potential buyer how great his or her goods or services are.

**Punitive Damages**—Damages which the courts have allowed as increases over compensatory damages because of the behavior of the defendant. They have been allowed in cases where the defendant has been reckless and malicious in his or her behavior toward the plaintiff or toward individuals who are similarly situated to the plaintiffs.

**Purchase Money Security Interest**—A security interest under the Uniform Commercial Code or similar laws which is created when a seller of goods lends the buyer money or when a finance agency lends money to the buyer to purchase goods. Therefore, it is called the purchase money security interest. Generally, under the Uniform Commercial Code it has a priority over most other types of security interests, but this is not always the case.

**Qualified Endorsement**—Limits, qualifies or even enlarges the liability of the endorser or transferor and does this in a manner which changes his or her liability under the law. It is also called a conditional endorsement.

**Quid pro Quo**—the consideration or the bargain for consideration for a contract. In other words, it is what one party gave up to get what the other party is giving or has given up.

**Quorum**—The number of directors or shareholders who are required to be present or represented as present at a meeting in order for action taken at the meeting to be valid and enforceable. For directors' meetings a majority of the directors—meaning anything over half—is generally required for a quorum unless the articles of incorporation or bylaws state otherwise. For a shareholders' meeting there is often times a different number, and may on occasion be less than a majority.

**Regulation A**—A regulation of the United States Security and Exchange Commission which allows a company or an issuer of securities an exemption from the detailed requirements of filing full registration. It nevertheless requires an offering circular and financial statements that meet certain standards.

**Release**—A writing whereby the parties to the release discharge any duty owed by the person being released. The release may or may not release all parties; it may release only certain named individuals. One that releases all parties would generally be considered a mutual release.

**Remedy**—Under the Uniform Commercial Code, any right that a party would have to cure some contract breach or other harm or damage to which the party had been subjected. This may involve a judicial determination, or it may be what is known as

a self-help remedy— done pursuant to contract but still in accordance with the law.

**Renunciation**—The giving up or elimination of a legal right a person has. This is done voluntarily. It may also involve disclaiming an interest a party may have in a negotiable instrument or an estate or in a contract.

**Repudiation**—A party to a contract denies its validity or its authority or refuses to even acknowledge the existence of an agreement.

**Res Judicata**—When a legal matter has already been decided. Thus, if there has been a final judgment in a given controversy, the matter effectively cannot be re-examined; it would generally be dismissed based on <u>res</u> <u>judicata</u>, meaning that the matter has already been decided.

**Rescission**—An agreement among the parties to the contract in which each party agrees to discharge all of the other parties' duties or performance under the existing contract.

**Restitution**—A condition whereby one person restores to another person everything the first person wrongfully lost at that party's hands. In other words, to put things back to where they were before any damages were done.

**Restraint of Trade**—A prominent term in antitrust laws. It generally involves horizontal and vertical price-fixing. Horizontal would involve competitors and vertical price fixing would be among suppliers anywhere from the manufacturer to the marketplace. All the participants in that chain would agree to the price-fixing. Additionally, it means division of territory or customers, involves refusal to deal, involves certain types of anti-competitor mergers, involves reciprocal dealing arrangements, time arrangements, exclusive dealing arrangements. Many of these behaviors are considered illegal because they restrain trade and diminish competition for the benefit of the consumer.

**Restrictive Covenant**—An agreement restricting the use of real property or the kind, type, location, size and value of buildings or improvement of structures on such property. You may find restrictive covenants in subdivisions that want to maintain exclusivity. Sometimes restrictive covenants are required legally by zoning restrictions.

**Restrictive Endorsement**—These endorsements are explained in the Uniform Commercial Code. They can be conditional or may attempt to prohibit further transfer which may restrict the behavior of the transferee by using words as "for collection," "for deposit," or used for the benefit of a third party.

**Retainer**—Engaging a lawyer for professional purposes by either a preliminary fee or a continuing fee. Sometimes you see a general retainer, which is often a continuing fee, vs. a special retainer, which may be for a specific price.

**Rule of 78**—Formally used for determining the amount of interest that has been paid on a loan or is left to be paid. The Rule of 78 is similar to accelerated depreciation in that it assumes that a significantly greater amount of interest has been paid at the beginning of the loan than would be the case if the interest payments were calculated on an unpaid balance. Needless to say, this is to the advantage of lenders and the disadvantage of borrowers.

**Rule of Reason**—Used in the antitrust, anti-competitive-behavior area. It generally means that the court will examine a particular behavior, weighing all of the factors of a case to determine whether the behavior is reasonable. Contrasting rule of reason would be the per se rule. Certain types of behavior under the antitrust laws are considered per se illegal, and the courts will not apply any weighing of all of the factors; it would be automatic. Again, the Rule of Reason allows the courts to examine the history of the behavior and the competitive effects of the behavior to determine whether a reasonable result has occurred.

**Secured Bonds**—Debt obligations of a corporation or other similar entity which give the purchasers of such bonds a security interest in certain assets of the corporation. The secured party is defined as a lender, seller or other person in whose favor there is a security interest. The Uniform Commercial Code uses the term in several articles.

**Secured Transaction**—A transaction involving a security device in the lending of money either to purchase goods or services or merely in the process of securing the loan which is sought by a borrower.

**Securities and Exchange Act of 1934**—A federal statute that not only created the Securities and Exchange Commission but provided for the registration of security issues that are publicly held and for the creation and registration of the Security Exchanges and also for the registration of broker-dealers. The Securities Act of 1933, passed by Congress in 1933, requires the disclosure of material information prior to a company's issuing securities to the public. The process of registration requires detailed disclosure and requires certain of the registrant's directors and officers to take part in standing behind the statements and disclosures made. It also prohibits fraud and creates a remedy in the issuance process.

**Security**—An instrument that can be issued in bearer or registered form. It is the type commonly dealt in on securities exchanges and public markets, and may come in one or more classes or series. It evidences a share of participation or other interest in property or an enterprise, or it may also evidence a debt obligation on the part of the issuer.

**Security Agreement**—A contract or agreement whereby the lender receives a security interest—in effect a partial ownership right—in the collateral being used as security for a loan.

**Security Interest**—An interest in personal property such as fixtures. This interest solidifies or secures payment or the performance of a payment of an obligation. It entitles the person holding such security interest to seize either the property or the fixtures upon default, at least to the extent of any debt owed plus any additional amounts to which the parties have agreed. It replaces the concept of lien of title retention under some common law or other statutory based security interest.

**Service Contract**—An agreement to perform services, as contrasted to the providing of goods under a contract.

**Servicemarks**—A mark is used in the sale and advertising of services to identify the services of one person from the services of others. The term can include titles, character names and distinctive features of radio or television programs.

**Shareholder Agreement**—An agreement among shareholders, usually in a closely held corporation or among the shareholders of such corporation, and the corporation itself. Subject matter of such agreements includes the corporate management, method of voting shares, how shares will be disposed of, and other related matters. There is sometimes a way of allowing a family or a group of individuals to control a corporation where none of them could do so individually.

**Slander**—Using defamatory words in an oral manner to injure someone's reputation, business, trade or means of livelihood.

**Sole Proprietorship**—A form of business ownership whereby the individual is also the business. There is no intervening entity.

**Special Endorsement**—Under the Uniform Commercial Code, a special endorsement is one that states specifically the person or entity to whom or to whose order the person makes the instrument payable. A special endorsement is important because only that person, or another with a legitimate endorsement from that person, transfer or negotiate this instrument. It is a valuable protective device.

**Specific Performance**—A remedy developed in the equity courts that requires an offending party to perform a specific kind of contractual obligation according to the terms agreed upon in the contract. This is used where money damages would not adequately cure the problem. This is considered an unusual remedy, and at times may be difficult for the courts to enforce. It is safest to put such specific provisions in a contract allowing the non-offending party to use this.

**Statute of Limitations**—This statute prohibits a party from taking legal action after the allowable time period since the cause of action arose has expired.

**Statute of Frauds**—This statute was passed by England's Parliament approximately 300 years ago to require that certain contracts be in writing in order to be enforceable. Thus, if a contract cannot be performed within a year, or involves someone's guarantee to another's debt or involves the guarantee of the debts of a decedent's estate, or involves the interest of the sale of land or sale of personal property for a price greater than a specified amount, or involves the sale of personal property in consideration of marriage, there must be some written documents giving evidence to the transaction. The Uniform Commercial Code gives such provisions, and almost all, if not all, states have similar provisions.

**Straight Vote**—In the corporate law context, this means that each shareholder receives one vote for each share of stock the shareholder owns. This is contrasted to cumulative voting, whereby each individual's total number of votes can be multiplied by the number of directorships at stake.

**Subchapter S Corporation**—A corporation that elects not to be taxed as a corporation for federal income tax purposes. The tax burden is passed through to the stockholders. Some states have provisions similar to the federal statute, but not all states.

**Subpoena**—An order from a court to appear and give testimony.

**Subpoena Duces Tecum**—An order from a court to appear and give testimony and to also produce certain specified documents.

**Subscribers**—Individuals or entities who have agreed to purchase shares in a corporation or an issuing entity. This could be a partnership or other similar type of entity.

**Subservient Party**—A party who is in a trust relationship with another individual (see Dominant Party, above). It can also involve real property where one of the parties has a right to drain water on another property, where the drainer is the dominant party and the party who must receive the water is the subservient party.

**Substantial Performance**—A procedure which the courts have dictated in certain cases. Generally under the common law in the contractual area, a party must perform the contract in a manner identical with the agreements. For instance, if you purchase someone's automobile for $2,000, you cannot show up with $1,999.99 plus some Super Bowl tickets. You must produce exactly $2,000. On the other hand, in the area of home construction there are no homes which are exact. Therefore, the courts have allowed the concept of substantial performance meaning that if the contract was performed in good faith and generally complied with except for some relatively minor deviations, the courts will enforce the contract. Sometimes the courts will decrease the penalty that might have to be paid under a home construction contract for the irregularities. Under most circumstances a person cannot refuse to pay because the house is not perfect, because there are no perfect houses.

**Subterfuge**—Resorting to concealment or some hiding scheme to avoid one's responsibility.

**Tangible Goods**—Property with material substance; property you can touch physically, as opposed to intangible personal property which might involve a promissory note or a loan secured by a promissory note or common stock in a corporation.

**Temporary Injunction**—An injunction that a court may issue pending a hearing of all the facts. On occasion the courts may have to make a quick decision where someone's rights are being injured but prior to the courts and the party being able to obtain all the information that may be necessary for a final decision.

**Temporary Perfection**—A process whereby someone may be able to obtain under the Uniform Commercial Code or certain state laws temporary perfection of their interest in the property, but it also means that they will have to follow up with some additional action, otherwise they may lose their temporary perfection.

**Tenancy**—Occupancy of property by a tenant. It can also mean possession under some right or legal title. There are various types of tenancies that can be tenancies at will, at sufferance, for life, for years, from month to month, and numerous other types.

**Tenancy at Sufferance**—A condition which exists when a tenant has had an initial right of possession, the term has ended, but the tenant has continued to possess the property with the absence of objection on the part of the landlord.

**Tenancy at Will**—The tenant continues to possess the property for as long as the landlord agrees. In some states, a tenancy for a fixed term has expired it is converted into a tenancy at will, as opposed to a tenancy at sufferance.

**Tenancy for Life**—A tenant can remain on the property for the entire lifetime of the tenant, there being no requirements for payment or whatever means were used to procure the tenancy for life.

**Tenancy From Period to Period**—A generic description of what could be from month to month, from quarter to quarter, from week to week, from year to year or for any other term. This would exist in many states where there has been an initial term of months with a fixed rate for that month. The tenant has remained on the property with the assent of the landlord, so therefore, if the initial term was for a month then any subsequent holdover would be on a month-to-month basis. If the initial term had been a quarter of a year and the tenant had remained, in the agreement of the landlord, with no other agreements as to terms, then the original term would carry over. Thus, the same would be for the week to week and for the year to year.

**Tenancy in Fee**—A right to occupancy of real property by a tenant under a lease for a specific term, which is renewable forever except for non-payment of rent.

**Tender Offer**—A offer made by a potential purchaser to a holder of certain securities to transmit for his or her purchase the securities at a certain price typically for cash. It could also be for securities or for a combination of securities and cash.

**Testimonial**—A comment of praise which an individual gives to a manufacturer of a product. You see it where someone gives a testimonial for the benefits of using a particular underarm deodorant. Some individuals are paid to give testimonials, whereas other individuals give testimonials based on their personal opinion.

**Tie-In Arrangement**—Whereby a seller of a product or products requires that the buyer of products and services must purchase other products of the seller if the buyer wants to get the initial products. These arrangements generally involve larger corporations forcing smaller corporations to buy products they do not want in order to get the products they do want. For most purposes this type of behavior is illegal.

**Tort**—A wrong or a violation of an individual's or an entity's or a business's rights. This can be rights to a good name or a right to possession of your house, but nevertheless it is the illegal taking of your civil rights.

**Trademark**—A word, symbol, device or any combination used by a manufacturer or merchant to identify his goods and distinguish them from those manufactured by others. It can be used more broadly by including both trademarks and service marks, meaning marks used in conjunction with services, certification marks which are used as stamps of quality, regional product marks, and collective marks.

**Trade Libel**—False words which are published concerning a business or person which attempt to injure the business's reputation or the person's reputation for professional, business or occupational employment reasons.

**Trade Secrets**—A formula, patent, device, or compilation of information used in a business. It can involve any of these or any other types of information which give a person an opportunity to attain an advantage over competitors who do not have this particular information. It can involve a formula for a chemical compound or a process for manufacturing or treating or preserving materials, a patent for a machine or other device, or a list of customers. The focus in this definition is something that would continue over time and would be of some lasting value to a business, such as a list of potential customers, as opposed to what would be one-time customers who could never be used again for any future business. In any event it involves generally an unpatented, non-protected, non-copyrighted secret which has commercial value as a plan or an appliance or as a formula or as a process which can be used in making products or treating products or materials that can be used to benefit a business.

**Treasury Stock**—A stock issued by a corporation and owned by the same corporation and not canceled. Such shares of stock are issued but are not considered outstanding and cannot be voted by the corporation.

**Treble Damages**—Several federal and state statutes allow, as an additional deterrent to the anti-social behavior banned by the statute, the trebling of any damages. In a price-fixing case, if the court were to determine that $1 million of overcharges resulted from price-fixing, the law would require a trebling of the damages, so the total judgment would result in a $3 million damages plus certain additional fees that might be allowed under the law.

**Trustee**—An individual or an entity which has the responsibility to administer the property of a trust. The trustee would be the nominal owner of any property or any securities, and would not only be required to invest it wisely for the benefit of the second party, but also would be held accountable for keeping track of all the money, and also would be held to being a wise investor.

**Truth-in-Lending**—A federal statute passed to assure that every borrower who is covered by the act would have the proper consumer credit information in a meaningful form prior to making such a loan. The Act requires that the cost of credit be developed and calculated in a uniform manner. It must include the calculation of the total dollar amounts of any finance charges, the annual percentage rate computed on the unpaid balance, the amount financed, and other relevant credit information.

**Ultra Vires**—A behavior undertaken by a corporation that is beyond its corporate powers. It generally implies that the corporation has acted in excess of its authority. This type of defense, or even this concept, has been diminished drastically over the years, and unless something is criminal in nature, a third party that deals with the corporation cannot plead *ultra vires* any more than the corporation itself can use the doctrine.

**Unconscionable Contracts**—These types of contracts are discussed and addressed in the Uniform Commercial Code. This concept also exists in several forms in the common law. What happens is, the courts may refuse to force any contract for the sale of goods or a portion of such a contract if the contract contains any unconscionable provisions. This could include certain terms such as taking advantage of the buyer, certain unconscionable damages, say, for a consumer. If a business sells a product which it knows is pretty risky to put in the marketplace but does it anyway, and requires that everyone sign a limitation of liability contract, the courts may not enforce that particular protective provision if it deems it to be unconscionable. This is not a common occurrence in business, but it does happen.

**Undue Influence**—An offshoot of fraud or constructive fraud by a dominant party who takes advantage of his or her dominance over another person to limit the information the other person gets or to frighten the person into agreeing to a contract. Undue influence amounts to a version of fraud implying mental constraint or coercion, which can make a contract voidable.

**Uniform Commercial Code**—A uniform law developed by the American Law Institute and the National Conference of Commissioners on State Laws. As mentioned above about the Model Business Corporation Act when developed it was not a law. It is up to the states to adopt the Uniform Commercial Code; 29 states have adopted it almost totally, and all 50 states have adopted substantial portions of the Uniform Commercial Code. Even though it per se is merely the compilation or ideas of a number of individuals, the state legislatures have adopted substantially all of its provisions. It was designed to resolve problems involving commercial transactions which included sales of goods, commercial paper, bank deposits, collections, and documents of title to personal property, problems involving investment securities, and methods of procuring secured interest in personal property.

**Uniform Limited Partnership Act**—A model developed by the National Conference of Commissioners on Uniform State Laws. Once again, it has been adopted by a number of states. It has been revised, and the revised version, called the Revised Uniform Limited Partnership Act, was created by the same conference of commissioners.

**Uniform Partnership Act**—An act developed by the National Conference of Commissioners on Uniform State Laws.

**Unilateral Contract**—A contract in which only one of the parties has made a promise. In order for this contract to truly rise to the level of a contract, it would require one of the other parties to whom the offer is made to do something, to perform an act. An example might be one person speaking to an audience of 40 individuals and throwing out the suggestion that if any of you will paint my house by the first of next month I will pay you $500. Only one of the parties is obligated to meet the requirements of that contract unless the person making the offer, the one in the audience, is obligated to do anything. On the other hand, if one of the parties in the audience does perform the act of painting the house then that individual would be due the $500.

**Unliquidated Damages**—Damages that cannot be easily calculated on the face of a contract. Most tort actions involve unliquidated damages, because there was no agreement with which to calculate damages. A lot of the injuries in automobile accidents might involve different opinions of the value of the injuries. On the other hand, in a contract it is possible to have known damages because they can be stated. When discussing a promissory note that is for $500, that would be a known quantity. On the other hand, if we have a contract which has some consequential damages as the result of the contract being breached, we have what is known as unliquidated damages, which cannot be easily calculated.

**Unsecured Bonds**—This can be considered an unsecured debt, but it means money lent to a corporation or an entity with no security interest in any specific property. The lender can then be a general creditor of that corporation.

**Usury Law**—A law that prohibits a lender from charging interest in excess of an allowable maximum interest rate. The limit can be called lawful interest, it may be called the legal rate of interest. These laws place caps on the interest rate the lender can require. There must be a loan or some giving up of the use of money.

**Verbum Sat Sapiente**—This is not a legal term that would show up in many legal opinions and is not a legal principle—it only means "A word to the wise is sufficient." It is the focus of this entire book. It is to make you wiser—hopefully, before you are poorer.

**Vertical Merger**—A process of a supplier and its customer merging or combining. It creates anti-competitive results.

**Workers' Compensation Act**—These are state statutes that provide for scheduled or fixed awards to employees and their dependents with employment-related accidents, injuries or diseases. One of the benefits of this sort of Act is that it dispenses with proof: That is, the plaintiff or employee need not prove that the employer or anyone else was negligent. The employee need only prove in general that the accident was work-related, and he or she is allowed to recover under the law. On the other hand, there are limitations on the amounts of money which can be recovered. Here the trade-off is assurance of recovery under the Act without having to prove negligence or without having to prove anything else other than that the injury or disease was work-related.

Adams, Paul. *The Complete Legal Guide for Your Small Business.* New York, NY: John Wiley & Sons, Inc., 1982. 218 p.

ALI-ABA, Committee on Continuing Professional Education, IV; Haynsworth, Harry J. *The Professional Skills of the Small Business Lawyer.* Philadelphia, PA: American Law Institute, 1984. 255 p.

Allen, Paul A. *How to Keep Your Company Out of Court: The Practical Legal Guide for Growing Businesses.* Englewood Cliffs, NJ: Prentice-Hall, Inc., 1983.

Allen, Paul A. *How to Keep Your Company Out of Court.* Englewood Cliffs, NJ: Prentice-Hall, Inc. 1984. 282 p.

*American Law of Products Liability.* 13 Binders; Quarterly Supplements, 3rd ed., Rochester, NY: Lawyers Co-Operative, Date Not Set.

Barlett, Joseph W. *Venture Capital: Business Strategies, & Investment Planning.* New York, NY: John Wiley & Sons, Inc., 1988. 514 p.

Beam, Burton T., Jr.; McFadden, John J. *Employee Benefits.* 2nd ed., Homewood, IL: Richard D. Irwin, Inc., 1988.

Bequai, August. *Every Manager's Legal Guide to Hiring.* Homewood, IL: Dow Jones-Irwin, Inc., 1989.

Berry, Don. *Small Business Borrowers Guide.* Seattle, WA: Law Forum Press, 1988. 52 p.

Bloomenthal, Harold S. *Securities Law Handbook, 1987-88.* New York, NY: Clark Boardman Co., Ltd., 1988.

Bond, Robert E. *The Source Book of Franchise Opportunities.* Homewood, IL: Dow Jones-Irwin, 1985. 509 p.

Breit, William. *The Antitrust Casebook.* Hinsdale, IL: Dryden Press, 1988. 480 p.

Brennan, Mary E., Editor. *Corporate Benefit Plans—International and Domestic Perspectives.* Brookfield, WI: International Foundation of Employee Benefit Plans, 1988.

Brombers, Alan R.; Ribstein, Larry E. *Brombers & Ribstein on Partnership.* 2 Vols. Boston, MA: Little, Brown & Company.

Brown, Gordon W.; Byers, Edward E.; Lawlor, Mary A. *Business Law with UCC Applications.* 7th ed., New York, NY: McGraw-Hill Book Company, 1988. 704 p.

Callaghan. *Products Liability Litigation: Case Evaluation, 1988.* Deerfield, IL: Callaghan & Company, 1988.

Cameron, Scalette. *Business Law: Legal Environment, Transaction & Resulation.* 3rd ed., Homewood, IL: Richard D. Irwin, Inc., 1989.

Cartwright, Robert E.; Phillips, Jerry J.; Lambert, Thomas F. *Products Liability.* Charlottesville, VA: The Michie Company, 1986.

Cihon, Patrick K.; Castagnera, James O. *Labor & Employment Law: Text & Cases.* Boston, MA: PWS Kent Publishing Company, 1988. 690 p.

Clark, Barkley; Smith, Christopher. *The Law of Product Warranties.* New York, NY: Warren, Gorham & Lamont, Inc., 1984.

Collins, Hugh. *The Law of Contract.* Littleton, CO: Fred B. Rothman & Co., 1986. 236 p.

Coltman, Michael M. *Buying & Selling a Small Business.* Blue Ridge Summit, PA: Tab Books, Inc., 1986.

Coltman, Michael M. *Buying (and Selling) a Small Business.* WA: Self-Counsel Press, Inc., 1983. 137 p.

Comesys, Walker B. *Antitrust Compliance Manual: A Guide for Counsel, Manager and Officials.* New York, NY: Practicing Law Institute, 1986. 209 p.

Commercial Law and Practice Service. *Franchising, 1988: Business Strategies and Legal Compliance.* New York, NY: Practicing Law Institute, 1988.

Coppola, Andrew J. *The Law of Commercial Paper.* Totowa, NJ: Littlefield, Adams and Company, 1977.

Covington, James S., Jr. *Introduction to Agency & Partnership.* 2nd ed., Austin, TX: Butterworth Legal Publications, 1988.

Crawford; Beadles. *Law & the Life Insurance Contract.* 6th ed., Homewood, IL: Richard D. Irwin, 1988.

Douglas, F. Gordon. *How to Profitably Sell or Buy a Company or Business.* New York: Van Nostrand Reinhold Co., Inc., 1981. 286 p.

Dunfee, Thomas W.; Gibson, Frank F.; Blackburn, John D.; Whitman, Douglas; McCarty, F. William; Brennan, Bartley A. *Modern Business Law.* 2nd ed. New York, NY: Random House, Inc., 1989. 1192 p.

Dunfee, Thomas W.; Ballace, Janice R.; and Rosoff, Arnold J. *Business and Its Legal Environment.* Englewood Cliffs, NJ: Prentice-Hall, Inc., 1983. 656 p.

Employee Benefit Research Institute Staff. *Fundamentals of Employee Benefit Programs.* 3rd ed., Washington, DC: Employee Benefit Research Institute, 1987.

Epstein, David G.; Henning, William H.; Nickles, Steve H. *Basic Uniform Commercial Code, 1988 Supplement.* 3rd ed., St. Paul, MN: West Publishing Co., 1988.

Farnsworth, E. Allan; Young, William F., Jr. *Selections on Contracts: Statutes, Restatement Second, Forms.* Mineola, NY: Foundation Press, Inc., 1988. 250 p.

Farnsworth, E. Allan. *Commercial Paper: Cases and Materials.* 3rd ed., Mineola, NY: Foundation Press, Inc., 1984.

*Federal Bankruptcy Law Handbook.* Binghamton, NY: Gould Publications, 1985. 750 p.

*Federal Securities Laws: Legislative History, 1983-1987 Supplement.* Washington, DC: BNA Books, 1988. 484 p.

Fischer, David A.; Powers, William C., Jr. *Products Liability, Cases and Materials.* St. Paul, MN: West Publishing Company, 1988.

*Franchise Opportunities Handbook.* Washington, DC: U.S. Government Printing Office, 1982. 430 p.

Freedman, Warren. *Product Liability for Corporate Counsels, Controllers and Product Safety Executives.* New York, NY: Van Nos Reinhold, 1984.

Freedman, Warren. *International Products Liability.* 2 Vols. Charlottesville, VA: The Michie Company, 1986.

Gellhorn, Ernest. *Antitrust Law & Economics in a Nutshell.* 3rd ed., St. Paul, MN: West Publishing Co., 1986. 472 p.

*General Information Concerning Trademarks.* Washington, DC: U.S. Department of Commerce, Patent and Trademark Office, 1984. 21 p.

Goldstein, Arnold S., Editor. *J. K. Lasser's Complete Legal Form-File for Small Business.* Austin, TX: S & S Press, 1988.

Goldstein, Arnold S. *The Small Business Legal Problem-Solver.* New York, NY: Van Nostrand Reinhold, 1983. 240 p.

Goldstein, Arnold S. *The Small Business Legal Problem Solver.* Boston: CBI Publications, 1983. 270 p.

Goldstein, Arnold; Knox, Peter; Frey, Audrey M., Editor. *The Complete Book of Corporate Benefits.* Washington, DC: Enterprise Publishing, Inc., 1988.

Grant, Anne R., Editor. *Product Liability, 1984.* Washington, DC: Association of Trial Lawyers of America, 1985.

Greenwood, Mary. *Hiring, Supervising & Firing Employees: An Employer's Guide to Discrimination Laws.* Deerfield, IL: Callaghan & Company, 1987. 122 p.

Griffith, John R. *Business Law & Cases: A Comparative Approach.* Dubuque, IA: Kendall/Hunt Publishing Co., 1988. 1168 p.

Hancock, William A. *The Small Business Legal Advisor.* New York: McGraw-Hill Book Co., 1982. 258 p.

Harris, Donald. *Remedies in Contract & Tort*. Littleton, CO: Fred B. Rothman & Co., 1988. 411 p.

Hawkland, William D. *Commercial Paper*. 2nd ed., Philadelphia, PA: American Law Institute, 1979.

Hawkland, William; Bailey, Henry J. *Commercial Paper*. 3rd ed., Santa Monica, CA: Herbert Legal Series, 1985.

Haynes, William J., Jr. *State Antitrust Laws*. Washington, DC: BNA Books, 1988. 435 p.

Hearn, Patrick. *The Business of Industrial Licensing: A Practical Guide to Patents, Know-How, Trademarks and Industrial Design*. Brookfield, VT: Renouf USA, Inc. 1981. 626 p.

Hicks, Tyler G. *Franchise Riches Success Kit*. 4th ed., Rockville Centre, NY: International Wealth Success, Inc., 1990.

Holmes, William C. *Antitrust Law Handbook*. New York NY: Clark Boardman Co., Ltd., 1988.

Hopfenmuller, Steven A. *Fringe Benefits Guidebook for Small Businesses*. Melville, NY: Hooksett Publishing, Inc., 1987.

*How to Protect Your Ideas*. Los Angeles: American Entrepreneurs Association, 1981. 44 p.

*Howell, John C. Forming Corporations & Partnerships*. Blue Ridge Summit, PA: Tab Books, Inc., 1986.

Howell, Rate A.; Allison, John R.; Prentice, Robert A. *Business Law* 4th alternate ed., Hinsdale, IL: Dryden Press, 1989. 1168 p.

Hoyes, Donald J., Editor *Insurance Law Anthology*. Vol. II, Bethesda, MD: International Library Book Publishing, Inc., 1989.

Hoyes, Donald J., Editor. *Insurance Law Anthology*. Vol. III, Bethesda, MD: International Library Book Publishing, Inc., 1989.

International Franchise Association. *What You Need to Know When You Buy a Franchise (Plus a Listing of the World's Leading Franchising Companies)*. Washington, DC: International Franchise Association, 1987.

Jackson, Stanley G. *How to Proceed in Business Legally: The Entrepreneur's Guide, Federal Edition*. Englewood Cliffs, NJ: Prentice-Hall, Inc., 1984.

Jackson, Stanley G. *How to Proceed in Business—Legally*. Englewood Cliffs, NJ: Prentice-Hall, Inc., 1984. 232 p.

Jacobsen, Jay; Lefevre, Julie, Editor. *Surviving & Prospering in a Business Partnership*. Milpitas, CA: PSI Research, 1988.

Johnson, Richard E. *Flexible Benefit Plans—A How To Guide*. Brookfield, WI: International Foundation of Employee Benefit Plans, 1988.

Jordan, Robert L.; Warren, William D. *Commercial Paper*. Mineola, NY: Foundation Press, Inc., 1983.

Jordan, Robert L.; Warren, William D. *Commercial Paper*. 2nd ed., Mineola, NY: Foundation Press, Inc., 1987.

Kaufmann, David J. *Franchising Nineteen Eighty-Seven: Business Strategies and Legal Compliance*. Washington, DC: International Franchise Association, 1987.

Keeton, Page W.; Owen, David G.; Montgomery, John E.; Green, Michael. *Products Liability & Safety, Cases and Materials*. 2nd ed., Mineola, NY: Foundation Press, Inc., 1989.

Kosel, Janice; Allison, Linda, Illustrator. *Chapter Thirteen: The Federal Plan to Repay Your Debts*. 3rd. ed., Berkeley, CA: Nolo Press, 1984. 153 p.

Lane, Marc J. *Legal Handbook for Small Business*. rev. ed., New York, NY: Amacom, 1989. 250 p.

Lieberman, Jethro K. *Business Law & the Legal Environment*. 2nd ed., San Diego, CA: Harcourt Brace Jovanovich. 1988. 1226 p.

Litigation & Administrative Practice Service. *Securities Litigation 1988*. 2 Vols. New York, NY: Practicing Law Institute, 1988. 1351 p.

Lorimer, James J. *Legal Environment of Insurance*. 2 Vols., 3rd ed., Malvern, PA: American Institute for Property and Liability Underwriters, Inc., 1987. 894 p.

Loss, Louis. *Fundamentals of Securities Resulation*. 2nd ed., Boston, MA: Little, Brown and Company, 1987. 1,400 p.

Lynch, Gary G.; Mathews, Arthur F. *Securities Enforcement Institute 1986*. 2 Vols. New York, NY: Practicing Law Institute, 1986. 1,026 p.

Maurer, Virginia, G. *Business Law: Text & Cases*. San Diego, CA: Harcourt Brace Jovanovich, 1987. 1228 p.

McCaffery, Robert M. *Employee Benefits*. Boston, MA: PWS Kent Publishing Company, 1988.

McGuire, E. Patrick. *Industrial Product Warranties: Policies & Practices*. New York, NY: The Conference Board, Inc., 1981.

Mendelsohn, M. *The Guide to Franchising*. 4th ed., Elmsford, NY: Pergamon Books, Inc., 1984.

Miles, Raymond C. *How to Price a Business*. Englewood Cliffs, NJ: Institute for Business Planning, 1982. 133 p.

Mohn, Reinhard. *Success Through Partnership*. New York, NY: Doubleday and Company, Inc., 1988.

Moran. *Practical Business Law*. 2nd ed., Englewood Cliffs, NJ: Prentice-Hall, Inc., 1988. 432 p.

Muncheryan, Hrand M. *Patent It Yourself*. Blue Ridge Summit, PA: Tab Books, 1982. 172 p.

Nicholas, Ted. *How to Form Your Own Corporation Without a Lawyer for Under Fifty Dollars*. 10th ed., Wilmington, DE: Enterprise Publishing, Inc.

Nickles, Steve H. *Commercial Paper*. St. Paul, MN: West Publishing Company, 1988.

Norris, Kenneth. *The Inventor's Guide to Low-Cost Patenting*. New York: Macmillan Publishing Co., 1985. 233 p.

Parker, Allan J. *Incorporating a Small Business*. New York, NY: Practicing Law Institute, 1984. 229 p.

Peters, George A., Editor. *Readings in Product Liability & Civil Liability*. Des Plaines, IL: American Society of Safety Engineers, 1985.

Phillips, Jerry J. *Products Liability in a Nutshell*. 3rd ed., St. Paul, MN: West Publishing Company, 1988.

Prentice-Hall Editorial Staff-Editor. *Employee Plans Under ERISA: Federal Resulations*. Englewood Cliffs, NJ: Prentice-Hall, Inc., 1989.

Raab, Steven. *Buying the Franchise That's Right For You: What to Look For, What to Look Out For*. New York, NY: John Wiley and Sons, Inc., 1988.

Rabin, Robert J.; Silverstein, Eileen; Schatzki, George. *Labor & Employment Law: Statutory Supplement*. St. Paul, MN: West Publishing Company, 1988. 212 p.

Ratner, David L. *Securities Regulation: 1988 Supplement*. 3rd ed., St. Paul, MN: West Publishing Company, 1988.

Redden, Tim. *Franchise Buyers' Handbook*. Glenview, IL: Scott, Foresman & Company, 1989.

Reitz, Curtis; Wolkin, Paul A. *Consumer Product Warranties Under Federal and State Laws*. 2nd ed., Philadelphia, PA: American Law Institute, 1987.

Rice, Jerome S.; Libbey, Keith. *Making the Law Work for You: A Guide for Small Businesses*. Chicago, IL: Contemporary Books, Inc., 1980.

Roberson, Cliff. *The Businessperson's Legal Advisor*. Blue Ridge Summit, PA: Tab Books, Inc., 1986. 240 p.

Roberts, Duane F. *Marketing and Leasing of Office Space*. Chicago: Institute of Real Estate Management, 1979. 289 p.

Rosenbloom, Jerry S. *The Handbook of Employee Benefits: Design, Funding and Administration*. 2nd ed., Homewood, IL: Dow Jones-Irwin, Inc., 1988.

Shaver, Alan M., Editor. *Successful Model Business Contracts & Agreements*. Dover, DE: Weka Publishing, Inc., 1988. 550 p.

Siegel, W. L. *Franchising*. New York: John Wiley & Sons, Inc., 1983. 206 p.

Simpson, A. W. *A History of the Common Law of Contract*. Vol. 1, New York, NY: Oxford University Press, Inc., 1987. 650 p.

Steinberg, Marc I., Editor. *Contemporary Issues in Securities Regulation*. Stoneham, MA: Butterworth U.S. Legal Publications, Inc., 1988.

Steingold, Fred. *Legal Master Guide for Small Business*. Englewood Cliffs, NJ: Prentice-Hall, Inc., 1983. 242 p.

Tax Law and Estate Planning Service. *Employee Welfare Benefit Plans*. New York, NY: Practicing Law Institute, 1987.

Tax Law and Estate Planning Service. *Employee Welfare Benefit Plans*. New York, NY: Practicing Law Institute, 1988.

Twomey, David P. *Labor & Employment Law: Text & Cases*. 8th ed., Cincinnati, OH: South-Western Publishing Company, 1988. 648 p.

Van Cise, Jerold G.; Lifland, William T.; Sorkin, Laurence T. *Understanding Antitrust Laws*. 9th ed., New York, NY: Practicing Law Institute, 1986. 391 p.

Ward, Peter D.; Goldblatt, Margaret A. *Trade Regulation, Antitrust & Economics: A Bibliography*. 4 Vols., Buffalo, NY: William S. Hein & Co., Inc.

Weber, Charles M.; Speidel, Richard E. *Commercial Paper in a Nutshell*. St. Paul, MN: West Publishing Company, 1982.

West Editorial Staff. *Bankruptcy Code, Rules & Forms, Including: Federal Rule Procedure & Federal Rules of Evidence*. St. Paul, MN: West Publishing Co., 1987. 1255 p.

White, Jeffrey R., Editor. *Products Liability: The First 25 Years*. 2 Vols. Washington, DC: Association of Trial Lawyers of America, 1983.

Windt, Allan D. *Insurance Claims & Disputes: Representation of Insureds & Insurers*. 2nd ed., Colorado Springs, CO: Shepard's/McGraw-Hill Publishing Co., Inc., 1988. 788 p.

York, Kenneth; Whelan, John W. *Insurance Law*. St. Paul, MN: West Publishing Co., 1988. 89 p.

# Index

# FRANCHISE SELECTION: Separating Fact From Fiction

By Raymond J. Munna
ISBN 0-935669-12-4 (PBK) · 8½ X 11 · 216 Pages · $19.95

## Complete Information On:

· The Franchising method of doing business;

· Categories and different types of Franchises;

· The origins and development of Franchising;

· How to self-evaluate your financial position prior to beginning your Franchise;

· The pros and cons of realistic Franchising;

· The best offense and the best defense to increase your chances of success;

· How to choose the right professionals to help one get started;

· How to locate the potential "hot" Franchises;

· Understanding the laws that affect Franchising, and how to understand the Franchise contract;

· A how-to check list to keep the investors on the right track and to put all the information together;

Plus, a complete Appendix containing listings of SBA Offices, Small Business Administration, SBA Business Development Aids, SBA Management Aids, National Directories for use in Marketing and other vital information for Franchising.

## WHAT OTHERS ARE SAYING ABOUT THIS BOOK:

"Analyzes franchisee contracts and gives instructions on where to get help picking a franchise." —*USA Today*

"A broad range of useful insights. —*In Business* Magazine

Sound basic advice . . . excellent general tips on how to find answers in order to protect oneself in this often risky field." —*Booklist*

The "two birds in the bush" touted in franchising often lead to "a turkey in hand." Good financial evaluation starts with *good assumptions* through market research. The book provides excellent points on market consulting and on proper documentation of representations of franchisors." —Gary B. Nunemacher, C.P.A.

# Franchise Selection: Separating Fact From Fiction
by Raymond J. Munna, Attorney

**Chapter 1: The Franchising Method of Doing Business**
Overview of franchising and the approach taken by this handbook.

**Chapter 2: Categories of Franchises**
Gives you a description of various types of franchises and different frameworks. Discusses various definitions of franchising and various exemptions from Federal Trade Commission and state disclosure requirements. You'll learn to be more cautious if a business opportunity might be exempt from telling you important information.

**Chapter 3: How Did Franchising Get Here**
Traces the development and stages of franchising.

**Chapter 4: Owning Your Own Business**
Studies reveal reasons individuals begin businesses. Also other studies indicate differences in degrees of independence versus type of managerial activity. Distinguishes independent entrepreneurs from franchise entrepreneurs. Examines personal financial information you need as part of your self-evaluation.

**Chapter 5: Franchising: Advantages and Disadvantages**
Outlines and *explains* the advantages and disadvantages in realistic terms.

**Chapter 6: The Best Offense**
Emphasizes the positive types of information which significantly raise your chances of success. Describes what information you need, where to get it and where you will not get it.

**Chapter 7: The Best Defense**
New approach to self-protection. Allows you to create your own life-preservers.

**Chapter 8: Choosing Professionals**
Gives a unique view for finding and using your professionals. Includes the most important professional who has been kept hidden for too long (it's not the lawyer or accountant).

**Chapter 9: Locating Potential Hot Franchises**
Examines the customary industries where franchising is common. Gives you readily available sources of listings of thousands of franchises. Shows how to find "hot" sources with many ideas.

**Chapter 10: Vital Information**
Checklist of information to fill in the many puzzle pieces with explanations about each item. You'll understand why you are looking for specific data.

**Chapter 11: Laws Affecting Franchising**
You'll learn why you have to learn the laws affecting franchising. You'll understand the information required in the franchisor's offering circular.

**Chapter 12: Analysis of the Franchise Contract**
Learn why you have to understand this contract. Plain language descriptions of these lengthy documents.

**Chapter 13: Selecting a Franchise**
Putting all the information together. Bringing together the many factors.

Also includes Small Business Administration information and national directories for use in marketing.

# ORDER FORM

## A★GRANITE PUBLISHERS

### 80 GRANADA DRIVE
### KENNER, LA 70065-3145

| QUANTITY | TITLE | PRICE EACH | PRICE TOTAL |
|---|---|---|---|
| | Legal Power for the Small Business Owner and Manager | $19.95 | |
| | Franchise Selection: Separating Fact From Fiction | $19.95 | |

| | |
|---|---|
| BOOK TOTAL | |
| Louisiana Residents add local sales tax | |
| SHIPPING | |
| **TOTAL** | |

*I understand that I may return any book within 30 days for a full refund if I am not satisfied.*

SHIPPING:
$3.00 for the first book
$1.50 for each additional book

## FORM OF PAYMENT

☐ Check or Money Order

☐ VISA

☐ MasterCard

Account Number ☐☐☐☐ ☐☐☐☐ ☐☐☐☐ ☐☐☐☐

Signature _____

Exp. Date ☐☐/☐☐

## SHIP TO

NAME

ADDRESS

CITY/STATE

ZIP